Suicide as a

Cultural Institution

in Dostoevsky's Russia

Suicide as a Cultural Institution in Dostoevsky's Russia

IRINA PAPERNO

CORNELL UNIVERSITY PRESS

Ithaca and London

First published 1997 by Cornell University Press.
First printing, Cornell Paperbacks, 1997.

Printed in the United States of America

Library of Congress Cataloging-in-Publication Data

Paperno, Irina.
    Suicide as a cultural institution in Dostoevsky's Russia / Irina Paperno.
        p.   cm.
    Includes index.
    ISBN 0-8014-3397-5 (cloth : alk. paper). — ISBN 0-8014-8425-1 (pbk. : alk. paper)
    1. Suicide—Russia—History—19th century. 2. Suicide—Social aspects. 3. Dostoyevsky, Fyodor, 1821–1881—Criticism and interpretation. 4. Suicide in literature. 5. Russia—Civilization—1801–1917. I. Title.
HV6548.R9P36   1997
362.28'0947—dc21   97-22593

Cornell University Press strives to utilize environmentally responsible suppliers and materials to the fullest extent possible in the publishing of its books. Such materials include vegetable-based, low-VOC inks and acid-free papers that are also either recycled, totally chlorine-free, or partly composed of nonwood fibers.

Cloth printing   10 9 8 7 6 5 4 3 2 1
Paperback printing   10 9 8 7 6 5 4 3 2 1

Contents

Acknowledgments

I wish to convey my gratitude to the organizations, colleagues, students, and friends who have helped me in many different ways. I am very much indebted to the people who assisted me in obtaining information and materials: Albin Konechnyi, Ksenia Kumpan, Susan Morrissey, Alexander Sobolev, Kirill Rogov, John Randolph, and Molly Wesling. To Larisa Ivanova, whose expert knowledge of the Dostoevsky archives was indispensable to my research, I owe a special debt of gratitude. I am most grateful to all those who read drafts of this book for their comments, criticisms, and suggestions: Laura Engelstein, Boris Gasparov, Liza Knapp, Thomas Laqueur, Olga Matich, Robin Feuer Miller, Susan Morrissey, Eric Naiman, Anne Nesbet, Viktor Zhivov, and others. I want to express my profound appreciation to Reginald Zelnik, whose thorough and thoughtful reading of the whole manuscript proved invaluable. I owe a special debt to Joachim Klein for his critical reading and kind encouragement. I am grateful to the members of the staff of the Suicide Prevention Center of Alameda County in California; working alongside them as a volunteer added an extra dimension to my understanding of suicide.

This book has benefited from editorial revisions performed by Sarah Pelmas and John Randolph. Robert Wessling expertly translated most of the Russian quotes.

I gratefully acknowledge major financial support from the John Simon Guggenheim Memorial Foundation (1992/93) and the Humanities Research Fellowship at the University of California, Berkeley (Spring 1996). In Spring 1992, I profited enormously from the opportunity to use the research facilities of Harvard University and from the collegiate support of the members of the Department of Slavic Languages and Literatures. I am grateful to the Rockefeller Foundation and the Bellagio Study and Conference Center, whose hospitality I enjoyed in March 1996. Over the years I have relied on the generous moral and financial support of the University of California,

Acknowledgments

Berkeley: Department of Slavic Languages and Literatures, Center for Slavic and East European Studies, the Doreen Townsend Center for the Humanities, the Academic Senate Committee on Research, and the Office of the Dean of Humanities.

I. P.

A Note on Language

In the text, Russian names and words have been transliterated according to the Library of Congress system, adopting the traditional *-sky* and *-y* for personal name endings. References consistently follow the Library of Congress system, including the name endings. An appendix provides the original Russian text of quotations from primary sources. I have used the traditional masculine forms to apply to both sexes.

A Note on Language

In this book, Roman letters and word-boundaries are used throughout, both anglophone and other. By convention, apostrophes indicate the traditional ... index to transliteration system. Liberties here are not strict. A line ... above element of complexity seeks to illumine the truncation as on special ... which provides the necessary decision list of equivalences from each ... opinion. Liberties served as making and approximations for as it spoke to both

Suicide as a

Cultural Institution

in Dostoevsky's Russia

Introduction

The Symbolic Meanings of Suicide

We have always believed we know what a cause is: but whence did we derive our knowledge, more precisely our belief we possess this knowledge? From the realm of the celebrated "inner facts," none of which has up till now been shown to be factual. We believed ourselves to be causal agents in the act of willing; we at least thought we were there *catching causality in the act*. It was likewise never doubted that all the *antecedentia* of an action, its causes, were to be sought in the consciousness and could be discovered there if one sought them—as "motives": for otherwise one would not have been *free* to perform it, *responsible* for it. Finally, who would have disputed that a thought is caused? that the ego causes the thought? . . . Of these three "inner facts" through which causality seemed to be guaranteed the first and most convincing was that of *will as cause;* the conception of a consciousness ("mind") as cause and later still that of the ego (the "subject") as cause are merely after-products after causality had, on the basis of will, been firmly established as a given fact, as *empiricism*. . . . Meanwhile we have thought better. Today we do not believe a word of it. The "inner world" is full of phantoms and false lights: the will is one of them. The will no longer moves anything, consequently no longer explains anything—it merely accompanies events, it can also be absent. The so-called "motive": another error. Merely a surface phenomenon of consciousness, an accompaniment to an act, which conceals rather than exposes the *antecedentia* of the act. And as for the ego! It has become a fable, a fiction, a play on words: it has totally ceased to think, to feel and to will!

. . . What follows from this? There are no spiritual causes at all! The whole of the alleged empiricism which affirmed them has gone to the devil! *That* is what follows!—And we had made a nice misuse of that "empiricism," we had *created* the world on the basis of it as a world of causes, as a world of will, as a world of spirit. The oldest and longest-lived psychology was at work here—indeed it has done nothing else: every event was to it an action, every action the effect of a will, the world became for it a multiplicity of agents, an agent ("subject") foisted itself on every event. Man projected his three "inner facts," that in which he believed more firmly than in anything else, will, spirit, ego, outside himself—he derived the concept "being" only from the concept "ego," he posited "things" as possessing being according to his own image, according to his concept of the ego as cause. No wonder he later discovered in things only *that which he had put into them!*— The thing itself, to say it again, the concept "thing" is merely a reflection of the belief in the ego as cause. . . . And even your atom, *messieurs* mechanists and physicists, how much error, how much rudimentary psychology, still remains in your atom!—To say nothing of the "thing in itself," that *horrendum pudendum* of the metaphysicians! The error of spirit as cause mistaken for reality! And made the measure of reality! And called *God!*

   Friedrich Nietzsche, *Twilight of the Idols* [*Götzen-Dämmerung*, 1889]
            trans. R. J. Hollingdale

The Problem and the Method

Suicide has figured in the popular and scientific imagination as an enigma, an act that defies explanation.[1] In the twentieth century, psychologists have eagerly accepted their failure to find a solution to the problem (without, however, abandoning the enterprise, which has crystallized into a special field—"suicidology").[2] In April 1910 the Vienna Psychoanalytic Society held a discussion on the nature of suicide. In his concluding remarks Freud said: "Let us suspend our judgement until experience has solved this problem."[3] In 1936 the psychoanalyst Gregory Zilboorg claimed: "It is clear that the problem of suicide from the scientific point of view remains unresolved. Neither common sense nor clinical psychopathology has found a causal or even a strict empirical solution."[4] In 1973 the dean of American suicidology Edwin Shneidman began his article "Suicide" for the *Encyclopaedia Britannica* with the statement "No one really knows why human beings commit suicide."[5] The psychologist Antoon Leenaars opened his 1988 study of suicides' farewell notes with the same words.[6] No one really knows, not even suicides themselves.

A "black hole"[7] left upon man's final departure, suicide creates a void that asks to be filled. Throughout the centuries, philosophers, writers, journalists, and scientists have attempted to endow suicide with meaning, writing over the "black hole." The act of suicide has been associated with specific patterns of meaning. While an individual may have drawn on these meanings in defining his experience, culture has come to use suicide as a laboratory for the investigation of crucial philosophical and social problems, such as the immortality of the soul, free will, the connection between the individual and God or society, and the relationship between subject and object. Understood as a meaningful action, suicide has become a subject of sociological and historical research.[8]

In this book, I endeavor to show how suicide—an individual act—becomes a cultural artifact. It is in this sense that I call suicide "a cultural institution": a practice associated with patterns of symbolic meaning adapted to the general ends of culture and specific needs of a society.[9] A historical enterprise, my study is concerned with nineteenth-century Russia, viewed in the context of Western Europe. While some of the issues I discuss are specific to Russia in the nineteenth century, others are common to Western culture. I neither purport to find out "why human beings commit suicide," nor attempt to analyze suicidal behavior, its forms and occurrences; this book is about the cultural construction of the meaning of human experience.

The design of my book has been shaped by the available material. And yet, because human action becomes an institution when written down in historical records, the book necessarily reflects the changing configurations of the cultural institution of suicide in Russia. In Russia, suicide made its first, brief appearance in the prescriptions of medieval canon law. In the 1790s, when the Sentimentalist cult of Goethe's *Werther,* the Enlightenment notion of heroic suicide, and the echoes of the French Revolution reached Russia, suicide became a popular topic for fiction. In the 1830s data on suicide first appeared in statistical surveys and brief newspaper reports. But it was only in the 1860s, during the Great Reforms, which created many new public institutions (organs of the press, open courts, statistical bureaus), that suicide became an object of vigorous discussions in science, law, fiction, and, above all, the periodical press. Between the 1860s and the 1880s, Russia was believed to have experienced an "epidemic of suicides," which left voluminous records. A time of radical change in Russian society, coincidental with an intellectual revolution—the rise of positivism—the reform era created a cultural context in which suicide acquired an array of meanings and became a symbol of the age. After the 1905 revolution suicide once again came to symbolize society's current state. Between 1906 and 1914, discussions of another "epidemic" filled the periodical press, scientific publications, and fiction.[10] Suicide was still largely discussed in terms introduced in the nineteenth century, but in the new context some concepts acquired different overtones while others lost their topical poignancy.

The period covered in this book, in fragments, constitutes a more or less coherent cultural epoch—"the nineteenth century." On several occasions (most importantly, in codas to chapters 3 and 5), I briefly address the twentieth-century discussions of suicide—not so much to show how some of the themes developed in the next century as to reflect on the nineteenth-century material by providing selected reference points in the future.

The book opens (chapter 1) with a survey of discussions of suicide in Western European science, between the 1830s and the 1890s—it was in Western Europe that science at that time took suicide as an object of study. Investigations of suicide, treated as a test case in the study of human action, played a large role in configuring the nineteenth-century sciences of man. Accordingly, I deal with broader concerns than explanations of suicide, focusing on how the object—man and his action—was transferred from the metaphysical and moral to the scientific domain, and from medical to social science.

Turning to Russia (chapter 2), I give a brief overview of the status of suicide in Russian civil and canon law and in popular belief (from the Middle Ages to the end of the nineteenth century), discuss the Russian appropriation of Western ideas on suicide, and survey the nineteenth-century studies of suicide in Russia.

I then turn to the periodical press of the 1860s–80s (chapter 3), tracing the theme of suicide from the brief newspaper reports on concrete cases to the extensive discussions of general issues on the pages of the "thick journals." Combining belles lettres, literary criticism, popularization of science, reviews of current affairs, and discussions of social issues, the "thick journals" addressed suicide in all of their sections. Equipped with such organs, the press mediated among science, politics, and literature as well as between these authorities and the public.

With science and the press attempting to provide an explanation of suicide, what about the subject? I analyze (chapter 4) the records left by suicides—letters, notes, and diaries—and show how these documents were read by others.

In the nineteenth century (and especially in nineteenth-century Russia), it was literature that promised solutions to problems that could not be solved by religious, social, and scientific authorities.[11]

Moreover, the writer aspired to know human motivations better than the subjects themselves. Dostoevsky, who wrote extensively about suicide, took upon himself the roles of scientist, examining the hidden depths of the human soul; philosopher, giving a transcendental dimension to individual experience; and priest, teaching men that God is still present in their lives. Dostoevsky also tried his hand at journalism. In the *Diary of a Writer,* a journal he wrote and published single-handedly, Dostoevsky reviewed cases of suicide reported in newspapers. The *Diary* was the writer's attempt to step from the pages of his text into real life: Dostoevsky corresponded (and occasionally met) with readers, among them would-be suicides. I consider Dostoevsky's various attempts to resolve the question of suicide (chapters 5 and 6).

When dealing with interpreters, we confront the Nietzschean question dramatized by Foucault: Who is speaking? And does it matter who is speaking? Throughout this book, I make attempts to describe the relationship between interpreters and interpretation. In the concluding chapter, I reconstruct the personality of one newspaperman, Albert Kovner, a feuilletonist from the Petersburg daily *Golos*. With this, the circle of interpretation is complete: the construction of the meaning of a human action has been traced through various interrelated cultural spheres in which the subject (whether actor or interpreter) is firmly embedded.

In recent decades, interpretive approaches to human experiences and actions, treated as cultural constructs, or texts, have been advanced, independently of one another, by several authors working in different disciplines (among them, Clifford Geertz in cultural anthropology, Paul Ricoeur in hermeneutic phenomenology, and Iurii Lotman in the semiotics of culture). In his monumental works, Michel Foucault created an epistemological basis and a discourse for the historical study of experience—and problematized the whole endeavor by revealing the precarious status of the individual as both the subject and the object of knowledge. Cultural historians have produced illuminating empirical studies: histories of death, sexuality, guilt, fear, senses, and the body. This book shares some of the concerns and methodological strategies of these works and, inevitably, transforms them. Thus, my understanding of the nature of meaning has been influenced by studying literature, perhaps the most complex of all meaning-making systems. I emphasize the role of symbolic renderings of experience and view metaphor as a powerful cognitive instrument that propels cultural development. I treat medicine, social science, law, and the press as modes of knowledge formed by different heuristic strategies and rhetorical conventions, as well as rhetorical conventions that work as heuristic strategies. In analyzing the discourses shared by science, the press, and fiction, I show how, using the same words, they ascribe different meanings to these words. As a former structuralist, I cannot help seeing patterns that underlie themes. Working with nineteenth-century Russian material, I deal with the appropriation of Western ideas—an opportunity to show the creative potential of distortion. Trained in psychology as well as in literary studies and cultural history, I attempt to access the subject, the actor and the interpreter. Literature and the great writer Dostoevsky occupy a privileged position in my study—not because (as many of his readers chose to believe) he offered solutions to the enigma of suicide, but because of all students of human action Dostoevsky came

5

closest to calling into question the belief that the meaning of suicide can be accessible to either the subject or the investigator.

Historical Survey: Paradigmatic Cases

In the nineteenth century, a study of suicide usually opened with a survey of celebrated cases, from Socrates to Goethe's Werther.[12] I will follow this practice; however, my purpose is different. For me, celebrated cases constitute not "the stuff of history," but units of meaning. Symbolic meanings associated with the act of suicide found their focal points in such cases. Reinterpreted in different cultural contexts, they became major vehicles for the transmission of meaning. Informing other acts, these cases acquired a paradigmatic quality. Before proceeding to analyze concrete historical material, I will review some of these cultural resources. The examples that follow do not amount to a brief history of the symbolism of suicide, but are meant to show the dynamics of the formation and mutation of meaning, which does not render itself easily to exhaustive treatments or generalizations.

Beginning with Socrates, self-inflicted death has been associated with the idea of the immortality of the soul, attained through separation of the soul from the body. In Plato's *Phaedo,* a dialogue that presents Socrates "practicing death,"[13] the Western concept of the immortal soul was born.[14] Reflecting on the nature of death as he prepares to take the poison, Socrates offers several logical proofs of immortality (to be frequently contested in the ensuing tradition), but it is Socrates' own death, the exemplary death of the philosopher/poet, that generations of readers have come to associate with immortality. Socrates anticipates dying and liberates himself from the constraints of the body while still alive. The cup of poison that he drains becomes the "drink of immortality."[15]

But is Socrates a suicide? The question has a long history. Arguing that the individual is inextricably connected to God, who alone can set him free, Socrates seems to imply that taking one's life means usurping divine authority. Many interpreters have taken this as a condemnation of suicide. But Socrates left a loophole, claiming that the "necessity to die" had been given to him by God—a loophole accepted by many. Socrates was condemned to death (by self-poisoning) by the Athenian state, but he chose to drink the poison before the appointed time.[16] In the eyes of philosophers, Socrates' willingness to die (evident also in his other actions) has been a deciding factor.

"Socrates *wanted* to die," claimed Nietzsche,"—it was not Athens, it was *he* who handed himself the poison cup, who compelled Athens to hand him the poison cup."[17] To this day philosophers debate whether Socrates' death can be considered a suicide.[18]

The death of Socrates became a productive paradigm in Western culture, a model that influenced the interpretation of one's own or another person's suicide. In Plato's immediate circle, we know of a man, Cleombrotus, who enacted the paradigm: he is said to have thrown himself into the sea after reading *Phaedo*.[19] Centuries later, Milton read his suicide in this vein—as an act aimed at attaining immortality, after the example of Plato's Socrates: "And he who, to enjoy Plato's Elysium, leaped into the sea, Cleombrotus" (from Book III of *Paradise Lost*). Augustine, by whose authority condemnation of suicide was established as the dominant Christian view, read (and admired) the act of Cleombrotus as a philosophical statement on the nature of death. John Donne quoted Augustine's words in his Christian apology of suicide, *Biathanatos*: "When no calamity urged him, no crime either true or imputed, nothing but greatness of mind moved him apprehend death."[20]

Those who used the death of Socrates as a paradigm seem to have reasoned in the following way:

> Socrates is immortal.
> Socrates is a suicide.
> Therefore, all suicides are immortal.[21]

These reactions demonstrate how a celebrated suicide case *informs* other acts. Bound by the hermeneutic framework, however, I would stop short of claiming that it *causes* other acts.

The connection between voluntary death and the immortality of the soul was reinforced and elaborated in interpretations of the death of Christ, viewed by some as a suicide. Early Christian thinkers frequently discussed the death of Christ in terms similar to those Plato used in discussing the death of Socrates: executed as criminals (accused of similar crimes), both Socrates and Christ nevertheless died willing deaths, and in both cases it was death that released the soul from the body.[22]

Christ was seen as a model to be imitated by every Christian, one that endowed human life and death with higher meaning. Thus early Christian martyrs, who died willingly, hoped to have taken a "short-cut to immortality."[23] The martyrs' deaths reinforced the interpretation of Christ's death as a suicide. In this context, Jesus's Gethsemane prayer was read as a death wish.[24] Voluntary martyrdom prompted Augustine's condemnation of suicide, but the question of whether or not Christ could be considered a suicide continued to be debated, from the early Christians to the nineteenth-century Romantics (and beyond).[25] Locating the will to die was crucial in these debates, and Christ's appeal to the divine will in the Gethsemane prayer, "Let Thy will be done," often figured as a decisive argument against suicide.[26] But the issue has not had a definitive resolution.

Throughout the centuries, the cases of Socrates and Christ have been viewed as embodiments of the same paradigm: (voluntary) death overcoming death.[27] For the eighteenth-century philosophes, the death of Socrates, who sealed the truth of his teaching by his own death, provided a model for the philosopher's secular immortality. From Voltaire's point of view, Jesus Christ, "le Socrate de la Galilée," was an inferior Socrates.[28] Hegel, however, while he also saw the story of Christ as "quite similar to that of Socrates, only on a different soil," emphasized that the death of Christ revealed the superior truth—the absolute and eternal truth of the divine. But for the unbeliever, for the human view (claimed Hegel), Christ's story was just another version of Socrates'.[29]

Dostoevsky, describing the death of Kirillov in *The Possessed,* rearranged the pattern, adapting it to the needs of the age of atheism and positivism. In a reversal of the Platonic and Christian views of death, Kirillov, striving for immortality here on earth, fuses body and soul in his suicide, uniting them (as Feuerbach saw it) after centuries of separation. A "man-God," Kirillov consciously usurps the right of God, dying by his own will. And (paraphrasing Augustine) no calamity or crime urged him—his suicide was a philosophical statement. In its turn, the death of Dostoevsky's Kirillov became a productive paradigm: rewritten by Nietzsche and Camus, it informed the atheistic view of death in the twentieth century. (The death of Kirillov and its legacy will be treated in detail later in this book.)

While philosophers and artists made a symbolic connection between suicide and the immortality of the soul, psychologists in our days claim that a sense of immortality is a part of the subjective experience of suicide.[30] The sociologist Jack Douglas has described the understanding of suicide as "a means of transforming the soul from this world to the other world" as fundamental to the social meaning of suicide.[31]

Suicide became a test case for another basic philosophical problem: the relationship between subject and object. For centuries, legal philosophers have struggled with the dilemma of a crime in which the perpetrator and the victim are the same person.[32] Confusion between self as subject and self as object was described by psychologists as an essential part of the suicidal experience.[33] (It is the separation of "I" as the subject of death from "I" as the object of death that leads to a sense of immortality—an illusion that the self will be able to exist after death.)[34]

Thus, over the centuries, a whole set of cultural issues was connected with the act of suicide—in this act, the philosophical, the social, and the psychological merged.

Associated with the same cases—Plato's Socrates, Christ, Dostoevsky's Kirillov—is the notion that suicide defines the relationship between man and God. Discussing whether or not suicide is legitimate, Socrates argues that men are "one of the gods' possessions."[35] In Christian terms, man is a part of God, and therefore, ought not to take his own life. From Plato's *Phaedo* to Augustine to the regulations of canon law to Dostoevsky, moral discussions of suicide focused on this idea. In a secular context, suicide provided a model for defining the relationship between the individual and society, with the individual seen as a part of the "body social." This principle was challenged in the legal thought and legislation of the French Revolution, which asserted man's autonomy by decriminalizing suicide. In Emile Durkheim's *Suicide: A Study in Sociology* (1897), which viewed the incidence of individual suicide as a function of the integrity of society, the idea reemerged, this time within a scholarly context (a matter for further comment). Underlying all these discussions is the basic problem of the relationship between part and whole.

A long-lived tradition, which goes back to the figure of Cato of Utica, associates suicide with political freedom and personal autonomy. In the reading of Cicero as well as Plutarch, the death of Cato, who killed himself at the fall of the Roman republic rather than surrender to Caesar's dictatorship, stood as a model act of citizenship. (The story of the rape and suicide of Lucretia, which led to the expulsion of the tyrant from Rome and the foundation of the republic, poses a similar connection, creating a female counterpart for the model of human autonomy.)[36] But Cato's situation is ambiguous. Is the act of Cato an affirmation of autonomy or a surrender? A victory or a defeat? Plutarch presents Cato's suicide as an act that turns the one into the other. It is a surrender to the authority of the fallen Roman republic, and thus a patriotic act. His Cato refuses to ask Caesar to spare his life, claiming that, while "those who are conquered, entreat," "he had got the victory and had conquered Caesar," and that "it is but usurpation in him [Caesar] to save, as their rightful lord, the lives of men over whom he has no title to reign."[37]

9

Seneca treated Cato's suicide as an act of civil disobedience. More-over, he presented the act of suicide itself as the affirmation of human freedom and "the only genuinely free act."[38] In the context of Stoicism, Cato's suicide was also seen as an example of ultimate self-control (the Stoic virtue of personal dignity).

Variations of the story of Cato can be traced through the Middle Ages and Renaissance to the Enlightenment.[39] The classic tradition was revived in eighteenth-century neo-Stoicism, culminating in the culture of the French Revolution. Beginning with the early eighteenth century, Cato made frequent appearances on stage. One of the first (and most popular) of such appearances was on English soil, in Joseph Addison's tragedy *Cato* (first performed in 1713), for which Alexander Pope wrote a prologue.* The play showed Cato struggling both with the personal tyranny of Caesar and with the tyranny of fate. Pope in his prologue presented him as a man "falling with the fallen state."[40] The French in the eighteenth century viewed Cato in several different ways. For one author, Cato exemplified "the situation of a man who, jealous of liberty, prefers a glorious death to a shameful slavery."[41] Friedrich Grimm thought that the sight of Cato disemboweling himself was the only suicide fit to appear on stage, "because he sees his destiny as bound up with that of his country."[42] His Cato performs an act not of affirmation of personal autonomy, but of patriotic surrender to the country. In these debates on Cato, suicide is viewed as a test case in the relationship between the individual and society.

In French revolutionary culture, Cato's suicide was associated with freedom—understood as political freedom and personal autonomy—with republicanism, and with dignity—understood as control over one's destiny, one's body, and one's emotions. Heroic suicides by defeated political figures, often committed in anticipation of the imminent death sentence (and sometimes committed publicly), became relatively common, as were cases where an arrest and death sentence seemed deliberately provoked. Cato was frequently cited as an example worthy of emulation or a "reference-figure" for the interpretation of one's action.[43]

Though Cato's suicide seems to be about freedom, the shadow of

---

*The play was an enormous success. It also provided a reference point for real-life suicides. In 1737 the writer Eustace Budgell (Addison's cousin, who suffered financial loss in the Bubble) committed suicide, leaving a note in verse: "What Cato did and Addison approved/ Cannot be wrong." It became the subject of Pope's *The Dunciad* (1742). The play also provoked a debate on the moral acceptability of suicide.

Socrates and the theme of the immortality of the soul are ever present. Plutarch's Cato read "Plato's dialogue concerning the soul" on the night he committed suicide. So did Addison's Cato: as the last act opens, Cato is sitting with "Plato's book on the immortality of the soul" in his hand. His deliberations on human longing for immortality and "the secret dread and inward horror of falling into nought" echo Plato, as well as eighteenth-century debates on immortality in which the new rationalism came into conflict with Christian faith. By association with Socrates, Cato is immortal.

The death of Cato influenced interpretations of the death of Socrates, emphasizing its civic aspects. The civic aspects were inherent in the very situation of Socrates, who faced the dilemma of whether to attempt escape or surrender to the will of the state. Like Cato, Socrates died caught between the struggle against the state and loyalty to it. Philosophes and participants in the French Revolution used Cato interchangeably with Socrates and Christ. "Our position," Diderot told Grimm in 1762, "is that of Socrates."[44] J.-L. David's famous painting *The Death of Socrates* (1787) provides a visual icon of the death of Socrates as a civic affair.[45] For Hegel, the deaths of both Socrates and Christ were examples of civic death. "Inasmuch as his teachings were revolutionary, Christ was accused and executed, and thus he sealed the truth of his teaching by his death." This story is "quite similar to that of Socrates. . . . He also taught that humanity must not stop short at obedience to ordinary authority." According to Hegel, however, there is a significant difference: Christ's divine nature.[46] Ultimately, in many interpretations the civic and the divine were inextricably intertwined. Thus the heroic suicide of a French revolutionary—a willed and controlled death—not only evoked the Stoic ethos associated with Cato, but also (in the words of historian Dorinda Outram) "prevented any acceptance of the finality and irrevocability of actual physical death."[47] A contemporary described the Girondins after the announcement of their death sentence: "they passed the night discussing the immortality of the soul; each of them represented Socrates among his disciples after he had drunk hemlock."[48] Different meanings of suicide converged.

We have seen that in different cultural contexts, suicide—like a sponge—absorbed a variety of meanings. In the age of Sentimentalism, suicide acquired additional connotations: it became a test of sensibility and a celebration of the power of man's irrational feelings. The same people who, inspired by eighteenth-century neo-Stoicism, admired the self-control of Socrates and Cato, also admired the out-

11

pouring of affect in Julie or Saint Preux from Rousseau's *La Nouvelle Héloise* and in Goethe's Werther.[49] The merging of paradigms did not stop there. In a deliberate paradox, Goethe superimposed the passion of young Werther on the passion of Christ. (Goethe's title, *Die Leiden des jungen Werther,* echoes the liturgical formula applied to the suffering of Christ, *Das Leiden unseres Herrn Jesu Christi.*) While Werther himself saw no difficulty in interpreting his suffering as an analogue of Christ's (he describes his suicide as "going unto my Father" and quotes the Gethsemane prayer in his last letter to Lotte), Goethe revealed the contradiction inherent in the Christian doctrine: (in the words of Maurice Funke, a Goethe scholar) "the simultaneous condemnation of suicide and the demand that the virtuous Christian rejoice at the prospect of entering into eternal life through physical death."[50]

There is yet another layer of meaning: the concept of "sensibility," or "feeling," associated in the late eighteenth century with Sentimentalism, had its roots in medical science. For the eighteenth-century scientists, "sensibility" (response based on or accompanied by feeling, as opposed to unfelt automatic response to stimuli) was a physiological property, expressed in parts of the body and nervous system, or the "sensorium commune."[51] A bridge between the mental and the physical, the concept of sensibility promised access to the soul through its instrument, the nervous system. Specifically, people expected experiments on convulsions to reveal the seat of the soul within the sensorium commune. As Karl Figlio puts it, the physiologists' language "wandered easily among the related concepts of soul, sensorium commune and convulsions."[52] This language created rich possibilities for using the nervous system as a metaphor for human nature and human society.

Thus in *Werther,* Goethe relied on discourse shared by natural science, social thought, religion, and imaginative literature. Few readers noticed that Werther's own testimony on his last days, modeled on the experiences of Christ and Hamlet, is juxtaposed with the "editor's" descriptions of Werther's condition as a succession of physiological states indicative of psychopathology (melancholy, oppressed spirit, fever, and frenzy). The description of Werther's body is couched in terms fit for a pathologist's report: "He had shot himself above the right eye, blowing out his brains. . . . From the blood on the backrest of the chair it could be deduced that he committed the deed sitting at his desk, then sank to the floor, thrashing convulsively about the chair."[53] At the beginning of the nineteenth century, when he wrote *Dichtung und Wahrheit,* Goethe acknowledged that he was prepared to share "jurisdiction" over suicide with at least two other authorities. "The loathing of life," he wrote, "has its physical and moral causes; the former we hand over to the physician, the latter to the moralist for investigation."[54] After *Werther,* Funke says, "religious transcendence and the negation of life, emotional expansion and pathology are no longer separable."[55]

As in antiquity, the case was taken as a model to emulate. "Werther fever" hit Europe, extending into the 1820s to inspire the Romantics. Literary works imitated *Werther,* adapting the novel to local conditions; Werther paraphernalia became fashionable, signifying adoption of a particular form of sensibility in daily life. Contemporaries also believed that *Werther* caused an "epidemic of suicides."[56] Although the suicide epidemic has not and cannot possibly be confirmed, the belief that this had happened, or what Martin Swoles called "the anxiety that this might have happened," was real.[57] Some people, including Goethe scholars and students of suicide, hold this belief to this day, testifying to the power of the idea that human action can be caused—rather than informed—by a cultural model.[58]

Western models of suicide reached Russia in the late eighteenth century, undergoing further metamorphoses. Goethe's *Werther* appeared in Russia (in 1781) under the title *Strasti molodogo Vertera* (literally, *The Passion of Young Werther*).[59] The word chosen by the first Russian translators, *strasti,* obliterated the difference between **die** Leiden, a word used by Goethe, and **das** Leiden, a word applied to Christ, intensifying the Christological connotations of Goethe's title.[60] Further complications arose when Russians (following the example of the French and the English) produced their own versions of *Werther.* One of the first such rewritings was undertaken by a young nobleman Mikhail Sushkov, whose novel *The Russian Werther* (*Rossiiskii Verter*) was based on a situation similar to Goethe's, using Russian characters. Sushkov did not stop at literary imitation: in 1792, soon after completing his *Russian Werther,* the sixteen-year-old author committed suicide.[61] The case attracted considerable attention. Both the death of the author, Sushkov, and the death of his hero, *Verter,* were hybrids, informed by an array of cultural sources. Sushkov's hero commits suicide, motivated (like Goethe's Werther) by unrequited love for a married woman, with "the English tragedy Cato" (Addison) open on his desk, combining the Sentimentalist cult of feeling with the heroic rationalism of eighteenth-century Stoicism. The book is open to Cato's last monologue, a popular text among Russian readers. Small deviations from the original lead to telling distortions of meaning. Sushkov quoted only the closing lines of the monologue, which contain an affirmation of Cato's decision, and omitted his reflections on the immortality of the soul (with a copy of Plato's *Phaedo* in hand). Moreover, in his translation of Addison, Sushkov emphasized man's complete mastery over his life and death.[62] Apparently, the Russian Cato (unlike Addison's) was a confirmed atheist who had no use for Plato's *Phaedo*. So was the Russian Werther. Sushkov's hero is a Voltairean freethinker: "He left many philosophical writings which were never published, and never could be. He ordered that his remaining money . . . be distributed to the poor and that nothing be given to the priests."[63] The hero also left a document liberating his servant from serfdom.

Sushkov's own suicide further emphasizes his rejection of belief in the soul's immortality. His last letter (which he calls "credo," *simvol very*) is a confession of nonbelief (and evokes the name of Voltaire): "No one has ever been as convinced of the nonexistence of the soul as I."[64] It appears that conviction in man's finitude invites the act of willful self-destruction. Sushkov's letter became a public document: it circulated in handwritten copies.

Sushkov's suicide is a peculiar amalgamation of paradigms: the Sentimentalist cult of irrational human passions, exalted *imitatio Christi,* Stoic indifference to life, and atheistic rationalism of the Enlightenment joined hands, converging in one case. The Russian Werther was Werther cum Cato cum Christ cum Voltaire.[65]

In the late eighteenth century, Sushkov was by no means unique in connecting suicide to a rejection of the soul's immortality. We know of another atheist inspired by Voltaire, a provincial landowner Ivan Opochinin, who killed himself in 1793. His last letter gives an extended justification of his act, which takes the rejection of immortality as its starting point, but cites profound disgust with Russian life as an important incentive:

> There is nothing after death!
> Corresponding to the most truthful principle, this just argument . . . made me take a pistol into my hands. I had no reason for putting an end to my existence. Because of my position, the future presented me with a self-willed [*svoevol'noe*], pleasant existence. But the future would pass forthwith; in the end my aversion for Russian life was the incentive that compelled me to decide my fate in an act of self-will.
> Oh! If only all unfortunate men had the courage to use sound reason . . .

Opochinin handed over his body (a "machine" that he believed to have existed solely by force of nature) to the legal authorities ("Gentlemen Judges of the Lower Assembly [*Gospoda nizhnie zemskie sud'i*]! I leave my body in your command. I despise it so much... You may be assured of that") and instructed his heir to free his serfs. He claimed to have spent his last minutes translating a poem by Voltaire into Russian.[66]

This eighteenth-century Voltairean assumed that, were his beliefs to be shared by all, a mass suicide would follow. In the 1870s, Dostoevsky, thinking in similar terms (*svoevolie* is a key concept of Kirillov's credo), saw this scenario as the social destiny of the European civilization and a matter for the not-too-distant future.

Another Russian Cato, Alexander Radishchev, the preeminent thinker of the Russian Enlightenment and a master of Sentimentalist prose, took a different stand in the argument on the immortality of the soul.[67] An outspoken opponent of despotism, Radishchev saw suicide as the act of ultimate liberation—from the fear of death and the power of earthly tyrants. He found an example of such a death in Addison's Cato. One protagonist of *The Journey from St. Petersburg to Moscow* (Puteshestvie iz Peterburga v Moskvu, 1790), a virtuous father in the chapter "Kresttsy," advises his children to die if they can find no protection from oppression: "I bequeath to you the words of the dying Cato." A radical statement against despotism, *Journey* earned its author a death sentence, which was commuted to exile in Siberia. For Radishchev, the message of Cato's suicide was not limited to a political statement. Another chapter ("Bronnitsy") cites Cato's reflections on the immortality of the soul. Radishchev's Cato is a believer. In his *Vita of Fedor Ushakov* (Zhitie Fedora Vasil'evicha Ushakova, 1789), a biography that follows the generic conventions of hagiography, Radishchev made his views on immortality—conceived in a Christian context—explicit: "It happens—and we see many examples of it in literature—that the man who is told he must die beholds his approaching death with contempt and without trepidation. We have seen and do see people who courageously take their own lives. . . . Often such a man sees beyond the boundaries of the grave and trusts in his own resurrection."[68]

In Radishchev's case, the influence of Addison's Cato was not confined to literature. According to Iurii Lotman, Radishchev's enigmatic suicide in 1802 (a year after Emperor Alexander I brought him back from exile) was an act affirming his ultimate freedom, after the example of Addison's Cato. Unlike Sushkov and his hero, however,

Radishchev was a Russian Cato who knew his *Phaedo* well. In Siberia he wrote his own *Phaedo,* a treatise entitled *On Man, His Mortality and Immortality* (O cheloveke, o ego smertnosti i bessmertii). Radishchev's treatise resembles a Platonic dialogue: the text presents different viewpoints, with books 1 and 2 arguing for man's finitude, and books 3 and 4 for the immortality of the soul. The treatise is a compendium of eighteenth-century views taken from a broad range of Western European sources. The views of materialists (Holbach and Helvétius, among others) are confronted by the arguments of believers, specifically by Moses Mendelssohn's *Phaedo or On the Immortality of the Soul* (Phaedon oder über die Unsterblichkeit der Seele, 1767), a reworking of Plato's dialogue.[69] In Radishchev's "dialogue," the rationalist meets the Sentimentalist: while his reason sides with the logical coherence of the arguments for man's finitude, his feeling opts for the idea of the immortality of the soul. This Russian Cato was Cato cum (Mendelssohn's) Socrates cum Christ.

The meaning of suicide gained a whole new dimension in the nineteenth century. Western European Romantic literature cultivated the image of suicide—a self-created, aesthetically organized death—as *le mal du siècle.*[70] (Romantic preoccupation with suicide, well documented in the annals of Western European culture, left very few traces in Russia.) In addition, beginning in the 1830s, suicide was not only a topic of *les méditations poétiques,* but also an object of positive science. With the development of science, celebrated cases of suicide lost their role as the primary units bearing the meaning of suicide. In the words of Foucault, modern man, conceived in his finitude, entered the field of positive knowledge, "imposing the brutal fact of his body."[71] Investigations of death played a crucial role in the development of the scientific discourse concerning the individual: "Western man could constitute himself in his own eyes as an object of science . . . only in the opening created by his own elimination."[72] Science faced a crucial problem: the redefinition of the Christian view of man, a creature with a body, immortal soul, and free will. I believe that suicide, a subject uniquely suited for the investigation of these concerns, played a special role in the construction of the positivistic model of man.

Indeed, from Plato's Socrates to Goethe's Werther, suicide focused attention on the relationship between soul and body. And from the days of Greek Stoicism to the French Revolution, "the problem of suicide [was] a problem of free will."[73] In the 1830s, medical scientists, renewing the efforts undertaken in the eighteenth century, sought to fix the site of suicidal action—and the seat of action as such—neither in the soul nor in the will, but in the physiology of the human body. Suicide was now considered a "malady" in the literal sense. Thus the French doctor Bourdin saw clear signs of brain pathology in the behavior of Plutarch's Cato (according to Bourdin, the illness's grave progress took place while Cato was reading Plato's dialogue on the immortality of the soul).[74]

In the middle of the nineteenth century, social science competed with medical science. Social science investigated not the individual, but the collective body: the metaphor of the *corps social* organized social discourse. Science clashed with metaphysics. While Schopenhauer maintained that suicide was a phenomenon of the will's strong affirmation, positivists made suicide into the main object of a new discipline, "moral statistics," which used numerical methods to demonstrate that, when treated collectively, human actions answered to natural laws and were subject to determinacy. Henry Buckle believed that moral statistics proved that individual actions were determined not by individual will, but solely by social causes working not on individual members of society but on the aggregate of the social organism. Thus, the metaphor of the "body social" helped to transfer the object, man, from one area of knowledge to the other. At the end of the century, the work of the social scientists reached its climax in Durkheim's *Suicide,* a study that launched sociology as an independent discipline in the study of man. But the new model of man combined characteristics posited by medical and social science with those of the Christian model. (These nineteenth-century developments constitute the focal point of my study.)

In addition to displaying some of the resources that nineteenth-century Russian culture placed at people's disposal, these fragments from the history of the symbolic meaning of suicide suggest several general principles. Most important, they demonstrate that both culture and concrete individuals experience and interpret suicide as a symbolic act that illuminates fundamental problems of human existence; that suicide, an act of intense emotional ambivalence and varied cultural functions, readily absorbs multifarious meanings; and that, in the course of its historical and cross-cultural transmission, these meanings mutate.

1 Suicide and Western Science: Man's Two Bodies

Toward the end of the eighteenth century, it was becoming increasingly clear that man no longer lived exclusively under the dispensation of Christian principles. Philosophers challenged the Christian view of man. In spite of special efforts, pathological anatomy and medical physiology could find no clear location for the soul. The forces responsible for human consciousness and human action were sought within man's body. Throughout the nineteenth century, with the rise of positivism the sciences continued to encroach on the ground held by theology and metaphysics; advances of physics, chemistry, and physiology were followed by the rise of social science. The new sciences worked on creating a new, positive mode of knowledge and a new model of man. The "new man" had to shake off "the old Adam" created in the image and likeness of God: mental life had to be described without using the notion of the soul; human action had to be explained without resorting to free will; man had to be reconnected to a larger whole, if not to God, then to society; and the ultimate problem—mortality—had to be faced. Underlying these efforts was another concern: constructing the object of investigation. The problem was especially poignant and lasting for social science. In his 1897 *Suicide: A Study in Sociology,* Durkheim argued that "for sociology to be possible, it must above all have an object all its own."[1] The new man—an object of positivistic science—was created to fit the emerging disciplines.

In this chapter, I review discussions of suicide in biological and social studies concerned with human action. Between the 1830s and the 1890s, such discussions preoccupied dozens of scientists, mostly medical pathologists and statisticians, in different parts of Europe. Suicide became a laboratory for the investigation of problems posed by positivism.

Suicide and Medicine

Considered medically, suicide was a symptom of disease, a form of insanity, or mental alienation. Associated with the name of Etienne Esquirol, this view dates back to the early 1820s. In his 1838 classic *Mental Maladies* (Des maladies mentales), Esquirol claimed to have proven that "suicide offers all the characteristics of mental alienation, of which it is, in reality, a symptom," and that "man only makes attempts upon his life, when in a state of delirium, and that suicides are insane persons."[2] From this, it followed that suicide, as an involuntary act, should not be punished by law. The argument was meant to settle the issue of which authority was responsible for suicide: in the 1830s the "jurisdiction" over suicide shifted from metaphysical, moral, and legal authority to medical.[3]

Esquirol made his mark on European thinking about suicide; moreover, he had a following. His student J.-P. Falret in *On Hypochondria and on Suicide* (De l'hypochondrie et du suicide, 1822) connected suicide to hypochondria. Another medic, C. E. Bourdin, in *Du suicide considéré comme maladie* (1845), presented suicide as a disease in itself (suicidal monomania). Although in the course of the 1840s and 1850s the exclusivity of the medical view came under attack by clinicians and statisticians,[4] the view of suicide as a distinct form of insanity and the belief that suicide could occur *only* in a state of insanity persisted throughout the nineteenth century. Durkheim found it essential to combat these often-debated views in the opening chapter of his 1897 treatise.

Striving "to fix upon the seat of suicide,"[5] Esquirol considered the data of postmortem reports. If suicidal pathology were to be located inside the body, grounding the mental in the physical, the question of the cause of suicide would be settled. This would also illuminate a larger question: the nature of human action. But a definitive answer was not to be found. Esquirol had to admit that "the opening of the dead bodies of suicides has shed little light on this subject"; the changes (mostly in the brain and the organs of digestion) were "so varied, that we could infer nothing from them."[6] However, attempts to fix the seat of thought, sentiment, and action in the body continued and some scientists were inclined to see them as successful.

In England, Forbes Winslow, the author of the popular *Anatomy of Suicide* (1840), also emphasized the importance of tracing suicide and other mental phenomena to the physical condition of the body. He claimed as a fact that "the disposition to commit self-destruction is, to a great extent, amenable to those principles which regulate our treatment of ordinary disease; and that, to a degree more than is generally supposed, it originates in derangement of the brain and abdominal viscera."[7] In a chapter titled "Appearances Presented after Death in Those Who Have Committed Suicide," he reviewed evidence offered by Esquirol, Falret, and other authors who reported a variety of structural changes to the organs of suicides: the cranial bones and the membranes of the brain are variously affected; "the heart is sometimes found seriously disorganized"; "the stomach, liver, and intestines, are the most frequent seats of morbid phenomena."[8] Though in many cases the evidence was inconclusive, this did not shake Winslow's belief in the primacy of physical causes: "In many cases, the brain is apparently free from structural derangement; and yet, reasoning physiologically, we must believe that in every case the sentient organ must be affected, either primarily or secondarily. There are many instances in which there cannot be a doubt but that the cerebral organ is the seat of the disease, but in which, after death, no vestige of the malady can be discovered!"[9] In an earlier chapter, "The Result of Insanity?" he insisted that suicidal madness had an organic cause: "Insanity results from a disease of the brain. Although after death, in many cases, no appreciable structural lesion can be detected in the cerebral mass, it would be illogical for us to conclude that the sentient organ has not been physically affected. Derangement of mind is but the effect of physical disease."[10] Clearly, this statement resembles the recitation of a credo rather than a product of logical reasoning.

Although attempts to locate the causes of suicide in the body yielded few results, the practice continued all over Europe throughout the nineteenth century and well into the twentieth. As early as 1828, the Englishman G. M. Burrows (in the words of Ian Hacking) "marvelled at the excessive 'zeal and labor' spent on cutting up cadavers in order to find out the proximate causes of suicide."[11] But in 1889, the Russian Ivan Gvozdev, who had opened more than a hundred corpses, concluded that "even if we were to use the whole power of our reasoning, we cannot accept any other reason but cerebral pathology as the immediate cause of *every* suicide."[12] As late as 1909 (to give just one common example), in Vienna, the physician Anton Brosch (inspired among others by Falret and Bourdin) opened 371 corpses—to conclude that definite and unquestionable traces of mental abnormality were evident in 7.6 percent of cases.[13]

The beliefs and patterns of reasoning that guided Winslow and Gvozdev were encouraged by the main authorities of positivistic and materialistic thought. As Claude Bernard put it in his widely acclaimed *Introduction to the Study of Experimental Medicine* (Introduction à la médicine expérimentale, 1865), not being able to find an "anatomical relation" (a lesion indicating the presence of disease in the body) "amounts to acknowledging an effect without a cause."[14] This would undermine the whole enterprise of positivism; therefore, it was crucial to find a way to account for the absence of visible manifestations of mental affliction in matter. In *Force and Matter* (Kraft und Stoff, 1855), a work that popularized materialism, inspiring a whole generation of German (and Russian) radicals, Ludwig Büchner, stated that it was only "owing to the imperfections of our senses" that it might not be possible, in all cases, to detect material manifestations of a mental affliction in the body.[15] In his view, strong evidence of a direct causal connection between mind and matter was provided by "the remarkable vivisections and experiments of Flourens." Working with live fowl, Flourens removed parts of the brain in layers, concluding from the reactions of the animals that "the mental capacities were removed in the same ratio," until "every mental function, every capacity to perceive sensual impressions, was obliterated, without extinguishing life." (Preserved by artificial feeding, the fowl remained in this state for years, and even gained weight.) "Can we desire any stronger proof as to the necessary connection of the soul and the brain than that afforded by the knife of the anatomist, who cuts off the soul piecemeal?" asked Büchner.[16]

Suicide and Moral Statistics

Beginning in the 1830s, a new discipline, moral statistics, took upon itself the investigation of suicide.[17] By recording human actions, calculating their rates, and arranging these figures in relation to physical and social factors such as age, sex, race, climate, seasons, soil, religion, profession, and economic conditions—that is (in the words of Frederick Lange), "by skillful combination of the numbers to be compared"—statisticians sought to gain insight into the "machinery of social life" that underlies an individual act.[18] Moral statisticians dealt with marriages (and occasionally births), crimes (especially murder), prostitution, and alcoholism, but they clearly emphasized suicide. They saw a close affinity between their discipline and pathological medicine. A later practitioner, Enrico Morselli (a medical doctor), in his classic *Suicide: An Essay on Comparative Moral Statistics* (Il suicidio: saggio di statistica morale comparata, 1879), found a similarity of origin between sociology and "psychological physical pathology"—"both the progeny of our times, both arisen out of the ruins of metaphysics."[19] The main thesis of moral statistics was the same as that of medicine: suicide is an involuntary action; it is aimed at a common enemy, metaphysics. But while medicine looked for the cause of suicide within man's body, social science looked outside the individual. In the words of a Russian popularizer of moral statistics, the cause of *every* suicide has its roots not within the individual, but in the society that surrounds him.[20]

The argument ran as follows. Statistics shows that certain phenomena of human action commonly considered to be willful repeat themselves with remarkable regularity. The coincidence of individual acts suggest that, rather than being a function of free will, they result from strict causality and are subject to forces lying outside the individual.[21] Statistics shows that the recurrence of suicide and murder is as regular as the recurrence of natural death. Thus moral phenomena resemble physical phenomena, which are subject to underlying laws, hidden from the naked eye. The logic of this argument implied not that suicide was a disease, but that it was *like* a (bodily) disease: it called for a metaphor.

The first person to draw such inferences from statistical data was L. Adolphe Quételet (around 1828).[22] Henry Buckle, in his famous introduction to the *History of Civilization in England* (1857), laid bare the philosophical implications of statistical investigations into human action: they revealed the "incontestable truth" that settled the controversy between free will and determinism. "Expressed in mathematical language," the uniformity of mental phenomena attested to the impossibility of free will, thus rejecting "metaphysical and theological dogma."[23] In Buckle's terms, crime and suicide are results of social laws, "more capable of being predicted, than are the physical laws connected with the disease and destruction of our bodies." Human actions "are the result of large and general causes, which, working upon the aggregate of society, must produce certain consequences, without regard to the volition of those particular men of whom the society is composed." Thus, "suicide is merely the product of the general condition of society."[24]

Twenty years later, drawing on comparative data accumulated by a generation of moral statisticians who worked in different European countries, Enrico Morselli echoed Buckle's argument: "By the statistical returns of suicide is disclosed then, through a long series of years, such a regularity as to surpass, as Wagner proved, the statistical laws of births, deaths, and marriages. This fact has helped to change radically the metaphysical idea of the human will, and in the hands of Quételet, Wagner, and Drobisch, has served as a formidable weapon to deny the reality of independent human actions, and to declare that the same laws exist in the moral as in the physical world."[25] Morselli joined Quételet in asserting that "the philosophical dogma of spontaneity of acts is one of the usual forms under which and at all times human pride and sentimentalism have been concealed."[26]

Moral statistics challenged not only "metaphysics," "sentimentalism" and "the old [Romantic] philosophy of individualism," which "had given to suicide the character of liberty and spontaneity,"[27] but also medical science. As a positivist and medical doctor, Morselli shared the view that human actions (as well as thoughts and feelings) are nothing but manifestations of the organic functions of the brain, no different than muscle contractions or reflexive actions.[28] But as a social scientist, he believed that even "the most positive" mode of study, when applied to individual cases, would not suffice to reveal those numerous influences to which "the most fatal and at the same time apparently most arbitrary actions, suicide and crime," are subject, influences "which collectively are universal, perpetual, and intense."[29]

The basic differences in the modes of knowledge offered by the Christian ("metaphysical") worldview, medicine, and social science lay in how each of them constructed its object, man. Christian anthropology endowed man with free will and an immortal soul. For positivistic medicine, man was the body. Social science, engaged in constructing its object throughout the second half of the nineteenth century, offered yet another model. Let us take a closer view at this process.

The first attempt was made by Quételet, when, in *On Man* (Sur l'homme, 1835), he postulated what he called an "average," or "mean" man (*l'homme moyen*), a "fictitious being" (*être fictif*), whose physical and moral characteristics were determined by taking the arithmetical mean of many individual cases. For Quételet, there was a reality to the mean man.[30] He claimed that the majority of individual cases reproduce, with a degree of fluctuation, this average type, from which, under the influence of "disturbing causes," only a minority deviate. Moreover, as civilization advances, deviation of individuals from the average type tends to disappear. One could say that the fictitious being was taking over the living person.

As Quételet admitted, the take-over indicated a change in the cultural climate: "It would seem at first sight that the fine arts and literature must suffer from this state of things . . . [for] whatever is more picaresque in society . . . ought ostensibly to disappear. Even during the last half century, and within the limits of Europe alone, we see how great the tendency is for people to lose their national character and be amalgamated in one common type (109/2:327)."[31]

In Quételet's personal development, the Romantic sentiments that had nurtured him as a young man who grew up during the Napoleonic era and aspired to a literary career gave way to social concerns, which motivated his activities as a statistician in the 1830s.[32] In both social and personal life, individualism was on the decline.

Some forty years later, Durkheim, in his *Suicide*, declared Quételet's theory of the average man to be entirely unsatisfactory, because it made the origin of morality an insoluble problem. "For since the individual is in general not outstanding, how has a morality so far surpassing him succeeded in establishing itself, if it expresses only the average of individual temperament?"[33] Such questions preoccupied many nineteenth-century thinkers. To make morality possible in a godless world, one had to relate the individual to a higher, external reality other than God. Had moral statistics offered a new model of man, a model that both accounted for the remarkable regularity of human action and satisfied this requirement?

According to Durkheim, the theory of the average man "has remained the only systematic explanation" of the discovery made by moral statisticians—that is, of "the remarkable regularity with which certain social phenomena repeat themselves during identical periods of time."[34] I would argue that another explanation was, indeed, offered—not as a "systematic explanation," but as a metaphor. The new model of man can be found in the phraseology of moral statisticians: it was the metaphor of society as a collective personality—a social organism or social body.

Indeed, while arguing for the "average man," Quételet also operated with a different unit: the *corps social,* a large number of individuals to whom statistical rates, which have no direct application to an individual, apply. This collective man, or collective body, was the object of moral statistics: "It is the social body which forms the object of our researches, and not the peculiarities distinguishing the individuals composing it"; it is "the study of the social body" that "we have in view" (7/1:15). In the framework of this research, man led a dual existence, as a part of the social body and as a separate individual: "As a member of the social body, he is subjected every instant to the necessity of these [social] causes, and pays them a regular tribute; but as a man, employing all the energy of his intellectual faculties, he in some measure masters these causes, and modifies their effect, thus constantly endeavouring to improve his condition (7/1:13)." The notion of the dual existence of man allowed for a compromise between the social and the personal; individualism crept in.

About thirty years later, Morselli, writing in the context of social Darwinism, which deliberately and systematically merged biological and social concepts, used "the social organism" (*l'organismo sociale*) as his central metaphor. In Morselli's words, since the examination of every single case would not suffice, it was essential to study not the individual body (a subject of psychological medicine) but "the whole of society, in the expression of its wants and tendencies, that is, in the functions of its complicated organism" (10/45).[35] Morselli defined the object of the new discipline in terms that anticipated Durkheim's widely acclaimed definition of social science's object. He argued that while psychology investigates the development of individual thought, "sociology or moral statistics, on the contrary, determines manifestations and developments of the total thought, so that it could be called *a psychology of collective man* [*psicologia dell'umanita collettiva*]" (12).

This implies that the method of medicine works, but only when it is applied to a different object. The transition from the medical to the social model of man was achieved by transferring notions that traditionally described the individual body to the collective body of society. Social science did not replace medical science but engulfed it.

To appreciate the heuristic potential of the new model of man—the collective man, or the *corps social*—it is essential to trace the genealogy of this metaphor. In the pages that follow, I will demonstrate that the new model was a mutant, combining characteristics of the old, Christian model and the positivistic models offered by the physical and biological sciences.

The Genealogy of the Collective Man

Theology: the Mystical Body of Christ

The metaphor the "collective body" has a sacred lineage that goes back to the Pauline concept of *corpus Christi,* the mystical body of Christ. A symbol of the Church, by extension it represents the whole of the Christian society. The concept mediates between multiplicity and wholeness: "For as the body is one, and hath many members, and all the members of that one body, being many, are one body: so also is Christ" (1 Cor. 12:12). As Ernst Kantorowicz has shown, this theological notion found a parallel in medieval political doctrine.[36] Merging the theological and the political, medieval political and legal documents defined relations between the king and the people through the metaphor of the king's double body: the body natural and the body politic, the latter being the aggregate of the king's subjects. One is a human body, individual and personal; the other is a corporate body, "super-individual" and "collective." The first is mortal, the second immortal.

The notion of the king's two bodies, distinct yet one, is obviously a projection of the Christological dogma of the two natures of Christ. The use of this notion indicates the sacralization of secular power and the concomitant secularization of the sacred. Kantorowicz has demonstrated how, over the course of the Middle Ages, the concept of the mystical body of Christ, which originally had liturgical and sacramental meanings, took on legalistic and sociological connotations. It was transferred to secular social organizations—corporations, the state, people, mankind—an assemblage or aggregate of people that was seen as one body, as an organism.* But having acquired the sociological and "organological" connotations, the concept nevertheless preserved "its definitely sacramental ring."[37]

Secularization of the mystical collective body reached a climax in the eighteenth century, when widely used phrases such as "the body politic" (*corps politique*) and its parallel, "the body social" (*corps social*), entered the political discourse of the Enlightenment and the French Revolution. At this point, the concept was deliberately stripped of its sacramental aura. According to Dorinda Outram, since "the collapse of the symbolism of the king's body," the human body has taken the place of *corpus Christi* as a model for the social body.[38] In the age of the Enlightenment, and later in the age of positivism, science, not theology, provided models that described society as an aggregate of its members. Physics, which studied inorganic matter, and later biology and social science, played an important role. These disciplines addressed the same structural problem: the relations between element and compound, or part and whole.

---

*The concept had consequences for views on suicide in the Middle Ages and later periods. In the words of Kantorowicz (who was paraphrasing Edmund Plowden's *Reports*) "the suicide committed an act of felony not only because he acted against nature and God, but also (as the Tudor jurists pointed out) against the King in that hereby he . . . 'has lost one of his mystic members'" (p. 269; see also p. 15).

Science: Atoms, Cells, Individuals, and Society

In the first half of the nineteenth century, atomic and molecular theories showed that matter was made up of independent particles, atoms and molecules. (These theories, which date back to the early 1800s, were fully accepted by physicists and philosophers by the 1850s.) In theological terms, matter appeared divisible, yet whole. And a transformation of quality occurred in the transition from element to compound, for each of the components obviously had properties very different from those of the body they constituted.

Among the far-reaching metaphysical implications of atomic theory was the notion of the "immortality of matter" formulated by Büchner, who argued that, since an atom cannot arise anew or disappear but can only change its combinations, "matter is immortal." For the same reason, it was "impossible" for the world to have been created. Büchner reasoned: "There exists a phrase, repeated *ad nauseam,* of 'mortal body and immortal spirit.' A closer examination causes us with more truth to reverse the sentence. The body is certainly mortal in its individual form, but not in its constituents. It changes not merely in death, but, as we have seen, also during life: however, in a higher sense it is immortal, since the smallest particle of which it is composed cannot be destroyed. On the contrary, that which we call 'spirit' disappears with the dissolution of the individual material combination."[39] The quality of immortality relies on the indestructability of the smallest particle, the atom, as well as on the notion of the compound. While in the above passage each constituent is presented as permanent, while the combination is mutable, in another passage (on the same page of *Force and Matter*) it is the whole (mother earth) that appears to be imperishable: "We return visibly to the earth from which we were taken. But, whilst we change, the earth endures and is more and more developed; it is an immortal being."[40]

Interpreted by materialists of Büchner's bent, who were eager to replace religion with science, atomic theory was equivalent to the theological paradigm of division and wholeness, gave a scientific justification for the miracle of the transformation of quality, and, most importantly, promised "positive" immortality. What had been secularized in the age of Enlightenment was sacralized in the post-Romantic era.

Cell theory, formulated in the middle of the nineteenth century, offered a paradigm of relations between element and compound as it applied to organic, "living" matter. It used the same structural principles as atomic theory; in fact, the two developed in relation to one another. While elaboration of atomic theory initially stimulated cell theory, ideas of cell structure in turn influenced ideas about atomic structure.[41]

A central role in the development of cell theory was played by the cellular biologist and pathologist Rudolf Virchow, who also distinguished himself as a medical and political reformer, anthropologist, and archaeologist. Many of the concerns of the age converged in this man. In his classic *Cellular Pathology* (Die Cellularpathologie, 1858) Virchow postulated that each cell is an autonomous and vital unit (i.e., a unit "manifesting all the characteristics of life").[42] When it is organized, a multitude of cells forms a body (the individual) that has properties different from those of its constituent elements. Thus, just as a cell is both a whole and a part, an individual is both a unity and a plurality.*

Cell theory had broad sociological and philosophical implications, which Virchow elaborated in his essay "Atoms and Individuals" ("Atome und Individuen," 1859). He developed a concept of the individual as two distinct identities fused into one. In his phraseology (both in the philosophical essay "Atoms and Individuals" and in the specialized biological study *Cellular Pathology*), Virchow clearly invited an analogy between the individual (a "community of cells") and society (a community of individuals): "The structural composition of a body of considerable size, a so-called individual, always represents a kind of a social arrangement of parts, an arrangement of a social kind." (*Cellular Pathology*).[43] "What is an organism? A society of living cells, a tiny well-ordered state." ("Atoms and Individuals").[44] In the words of Virchow's biographer, "his political and biological opinions reinforced each other mutually at this point. Cellular pathology showed the body to be a free state of equal individuals, a federation of cells, a democratic cell state. It showed it as a social unit composed of equals, while an undemocratic oligarchy of tissues was assumed in humoral, or solidistic (neuro) pathology."[45] The two paradigms, biological and social, merged. The object of medical science and the object of social science were defined in the course of mutual projection.

---

*In an effort to create a philosophical genealogy for his scientific deductions, Virchow connected them to Goethe's work on the metamorphosis of plants: "Every living thing," says Goethe, "is not single, but multiple; even in so far as it appears to us as an individual it remains nonetheless an association of living self-sufficient beings, which, though alike in idea or plan, can in their manifestations be identical or similar, unlike or dissimilar" ("Atoms and Individuals," p. 132).

The metaphoric connection between the human organism and society finds a parallel in Virchow's life. A reformer concerned with constitutional and public health problems, he campaigned for the liberalization of society (and of the medical profession) and worked against "social pathology"—poverty and urban decay—investing considerable energy in the improvement of sewage disposal in Berlin, thus improving, as it were, the body social's circulation.

The use of social metaphors in biology also had philosophical implications: an analogy between the cell/individual and individual/society relations called the concept of individuality into question. Virchow reasoned: "Now are the cells or the human beings individuals? Can a single answer be given to this question? I say No!" He commented that "the 'I' of the philosopher is a consequence of the 'We' of the biologists." Refraining from giving a final answer to his question, Virchow considered distinguishing between "collective individuals" and "single individuals."[46] An individual in relation to his cells, and a society in relation to human individuals, are such "collective individuals." The difference between life and death, health and disease, depends on the degree of integration among the individual parts of this collective whole: "As in the lives of nations, so in the lives of individuals the state of health of the whole is determined by the well-being and close interrelation of the individual parts; disease appears when individual members begin to sink into a state of inactivity disadvantageous to the commonwealth, or to lead a parasitic existence at the expense of the whole."[47] It follows that whether or not human beings can be considered "individuals," "life" is a quality of the compound.

It appears that metaphors provided the only resolution to the question of individuality brought forth by the mid-nineteenth-century advances of science. In all likelihood, Virchow was neither oblivious to nor regretful of this fact; one of the greatest biologists of his age, in the assessment of his biographer, "he might also well qualify as a philologist."[48] Indeed, Virchow's writings are full of philological excursions. Moreover, he derived ideas about the underlying structure of natural phenomena from the etymological structure of concepts. In drawing an analogy between atoms and individuals, Virchow started with an observation on the common etymology of the two words: the Greek word "atom" means precisely the same thing as the Latin word "individual": something that can no longer be divided. In his search for the initial meaning of "word-roots," he sought the moment in which "consciousness unveils itself."[49] His biographer compared Virchow's bent for philology to his predilection for the microscopic (and,

I would add, anatomical) investigation of organic tissues, arguing that both inclinations had a "common root."[50] Like many in his generation of scientists, Virchow sought a synthesis of the sensual (scientific) and the metaphysical in his cultivation of metaphoric forms of expression.

While the analogy between the individual and society has been used extensively since the time of the Greeks, its immediate sources in the mid-nineteenth-century positivistic culture included Romantic mythology.[51] Earlier in the century, the problem of the relation between element and compound had troubled those Romantic social thinkers who sought to make a transition from the individual to the collective life of man. This problem was addressed by French Christian socialists. Saint-Simon and, especially, his followers, Lamennais, Leroux, and Enfantin, with their predilection for theological meta-phors and Christian mysticism, spoke of society as the *Homme collectif, Homme-humanité,* an echo of the androgynous Adam of the occultists—a symbol of a whole, undivided humanity that existed before the Fall precipitated division into individuals and sexes. The image of the single, collective man was widely used in the fiction of social Romantics such as Hugo and Balzac. Out of this context, the image of humanity as the *Grand être* and the concept of the social or collective organism (society as an ordered organism) arose. This idea was prevalent in the writings of Auguste Comte, whom some consider the founder of sociology.

In the second half of the nineteenth century, the age-old analogy between the living organism and society, with its mystical and Romantic connotations, received a new impetus from the advances of biological science and the theory of evolution.[52] Comte's image of society as an organism had its counterpart in Virchow's conception of the organism as a society of cells.[53] With the development of cell theory, what was previously a figure of speech ("social organism") or a mystical notion (the androgynous Adam) became a scientifically proven entity, in which biologists' formulations were reinforced by social theories. The appeal of the "social organism" was irresistible to positivistically inclined minds. By the 1880s, through the efforts of such social scientists as Herbert Spencer, Paul von Lilienfeld, Albert Schäffle, A. Espinas, J. Novicow, and René Worms, the discourse built on the notion of social organism became dominant in social theory.[54] In his 1895 *Social Pathology* (La pathologie sociale), Lilienfeld used this metaphor and appealed to cell theory in order to argue that sociology deserved the status of a positive science: "The condition *sine qua non* in order for sociology to be raised to the rank of a positive science and for the inductive method to be applicable thereto is . . .

31

the conception of human society as an actual living organism, composed of cells in the same way as individual organisms in nature."[55] Two years later, in *Suicide,* which successfully launched sociology as a scientific discipline, Durkheim also argued that the concept of society as a unified entity had a reality of its own (a matter for later discussion). Thus in the latter half of the nineteenth century, in the eyes of the students of society who followed in Comte's footsteps, the mystical androgyne of the Romantics became an object of positive science.

Each of the three scientific paradigms—atomic theory, cell theory, and moral statistics—addressed the same general philosophical problems. Mutual projection reinforced the solutions the paradigms offered to these problems. One issue was that of part and whole, division and wholeness. Positivistic science aspired to reveal the world as a unity, a connected whole subject to immutable laws, which were comprehensible and predictable.[56] Moreover, integrity was an essential condition for the vitality of the unit. In the eyes of social scientists, the social organism—an aggregate of individuals—became such a unity. So did the biological organism: all parts of a living body were interrelated and inseparable. In the words of Claude Bernard, "trying to separate one from the whole means transferring it to the realm of dead substances."[57] The principle of unity not only guaranteed predictability, but also helped to define the difference between life and death.

Underlying all three paradigms is an epistemological problem—a concern with the positive validity of knowledge. Büchner commented that, while for the ancients the atom was merely a philosophical category, natural science made the atom a physical reality. Yet as James Clerk Maxwell noted, the knowledge of matter advanced by atomic or molecular theories was "of essentially statistical nature." And "if the molecular theory of the constitution of bodies is true, all our knowledge of matter is of a statistical kind."[58] From this followed a parallel between knowledge of matter advanced by atomic/molecular theory and knowledge of man advanced by moral statistics: "those uniformities which we observe in our experiments with quantities of matter containing millions and millions of molecules are uniformities of the same kind as those . . . wondered at by Buckle, arising from the slumping together of a multitude of cases, each of which is by no means uniform with the others."[59]

The analogy between the nature of knowledge in moral statistics and physics highlighted the fact that the new science of man was incapable of dealing with individual cases. Maxwell continued: "If we betake ourselves to the statistical method, we do so confessing that we are unable to follow the details of each individual case, and expecting that the effects of widespread causes, though very different in each individual, will produce an average result on the whole nation, from the study of which we may estimate the propensities of an imaginary being called the Mean Man."[60] In order to become an object of positive knowledge, man had to be replaced by an artificial, constructed being. In this case, it was Quételet's mean man.

The analogy between moral statistics and cell theory offered different, and richer, possibilites. It suggested a model of man as a social organism; that is, not as the mean man, but as the collective man. The analogy appeared to have strengthened the positive validity of statistical knowledge. In Virchow's words, the individual, although a community of cells, is "an *actual* unity in opposition to the merely conceptual unity of the atom."[61] Unlike atoms and molecules, "not one of which ever becomes sensible to us," the constituent elements, the individual cells, could actually be perceived.[62]

Direct access to the composite nature of organic matter was granted by anatomical dissection. In *Cellular Pathology,* Virchow emphasized that cell theory was based principally on anatomical observations. With the help of elaborate techniques for dissecting tissues into minute particles, and aided by microscopes that permitted examination of infinitely small matter, biologists revealed to human senses the reality of the individual units composing the whole of the organism. Knowledge gained in this manner appeared to have the greatest validity—it could benefit not only biology (cell theory) but also sociology (moral statistics), which was defined by analogy with biology.

Medicine: The Symbolism of Autopsy

Throughout the nineteenth century, anatomy was the central metaphor of positive knowledge. According to Foucault, "pathological anatomy was given the curious privilege of bringing to knowledge . . . the first principles of its positivity."[63] As a symbolic act, anatomy connotes uncovering the hidden depths and revealing the underlying causes of life and death (the Russian term, *vskrytie,* "uncovering," reinforces these connotations). Working from the manifest to the hidden, dissection turns the body into a legible text.[64] In decomposing phenomena into their elements, dissection performs analysis.* For mid-nineteenth-century positivistic scientists, anatomizing also meant finding manifestations of the mental in the physical, assigning causality, and transcending the individual and the subjective to attain the objective truth in matter.

By dissecting the dead, the anatomist sought to reveal the secret of life. In pursuit of this goal, science also adopted another procedure: vivisection. "Vivisection," wrote Claude Bernard, "is only an autopsy on the living."[65] He elaborated: "After dissecting cadavers, then, we must necessarily dissect living beings, to uncover the inner or hidden parts of the organisms and see them work; to this sort of operation we give the name of vivisection, and without this mode of investigation, neither physiology nor scientific medicine is possible; to learn how man and animals live, we cannot avoid seeing great numbers of them die, because the mechanisms of life can be unveiled and proved only by knowledge of the mechanisms of death."[66] In the long run, autopsy and vivisection aimed at catching death in the act.

The practitioners of dissection in the positivist generation were acutely aware of the symbolic potential of their scientific method. Virchow viewed autopsy, which he understood as direct observation of the underlying connections, as "*the* method of natural science."[67] Instructing students in *The Technique of Dissection* (Die Sektiontechnik im Leichenhause des Charité-Krankenhauses, 1875), accepted as the standard manual throughout Europe and the United States, he decribed dissection of the brain poetically—as a procedure that turns the organ into an open book. It often happens (he argued) that it is desirable to reexamine the dissected organ at a later stage of investigation: "Very simple precautions are required to rearrange the parts of an organ thus dissected; it resembles a book, the leaves of which can be opened here and there, or even entirely separated, and then again closed. But the object in having a book bound is to secure to every leaf a definite place, where it can be found in a moment without much trouble."[68] To conclude the procedure, one needs to examine the cerebral ventricles in the depth of the brain, exposed "by digging, almost in mining fashion, with the handle of the scalpel."[69] Comparing anatomy to mining or archaeology, that is, to penetration

---

*This idea was propagated by Condillac (see Jordanova, *Sexual Visions,* p. 56). Foucault commented that, as an act of analysis, postmortem examination only extends what is done by death: "Death is the great analyst that shows the connections by unfolding them, and bursts open the wonders of genesis in the rigour of decomposition: and the word *decomposition* must be allowed to stagger under the weight of its meaning" (*Birth of the Clinic,* p. 144).

into the body of the earth—be it the layers of geological formations or the layering of historical accumulations—Virchow added another symbolic dimension to autopsy. The connections were not limited to discourse: Virchow made archaeology (along with physical anthropology) one of his professional pursuits. His excavations and reconstructions of sites in Northern Germany (in 1865) revealed the Slavonic origins of this area; in 1879 he participated in Schliemann's expedition in search of Homer's Troy.

The fact that diverse pursuits—anatomy, archaeology, etymology, and concern with cell theory, sewage disposal, and constitutional reform—converged in the personality of one man, reinforces the power of the metaphor.[70] In Virchow's activities, the connections between objects of knowledge—the human and the social organisms, or the human body and the earth—are powerfully emphasized. The symbolism of his investigative procedures is clearly revealed: they involve uncovering hidden connections, penetrating the layered past in matter and language, deconstructing the dead into parts and subsequently reconstructing the living whole. What also becomes apparent is the inherent connection between analysis and reform. In this sense, one can say that the individual—the scientist Rudolf Virchow—is a living metaphor of the knowledge attained by his age.

As if to increase the positive validity of sociological or statistical knowledge, moral statisticians and their proponents employed anatomical metaphors to describe the method of their discipline. In the opening pages of his *History of Civilization in England,* Buckle described statistical methods in sociohistorical investigation (measuring and registering information on the physical, economic, and moral constitution of the country) as "the anatomy of a nation." Morselli, in the introduction to his study of suicide, claimed that statistics, which "scrutinizes, measures and compares" various processes at work in society, thus investigating society's internal organization, performs a "genuine process of social autopsy" (*vero processo di autopsia sociale*).[71] By analogy with anatomical knowledge, sociological knowledge seemed to have attained true positivity.

However, in the strict sense, moral statistics is not autopsy, but vivisection, for the collective body of society, after all, is alive (and immortal). Moreover, it is vivisection performed on one's own body. This became apparent when Morselli's metaphors were translated into Russian. A. V. Likhachev, in his *Suicide in Western Europe and European Russia. An Essay in Comparative Statistics* (Samoubiistvo v Zapadnoi Evrope i Evropeiskoi Rossii. Opyt sravnitel'no-statistich-eskogo issledovaniia, 1882), reproduced Morselli's method, his rhetorical strategies, and his conclusions. In the Russian rendition, the procedure is defined as *self*-autopsy: "developing statistics, society, as it were, subjects itself to a forensic autopsy [*obshchestvo kak by podvergaet sebia sudebno-meditsinskomu vskrytiiu*]."[72] In an act of self-vivisection, society tears itself open to look at its own entrails. The metaphor promised that, as with Bernard's vivisections, the mechanism of (social) life could be fully exposed. It also revealed the dangers inherent in the position of a human science in which man was both the subject and the object of knowledge.

The metaphor of moral statistics as an autopsy of the body social appears to be well justified. Like anatomy, statistics strives to uncover the structures underlying the flux of external forms. Schlözer defines statistics as "history standing still" (a statement quoted by Morselli); it can also be seen as society standing still, or society as a corpse. In both disciplines, conclusions about life are made through recourse to death, and pathology plays an important role. And yet there is a discrepancy that passed unnoticed by those proponents of moral statistics who drew the analogy. While anatomy goes from the whole, which is a given, to the parts, which are made accessible through dissection, moral statistics reverses the process. Only the individual phenomena, that is, the parts, are a given. "Slumping together" many individual cases, statistics constructs the whole (society), which exists only as a conceptual unity. Presenting itself as anatomy or vivisection, moral statistics (and its outgrowth, sociology) actually reenacts the work of Frankenstein: it constructs an artificial human being by (to paraphrase Mary Shelley) assembling the parts furnished by charnel houses and the dissecting room. The social androgyne of the Romantics is replaced with an image fit for the age of science: the social organism as Frankenstein's monster—an indestructible, overgrown creature, capable of both exquisite sensitivity (which makes him akin to Werther) and murderous cruelty. In their search for the object of scientific investigation, the positivistic sciences of man, having proved incapable of dealing with individual cases, replaced the living man with an artificial creature, constructed mainly from materials furnished by those who had died by suicide.

The Metaphorical Structure of Durkheim's *Suicide*

Durkheim's 1897 *Suicide* has been viewed as an attempt to synthesize the principles and findings of moral statistics in order to demonstrate the need for sociology as an independent scientific discipline concerned with human action.[73] Durkheim's main problem is that of the object of investigation: "For sociology to be possible, it must above all have an object all its own"; "if no reality exists outside of individual consciousness [the object of psychology], it wholly lacks any material of its own" (38).[74] To create the science of sociology and construct "an object of its own" for it, Durkheim undertakes the investigation of suicide.

He starts by refuting the argument that medicine made to claim suicide as its object: "If a manifestation of insanity were reasonably to be supposed in every voluntary death . . . suicide would be a purely individual affliction" (58). He breaks the spell by questioning the "only" of Esquirol's influential argument ("a man attempts self-destruction only in delirium"): if "suicide of insane persons do not constitute the entire genus," then "psychopathic states constituting mental alienation can give no clue to the collective tendency to suicide in its generality"; that is, to the regularity of suicide rates revealed by moral statistics (67).

Durkheim's ultimate conclusion is that causes of suicide lie not in the individual (body or soul), and not in the physical environment, but in society; that is, in collective existence and collective activity. He argued that the coincidence of suicide with certain facts of physical and biological character, external or internal to the individual (such as climate, seasons, soil, sex, and age), which was noted by moral statisticians and attributed to the influence of material causes on "suicidal disposition," can be explained in terms of "collective existence": "if women kill themselves much less than men, it is because they are much less involved than men in collective existence"; "if suicide increases from January to June but then decreases, it is because social activity shows similar seasonal fluctuations" (299). Only when we relate suicide to certain states of social environment are we at last "face to face with real laws" (299). The reader is forewarned that every page of this book will give "the impression that the individual is dominated by a moral reality greater than himself: namely, collective reality" (38). This collective reality is society—the true object of sociology.

There also emerges from every page of *Suicide* a particular image of society: society as a "collective personality" (*la personalité collective*), a "social organism," complete with the "social body" and the "collective conscience" (*la conscience collective*), or "collective soul" (*l'âme collective*; 51/14).[75] Thus the object constructed by Durkheim is a metaphor that had already made its appearance in the works of social scientists who preceded him, from Quételet to Morselli, from

Comte to Spencer and Lilienfeld.[76] But unlike the moral statisticians, Durkheim developed the metaphor into a coherent model with remarkable explanatory power.[77]

As regards suicide, "collective personality" has a distinct identity that is bound to society's suicide rate: "the sum of all these individual cases has its own unity and its own individuality, since the social suicide rate is a distinctive trait of each collective personality" (322). It is an entity distinctly different from Quételet's "average man": it would be "a profound mistake to confuse the collective type of a society, as is so often done, with the average type of its individual members" (317/359). The collective type, Durkheim emphasizes, is qualitatively different from the sum of its parts: "Collective tendencies are of a different nature from individual tendencies and thoughts," "the former have characteristics which the latter lack." He anticipates the retort of a nonbeliever: "How can this be, it is objected, since there are only individuals in society?" (310). To convince the sceptics, he makes an analogy with atomic and cell theories: "reasoning thus we should have to say that there is nothing more in animate nature than inorganic matter, since the cell is made exclusively of inanimate atoms. To be sure, it is likewise true that society has no other active forces than individuals; but individuals by combining form a psychical existence of a new species, which consequently has its own manner of thinking and feeling" (310). A line of succession goes from atom to cell to individual organism to social organism. Ascending on this evolutionary ladder of sorts, we follow the generation of new species created by compounding. A series of mutations results in the appearance of a new, more complex being at each stage. At the top of the ladder stands a "social organism"—a highly sophisticated creature equipped with thinking and feeling.

Durkheim's famous classification of suicide into egoistic, altruistic, and anomic is worked into the same metaphor. Suicide occurs when "society allows the individual to escape it, being insufficiently aggregated in some part or even in the whole" (egoistic and anomic suicide) and when "society holds him in too strict a tutelage," the state "where the ego is not its own property, where it is blended with something not itself" (altruistic suicide) (221).

In many cases, however, the explanation for the causes of suicide does not come from the application of these categories: it is implicit in the use of metaphors, in the way that medical notions are transferred from the human body to the collective body of society.[78] For example, Durkheim claims that society's vitality depends on the degree of cohesion among its constituent parts, individuals—an image that can be found in the writings of many biologists in the mid-nineteenth century, such as Virchow and Bernard.[79] As Durkheim puts it, "in a cohesive and animated society [there is] a constant interchange of ideas and feelings from all to each and each to all" (210); these "currents" running through the social body (a circulatory system of sorts) allow the individual "to share in the collective energy" that nurtures him (210).[80] The life of each separate individual is a function of his integration into the social organism: "as we feel detached from society we become detached from that life whose source and aim is society" (212). Like a cell, a separate individual, although an autonomous and "vital" unit, cannot survive on its own. With the disintegration of the organism (society), an individual cell (the individual) necessarily dies—and this is how suicide comes about. Suicide is also the result of a morbid enlargement of a single cell (it is a cancerous growth, such as Virchow describes in *Cellular Pathology*). One could say that Durkheim explains individual suicide as a natural death, the death from a disease—not of the individual body though, but of the collective body.

Durkheim's narrative is informed by medical notions: "the relaxation of social bonds" is "a sort of collective asthenia," a "social malaise, just as individual sadness, when chronic, in its way reflects the poor organic state of the individual" (214). The notion of the "decay" and "decadence" of the collective body, identified as a cause of individual suicide, is probably related to Cesare Lombroso's theory of degeneration, which named "a decay of the organism" as a cause of a suicidal (and criminal) disposition. By transferring language used to describe the individual body to the social body, Durkheim literalized Lombroso's metaphor of degeneration: in Durkheim's discourse the "decay" of the body is understood literally, as decomposition of the whole into parts.

On the whole, the logic of his metaphors makes the author of *Suicide* a materialist. In his discourse, the mental activity of the social organism—ideology—is a symptom of the physical condition of the body social. At the time of "collective asthenia" which results in suicide epidemics (writes Durkheim), "metaphysical and religious systems spring up, which . . . attempt to prove to men the senselessness of life." He continues: "On their appearance they seem to have been created out of whole cloth by their makers who are sometimes blamed for the pessimism of their doctrines. In reality they are an effect rather than a cause; they merely symbolize in abstract language and systematic form the physiological distress of the body social" (214). The work of the pessimistic philosopher (such as Schopenhauer or

Hartmann), and the work of "the anarchist, the aesthete, the mystic, [and] the socialist revolutionary," all of whom are united by "a single sentiment of hatred and disgust for the existing order," merely indicates the disturbance of the "social organism"—the morbid development of a "collective melancholy that has reached the "higher centers of the social body" (369–70). Thus, in Durkheim's discourse, the idea is a "symbol" of the physiological condition. The ideational and the individual appear to have no real existence; the only reality is the collective body.

Apropos the "reality" of his construct, however, Durkheim seems to be an idealist—a proponent of philosophical realism. Having said that there is "nothing substantial or ontological" about the collective personality, since "it is merely a whole composed of parts," he adds that "it is just as real, nevertheless, as the elements that make it up" (319). Metaphors are "things": "It is not merely metaphor to say of each human society that it has a greater or lesser aptitude for suicide; the expression is based on the nature of things" (299). Again and again, Durkheim returns to this issue: "Usually when collective tendencies or passions are spoken of, we tend to regard these expressions as mere metaphors and manners of speech with no real signification but a sort of average among a certain number of individual states. They are not considered as things, forces *sui generis* which dominate the consciousness of single individuals. None the less this is their nature" (307).[81] As Jack Douglas has pointed out, Durkheim "faced up to the ageless conflict between the realists and the nominalists—and cast his lot with the realists."[82] And yet, as we saw earlier, the logic of his medical metaphors made Durkheim also cast his lot with the materialists.

I would argue that his theory and method are a synthesis of scientific positivism and philosophical realism (i.e., idealism). In Durkheim, arguments on the reality of metaphors are intertwined with analogies from physical and biological science. Discussing the forces of moral order, Durkheim argues: "Whatever they are called, the important thing is to recognize their reality and conceive of them as a totality of forces which cause us to act from without, like the physico-chemical forces to which we react. So truly are they things *sui generis* and not mere verbal entities that they may be measured, their relative sizes compared, as is done with the intensity of electric currents or luminous foci" (310). What imbues the object of sociology— the metaphor of "the collective personality"—with "reality" is the fact that it is constructed on the same pattern as the objects of natural sciences. Positivistic, scientific "realism" is compounded with philosophical, idealistic "realism."

What is the relationship between Durkheim's theory and the Christian view of man? Durkheim takes every chance to refute Christian notions. Having introduced the notion of the *collective soul,* he hastens to emphasize that "by the use of this expression we of course do not at all intend to hypostasize the collective conscience. We do not recognize any more substantial a soul in society than in the individual" (51). Speaking for science, Durkheim also explicitly rejects the morality that rests on the connection between man and God: "With good reason, religions and many philosophies with them have regarded morality as deriving its total reality only from God. For the pallid, inadequate sketch of it contained in individual consciences cannot be regarded as the original type. This sketch seems rather the result of a crude, unfaithful reproduction, the model for which must therefore exist somewhere outside individuals. This is why the popular imagination, with its customary over-simplicity assigns it to God. Science certainly could waste no time over this conception, of which it does not even take cognizance" (318). But despite such disclaimers, Durkheim borrows structural parameters and terms from Christian doctrine. Christian morality, as described by Durkheim, postulates a reality that, while being exterior and superior to the individual, dwells inside the individual. Indeed, in Christian anthropology, man, created in the image and likeness of God, is a model of God; simultaneously, man is a part of God, since his immortal soul represents the presence of the divine in man. Durkheim cites the theological definition of the soul as a "particle" of God (*une parcelle,* 334/379). He uses the same structural pattern and the same word to describe the relationship between the individual and society: individuals who "make up the great body of the nation" contain a "particle" of the collective current (316/357). Moreover, he casts society in the role of God, the creator of man: "just as society largely forms the individual, it forms him to the same extent in its own image [*elle le fait . . . à son image*]. Society, therefore, cannot lack the material for its needs, for it has, so to speak, kneaded it with its own hands" (323/366). Here, Durkheim transfers theological models and terms to social issues.

To conclude, in Durkheim's treatise, the object of the new science of sociology—the collective personality of society—appeared as a metaphoric construct, in which the configurations of both scientific theory and theological paradigm are clearly present.

The Mechanism of Meaning

In recent years the idea that bodily metaphors are central to nine-teenth-century social discourse has captivated historians of culture.[83] Arguably, the mutual projection and conflation of two concepts—that of the individual and that of society—structured mid-nineteenth-cen-tury thought on man. Revealing the rhetorical nature of cognition, the metaphor of the "body social" served as the force driving scientific knowledge. What is the mechanism by which the meaning of this metaphor is created and unfolded?

The metaphor of the collective body which pervaded the works of moral statisticians and Durkheim's synthesizing study inherited mul-tifarious characteristics from its several sources: theological thought, Romantic mythology, and various scientific theories. These charac-teristics contributed to the metaphor's rich resonance and explana-tory power. As a metaphor, it connected two separate domains. The old knowledge was transferred onto the new object: the discourse used to speak about the sacred, the physical, and the individual was applied to the secular, the mental, and the social. Moreover, the metaphor brought its own solutions to the problems that arose when the Christian view of man was challenged by positivism. It had the power to reconcile contradictions that the logical models of science had not resolved, and it generated new, at times unintended, mean-ings which resulted from the realization of the symbolic potential of its components. By a process of metaphoric osmosis, one object was endowed with the properties of the other. Thus the metaphoric con-nection between atomic theory and moral statistics made society sub-ject to the immortality that characterized matter. Moreover, the idea of the immortality of the corporate, collective body—the principle of medieval political theology—appeared to have received scientific cor-roboration. The projection of cell theory onto the relationship be-tween individual and society suggested a transfer of responsibility from individual to society. The cell analogy appeared to have deprived the individual of reason and will as well as the capacity to lead an au-tonomous existence. (For example, following the logic of the meta-phor, Morselli claimed that the individual's entire mental life was nothing but a reflexive action of the social body within which he lived.)[84]

In Durkheim's book, the transition from the individual to the col-lective body becomes an instrument for obliterating the difference be-tween the inanimate and animate (the dead and living), the external and internal, and the self and the other. Thus Durkheim implied that what is inanimate/dead as an element becomes alive when combined in a compound: an individual taken singly ("detached from society") is as good as dead, but within the collective personality, the individual receives life (212). In a similar fashion, the external can become the internal. Thus, what is external for the individual body is internal for the collective body. Moreover, because the individual is absorbed by the collective body, an external state actually becomes an internal state. In Durkheim's words, "collective states" (i.e., states exterior to the individual) within the group affect the individual by establishing in him "a new form of purely inner existence" (320). Egoism is transformed into altruism (and vice versa). It is often debated, writes Durkheim, "whether our feelings for our fellow-men are only extensions of egoistic sentiments or, on the contrary, independent of them" (359). He argues that "both hypotheses are baseless": "pity for another" is not a mere extension of "pity for ourselves," and yet "a bond of kinship exists between them"—they are both derived from "a single state of a collective conscience" (359). Within the collective personality, the self is the other.

Conflating the two planes of meaning, direct and metaphoric, proved to be a creative method capable of resolving the problems posed by the new age without abandoning established patterns. Thus, in accordance with the requirements of positivism, the model of *the body social* locates the seat of action within the "body"—not the physical body, however, but the metaphoric one, the body of society. And what was inaccessible in the individual body proved to be accessible in the collective body. While pathological anatomists had to admit (as Morselli lamented) that internal processes affecting suicide remained inaccessible to observation (it is impossible to "open up" mental processes as one opens up the brain in autopsy), moral statisticians claimed that they had uncovered the processes at work in the body social. Substituting one "body" for another created the impression that the "autopsy" could provide conclusive evidence.

By encouraging the conflation between the two planes of meaning, the metaphor reified the ambiguity. Questions about the individual (does the individual have a soul and free will?) and questions about suicide (is it caused by internal or external influences?) are "resolved" by accepting the ambiguity. The answer is: both. The individual is doubled. In Durkheim's words, "if . . . as has often been said, man is double, that is because social man superimposes himself upon physical man" (213). In other words, in the age of positivism, man, like Christ (and like the medieval king), has two bodies, the individual and the social.

The sociological model of the relations between the individual and society follows the same structural pattern as the theological model of the relations of man and God. And while the individuals making up a society "change from year to year," because they die (307), society itself (to borrow the phrase applied to the king's second body) "never dies." At the same time, the sociological model clearly parallels the model of relations between element and compound in atomic and cell theories. Sociology superimposed its object, the social man, upon Christ and upon the physical man, an object of natural science. The institutional shift among disciplines does not necessarily imply the epistemological shift: as if writing on the same slate, Christian anthropology, physiology, and sociology used the same structural pattern, or spatial model, and, frequently, the same terms. And their paradigms had similar implications for the ultimate problem: mortality. The "new man" of the positivistic age, constructed by social science as an object of scientific investigation, was inscribed on a palimpsest, over the visible contours of the "old Adam."

2 Russian Views: Church, Law, and Science

A Suicide Epidemic Hits Russia

In the 1860s, basing their impressions on newspaper chronicles and statistical data, Russian journalists noted that the suicide rate was increasing in all European countries: "Suicide is as old as humanity itself. . . . But in no other epoch in human history has it been as widespread . . . as in our enlightened and humane nineteenth century. Suicide has now become a kind of epidemic disease and furthermore a chronic disease claiming thousands of victims among the populations of all the civilized countries of Europe. That is what the statistics say, and any person who reads the city chronicle of events can tell you the same."[1]

Russia, considered more backward than most Western European countries, had recently caught up with the West in suicide rate. Journalists, hygienists, municipal authorities, scientists, writers, and the general public were united in the belief that, for the first time, Russia was hit by an epidemic of suicide. The suicide epidemic continued to preoccupy public attention until the 1880s. It was a matter of common opinion that suicide was both a "sign" and a "product" of the age—the era of the Great Reforms, associated with disintegration of the social and moral order.

The reforms started with the emancipation of the serfs in 1861—an act that incorporated millions of peasants into Russian society and involved a partial decentralization of authority. Local administrations in towns, cities and provinces (the reformed municipal organs and the newly created *zemstvos*) were to assume responsibility for public welfare and public health. Judicial reform (1864) liberalized legal proceedings and opened them to the public. The new censorship statute (1865) offered more freedom to the press and created conditions for expanding press coverage and increasing the circulation of newspapers and journals. A policy of glasnost ("openness," literally, "voiced-ness") opened the workings of the social mechanism and the daily lives of ordinary people to the public eye. Daily life became a matter of social responsibility and public concern.[2]

In the sixties, Russians experienced an intellectual revolution; in the words of a contemporary, a rebellion against "eighteen centuries of the rule of metaphysics."[3] Joining their European cohorts in the belief that the only reality was the world accessible through the senses and science, the world of fact and matter, subject to natural laws, Russian positivists frequently carried their "nihilism" to the extreme. Nihilism was, moreover, closely linked with political radicalism. Confrontations between the radicals and the government punctuated the reform years. It was a violent age. In the opinion of some contemporaries and historians, the reform era came to an end on March 1, 1881, when bombs blew up the Emperor's sleigh, killing both the tsar reformer and his assassin.

A coherent symbolic vocabulary developed in literature and in the popular press to describe these sociocultural processes. The sense of time was expressed in concepts such as "restructuring" (*perestroika*), (in a pessimistic vein) "decomposition" (*razlozhenie*) of the life order, "a time of difficult transition" (*trudnoe perekhodnoe vremia*), or "a transition between the old and new, between idealism and positivism."[4] Broad historical analogies were drawn: contemporary Russia was compared to France during the Revolution and to the Roman empire in the stage when "the former psychological world of man had entirely collapsed," giving way to Christianity.[5] Suicide was treated in this context and linked to these historical processes (these quotations come from discussions of suicide).

With the new age came the "new man" (a Pauline concept now appropriated by atheists), a man possessing neither immortal soul nor free will, who was prepared (in Büchner's words) to "readily submit to the jurisdiction of fixed physical laws."[6] Based on science, the new worldview relied on materialistic physiology as the source of knowledge about man. Medical metaphors pervaded the discourse of the press and belles-lettres. But the new scientific and the old Christian symbols were frequently used interchangeably. The following ironic overview of the "new faith," taken from a Christian pamphlet on suicide, *Our Time and Suicide* (Nashe vremia i samoubiistvo, 1890), contains some of the key words of the day:

> Not long ago, the idea was propagated among our youth, that . . . a
> person has neither soul nor spirit, but only reflexes of the brain; that

the terms "soul" and "spirit" must . . . disappear from our vocabulary, for a person has only a brain and "brains." . . . One also could not speak of responsibility for personal actions, because all things take place according to the invincible, autonomous force of external circumstances or under the influence of a disorder in "the reflexes of the thinking brain." Science declared . . . that man has power only in facts and experiences. Know the laws by which these facts and experiences occur, and man will subdue the entire world. "You will be gods," science tells us.[7]

The author clearly implies that science has replaced religion.

Literature offered a model of the "new man" in the "nihilist" Bazarov, an image created by the collective efforts of the novelist Ivan Turgenev and the critic Dmitrii Pisarev.[8] A medical student, an atheist (whose bible is Büchner's *Kraft und Stoff*), and (the reader suspects) a political radical, Bazarov views nature as man's "laboratory." Emblematic of his views is his preoccupation with anatomy, a standard symbol of positivistic knowledge, and with the dissection of frogs, which he deems to be made in the same way as men. (Ironically, Turgenev's Bazarov dies of an infection contracted during an autopsy he performs on a human body.) Overwriting Christian symbolism with the symbolism of science, the radical critic Pisarev made the spread-eagled frog, used in experiments on the reflexes of the brain, into a holy image, claiming that "it is here, in this frog, that the salvation and renewal of the Russian people lies."[9]

In Russia, as elsewhere in Europe in the 1860s and 1870s, the natural sciences competed with the social sciences. The main instrument of the nascent social science, statistics, was considered to be a major source of knowledge about man and society. Russian reformists focused their efforts on collecting objective, reliable facts about society to provide a "key to future change and reform."[10] In the meantime, statistics, along with medicine, provided an array of symbolic notions used to describe human actions and social processes.

Contemporaries frequently saw the social sciences as the successor to the natural sciences. One author described these developments in the following terms: "It has become clear that frogs and test tubes do little to move the Russian people to actions for the general good. Intellectually developed people have taken a moment to think and have decided to change the educational curriculum. The social sciences, rather than the natural sciences, will save the Russian people. . . . The salvation of the Russian people, it has been found, depends on the propagation of sociology. The social sciences talk about the *narod* [the people], about its well-being. . . . The new men have pointed . . . to the *narod*."[11]

From the vantage point of today, the process looks different: the concepts of natural science did not displace, but rather overlaid those of social science. The social sciences provided their key metaphor—the social organism. As I argued in the previous chapter, in the discourse of Western European science, the metaphor of the social organism, derived from the age-old analogy between the living organism and society, helped to resolve the tension between the two disciplines by transferring medical notions to the study of society. It also offered a paradigm for combining the two perspectives on phenomena in human life: the individual and the social. Over the course of the 1870s, the notion of society as a collective man, which dominated the writings of Western social scientists such as Herbert Spencer and Paul Lilienfeld,[12] came into general usage in Russia. In Russia, the organicist discourse in social science appeared concomitantly with the development of populism, with its ideal of collectivism. It was in the traditional Russian peasant commune, the *obshchina,* that populists found salvation from the chaos brought about by the postreform dissolution of social structures in Russia and from the alienation that capitalism had brought to the West. For the individual, the road to salvation lay in submerging one's personality to the collective desire of the Russian people.[13]

One could say that in the discourse of the 1870s, the collective man played the role of a newer and better "new man." Statistics showed that the collective man complied with the laws of science. Immortal, the collective man was a true equal of God. Reviewing studies in moral statistics for the journal *Otechestvennye zapiski,* one journalist wrote: "Birth, marriage, reproduction, death—this is the cycle of the individual person's external existence; but while individual people are born, live, and die, the human race—mankind—continues to live, developing as a whole according to definite, regular, and immutable laws."[14] Such are the key concepts in the language that contemporaries used to make sense of their time. The symbolic connotations of these concepts contributed to (and often directed) the solutions that were offered to the momentous problems of the day.

In the symbolic network outlined above, suicide came to occupy an important, if not a central, place. It became a symbol that absorbed many of the social and intellectual concerns of the age, some shared by European thinkers and some specific to postreform Russia. In this book, I trace the process by which the meaning of suicide was constructed in Russian culture in the 1860–80s. But first I present essential historical information on the status of suicide in Russian law, popular belief, and science.

Canon Law

Until Peter the Great's reforms in the early eighteenth century, secular law in Russia did not concern itself with suicide. Suicide fell under the jurisdiction of the Church, and its position was informed by the Eastern (Byzantine) Orthodox tradition. While the condemnation of self-murder was common to both the Western and Eastern Churches, their concrete formulations go back to different sources and show subtle differences in emphasis.

The position of the Western Church has its theological roots in St. Augustine's condemnation of suicide as it was elaborated in Thomas Aquinas's *Summa Theologica*. The Council of Arles (in 452 A.D.) declared suicide to be an act of diabolic possession; the Council of Braga (563 A.D.) penalized it by denial of funeral rites and masses for the repose of the soul. No exception was made for insane suicides.* Slight alterations were introduced in canon law over the course of the following centuries, and the final touches were added in 1284, when the Synod of Nîmes legislated the refusal to bury suicides in consecrated ground. From that date on, canon law in the Catholic Church remained fundamentally unaltered (and was confirmed by the Council of Trent in 1568, which reaffirmed Augustine's unconditional equation of suicide with murder).[15] The Reformation further intensified the religious condemnation of suicide in England and other Western European countries.[16]

In the Eastern Orthodox Church, regulations about suicide were based not on the decisions of the Councils of Arles and Braga (which are not acknowledged by the East), but on the Eighteen Answers (or Canons) of Timothy of Alexandria (a member of the Second Ecumenical Council of Constantinople in 381); they acquired canonical force through confirmation by the Sixth Ecumenical Council. Canon 14 says:

—If someone who is not in his right mind lays violent hands on himself or hurls himself down from a height: should an offering be made for him or not?

*In Western canon law, the distinction between sane and insane suicides appeared for the first time in the *Penitential* of Theodore, Archbishop of Canterbury (seventh century), which exempted insane suicides from penalty. (L. I. Dublin, *Suicide: A Sociological and Statistical Study* [New York, 1963], p. 139.)

—The clergyman ought to discern whether he was actually and truly out of his mind when he did this deed. For oftentimes those close
to the victim, wishing to have him accorded an offering and to have
a prayer said in his behalf, will tell an untruth and assert falsely that
he was out of his mind. It could be, however, that he did this deed
as a result of an insult received from other men, or somehow in another instance as a result of faint-heartedness, and no offering ought
to be made in his behalf, for he is a suicide. It is incumbent, therefore, upon the clergyman to investigate the matter with due dili-
gence, so that he not fall unto condemnation.[17]

As far as the letter of canon law is concerned, this formulation has
retained its force in the Orthodox Church to this day.

Recorded in a number of diverse sources, the laws of the Russian
Orthodox Church have never been strictly codified or systematized.
Their original source was the Byzantine collection *Nomocanon.*
Known in Russia primarily as *Kormchaia kniga,* the Russian collections of canon law, like their Greek prototypes, included diverse documents: statements made by the church fathers, decisions of the
ecumenical and local councils, selections from civil codes, and authoritative opinions (such as the Answers of Timothy of Alexandria).[18] Beginning with Christianization in the tenth century,
Nomocanon, or *Kormchaia kniga,* circulated in Rus' in different manuscript variants; the answers of Timothy of Alexandria are found in
the earliest (pre-Mongol) versions. The first published version, *Iosif-
skaia kormchaia* (1650), included in chapter 61 a ruling on suicide
that followed Answer 14 of Timothy of Alexandria. In a slightly revised edition, *Kormchaia kniga* circulated until the twentieth century; throughout that time, no changes occurred in the ruling on suicide.
In 1839 the Holy Synod (after Peter the Great, the governing body of
the Russian church) issued another comprehensive prescriptive document, *A Book of Rules of the Holy Apostles, Holy Ecumenical and
Local Councils, and Holy Fathers* (Kniga pravil sviatykh apostolov, sviatykh soborov vselenskikh i pomestnykh i sviatykh otsov), which also
contained the Answer of Timothy of Alexandria on suicide.

Scholars found it difficult to determine the scope of the authority
of *Kormchaia kniga* and *Kniga pravil.* E. Golubinsky, discussing both
the medieval and the modern church in his 1880 *History of the Russian Church* [Istoriia russkoi tserkvi], maintained:

The binding authority of church canon law is undeniable. It is not
church canon law, however, that takes direct effect in practice, but

custom, acting separately from (and in part in contradiction to) the laws on which it has been based. Practice requires the knowledge and observance of custom, rather than of canon law, the knowledge of which seems superfluous and unnecessary, and merely a scholarly luxury. For this reason, even at the present time, one cannot find a single clergyman who has a proper knowledge of the church canons and an even remotely satisfactory understanding of the book called the "Kormchaia" (aside from knowing that it is a rather thick book).[19]

The legal expert N. Suvorov concluded that "for the most part, church practice has been determined not by the 'Canons of the Holy Apostles and the Holy Fathers,' but by customs which have taken shape over the course of centuries."[20]

Liturgical practice was directed by prayer books, *Trebniki*. The most authoritative *Trebnik* in the early modern church, compiled in 1646 by Kievan Metropolitan Petr Mogila, instructed parish priests to deny Christian burial to "those who killed themselves in despair or anger, unless they displayed signs of repentance before death."[21] According to the legal expert N. S. Tagantsev, the *Trebnik* used by parish priests in the 1870s gave the same instructions, citing the formulation from the Byzantine *Nomocanon* of Basil the Great and appealing to Timothy of Alexandria as the authority.[22]

Detailed instructions were given in the circulars that the church hierarchs addressed to the clergy. The 1417 circular from the Metropolitan of Kiev Fotii (the head of the Orthodox Church in Rus') to the Pskov clergy, one of the most important prescriptive church documents of the medieval era, specified: "But he who dies by his own hand, hangs himself, or stabs himself with a knife, or casts himself into the water: it is not permitted by the holy rules to bury him at a church, to hold a service for him, nor to say prayers for his soul. But after having placed him into a pit in a remote place, he may be buried. The Lord will care for their souls as He Himself sees fit, according to his ineffable destinies, for the holy fathers name them victims of their own will, not a sacrifice given unto God."[23]

Still more, and gruesome, details were given in a letter to church inspectors assisting bishops (*popovskie starosty ili blagochinnye smotriteli*) by Patriarch Adrian (the last to occupy this post, which Peter the Great left vacant after 1700), on December 26, 1697. According to article 21: "Whosoever is possessed by a demon, or stabs himself, or drowns while swimming, rejoicing, and playing in the water, or dies as a result of drinking wine, or dies having fallen down from a swing, or by his own hand brings about his own death, or is killed committing robbery or thievery: do not bury the bodies of these dead near God's church and do not hold a service for them, but order them to be placed in the forest or the field, instead of the cemetery or charnel houses [*ubogie doma*]."*

The equation of suicides with victims of death through negligence, alcohol abuse, and criminal activity and the recommendation to abandon the body in the wood or field betray the heavy influence of Slavic pagan beliefs (specifically, the fear of the improperly dead, *zalozhnye pokoiniki*—a matter for later discussion). In the nineteenth century, Adrian's instruction was included in the complete laws of the Russian Empire, *Polnoe sobranie zakonov Rossiiskoi Imperii*.[24] This document and its history demonstrate the confusion between the Christian and the pagan, as well as between the prescriptive power of church authorities or state law and the force of tradition.

Guided more by tradition than by fixed law, the Russian church has always given a certain leeway to clergymen, who are instructed to consult higher authorities when in doubt. In many cases, parish priests were guided by precedents set by the most recent decisions of church authorities. In the mid-nineteenth century, Metropolitan Filaret (Drozdov, 1783–1867), a figure of considerable influence, established one such precedent. The mother of a young female suicide requested permission from her local bishop to perform funeral rites for her daughter and was denied; the request was then forwarded to the Holy Synod, which denied it as well. Finally, the document reached the Metropolitan, who wrote on the petition: "Satan has already laughed at the unfortunate woman once. Should he be given occasion to laugh at her once again? Give her an Orthodox burial."[25] For parish priests, this somewhat informal resolution, although it was not binding, had the authority of an official prescription. In the eyes of Russian clergymen, such ambiguous legal situations were justified by the Eastern Orthodox tradition, in which the community's authority as the "guardian of piety" superceded that of canon law. (This view was stated in the Eastern patriarchs' reply to Pope Pius IX in 1848.)

Actual church practice is difficult to determine. The author of a

---

Ubogie doma (or *bozhedomki*), widespread in medieval and early modern Russia, were charnel houses built beyond the borders of towns and villages, on unconsecrated ground, where the bodies of unknown people, victims of accidents and sudden death, were put to rest. Once a year, on the seventh Thursday after Easter, a priest served a funeral mass at the site. According to Golubinsky, in medieval Rus' suicides were sometimes buried in *ubogie doma*. See his *Istoriia russkoi tserkvi*, vol. 1, part 2, pp. 459–60.

manual for parish priests from the latter part of the nineteenth century lamented that at the very time suicide had become a social epidemic, leniency toward suicides was also on the rise.[26] Condemning the erosion of Christian principles, he offered a theological justification for denying funeral rites to suicides:

> The Church considers completely conscious, premeditated suicide—but not suicide committed in an attack of delirium—as severe a sin as the taking of another person's life (murder). Life is the most precious gift granted unto each person by God—both by Nature and by the Grace of Redemption. By placing a murderous hand upon himself, the Christian twice offends God—as the Creator and as the Redeemer. It is evident in and of itself that such an act can only be the fruit of complete nonbelief and despair in Divine Providence. . . . And he who has neither faith in God nor hope in Him, he is a stranger to the Church, which looks upon the intentional suicide as a spiritual descendent of Judas the Traitor, who, having denounced God and having been outcast by Him, went off to hang himself.* Hence, it is understandable that according to our church and civic statutes, the conscious and intentional suicide loses the right to a Christian burial and to the Church's prayers for the dead.[27]

The first argument (equating suicide with murder) follows Augustine, who insisted that suicide violated the commandment "thou shalt not kill." (Adopted by Thomas Aquinas in *Summa Theologica,* this argument was largely responsible for the classification of suicide as a felony in Western civil law.)[28] The view of suicide as an assertion of nonbelief befits the language of the time: beginning in the 1870s, Russian public opinion connected the rise of suicide with the advance of positivism and atheism. The clergy felt a need to reaffirm the original position of the church.

Popular Belief

From the Middle Ages until the twentieth century, suicide figured prominently in the popular belief of Eastern Slavs (shared by Russians, Ukrainians, and Belorussians), in which Slavic pagan mythology was overlaid with Christian notions. One ethnographer, S. V.

---

*Taking a cue from Augustine, early Christian theologians argued that Judas had sinned unredeemably not in betraying Christ, but in committing suicide. (See Fedden, *Suicide,* p. 113).

Maksimov, recorded: "Satan takes rides on those who have committed suicide in the other world in the following manner: instead of horses he harnesses some of the suicides up, he seats others in the coachman's place so that they may steer, and he himself takes a seat in the main place, whipping and goading them on. At times he rides them into the smithy. . . . Whenever Satan sits on his throne in the underworld, he always holds Judas, the seller of Christ and the suicide, on his lap."[29] Central to this mentality was not the notion of suicide as a mortal sin, but the sense of danger evoked by those who, having died improperly, might have become agents of evil forces infiltrating the world of the living.

The image of the wandering dead is prevalent in Eastern Slavic popular mythology. Known as *zalozhnye pokoiniki,* this category includes those who died an "unnatural death"—by suicide as well as by accident, or under circumstances that could not be ascertained.[30] Since the earth refuses to allow their bodies to repose in its depths (*zemlia ne prinimaet,* a pagan notion), and the Church will not perform rituals ensuring the repose of their souls, *zalozhnye pokoiniki* are not fully dead; disembodied, they continue to serve the term of their earthly existence. Anthropologists connect such beliefs, which are common to many cultures, to the mythological view of death as a transition between two worlds. Suicides are forever suspended in the liminal realm, belonging neither to the world of the dead nor to the world of the living.[31] The Russian *zalozhnye pokoiniki,* acting as evil spirits, wreak havoc and inflict harm on the living, ranging from childish pranks to droughts and famine.[32] The status of the suicide is defined by a popular saying: "a suicide is satan's ram" (*chortu baran,* i.e., satan's obedient servant and aid).[33] Women who drown themselves are accorded a special place: they join the ranks of *rusalki,* attractive female creatures populating various waters; as forces of evil, they rely on the power of sexual seduction. (A figure from pagan mythology, the *rusalka,* according to some scholars, was connected with suicide in later, Christian times.)[34]

In Russian folk belief, as in the West, suicide is sometimes seen as an act instigated by the devil. Russian evidence documenting this belief, however, is scarce.[35] By contrast, there is evidence that in medieval France, Italy, and England this was a widespread conviction, sanctioned by the Catholic Church.[36] In Protestant England, the idea of diabolic possession was perpetuated by Puritan writers.[37]

Common to both Western and Russian culture are rites accompanying the disposition of the suicide's body. Aimed at protecting the living by fixing the spirit of the suicide to the grave, they were practiced, with many local variations, from the Middle Ages to the twentieth century. In early Christian Rus', customs rooted in pagan beliefs proscribed burying the bodies of all those who died an "unnatural death" and ruled that they be abandoned in liminal locations,[38] although the Orthodox Church insisted on interment.[39] This custom survived into the modern age. Instances in which the body of a suicide was removed from its burial place, with the aim of thwarting the evil it might bring, occurred in rural Russia and Ukraine as late as the 1870s and 1880s.[40] On the whole, in modern times, suicides were usually interred, but custom emphasized the proper choice of the burial location and protective rituals. On one point, folk belief coincided with the prescriptions of the Orthodox Church: suicides were not to be buried in cemeteries. Popular custom prescribed a number of "proper" locations: by a road, at a crossroads, at the edge of a field; also in the wood, swamp, or ravine.[41] Since these locations figure in folk belief as the natural habitat of evil spirits, the choice betrays the belief in the dead person's connection to the realm of evil. The choice of the boundary locations also reflect the deceased's liminal status at the threshhold between two worlds. Protective measures included driving aspen stakes through the body[42] and throwing stones, wood, and hay on the grave.[43] Until the early twentieth century, in the countryside in Russia, Ukraine, and Belorussia, solitary graves with piles of stones and wood clearly indicated the burial places of the improperly dead—mostly suicides.

To conclude, the question of what was to be done with the body of the suicide—the improperly dead—retained its ritual importance in Russian popular belief and Christian practice from early medieval times to the beginning of the twentieth century.

Secular Law[44]

In the eighteenth century, with Peter the Great's reforms—considerably later than in the Christian West—suicide fell under the authority of secular law.[45] When Peter's ecclesiastical policy established the institutional dependence of the church on the state, limiting the church's judicial role, suicide, like many other problems formerly handled by ecclesiastical authorities, was simply taken out of clergymen's hands.[46] The ruling on suicide appeared in the first code of Petrine laws, the Military Code (*Voinskii ustav* of 1716), article 164: "If someone kills himself, the executioner will be ordered to drag away the corpse to a dishonorable place for burial, first dragging it through the streets or army camp." This measure was limited to sane suicides. The bodies of insane suicides, who committed the act in a state of delirium, illness, or melancholia, were to be buried in a "special place" (that is, beyond the cemetery), but not desecrated. The law also specified punishment for attempted suicide: "If a soldier is caught in the act of truly trying to kill himself but is prevented from doing so and is unable to carry it out, and attempted to commit this act in a state of torment or aggravation, wishing not to live any longer, or in delirium or shame, that person, in the opinion of the experts on law, will be dishonorably discharged from the regiment . . . and if he did this for reasons other than those mentioned above, he will be sentenced to death."[47]

The Naval Code (*Morskoi ustav*) of 1720 prescribed similar measures and further specified cases exempt from punishment: "If this murder was unintentional or committed on account of some kind of torment or an unbearable burden [*ot nesnosnoi nalogi*] or in the state of delirium that occurs in feverish or melancholic illnesses, the people found doing this will not be subjected to the above-mentioned execution."[48] The wording clearly equates suicide with murder. These formulations formed the basis for subsequent laws.

The immediate source of the Petrine laws was the legal practice of Saxony, but their antecedents went as far back as Roman law, which punished suicide only when a man's special status, such as soldier or slave, gave another man or the state a claim on his life.[49] True to the Petrine principle of secularization, these formulations do not show the influence of canon law. The same year, in 1716, the military code was extended to cover civilians by a special decree.[50] As far as suicide was concerned (as well as in many other respects), the subject of the Petrine state was treated as a soldier of the state and the sovereign, who had a claim on his life.

In the course of the eighteenth and early nineteenth centuries, several unsuccessful attempts were made to revise and codify criminal law; the rulings on suicide were affected by these projects. The project for the Criminal Code of 1754, undertaken under the Empress Elizabeth, considered replacing capital punishment for those who attempted suicide with "punishment with lashes or detention in prison for two months." The 1766 project prepared for Catherine the Great suggested demotion of attempted suicides within the ranks of the civil service (by one step); non-serving gentry and merchants of the first guild were to be sentenced to a six-month church penance (other social classes were not mentioned). In the early nineteenth century, the prominent liberal statesman Mikhail Speransky, assisted by Ludwig

Heinrich von Jacob, a professor of law at the University of Halle, once again attempted to reform the Russian legal code. The proposed articles on suicide read:

> 392. if a person attempting suicide is unable to complete the act or is hindered in doing so, he, as an insane person, will be handed over to the Church for penance after being treated in the hospital.
> 395. in relation to the body of a suicide, it is necessary to act according to church rules and police regulations.[51]

These formulations clearly implied that a dead subject was not to be prosecuted (a legal principle known in the West) and that all suicides were insane. An attempted suicide and a suicide's body (treated as separate legal subjects) were to be handed over to medical and ecclesiastic authorities. In essence, this project amounted to a decriminalization of suicide. Speransky's reformed code did not become law.

The first code to be adopted (published in 1832 as *Svod zakonov Rossiiskoi Imperii*, it was officially approved in 1835) relied on the original articles from the Petrine military and naval codes for its ruling on suicide. Laws about the indignities to be performed on the body of a suicide were repealed:

> 347. A suicide is denied a Christian burial if it is proven that he was not in a state of insanity or delirium when he took his life.[52]

The ruling on attempted suicide remained basically unchanged from Petrine times, equating it with attempted murder. Cases exempt from penalty were described in the archaic language of the Petrine code, which pointed to situations that in legal practice were clearly impossible to determine:

> 348. A person who was discovered in the act of attempting suicide, and was prevented from doing so only by an external obstacle, will be punished for attempted murder if the suicide attempt was not made in a state of torment, or on account of unbearable burden, aggravation, shame, or the delirium of a feverish and melancholic illness.

The 1842 edition of the 1835 code specified that attempted suicide by the insane should be treated in accordance with the general procedure applied to the criminally insane; that is, they should be committed to mental institutions for treatment (article 380).

In 1845, a major revision of the criminal code was undertaken under the direction of Count Dmitry Bludov. Ratified, these laws remained basically unchanged until after the revolution of 1917.[53] (In 1903, a draft for a new, radically reformed law was prepared, which simply omitted suicide from the criminal code, but the new law was never enacted.) Beginning in 1845, the criminal code said:

> 1943. A person who intentionally commits suicide—except in cases involving insanity, madness, or temporary delirium brought on by attacks of illness—will be denied the right to have his last wishes respected. Therefore, the will and all other expressions of the suicide's last wishes with regard to children, wards, servants, property, or anything else—no matter in what manner they were made—will not be administered and will be considered null and void. If the suicide belongs to one of the Christian denominations, he will be denied a Christian burial. (Article 2021 in 1857 edition; 1472 in all subsequent editions)
>
> 1944. If a person found guilty of attempted suicide—except in cases involving insanity, madness or a temporary fit of delirium brought on by attacks of illness—was prevented from carrying out his intentions by other people or by circumstances beyond his control, and if he is a Christian, he will be handed over to the ecclesiastical authorities for penance. (Article 2022 in 1857 edition; 1473 in all subsequent editions)

Beginning in 1845, the criminal code no longer regarded a suicide attempt as attempted murder. Moreover, suicide and attempted suicide now entailed ecclesiastical measures (denial of Christian burial), as well as civil ones (annulment of the will), but not punishment in the strict sense of criminal law. From the point of view of legal philosophy, this can be interpreted as a de facto exclusion of suicide from the category of crimes. In the 1870s, the liberal jurist N. S. Tagantsev claimed: "Since 1845 the law has regarded suicide predominantly from a religious point of view, although it is far from being consistent in this."[54] It should be noted that, while the 1845 code excluded secular penalties, it retained the article on suicide in the criminal code, thus emphasizing the state's interest in religious values and asserting the state's authority over the Church.[55]

The 1845 code made two exceptions, which applied to "cases involving disinterested patriotism in which a person subjects himself to obvious danger or even certain death for the preservation of state secrets and in other similar cases, and equally to a woman who commits suicide or attempts suicide in order to preserve her chastity and honor from otherwise inescapable rape threatening her" (article 1945/2023/1474).[56] There was also a clause on instigation of suicide, or participation in suicide, or driving someone to suicide, which—and which alone—survived in the Russian law after the revolution of 1917 (articles 1946/2024/1475 and 1947/2025/1476).[57]

The draft for the new code (*proekt*), submitted in 1843 to the State Council and the Emperor for ratification, contained extensive commentaries justifying the proposed changes, shedding light on the state of legal thought in mid-nineteenth-century Russia. Commenting on article 1943, the authors of the draft argued that "it seems more proper and appropriate to leave to the discretion of the ecclesiastical authorities the decision of whether the suicide be denied a Christian burial in each particular case." The reformers suggested changing the formulation to: "If the suicide belonged to one of the Christian denominations, the question of a Christian burial will be at the discretion of the ecclesiastical authorities of his faith."[58] In the ratified version and in all subsequent imperial codes, however, the formulation remained unchanged. Secular law stood firm in asserting Christian principles.

Concerning the exemption of certain cases, the draft's authors commented that some reasons, such as "torment, an unbearable burden, aggravation, and shame, are so difficult to determine that we have decided not to remark on them in our project," and defended their decision to extend a legal exemption to cases involving a disinterested patriot and a woman preserving her honor, "even though they are undoubtedly rare."[59]

At that point, the most serious legal consequence of suicide was the annulment of the will. The authors of the 1843 draft commented that legislation in other countries, ancient and modern, contained no such law,[60] but recommended retaining it on the grounds that it would serve as a deterrent.[61] This provision, which now appeared for the first time within the criminal code, had been part of civil law since the early 1830s (based on *Polozhenie gosudarstvennogo soveta* of December 1, 1831). The civil code stated:

> 1016. All wills must be drawn up in sound mind and memory. For this reason, the wills of the following will be null and void: (1) madmen and insane when the wills were drawn up during the time of insanity, and (2) suicides.[62]

At the same time, the criminal code exempted insane suicides from all legal consequences. Thus, there was an obvious contradiction between civil and criminal law, which remained unnoticed until the reforms of the 1860s. Laws on the suicide's will remained unchanged until after the revolution of 1917.

In proposing to repeal the ruling that treated suicide attempts as attempted murder (perhaps the most radical among the proposed changes in the law), the authors of the 1843 draft commented that "the administration of this ruling is as unjust as it is inconvenient," adding that "it is well known that this law has never been administered."[63] They suggested replacing penal servitude with a prison term of six months to a year, followed by church penance for Christians. The ratified version went still further and made church penance the only remaining punishment.

Such was the state of the Russian law and legal thought at the start of the reform age.

A Note on Suicide in Western European Law

Under the influence of canon law, suicide was considered a serious criminal offense in almost all Western European countries from the Middle Ages until (at least) the French Revolution, with denial of Christian burial, desecration of the corpse, and forfeiture of property commonly administered as punishments. In at least one continental country, Austria, attempted suicide was punishable by imprisonment. Until 1879, English law regarded suicide as murder. The Draft Penal Code of 1879, which no longer contained such an article, nevertheless prescribed the punishment for attempted suicide as two years' imprisonment with hard labor. Forfeiture of the suicide's property remained on the books until 1870; dishonorable burial until 1882. It was only after the Suicide Act of 1961 that English law no longer regarded either suicide or attempted suicide as a crime.[64] In France, on January 1, 1790, the National Assembly, upon the motion of Doctor Guillotin, abolished criminal prosecution against the suicide's corpse, memory, and property. Napoleon's criminal code (1810) did not mention suicide. In the course of the first half of the nineteenth century, many countries of Continental Europe, following the French example, repealed laws against suicide.[65] In the 1860s, however, suicide still remained in the criminal codes in Holland, Hungary, and some parts of Germany and Italy, as well as in England and several American states.[66] The distinction between sane and insane suicides was maintained in most, if not all, countries. In the words of

H. R. Fedden, it was "a loophole through which a large percentage of suicides may slip away without dishonor."[67]

Western legal thought on suicide changed drastically with the ascent of the positivist or sociological school of criminal jurisprudence in the late 1870s and 1880s, which advocated detaching laws from moral ideals and basing them on a view of man as an object of natural science, who acted in accordance with the laws of causality. Its founder, Enrico Ferri, took up the subject of reforming suicide laws in his *L'Omicidio-suicidio* (Turin, 1884).[68] According to Michel Foucault, "the Penal Code started out as a theory of right; then, from the time of the nineteenth century, people looked for its validation in sociological, psychological, medical and psychiatric knowledge."[69] In Western Europe, these processes reached their peak in the 1870s and 80s.

Suicide, Law, and the Church in the Reform Age

In Russia, the pace of development of legal thought was different from Western Europe. In the 1860s and 70s, in the course of judicial (and other) reforms, Russians struggled to create an autonomous sphere of law which would play an independent role in the new civic order. This involved separating different points of view (legal, on the one hand, and religious and moral, on the other) and different authorities (secular and religious, administrative and judicial), as well as separating conflicting legal jurisdictions.[70]

In the 1860s and 70s, procedural and structural reforms of the legal process, aimed at creating a system of independent courts governed by modern Western principles, were undertaken in Russia. The procedural changes were codified in the new *Ustav ugolovnogo sudoproizvodstva,* issued in 1864 (and amended in subsequent years in accordance with decisions of the Senate criminal and civil cassation departments). The reforms, however, did not entail changes in the legal code.[71]

In the reform age, laws on suicide, for the first time in Russia, became a matter of discussion and debate among members of the legal profession (but it seems that they did not attract the attention of the popular press). The most thorough treatment of the issue was offered by the prominent legal expert and influential reformist, N. S. Tagantsev, in his treatise *On Crimes against Life According to Russian Law* (O prestupleniiakh protiv zhizni po russkomu pravu, 1870; 2d ed.

1873). After a brief survey of the history of laws on suicide, Tagantsev criticized existing Russian legislation from the point of view of
modern legal philosophy. In his condemnation of Russian law, he appealed to the example of Western European countries, claiming that,
through the nineteenth century, legislation on suicide had disappeared from the codes of all the countries in continental Europe—a
clear exaggeration. (Acknowledging that the situation was different in
England, he commented that, since most coroners ruled that suicide
was caused by insanity, the English law had practically no effect.)
Tagantsev implied that Russia, because her legislation was untouched
by the legal arguments of Enlightenment philosophy,[72] lagged behind
the civilized West.

Tagantsev's main goal was to establish the independence of the judicial sphere from considerations of a religious, moral, psychological,
or medical order.[73] It was in this context, and in purely legal terms,
that he attempted to resolve the problems plaguing Russian suicide
legislation. Tagantsev rejected most of the arguments against the
criminalization of suicide made by theoreticians of law beginning in
the eighteenth century, including the argument (which goes back to
Esquirol) that suicide cannot be punished by law because it is a mental aberration. Referring to statistical data, which reported mental illness in about one-third of suicide cases, he argued that, since for the
remaining two-thirds of suicides their "mental state remained at least
'unknown' [*ostaetsia 'neraskrytym'*]," it cannot serve as a justification
for determining their legal responsibility.[74] Consistent in his attempt
to maintain the autonomy of judicial claims, Tagantsev sided with the
argument developed in the 1820s by Carl Georg Wächter[75]: law reg-
ulates social life, that is, a sphere of relations between people; since
a man cannot stand in legal relation to himself, suicide, whether or
not it is morally reprehensible, cannot fall under the domain of law.

In criticizing the existing Russian law, Tagantsev noted a number of
inconsistencies as well as violations of general legal principles. The
basic problem underlying the criminal prosecution of suicide was a
failure to distinguish between the subject and the object of crime. But
what seemed to trouble Tagantsev most was the overlapping of authorities and jurisdictions. He pointed out that, in deciding the validity of the suicide's will, criminal law came into contradiction with civil
law.[76] On a larger scale, by legislating such issues as Christian funeral rites and prayers, the law treated suicide as a sin, not a crime,
and intruded not only into the jurisdiction of canon law, but also into
"[the realm of] divine justice . . . which is completely independent of
the law."[77]

Rather than clearing up the confusion, the reform measures exacerbated the situation. Thus, article 16 of the new procedural regulations, *Ustav ugolovnogo sudoproizvodstva,* stipulated that "after the death of the accused criminal prosecution cannot be initiated." This was in obvious contradiction to article 1472 of the criminal code, stipulating criminal procedures against a suicide, which was still in force.

In the 1870s, the status of suicide became the subject of debates in newly created professional legal journals.[78] A heated exchange was started by the prominent reform activist Petr Obninsky. In his article in 1871 on the criminal prosecution of attempted suicides, Obninsky pointed out the inconsistency between article 1473 of *Ulozhenie* and the new *Ustav*. In legal practice, it led to disputes among different judicial authorities: it was unclear whether attempted suicide fell under the jurisdiction of the secular (*okruzhnoi,* circuit) court or the ecclesiastical (*dukhovnyi*) court. Most members of the legal profession held the opinion that, since article 1473 was "geographically" located in the criminal code, attempted suicide was regarded by the Russian law as a criminal offense. Others argued that, according to article 1002 of the new *Ustav,* crimes that entailed no punishment other than church penance (of which suicide attempted in sound mind was one) fell under the jurisdiction not of the criminal court but of the church. Obninsky upheld the latter view. He pointed to a qualification that hitherto had apparently escaped notice: "a person who has attempted suicide in sound mind, *if he is a Christian,* will be handed over to the ecclesiastical authorities for penance."[79] Thus Jews and Muslims were not subject to this law—a factor which, in Obninsky's view, clearly indicated its purely religious character.[80] (Suicide committed by insane individuals was a separate issue, since insanity was a medical condition that entailed certain civil and administrative consequences.) For Obninsky, to affirm that attempted suicide fell under the jurisdiction of the ecclesiastical courts meant to uphold the spirit of the new, progressive statute, which attempted at least partially to restore to the Church the power given to it "by the ancient ecumenical decrees of the Church that are always to maintain their binding force."[81] Obninsky also offered a personal—philosophical—opinion: "There are a host of actions that are contrary to the rules of morality and religion, yet these actions cannot be prosecuted by a secular code, which cannot capture the religious inner world of the human soul."[82] Thus, for nineteenth-centry Russians, the issue of the jurisdiction over suicide had both literal and metaphorical connotations.

Objecting to Obninsky's arguments, the jurist I. N. Shestakov reaffirmed what **he** saw as a progressive, Western principle, introduced by Peter the Great—the predominance of state authority over that of the Church.[83] Another jurist, I. A. Arevkov, agreeing with many of Obninsky's arguments, pointed out that there was a positive side to the existing confusion: the very overlapping of statutory laws left room for the decriminalization of suicide, "not a crime, not a misdemeanor, but something else."[84] In his turn, he focused on the conflict between criminal courts and administrative authority (police). Attacking the established practice of entrusting the official investigators attached to the circuit courts (*sudebnye sledovateli*) with the investigation of suicide cases, he insisted that suicide should be handed over to the police, who were to be assisted by medical doctors and pathologists. Moreover, these two authorities, legal and medical, should act independently of each other. The doctor, Arevkov argued, did not require the presence of a court-appointed criminal investigator in order to exercise his professional judgement in establishing the cause of death ("a doctor, as a competent subject, may perform an autopsy on the corpse even without an investigator present").[85] Were police to ascertain, on the basis of medical evidence, that a victim died as a result not of murder but of suicide (and that suicide did not occur at the instigation or with the assistance of another person), the case should be handed over to the church court, "which will be responsible for determining whether the person who has committed or attempted suicide did so of sound mind or under the influence of a mental illness."[86] Thus, in the opinion of this reform-minded legal expert, the body of the suicide fell under the "jurisdiction" of medicine, and the mind under the "jurisdiction" of the Church. Court officials were to be banished entirely from the scene, and instead the whole procedure was to be supervised by an administrative authority—the police.

In postreform Russia, clergymen were also concerned about the division of power between church and civil authorities. The suicide's body and mind were points of contention. S. V. Bulgakov's authoritative 1890 manual for parish priests instructed clergymen that, according to civil law, suicides were not to be buried without prior investigation by the medico-police authorities and specified the accepted procedure.[87] The manual emphasized that secular law took upon itself the decision about the suicide's state of mind and, consequently, the possibility of a Christian burial for his body: "civil law makes the question of whether the suicide may or may not be given a Christian burial contingent upon the judgment of the doctor and police."[88] The manual claimed, however, that those suicides who repented and took communion before dying, in keeping with ancient canon law, could be granted funeral rites[89]—the act of repentance, sealed by the sacrament of communion, returned the suicide to the "jurisdiction" of the Church.

What was to happen to the bodies of those who were denied Christian burial? The legal answer to this question could be found in the code on medical practice (*Ustav vrachebnyi*). *Ustav vrachebnyi,* which was incorporated into volume 13 of *Svod,* contained archaic and often conflicting regulations that "defined the state's jurisdiction over all health matters."[90] From 1835 to 1892 (the last prerevolutionary edition), *Ustav vrachebnyi* (part 2, *Ustav meditsinskoi politsii,* [the code on medical police]) directed: "the executioner must drag the body of a suicide away to a disgraceful place and inter it there."[91] The details of actual practices are difficult to ascertain, but it is highly unlikely that in the nineteenth century this ruling was obeyed literally.

One point on which clergymen challenged civil authorities was whether the rulings granting Christian burial to a suicide who was judged to be insane were binding on the clergy. The *dukhovnaia konsistoriia** of Tobolsk (in 1895) advised parish priests to form their own opinion of the state of a parishioner's body and mind (*fizicheskom i dukhovnom sostoianii*), in accordance with the true meaning and spirit of the rule of Timothy of Alexandria, and not to rely "unconditionally" on medical certificates.[92] The *dukhovnaia konsistoriia* of Samara instructed the clergy that authorization from the police did not constitute an order to bury the suicide in accordance with Christian rites, but only indicated that the civil authorities saw no obstacles to a Christian burial. According to Bulgakov's manual, however, when medical experts certified insanity based on an autopsy, which was to be taken as positive proof that suicide did not occur as a result of "despair" or "nonbelief," it was considered binding: "medical evidence based on an autopsy showing that the person committed suicide because he was in an abnormal mental state renders it obligatory for the clergy to inter the suicide's body, since this certifies that the cause of death was not despair or lack of faith."[93]

Thus, clergymen who, under the threat of civil penalties,[94] only reluctantly submitted to the authority of police, eagerly submitted to medical opinion. Erroneously assuming that autopsies provided pos-

*The *dukhovnye konsistorii* were local governing bodies, answerable to the Holy Synod. Regulated by the *Ustav dukhovnykh konsistorii* (first issued in 1841), they fulfilled the functions of the ecclesiastical courts, which dealt with such issues as unlawful marriages, divorces, and offenses entailing church penance.

itive evidence of the suicide's state of mind,* clergymen effectively granted the medical examiner who performed the autopsy the privilege of determining the state of sin.

To conclude, throughout the nineteenth century, different authorities—criminal, civil, ecclesiastical, administrative—guided by conflicting and often archaic or obsolete rulings, participated in regulating suicide.[95] Rather than competing for control of suicide, however, each authority strove to relinquish its share of responsibility to another. This tendency increased during the age of the Great Reforms. Reform-minded members of the nascent legal profession wanted to remove suicide from the sphere of law. They were willing to hand over the suicide's body and mind to the church, police, medical experts, and even "divine providence." Not eager to take over, the Church was prepared to submit to the authority of medical science.

Russian Interpretations of Western Science

In the 1860s, knowledge of Western scientific studies on suicide and crime, familiar to experts since at least the 1840s, reached general readers. The left-wing popular press, concerned with the idea of the "new man," paid much attention to the investigations of human action undertaken by the positivist sciences in the West.

The first edition popularizing Western views on suicide to appear in Russia, P. M. Ol'khin's *On Suicide from a Medical Perspective* (O samoubiistve v meditsinskom otnoshenii [St. Petersburg, 1859]), presented it as a medical phenomenon.[96] The second edition appeared in 1863, under the enticing title *Suicides' Last Days* (Poslednie dni samoubiits); however, Ol'khin's compilation was ignored by the periodical press. Beginning in the early 1860s, moral statistics, especially statistics on crime and suicide, ruled in the "thick journals." In 1868, looking back at the beginnings of this trend, the radical jour-

---

*In fact, medico-legal regulations provided no clue about how the suicide's state of mind could be ascertained through autopsy (the procedure of the autopsy was prescribed in *Ustav sudebnoi meditsiny* [the code on forensic medicine], part 3 of *Ustav vrachebnyi*, which has remained almost intact since 1835). The reports of the medico-legal autopsies that were at my disposal—those performed at the Department of Forensic Medicine of the St. Petersburg Medico-Surgical Academy in the early 1860s—contained no conclusion on the state of the suicide's mind and were descriptive in character. ("Perechen' sudebno-meditsinskikh vskrytii, proizvedennykh pri sudebno-meditsinskoi kafedre Imperatorskoi St. Peterburgskoi Mediko-khirurgicheskoi akademii [s 1 sentiabria 1860 goda po 1 iiulia 1863 goda]," *Arkhiv sudebnoi meditsiny i obshchestvennoi gigieny,* September 1865.)

nal *Delo* reflected: "The ear of the Russian reader long ago grew accustomed to talking about the importance of statistical figures in all branches of human activity. The enthusiasm for statistics, to which our society succumbed about five years ago, emerged at the same time that we were acknowledging the importance of the principle of realism, which has presently received the full right of citizenship in Russia."[97]

In 1865 and 1866, Russian translations of Quételet (published in France in the 1830s) appeared in Russia, giving rise to a vigorous debate.[98] Discussions focused on the philosophical and social implications of statistical regularities; most importantly, on the issue of free will versus determinism, a cornerstone in the dispute between positivism and the Christian worldview. In 1867, reviewing a compilation from Guerry, Wagner, and Drobisch, the publicist from the left-wing *Otechestvennye zapiski* presented the "new science" in this vein: "among its tasks is one of the most important and fundamental problems for each individual and all humanity: relating the law of necessity to an individual's actions, which people customarily view as arbitrary, independent and free."[99]

The debates around moral statistics were prepared by Henry Buckle's *History of Civilization in England* (1857–61), read as a book which, denying the freedom of will, proclaimed that only statistics, by performing "the anatomy of nations," could lay bare the objective, immutable laws that govern individual and collective actions. (According to the critic M. A. Antonovich, writing in *Sovremennik* in 1864, Buckle's fame in England was exceeded by his popularity in St. Petersburg and Moscow, where talk about Buckle was as common as talk about the weather.)[100] The prominent radical publicist and popularizer of science from *Russkoe slovo*, Varfalomei Zaitsev, introduced moral statistics as "the method that created Buckle."

Reviewing the Russian translations of Quételet, Zaitsev emphasized that Quételet's main achievement was the submission of man to statistical laws: "In all his actions, from the most important to the least significant, the individual obeys statistical laws. . . . Fateful figures, . . . like fate in ancient times, govern the destinies of man and do not allow him to take even one step away from their mathematical conclusions."[101]

In Zaitsev's interpretation, this led to the rejection not only of the Christian principle of free will, but also of the validity of law and of judicial proceedings:

> If of six hundred people—*a, b, c, d* and so on—*one person must* commit a crime, then can we say that this person committed the crime

of his own free will? People who talk about freedom of the will and who hold a dramatic opinion of humanity, think that a person can successfully resist the inclinations of the flesh. But a positive fact tells us that of these six hundred people one is absolutely *obliged* to commit a crime. Where is the freedom of will in that? Who can condemn this faceless individual while he remains faceless? And yet, as soon as it becomes known that *a* has committed the crime, he is judged and prosecuted. But we forget that if *a* had not committed the crime, *b* or *c* would have done so, and that there certainly must be a criminal. This completely excludes the possibility of prosecution.[102]

In this argument, not only suicide, but crime as well was, so to speak, removed from the jurisdiction of law. Jurisprudence was subjugated to science.

In an attempt to find the exact cause and locus of human action, Zaitsev appealed to the authority of the German physiologist Karl Vogt, who incorporated Quételet's statistical determinism into a radically materialistic view of human nature. Following Vogt, Zaitsev connected the propensity for crime to "the quality and quantity of the constituent parts of the brain, blood, and the nervous fibers": "Finally, we will state definitely that any crime, regardless of the circumstances in which it was committed, is an external manifestation of physiological or pathological processes in our organism and therefore may involve as little personal responsibility as some external deformity, such as a hunchback or a curvature of the neck. Statistics have already proven that crimes are committed independently of the human will; hence, crime depends on the physical state of the organism."[103] Thus, in the wake of moral statistics, the medical view on the causes of crime and suicide made its appearance in the periodical press.

But most Russian positivists subscribed to the view that crime and suicide were caused by the social environment (*sreda*); that is, by forces outside the individual, in the surrounding society.

On the whole, Russian readers, like their Western European counterparts, received mixed messages from science about the immediate cause and exact locus of human action. Did the cause lie in the body or in society? Did suicide fall under the jurisdiction of medical or social science? In Russia, science had remained underdeveloped until at least the 1860s, both as an intellectual force and as a social institution.[104] In this context, conflict among disciplinary discourses or disciplinary authorities seemed to have been less prominent than the conflict between the discourse of science, which was appropriated by radicals, and the authority of the autocratic regime. In the Russian context, where Orthodoxy was closely associated with government policy and positivism with political radicalism, moral statistics, along with materialistic physiology, became a weapon in the conflict between the radicals and the government.

The following episode serves as an illustration. The first issue of the radical journal *Delo* (January 1866) contained an article "Statistics on Suicide (apropos of Wagner's work *Statistik der Selbstmorde*)," subtitled "Part One." Signed "N. Radiukin," this extensive summary of Wagner's treatise was actually written by Nikolai Shelgunov, one of the major political activists and publicists of the 1860s, who spent most of his life in exile in remote areas of the Russian Empire. Shelgunov emphasized the same point as Zaitsev: statistical science, which had proven that suicide is an involuntary act, questioned free will (and, by implication, the Christian view of man).[105] However, unlike Zaitsev, Shelgunov sought the cause of human action not in the body, but in the society surrounding the individual. The censor found this article offensive, and the second part was banned, with the following comment:

> In the present article the author explains the causes of suicide. First, he considers it necessary to mock *ancient philosophies* in which man is considered a privileged creature governed by special laws independent of earthly forces . . . Examining suicide from this point of view, he tries to prove that suicide, like all other phenomena of human life, is not an arbitrary action but arises exclusively as the result of oppressive circumstances and abnormal conditions in the surrounding environment in which one lives . . . What follows is a series of vignettes of suicide during the French terror. The author's goal is to show that political persecution in particular increases the number of suicides.[106]

The censor's reading indicates that the far-reaching implications of moral statistics were quite clear to the authorities (and to the contemporary reader in general): discussions of suicide in this context signified "antireligious views" and aspirations for radical social change.

The shadow of revolution and violence haunted the reform years. In April 1866 a student, Dmitrii Karakozov, made an attempt on the life of the czar. In response, the government tightened its control over the press: a special decree prohibited criticism aimed at law courts, thus making any discussion of crime impossible (it was still possible to discuss suicide, though). Several radical journalists, Zaitsev among them, were arrested and several journals were shut down.[107] With this move, the intense debates around the philosophical implications of moral statistics came to a halt.

A new wave of interest in moral statistics arose in the 1880s. Enrico Morselli's magisterial study, *Suicide: An Essay on Comparative Moral Statistics,* was published in Milan in 1879, and Russian journalists, after a delay of several years, favorably reviewed and freely incorporated it into their discussions of suicide.[108] Welcoming moral statistics as a weapon in the struggle against "the rule of metaphysics," one reviewer also commented on what it meant for the disciplines of man: moral statistics had transformed the object of human sciences, and reconfigured their borderlines; by proving the existence of hidden laws that govern human behavior, it turned individual action into a social issue.[109]

Russian Studies of Suicide in Russia

In the nineteenth century, most of the scholarly studies of suicide produced in Russia were statistical.[110] Some attempts at gathering Russian data had been made in the 1820s–40s, but systematic efforts started only in the 1860s, in the wake of the reforms.

The first such attempt had been made in 1823, when a member of the Imperial Academy of Sciences, Ch.-Th. Herrmann, read to his fellow members a report on the number of suicides and homicides that had occurred in different provinces of the Russian Empire in 1819 and 1820 (compiled from official government censuses). The idea of publicizing data on criminal actions met with bewilderment and resistance from the authorities. When Herrmann's report was submitted to the annals of the Academy for publication, the Minister of Enlightenment, A. S. Shishkov, rejected it with the following note:

The article enumerating the murders and suicides that have taken place in the past two years in Russia, I regard as both pointless and dangerous. Firstly: What is the need to know the number of these crimes? Secondly: By what evidence can any reader be assured that this number is by no means exaggerated? Thirdly: What purpose can such a notice serve? Perhaps only that an unsure criminal, seeing before him many predecessors, can find assurance that he will not be the first to commit such a crime? It seems to me that similar articles, unsuitable for publication for the above-mentioned reasons, ought to be returned to the person who submitted them with the admonition that henceforth he no longer labor over such frivolous things. It is advantageous to inform people about good deeds, but deeds like murder and suicide ought to be plunged into eternal oblivion.[111]

The report was finally published, in French, in 1832.[112] Although, contrary to Shishkov's fears, it was highly unlikely that Herrmann's work reached potential criminals, it did succeed in making Russian suicide public: his data were cited by Quételet in *Sur l'homme* (1835).[113]

The first Russian work of moral statistics devoted solely to suicide, *Explorations in the Moral Statistics of Russia* (Opyty nravstvennoi statistiki Rossii) by K. S. Veselovsky, was published in 1847 in the official organ of the Ministry of Foreign Affairs.[114] Following the format used by Quételet and Guerry, Veselovsky presented limited data (based on government statistics) for 1803–41. This study, which appeared before the philosophical implications of moral statistics became clear to the Russian readers, drew no public attention; it became, however, a resource for future statisticians.

In the 1860s, an array of statistical studies of suicide appeared in Russia, some of them in the popular press. One of the earliest and most quoted sources was Iu. Gübner's survey of suicides in St. Peterburg between 1858 and 1867, which was published in 1868 in the new medico-social journal *Arkhiv sudebnoi meditsiny i obshchestvennoi gigieny* (Annals of Forensic Medicine and Public Hygiene), which became quite popular with the general reader and, especially, with radical journalists.[115] Gübner, who argued that official government statistics were highly unreliable, relied primarily on newspaper materials, taken from the official newspaper of the Petersburg police, *Vedomosti Sankt-Peterburgskoi gorodskoi politsii*, and also on autopsy reports published in a medical journal.[116] Publication of the official data in organs accessible to the general public started a little later; in 1876 the journal *Pravitel'stvennyi vestnik* published suicide statistics for the years 1870–74 (no. 100). In 1870, the prominent ethnographer S. V. Maksimov, who took over the editorship of *Vedomosti Sankt-Peterburgskoi gorodskoi politsii* in 1868, published a comprehensive review of suicide in the capital city (no. 7). Data for 1870–72, derived from various sources, were systematized by I. Pasternatsky in a study that appeared in 1872 and 1873 in a medical journal.[117] Between 1873 and 1882, A. S. Suvorin's annual *Russkii kalendar'*, an almanac that could be found in almost every educated family, included suicide statistics (mostly for Petersburg), which were largely based on newspaper, not government data.[118]

All the authors involved in the statistical investigation of suicide in Russia commented on the inadequacy and unreliability of their (varied) sources, from complaints about the scarcity of information to claims that the available data were simply "unusable"[119]—but this fact did not diminish their enthusiasm for statistics.

In the 1880s, two major Russian studies that went beyond a simple review of statistical data made their appearance. The first was N. V. Ponomarev's "Suicide in Western Europe and in Russia in Relation to the Development of Insanity," an extensive article published in 1880 in the serial edition of sources on forensic medicine.[120] It was followed by the first book-length study of suicide, a comprehensive moral statistics, A. V. Likhachev's *Suicide in Western Europe and European Russia. An Essay in Comparative Statistics* (1882). Both works were welcomed and reviewed by the popular press.[121]

Aiming at a synthesis of everything written on suicide, Likhachev opened his book with a detailed survey of Western statistical, medical, and historical studies. He also offered a systematic survey of the available Russian data, which covered the years from the 1830s to the 1880s (with one omission—no data for the years 1841–1858 could be found). In both studies, Western Europe was a reference point and the Russian material was treated in a comparative perspective. Several more studies appeared in the nineteenth century, to be followed by more extensive literature after 1905.[122]

The two Russian authors held different views on the nature of their topic. For Ponomarev, suicide was a phenomenon that belonged entirely to the domain of medicine; following Esquirol, he saw in every suicide either a person who was chronically mentally ill or one who acted under the influence of a sudden affective impulse. Likhachev, following Morselli, viewed suicide as a topic for sociology. To formulate his theoretical position, he paraphrased the introduction to *Il suicidio;* although he did name his source, Likhachev did not use quotation marks, merging his voice with Morselli's. Like his Western predecessors, the "Russian Morselli" fused the medical and social views in the metaphor "the body social." While psychiatry investigated individual thought (wrote Likhachev), sociology investigated collective thought, or the psychology of the collective man. By extension, the method adopted by sociology amounted to autopsy, or, as Likhachev insightfully put it, self-autopsy (a metaphor that accounts for the fusion of the subject and object in the body social), a procedure in which medical and legal authority intersected ("developing statistics, society, as it were, subjects itself to a medico-legal autopsy").[123] Thus, in the two years that separated Ponomarev's study and Likhachev's, Russia repeated the development of European science, from Esquirol in the 1830s to Morselli in the 1870s.

The general conclusion made by Russian studies were also similar to those reached by Western European statisticians: in the nineteenth century, suicide rates were increasing.[124] Likhachev arranged the Russian data to show that in the period between 1803 and 1875, the suicide rate doubled in Russia. Although he had to combine data derived from vastly different sources, he was encouraged by the fact that the tendency for increase in Russia corresponded in its general configurations to the Western European data. In terms of absolute figures, Russia occupied the last place among developed European nations, confirming a popular view that the increase in suicides was the result of civilization, still sadly lacking in most parts of Russia.[125] While Likhachev, following the statisticians who worked in the 1860s and 1870s, readily admitted that the data were incomplete and inadequate, he maintained the validity of the conclusion: Russia was experiencing a suicide epidemic. Many of his contemporaries shared this belief. It was not science, however, but mainly the periodical press that took upon itself the task of presenting the increase in suicide and interpreting its meaning. Law, the Church, and science relinquished their authority to public opinion.

3 Suicide in the Russian Press

Russian newspapers started printing information on suicides only in the late 1830s. (English newspapers reported suicides beginning early in the eighteenth century.)[1] A regular section called *Dnevnik proisshestvii,* a "diary" that recorded urban accidents, appeared in 1839 in two major Petersburg papers, the official government bulletin *Sankt-Peterburgskie vedomosti* and the private paper *Severnaia pchela.* Reprinted from the official bulletin of the capital's police, *Vedomosti Sankt-Peterburgskoi gorodskoi politsii,* which came into existence that year (1839), information was mostly limited to the description of unidentified bodies discovered in public places.[2] The following report, from the August 9, 1839, issue of *Sankt-Peterburgskie vedomosti,* is typical: "On July 31 at 10 A.M. in Chernaia Rechka (Narvsk. district, quarter 4), the corpse of an unidentified male was found. As it was in a state of complete decay, the corpse was interred."

By 1848 such reports had disappeared. In 1848, a year of revolution in Europe, the Russian government instituted a series of measures restricting the press, which remained in effect until the late 1850s. In the early 1860s, suicide reports reappeared, but were infrequent. A new publication, the liberal newspaper *Golos* [Voice], started in January 1863, printed the first (brief) suicide report in its fourteenth issue (on January 16).

In the course of the 1860s, the coverage of events in newspapers expanded and their circulation increased. Newspapers started to play an important role both as a source of information and as a vehicle for public opinion. In 1866 major newspapers began to report on the proceedings of the new open courts, making crime—for the first time in Russian history—one of their central topics. By the late 1860s, major newspapers and the "small press," aimed at the popular reader, featured reports of suicide in each issue.[3] Major newspapers also published comprehensive surveys of statistical data.[4] Selected cases of suicide (and suicide in general) became an object of discussion in the reviews of social events featured in daily, weekly, and monthly publications.

Interpretation of suicide was the prerogative of the liberal and left-wing press. Among the daily newspapers, the liberal *Golos* and *Sankt-Peterburgskie vedomosti* devoted most attention to the topic. Suicide figured prominently in the weekly populist paper *Nedelia* and in the left-wing monthly journal *Otechestvennye zapiski.* "Thick journals" such as *Otechestvennye zapiski,* the radical *Delo,* the populist *Russkoe bogatstvo* (along with *Nedelia*), and the progressive medical-social journal *Arkhiv sudebnoi meditsiny i obshchestvennoi gigieny* also featured reviews of scientific treatises on suicide. By contrast, the moderately liberal journal *Vestnik Evropy* devoted little attention to the topic, and the conservative *Russkii vestnik* ignored it altogether.

An exception to this rule was *Grazhdanin,* a weekly newspaper published (beginning in 1872) by the conservative Prince V. P. Meshchersky, who made it his goal to counteract the harmful effects of the liberal press. In the year 1873–74, during Dostoevsky's tenure as the paper's editor, *Grazhdanin* featured reviews and discussions of crime and suicide, treated as evidence of the social and spiritual pathology for which the nihilist spirit was held responsible.[5] M. N. Katkov's conservative *Moskovskie vedomosti,* another newspaper that combated nihilism, also commented on suicides in this vein.[6]

Most of the opposition newspapers and journals launched in the late 1860s went out of circulation by the late 1880s.[7] It was at that time that the prominence of suicide diminished: although suicide reports continued to appear, suicide lost its status as an event that symbolized society's current state. Thus the prominence of suicide in the 1860s–70s can be seen as a product of glasnost. As one journalist put it, "nowadays, as glasnost is becoming more widespread in our society, one continually hears of new cases of mental derangement and suicide." He concluded: "Such cases, of course, are one of the most unfortunate signs of our society's unhealthy condition."[8] But it was the newspaper coverage of crime and suicide that created the impression that social pathology was rampant: the rise of suicide coincided with the rise of the socially conscious press.[9]

The Suicide Epidemic of the 1860s–1880s

Beginning in the early 1870s, the press presented suicide as a regular and anticipated event. The newspaper chronicles reported: "Suicide after Suicide in Petersburg" (*Sankt-Peterburgskie vedomosti,* May 24, 1872); "another suicide attempt was discovered last night" (May 31, 1873). Journalists who wrote for the "thick journals" drew a connection between suicide and the historical moment. In March 1871, on the tenth anniversary of the Emancipation Edict, the "Internal Affairs" section of *Otechestvennye zapiski* focused on crime and suicide: "you need only to read the chronicle of daily events and the transcripts of circuit court sessions, and a kind of terror will unwittingly take hold of you. . . . If we take the last month of the past year and the first two months of this year, we see that in the capitals alone about ten noblemen have either shot or stabbed themselves to death. We do not take commoners into account, because they must be counted by the dozen."[10]

In reporting crimes and suicides, the press (the reporter claimed) provided "living illustrations" for statistical figures, which indicated a steady increase in the incidence of suicide. In the fall of 1873, drawing on the chronicles from Petersburg, Moscow, and provincial newspapers, the same author described the incidence of suicide in the following terms: "In the last few years in Russia, suicide has definitely become a sort of cholera that has gotten into a rotten place expressly created for its maintenance. In cities special weekly accounts of suicides have become a regular news item."[11] By 1872–73, the idea of "a suicide epidemic" had set in. The "Chronicle of Internal Affairs" (Vnutrenniaia khronika) section of *Nedelia* occasionally included a column entitled "Suicide Epidemic" (Epidemiia samoubiistv). Sometimes all the newspaper reported was: the suicide epidemic continues.[12]

The notion of an epidemic gained new prominence a decade later. In 1884, journalists were still struggling with the apparent coincidence of individual acts and they still linked suicides with modern means of transmitting information and media reports: "Among young people suicide mania has definitely become a social disease, taking on greater dimensions every day. Our young people are disappearing one after another. As if having agreed on an exact time and date by telegraph, they depart simultaneously from various places into the next world, providing inexhaustible material for the newspaper chronicle of daily events."[13]

At that time the epidemic raged with special force on the pages of *Nedelia,* one of the few reform-era publications to survive into the 1880s.[14] In 1886, *Nedelia* commented that the reporters now commanded a special language:

Suicide long ago became a common occurrence in Russian life. Nowadays, no one is surprised to see several reports of suicide in every issue of the newspaper: this man or that woman has put a bullet into his or her skull, taken some kind of poison, thrown himself or herself under a railroad train, or by some other means has settled the score with life. Special expressions have even gained currency, attesting to the regularity of this sad affair and to the vast extent to which it has spread: rare is the correspondence on suicide in which we do not come across expressions such as "the usual spring or autumn epidemic of suicides has already begun," or: "the victims of this season of suicides are...." and so forth.[15]

This terminology was a compromise. In the early 1870s, soon after it started regular coverage of suicide, the press announced the onset of the "suicide epidemic"; in the 1880s, metaphors were adjusted: suicide was now presented as an annual, seasonal epidemic (on the model of influenza, not cholera).

Most newspapermen and their readers took the reality of the suicide epidemic for granted. In its last years, however, one skeptic voiced his doubts. The prominent radical publicist Nikolai Shelgunov (who had studied natural science at the Academy of Forestry), commenting on the fact that the press noted an increase in suicides for the year 1888, suggested: "In Russia suicides started occuring neither today nor yesterday. Whether the number of suicides is generally increasing, and whether it has increased in the year 1888, is truly unknown, because there are no exact suicide statistics for Russia. But those who need suicides as their 'material' claim (and this can be done without evidence) that suicide is on the rise."[16] There is no evidence, however, that any of his contemporaries joined Shelgunov in his skepticism.

Case Study: A Public Drama of Intimate Life

In 1873, the Russian press was preoccupied with a crime committed in a fashionable hotel in St. Petersburg, the Hotel Belle Vue. A murder followed by a suicide, the "Hotel Belle Vue case" became a focal point for debates on crime and suicide, their causes and social implications, as well as the implications of making such cases public. (The press referred to the case as "suicide-murder" or "murder-suicide,"[17] treating them as two sides of the same phenomenon.) On

September 19, 1873, in the Hotel Belle Vue, a young man shot a woman, the object of his unrequited passion, and then shot himself. The perpetrator was Timofei Komarov, a candidate in law at St. Petersburg University. The victim was Anna Suvorina. A publisher and author,* she was the wife of the prominent journalist A. S. Suvorin, who then worked for the liberal newspaper *Sankt-Peterburgskie vedomosti,* where he published a weekly feuilleton called "Sketches and Vignettes" (*Ocherki i kartinki*) under the pseudonym Stranger (*Neznakomets*). (In 1876, Suvorin began publishing his own newspaper, *Novoe vremia,* and soon gained the reputation of one of Russia's most prominent conservative activists.) The connection of the heroes of this drama to the press heightened public interest in the incident. *Nedelia* introduced it as "the case of Suvorina, the wife of the contributor to *Sankt-Peterburgskie vedomosti,* who is known in her own right among the reading public as the publisher of several children's books."[18] The death of Suvorina had all the characteristics of a sensation: a thirty-three-year-old mother of five children, she was sharing supper with Komarov in a hotel room. Her husband, who was supposed to join the couple, arrived at the scene at about midnight— shortly after the shots were fired—having just completed an urgent report for his newspaper.[19]

It is hard to say what shocked readers more—the crime, the revelation of the unconventional mores of men and women of letters, or the very fact that intimate details of their lives were revealed to the public. The theme of exposure and publicity (*glasnos'*) figures prominently in the accounts of the drama. What glasnost meant in this case was exposing the private to the public eye. The article in *Nedelia,* in which this case was discussed as a characteristic social fact, was entitled "Public Dramas of Intimate Life" (Glasnye dramy intimnoi zhizni). (Signed E. K., it was written by left-wing journalist Evgeniia Konradi).

Exposed to the public eye in numerous accounts in many organs were not only the circumstances of the Suvorins' personal drama, but also the woman's body, whose condition, as well as that of the suicide's body, was described in the papers in considerable detail. A reporter from the gossipy *Novosti,* which published its coverage of the

---

*Working in cooperation with Elena Likhacheva, a journalist known for her writings on women's issues, Suvorina published several anthologies for children and compilations of popular science readings, one of which (*Dlia chteniia,* 1866) was branded by a reviewer as "nihilist." In 1881, Suvorina's co-author, Likhacheva, devoted an extensive review article to suicide, treated—along with crime—as a "social disease" (Likhacheva, "O samoubiistve").

case on the front page, claimed that he saw the body in the morgue and described its "large lacerated wound" in the terms of a forensic report.[20] *Golos* gave a similar description.[21] *Sankt-Peterburgskie vedomosti* found it essential, speaking for Suvorin, to announce that the victim's husband (contrary to the reports of the rival newspapers) did not object to the autopsy of his wife's body.[22] In itself the operation performed by the press—opening the intimate and the physical to public view—was tantamout to an "autopsy" (*vskrytie*). In this context, the name of the hotel—Belle Vue—became emblematic.

Members of the press were clearly ambivalent about such practices. An author from the radical monthly journal *Delo,* B. Ongirsky, after reviewing various newspaper accounts of the Suvorin case in his "Statistical Results on Suicide," reproached the reporters from *Sankt-Peterburgskie vedomosti* for sounding the alarm "throughout the entire precinct of the liberals" (*na ves' liberal'nyi okolotok*) rather than relieving their colleague's grief "in the family circle."[23] The sensationalist newspaper *Novosti* preceded its revelation of the scandalous details with a disclaimer: "When describing the bloody drama in Belle Vue in yesterday's issue, we found it necessary, out of a completely understandable feeling of delicacy and respect for the honor of the family of Mr. Suvorin, to be silent on one important fact. . . . This fact consists of the following: as told to us by the owner of the Hotel Belle Vue, Mr. Lomach, everything in the hotel room that had been occupied by Mr. Komarov was found exactly in place, and the bedding had not been touched."[24]

The socially minded weekly newspaper *Nedelia* reported the scandalous fact that this detail was exposed: "One newspaper had even voluntarily taken on the role of forensic investigator and triumphantly reported to the public that, according to inquiries conducted by the newspaper, the hotel room where the event occurred had been in perfect order and the bedding had not been crumpled!"[25]

Social language and social argument prevailed over everything. Even *Novosti* concluded their graphic description of the dead woman's body with an appeal to the social significance of the event, treating it as a part of a series and a sign of a social pathology characteristic of the age: "The frequent repetition of such facts, in part, points to the abnormal condition of the developed sector of our society, and the causes for this condition, in our opinion, lie in the changes that our society has undergone in the last decade."[26]

Journalists writing in the serious press followed the same strategy: indecent exposure could be counteracted by moving from discussions of "personalities" (a product of "our homemade glasnost") to the "general meaning of events."[27] In their weekly and monthly reviews these journalists indeed passed from the individual to the collective. For the author from *Delo,* "the romantic death of Suvorina, who was killed by Komarov in The Hotel Belle Vue" was a part of a continuum that extended to "the prosaic death of a poor peasant woman who had hanged herself from a city streetlight near the Mytninsky dvor."[28] As such, these events became social phenomena and therefore a matter of social concern. *Nedelia* attributed the two Hotel Belle Vue deaths to an "epidemic" of violence. And of such epidemics "it is hardly possible to doubt that they obey known laws with the same fatefully undeviating regularity as do phenomena of the physical world."[29] Appeals to science and its laws made the procedure appear legitimate.

About a year later, in his feuilleton in *Sankt-Peterburgskie vedomosti,* Suvorin himself alluded to his wife's death, along with three similar cases that he had witnessed in the course of the year. Comparing contemporary young men to the serfowners of former times, who punished serf girls for rejecting their amorous advances, he appealed to his progressive readers to pass sentence: "But are these murderers from the ranks of the youth of today, who treat the life of another person as their own property, really better than the landowners of the good old days whom you have consigned to perdition?"[30] The journalist seems to have drawn far-reaching social conclusions from his private drama.

The status of the event was clear, but there was no consensus on the cause. The confusion became painfully obvious in a debate between *Nedelia* and *Delo.*[31] (In *Delo,* B. Ongirsky, in the essay "Statistical Results of Suicides" [Statisticheskie itogi samoubiistv] written largely in response to E. K.'s "Public Dramas of Intimate Life," treated the Hotel Belle Vue case among other recent suicides.) Ongirsky bitterly lamented the fact that the public, alerted to the issue of murder and suicide by the Hotel Belle Vue case, subscribed to widely diverse views: "some, as usual, saw the root of the evil in nihilism and atheism"; some looked for an explanation in the pages of a psychiatric study; and still others did not look for a cause at all, attributing the events to fate. Much to Ongirsky's dismay, E. K. from *Nedelia* had turned the power of her pen against herself, suggesting that the suicide epidemic was a product of glasnost.[32] She argued that newspaper coverage of crime and suicide provoked those who desired to appear in the spotlight to imitate such acts. To give "the real reason," Ongirsky from *Delo* [Deed] turned to "facts"—that is, to statistical data. The figures, in his opinion, hardly required comment, "clearly" indicating that poverty was the real cause of the private dramas behind the numbers (Ongirsky used the statistical data on suicide published by I. Pasternatsky).[33] A social law was at work. That poverty was not actually an issue for Komarov did not trouble the journalist, but he was troubled, as were many others, by the contradiction between the social explanation of suicide and the traditionally accepted medical view. He tried to combine the two paradigms: perhaps poverty caused mental aberration, which then led to suicide? The issue remained unresolved.

In her retort, Konradi gave a penetrating analysis of her colleague's difficulties, pointing out that, like many others, the "publicist" from *Delo,* confused by knowledge derived from several Western sciences, passed from the social argument to the medical, "simply changing horses midway": "statistics are cast aside, and another fashionable horse is saddled—the laws of the human organism and psychology. . . . [S]ince we first learned about the existence of statistics as a science and also of several other sciences that study the laws of organic and inorganic nature . . . the number of such articles in Russia has greatly multiplied."[34]

Indeed, there were many such articles. Shaken by the collapse of the absolute authority of the Christian worldview, caught in the contradiction between social and medical explanations of human action (which also troubled Western scientists), bewildered by the novelty of publicity and by the contingencies of the historical moment, Russian publicists—like the Russian public—were profoundly confused. The confusion involved the general frame of reference (Christian and scientific); specific disciplinary authorities (medical and social science); and the basic categories of social thinking, such as individual and social, public and private.

Discursive Strategies

Possible solutions to conceptual confusion were found in the very discourse used to discuss suicide. In the 1860s–80s, a discourse that invested body images with an array of symbolic meanings—a discourse pervaded by intended and unintended metaphors—was prevalent in the Russian press. Fed by organicist trends in Western social theory and utilizing the phraseology of Russian populism (adopted even by those who did not subscribe to the populist program), this discourse abounded in metaphors of society as a collective body. The pathology of the social body was a common theme. In the words of Petr Lavrov (in a populist manifesto serialized in *Nedelia* in 1868–69),

"The present social order is a pathological order."[35] Autopsy was a common metaphor, used to comment on the power, limitations, and dangers of knowledge and exposure. The idea of pathology was also articulated in the images of the disintegration of the social body. Presented as a consequence of this disintegration, individual suicides were implicated in the destiny of Russian society. Metaphoric categories of science were correlated with political metaphors and suicide acquired a political twist. Various specific explanations of suicide were offered: suicide was connected to atheism and nihilism, growing poverty, development of civilization, social alienation brought by capitalism, or mental illness. What united those who held divergent views was a common language—a set of metaphors and rhetorical strategies derived from the image of the disintegrating social body. This metaphor offered solutions to many contradictions: created by conflation of the two concepts, the individual body and society, the metaphor encouraged the conflation of the two points of view, the individual and the collective, the medical and the social, the public and the private. It also encouraged the confusion of direct and metaphoric meaning.

In many texts, metaphor alone provided an (implicit) explanation for the suicide epidemic. A journalist from *Otechestvennye zapiski* (in 1872) topped a long list of suicides and crimes with the comment that a society under reform is a victim of vivisection, in danger of losing its limbs: "The sudden reforms are very similar to excruciatingly painful surgical operations or amputations."[36] An author from *Nedelia* (in 1873) described a healthy society as a well-integrated organism and lamented that this condition was not currently to be found: "In vain would you search for that life-giving stream of powerful, fresh, and bold thought that in other epochs runs like an electric current from individual to individual, branching out along various layers of the social formation, as if making up the collectively thinking and feeling whole in which the individual worlds of thought and feeling fuse together."[37]

At present, he thought, the individual "detaches himself from the solidarity of general interests": it was the morbid overgrowth of individual interests and passions (cellular pathology of sorts) that accounted for murder and suicide, such as the Hotel Belle Vue case.[38] The reason for the suicide epidemic was also clear to a journalist from *Otechestvennye zapiski* in 1882: it was brought about by the "decomposition [*razlozhenie*] of communal principles" in Russian society.[39] Another author, writing in *Slovo* in 1880, offered a philosophical explanation of suicide, connecting the epidemic to the Buddhist ideal of nothingness ("nirvana") derived from Schopenhauer. Being sucked into the "abyss of nirvana," however, was not a danger to the individual who was firmly connected to a larger whole, society, the source of life: "when this is the case, a person feels beneath him the firm ground from which he extracts his living juices and his living energy."[40] Severed from the social body, the individuals lost their vitality and naturally succumbed to death by suicide: "Because they do not take nourishment from the flow of the life force in society, their energy weakens and becomes exhausted, and day by day the person unnoticeably approaches a psychological state in which further toiling becomes completely impossible."[41] Adapted to a national context, the image of the social organism resembled the Russian folk symbol of moist mother earth. In this metaphor, the social argument conquered the metaphysical one.

In their discussions of suicide, publicists from the anti-nihilist camp also focused on the relationship between the individual, body and soul, and a larger entity. In their case, this larger entity was not only society but also God. The author of the Christian pamphlet *Our Time and Suicide* (Nashe vremia i samoubiistvo), Klitin, claimed that when a man loses faith, thus severing his connection with "the source of life—God," he is already dead.[42] In *Grazhdanin,* Meshchersky reasoned that because a nihilist gives up the immortal soul (a particle of God within his body), and becomes matter alone, he is subject to total annihilation: "Our young generation is *nihil,* and nothing more [*nichto i nichego bolee*]."[43] The end for a nihilist is, inevitably, suicide; what remains is "smoke and a dead body." Meshchersky discussed the situation in terms of its effect not only on the individual body but also on the society: "we are all headed for suicide by a rapid or slow process of self-deception and self-decomposition (*samorazlozheniia*) . . . nihilism is the common plague of our society."[44] Like an individual without faith, a society without religion is a body without a soul—a suicide's body in a state of (self)-decomposition.[45] Thus two antagonistic languages—Meshchersky called them "the language of the spiritual Russia" (*Rossii dukhovnoi*) and "the language of the realistic Russia" (*Rossii real'noi*)[46]—used metaphors built on the same pattern: conflation of the two bodies.

The Suicide's Body as a Locus of Meaning

Most newspaper accounts of suicide followed a standard pattern: a brief description of the location, the victim's identity (which was frequently unknown), and the method of self-destruction, as well as a detailed description of the suicide's body. The report concluded with a remark: "causes unknown," or "an investigation is being conducted." The description of the body was usually taken from official police bulletins, which quoted the post-mortem reports. As might be expected, images of corporeal disorder (dismemberment, disfigurement, and decomposition) dominated these descriptions. From the newspaper reports, these images made their way to the reviews of suicides in monthly journals. In the following example from the October 1873 issue of *Otechestvennye zapiski,* the reader is invited to view the body with the eyewitnesses. On a Volga ship approaching Samara, a passenger had leaped into the ship's engine: "curious onlookers saw a kind of bloody pulp, not at all like any living being. . . . The upper part of the unfortunate man's body was already ground up into a solid bloody pulp. An official report has been filed, of course. Apparently, the suicide was a petit bourgeois of the city of Samara. It is not known what caused him to take his own life."

On another Volga ship, a passenger was found dead in his cabin: "the corpse of a passenger, a merchant, was found in a second-class cabin. A young man of average height with a light brown beard stood near the corpse and looked apprehensively at the dead man's face, which had been disfigured by the shot. This was the deceased man's shop assistant."[47]

This review ends with a reference to numerous other suicides, such as suicides of common peasants, which are not committed "in such a prominent [*vidnom*] place as a hotel on Nevsky [Prospekt] or a passenger ship," and which lack witnesses: "In several months to a year, when the spring waters subside, a missing person's corpse will be found accidentally. They will write about this event briefly: 'the completely rotten body of a man or a woman was found.' Another time, someone's decapitated head will simply be fished out of the water near the steamship bureau, but whose head is it? To what poor fellow does it belong? Who knows! Who knows him, where is he from, what kind of person is he to have lost his head so carelessly?"[48]

Such a case of a severed head appeared in the newspaper *Golos,* which, in its turn, borrowed it from the bulletin of the provincial government, *Samarskie gubernskie vedomosti.* This is what *Golos* reported:

On August 2nd at 2 P.M. on the Volga River near the bureau of the Samolet steamship company *a severed head was extracted from the water.* The head belongs, it seems, to a man. There is no hair on it.

The outer covering of the head, the face and what remained of the neck are of a dirty green color. They have swelled up and are covered with slime. The membranes of the eyes are wrinkled. The nose, lips, and ears show signs of decomposition. A total of eight teeth are missing, four from each of the upper and lower mandibles. The places where the teeth were located are not covered over by gums. The skull bones are intact. Only half of the neck is attached to the head; it ends with the fourth cervical vertebra. On the lower part of this vertebrae, a piece of bone was severed in a horizontal direction. The soft tissue surrounding the cervical vertebrae terminate parallel to the fourth cervical vertebra. Despite the decomposition, it is still possible to determine that they were cut through by a sharp cutting implement.[49]

Since nothing was known about the victim or the circumstances of his death, the newspaper account was largely limited to a forensic report on the condition of the only remaining part of the body, the head. The author of the journal review (N. A. Demert from *Otechestvennye zapiski*) turned the image of the severed head taken from the autopsy report into an explicit metaphor: a folk idiom, *poteriat' golovu* [to lose one's head], which means "to die recklessly." The reader was thus invited to ascribe symbolic meaning to the whole picture: it could be read as an emblem of the decomposition of postreform Russian society, the result of self-destructive social policies, which the press exposed to the public eye. And the very fact that the journalist chose to discuss death by decapitation (a violent act more likely to have been murder) among suicides, testifies to the symbolic power of the image of suicide.

In conclusion, a note on the mechanism of meaning. Newspaper accounts, in which the information on suicide originated, did not call for developed interpretations. In the absence of interpretation, descriptions of the body borrowed from forensic reports—an essential part of newspaper accounts of suicide—became the locus of textual meaning and carried the weight of explanation. The implied explanation relied on possible metaphoric readings: images of the disintegrating body of a (frequently unidentified) victim could be seen as symbols of the disintegration of the Russian society. On another plane of meaning, these pictures of corporeal disorder, almost always followed by the statement "cause unknown," stood as symbols of the tragic inaccessibility of knowledge about man and society. The reader well versed in this discourse received poetic license to read statements about the physical body metaphorically, as statements about society and as comments about knowledge. Other genres often made such metaphors explicit and used them deliberately. With the newspaper reports, it was the formal requirements of the genre that transformed the descriptions of disfigured bodies into a symbol—the medium created the message.

Between Metaphoric and Literal Meaning

Constructed in this manner, discussions of suicide in the press were pervaded by intended and unintended conflations of direct and metaphoric meaning. In an article titled "On One Death" (Po povodu odnoi smerti),[50] published in the populist monthly *Ustoi* (in 1882), the metaphor is made literal in the image of the body of a suicide dissolving in the body of Russia. First, the author presents the reader with a vivid picture of suicide: "before you lies a disfigured corpse." The journalist wants to show death "in the form of a shattered skull, of bloodied integuments, of brains that have dried and stuck to the wall"[51]—as it would be presented in a forensic report. But at the next stage, the writer takes over from the medical examiner, suggesting that the bones of honest young Russian men who have died by suicide—"the salt of the earth"—"are spread on the face of our earth" (*rasseiany po vsemu litsu nashei zemli,* a folk idiom applied to fallen warriors). Further, we see the bodies "buried in the humid earth." And a year later, "the lonely graves will be level with mother earth, and next summer no one will notice or remember that here have decayed the best hearts and the best brains that Russia has ever produced."[52]

From a graphic description of disintegrated bodies (couched in medical terms) the text progresses, by way of a sequence of idioms evoking the folk symbolism of Russia as mother earth, to an image that merges the body of the suicide with the body of society. The metaphor is made literal: the individual and the social body converge physically.

Although journalists took recourse in metaphor, they were nevertheless deeply concerned with "reality." According to *Delo* (in 1868), scientific data (statistics), in themselves, lacked reality, but in the hands of a journalist "that raw material can be put to good use."[53] True to the journal's name ("deed"), one author argued for the deed, not the word. Taking statistics as his starting point,[54] he chose to enlarge on the relationship between such environmental influences as "the decay of the atmosphere and the rottenness of the soil" (*gnilost' atmosfery i isporchennost' pochvy*) and the high morbidity in the capital. He explains that it was recently revealed (in *Arkhiv sudebnoi meditsiny i obshchestvennoi gigieny,* "the best and most useful of all the periodical publications in Russia")[55] that in Petersburg waste is not removed through sewers, but absorbed into the soil. Petersburg's soil is nothing but a repository of decaying matter that poisons the air: "the soil of Petersburg is bit by bit turning into a common garbage pit emitting miasmas." This circumstance is responsible for the epidemics of infectious diseases and the birth of unhealthy children in families who live in basement apartments, in direct contact with the poisonous soil. This "murderous" soil is also responsible for suicides: "a statistician would make a tremendous error, if, while discussing, for example, suicides in Petersburg, he did not consider such circumstances as I have just mentioned."[56]

How is this connection established? Looking through statistical data, the journalist notes a considerable number of cases under the heading "students." He speculates on the cause of high mortality among students, specifically, among medical students. The cause lies in their "material environment." Given the cold, dark, humid cells ("frequently, with cracks in the floor") in which students live, scarce food, intense daily studies, and, moreover, their "work with decomposed corpses in the hospital, the soil would be prepared for developing pulmonary tuberculosis." The journalist concludes: "Is it any wonder, given the circumstances, that the number of student suicides is a sizable figure?"[57]

Guided by a sequence of rhetorical figures, the reader comes to accept suicides among medical students as no surprise. Central among these figures is the image of the "soil" that "prepared" the development of disease. In this case, no real soil is involved, "soil" is purely a metaphor, a part of the common idiom *podgotovit' pochvu.* But the author also evokes images of real, not metaphoric soil: the miasmic soil soaked in the city's wastes, its "murderous" influence reinforced by the decomposing bodies with which medical students deal in the anatomical theater. At the start of his project, the journalist declares that his goal is to discover "the root causes" of suicide.[58] Were they to be found, the figures would serve not only as material for moral statistics, but also as "positive data," of practical use to society. In searching for this "positive data," the text vacillates between the literal and the metaphoric meaning of the word "soil," conflating the two. The procedure (looking for the "root cause") is directed by the metaphor: the "root" of the matter is found in the "soil."

Behind these deductions stands the age-old concern over the danger of evaporations from the earth, "miasmas," which has haunted the popular imagination and scientific discourse since the eighteenth century. As Alain Corbin showed in his study of the French social imagination, the foul-smelling soil that absorbed products of decay (excrement, kitchen refuse, dead bodies) was regarded as morbid in eighteenth- and nineteenth-century France; "death was seen as circulating in the atmosphere with the odor of [decomposition]."[59] Anxieties concerning the urban subsoil, which "aroused the vigilance of sanitary reformers," were reinforced "by the survival, conscious or unconscious, of collective beliefs about the living nature of the earth."[60] The same hygienic problems and the same deep-rooted mythological fears obviously preoccupied the reform-minded Russian journalist in the 1860s–70s.

The persuasive power of the journalists' arguments seems to lie in the rhetorical connections and symbolic associations. The lull of familiar idioms (such as "to prepare the soil") as well as, for a well-informed reader, the story of Turgenev's character, the medical student Bazarov whose death resulted from contact with a corpse during an autopsy, all contribute to the general impression that the causal connection between the "soil" (a product of decomposing matter) and social ills such as suicide has been positively established. The project of making word into deed undertaken by *Delo* turned into a rhetorical operation of realizing metaphors and making scientific concepts metaphorical.

Two Autopsies

In the popular press as well as in scientific publications, "autopsy," understood literally and metaphorically, figured as a predominant method of determining the cause of suicide. The idea of autopsy as an operation aimed at uncovering material manifestations of mental phenomena was consonant with contemporaries' desire for positive knowledge. The symbolic connotations of glasnost and the practice of exposing the workings of social mechanisms to the public view added to the metaphor's meaning. The image of a medico-legal autopsy, which combined the authority of science with that of law, doubled, as it were, the symbolic power of penetration. (It was in this context that the journal *Annals of Forensic Medicine* was judged to be the most reliable and effective of the Russian periodicals.) Journalists and popularizers of science who wrote in the popular press and medical scientists who actually performed autopsies frequently fell victim to the power of this metaphor.

One such scientist was Ivan Gvozdev, professor of forensic medicine at Kazan University, author of the brochure *On Suicide from a Social and Medical Point of View* (O samoubiistve s sotsial'noi i meditsinskoi tochki zreniia). Published in 1889, this book summarized the results of twenty years practice, beginning in the late 1860s. On the whole, Gvozdev subscribed to Büchner's views, claiming that the "force of matter," a concept "used at present to explain all phenomena of the visible world," can also serve as an explanation for the normal and abnormal functions of mental capacities, including suicide.[61] As a scientist, Gvozdev limited his material to "positive data," that is, to evidence of mental activity deposited within cerebral matter. As a positivist, he relied exclusively on his own life experience, "[using] only what we have personally experienced in the course of life in general, and from the data of forensic medical dissections of suicides in particular."[62] On the basis of over one hundred autopsies performed by himself and his students, Gvozdev claimed that the adhesion of the dura mater (the outermost of the three membranes covering the brain) to the skull was "one of the characteristic features of death by suicide as such." Though he admitted that the exact role played by the dura mater in mental activity was unknown, Gvozdev argued that its fusion with the skullcap could not have left molecular movement in the brain (that is, mental activity) unaffected.[63] It proved harder to pinpoint the material manifestations of suicidal disposition in the pia mater (the inner membrane), that is, in deeper, and softer, layers of matter:[64]

Although the brain ought to display physical changes corresponding to any mental disorders present, including suicide, these changes are sometimes so elusive or ephemeral that even with acute forms of insanity, they often evade appropriate detection.

With suicide, physical changes in the brain tissue itself are ephemeral and elusive to detection; this is an almost constant phenomenon, especially when we are dealing with people of apparently good mental health who have made an attempt on their lives.[65]

Despite the lack of hard evidence, Gvozdev stood firm in his beliefs, assuming that the physical changes in the brain tissue merely eluded the scientist. He struggled with the two entities that defied the principles of positivism—people who were "apparently" (*po-vidimomu*, literally, "visibly") mentally healthy and brain tissue which had no visible manifestations of pathology. In both cases, the perception was declared to be false: suicides were known to be mentally ill (an axiom going back to Esquirol); mental was known to be inscribed in matter (a tenet of positivism). (In Büchner's words, "there must have been material pathological alterations, though they were not visible.")[66] "Reality" was believed to lie beneath the deceptive surface of appearances, even though it constantly eluded appropriate detection.

A central symbol of positive knowledge, anatomy was also used as a symbol of positivistic education. Gvozdev, who approached suicide not only from a medical but also from a social point of view, devoted a chapter to the role of education in causing (or failing to prevent) suicide. Statistics showed that the propensity for suicide increased within the educated classes of society and was higher among the young than among the general population. "Can contemporary education be a reason for suicide, if only a remote one?" asked Gvozdev. In approaching this question, he remained true to the principle of basing conclusions on his own experience and trusting the evidence provided by autopsies. Because he had seen students mainly over the bodies of suicides as he supervised them in performing autopsies, he based his judgment about the quality of education on the quality of the students' autopsy reports.[67] (His sample included about two thousand student reports, accumulated over twenty years of teaching, beginning in the late 1860s.) Gvozdev was struck by mistakes in spelling, grammar, and diction in these reports and surprised to discover ignorance about the basic principles of physiology. But "nothing made such an impression [on him] as did the almost complete ignorance of the classical languages among the majority of students finishing their medical education."[68] For Gvozdev, the fact that a typical student allowed his knowledge of Latin to fall into oblivion amounted, in the long run, to a mockery of life itself: "In our opinion, this is nothing but a direct insult to Latin and an indirect insult to the time spent learning this language—and after all, time is life!"[69] With this argument, Doctor Gvozdev came closest to establishing a connection, albeit a symbolic one, between education and suicide (rejection of life). Of the two types of autopsy, a medical procedure and a metaphor, the metaphor seems to have had a stronger explanatory power.

Dead Languages: Suicide and Classicism

In the Russian press, suicide was often connected to the classical languages: the requirements in Latin and Greek were frequently identified as a cause of suicide among gymnasium students. This argument had ideological significance: in the reform era traditional classical education came under attack in favor of a more democratic, reality-oriented (*real'noe*) education. One case that attracted attention of the press was the suicide of Platon Demert, an adolescent seeking admission to a classical gymnasium in the city of Kazan. To enter the fifth grade, the boy was required to pass examinations in Latin and Greek. In the course of preparation, on January 5, 1871, he shot himself dead. The victim's uncle, P. A. Demert, described this case in a letter to the newspaper *Sankt-Peterburgskie vedomosti* (promptly published in no. 16), laying the blame for the young Platon's death on the educational system, which put such emphasis on "dead languages." (To prove his point, he referred to another Kazan student suicide, Sergei Puparev, who killed himself in July 1870, reminding the reader that in Kazan alone "this is not the first case of suicide caused by dead languages.") At the request of the minister of education, the head of Kazan's Board of Education, P. D. Shestakov, prepared a detailed report on the case (published in *Zhurnal Ministerstva narodnogo prosveshcheniia,* an official organ of the Ministry of Education, in February 1871). According to Shestakov, the elder Demert, overcome with "a hatred for classicism," slandered the dead (Puparev, for one, had an easy command of dead languages). The pedagogue claimed that the cause of suicide lay not in the education students received at classical gymnasiums, but in the "education" they received through "literature" (as he called articles that appeared in the popular press), which did nothing less than serve as an instrument of "decay" and "destruction": "by surrounding suicides with a halo of martyrdom, writing articles about them, glorifying and mourning them . . . literature acts perniciously (*tletvorno*) and destructively, inculcating young people with the notion of a great heroic deed performed by the people who take their own lives."[70] Moreover, by glorifying young suicides, literature strove to strike a blow against the classical system in secondary education.[71] If classical languages caused suicide, argued Shestakov, there would be thousands of such cases. In conclusion, he appealed to his own experience: having studied Latin and Greek, Shestakov had never been tempted to kill himself on their account.[72]

The topic was picked up by the press. *Otechestvennye zapiski* alluded to the case (without mentioning young Demert's name) in its "Internal Chronicle" for March 1871, commenting with bitter irony that it might be in order to publish lists of classicists who neither hanged nor shot themselves. *Otechestvennye zapiski* returned to this incident in the July 1872 issue. At this time, the observer noted that there were two or three such cases annually. He discussed yet another suicide of a gymnasium student, Gartvikh in Odessa, which official investigation linked, on the basis of the autopsy report, to the fact that the boy's skull "did not have sufficient firmness."[73] Recalling the "clarification" of the Platon Demert case offered in *Zhurnal Ministerstva narodnogo prosveshcheniia* in 1871, the journalist ironically suggested that the difference between the gymnasium students who died by suicide and those who survived classical education lay in the degree of firmness of their skulls.

Trivial as it might seem, this episode reveals the network of associations woven around the theme of suicide. Thus the theme of Latin and Greek evoked the paradigm "suicide in antiquity," associating suicide with heroism and martyrdom. (The very name of the young suicide, Platon [the Russian spelling of Plato], could have contributed to this reading.) In this context, suicide was discussed as a consequence of imitation, dependent on literature. When a positivistic notion of autopsy was evoked, it seemed incompatible with the whole context. Two different cultural paradigms—classicism and positivistic medicine—clashed.

Who Is Speaking? N. A. Demert, the Observer

The "Internal Chronicle" section of *Otechestvennye zapiski* that alluded, with such bitter irony, to authorities' feeble attempts to explain students' suicides was written by the journal's regular correspondent Nikolai Aleksandrovich Demert. Signing his reviews of internal affairs D., he remained anonymous. The young suicide, Platon Demert, was the journalist's nephew.

To his fellow journalists, Demert's identity was no mystery. Upon his untimely death in March 1876, newspapers and journals eulogized the author of the "Internal Chronicle" as a keen observer of Russian life, an examiner of society's ills, and a reporter of its acute problems, who himself fell victim to the vicissitudes of Russian life and the pressures of a journalist's work.

The son of a landowner and a graduate (in law) of Kazan University, Demert started his public career as an active participant in peasant reform, holding official positions in the reform administration. For several years, he combined civil service with journalism, also trying his hand at fiction. Beginning in 1866, Demert devoted himself entirely to writing. He excelled as the author of "internal chronicles," or "internal observations"—reviews of domestic affairs, complete with social commentary, which were among the most popular genres in the periodical press of the time. Demert's reviews appeared in a number of publications: *Sankt-Peterburgskie vedomosti* (1865–67), satirical journal *Iskra* (1865 and 1867–73), newspaper *Birzhevye vedomosti* (1874–75), *Nedelia* (1868–69), and, most notably, *Otechestvennye zapiski* (1869–75).[74] Widely read, these writings were a vehicle of public activism, and a trade mark of the public and professional role of a "publicist."

"The internal observer Demert is known to everyone who is interested in the manifestations of the inner, 'black-soil,' side of Russian life"—wrote Gleb Uspensky in an essay devoted to Demert's memory.[75] But it was the circumstances of Demert's untimely death in March 1876 (at the age of 42) that preoccupied Uspensky, as well as those authors who remembered him in their memoirs. According to Uspensky, the famous publicist died in the Moscow city hospital (a hospital for the poor), where he was brought by police, who picked him up, unconscious, in the street—"he was mad."[76] A. M. Skabichevsky claimed that Demert died in a prison hospital. He was put under arrest when found, deranged and drunk, in the company of swindlers in a disreputable Moscow tavern. Apparently (lamented Skabichevsky), Demert's literary fame did not reach the ears of an overzealous police officer.[77] All memoirists agree that Demert suffered from alcoholism and was mentally ill at the end of his life. By the middle of 1875, his chronicles became incoherent; *Otechestvennye zapiski* refused to publish them.[78]

Gleb Uspensky elaborated on the diagnosis. According to him, Demert's main weakness was not alcoholism, but "excessive sensitivity" and a "passion for his work"—"and the work of an internal observer is a difficult task for a sensitive man."[79] Appealing to his own experience, Uspensky claimed that Demert's illness and death were caused not by alcohol, but by the "*properties*" of his work. An occupational disease of sorts, mental derangement was caused "precisely by this *internal observation*." Uspensky's phraseology (and his use of italics) is suggestive; in the end, he creates a metaphor: "internal observation" (*vnutrennee obozrenie,* the title of Demert's chronicle) is a hazardous occupation, which "consumed the whole of Demert's private life."[80] Like Turgenev's Bazarov, who died from an infection he caught performing an autopsy, Demert was killed by his pursuit: the observation of internal processes.

There were also personal circumstances: unhappy love and suicide in the family. After these experiences, writes Skabichevsky, Demert himself was a "living corpse."[81] Demert's young nephew Platon killed himself in January 1871. Suicide figured prominently in his chronicles in *Otechestvennye zapiski* in 1871, 1872, and 1873. It was during these years that a "suicide epidemic" raged on the pages of the Russian press—in no small measure, through the efforts of Demert himself. Seeing his personal tragedies as a social fact, he devoted special efforts to publicize society's ills, especially suicide and crime, the cause of which remained a mystery to him. "What is, after all, the reason for all these horrors?"—he asked in the chronicle that discussed the suicide of a gymnasium student in Kazan, who remained nameless.[82] When he met with a horrible end himself, his colleagues described his death in the language they shared with the diseased. In the imagination of a fellow publicist, Demert's body—the dissected body of a nameless prisoner—merged with the bodies of suicides and criminals whose fate Demert described in his chronicles: "And where is his grave? Does he even have one? Perhaps he, as an unidentified person who died under arrest, was sent to the university's anatomical theater and opened up there, side by side with the corpse of one of the swindlers with whom he was detained."[83] In the end, the personality of the journalist was completely entangled in the web of metaphors he himself spun.[84]

Suicide as Symbol

Different themes converged in the image of suicide, different ideological groups invested it with meaning. The suicide's body, presented in graphic images of corporeal disorder, became an emblem of the disintegrating social body—Russian society after the Great Reforms. For positivists, suicide was a test case for the issue of free will versus determinism (and a strong argument for the latter). Those troubled by positivism and atheism saw suicide as the direct result. For them, the fate of a suicide exemplified the fate of an atheistic society—willful reduction of the self to nothingness, a body deprived of a soul. The suicide's body was also the positivist's worst nightmare: the evidence of man's inability to determine what causes observable phenomena. The obvious inability to determine causation put a heavy emphasis on discourse itself. In this context, in the Russian press of the 1860s–80s, the body of the suicide assumed a second existence as a symbol.

Coda: The Second Suicide Epidemic, 1906–1914

At the beginning of the twentieth century the press was once again preoccupied with a "suicide epidemic." These discussions began soon after the first (1905) Russian revolution and came to an abrupt end in 1914, at the start of the First World War. In this section I show how some of the themes prevalent in the discussions of the 1860s–80s suicide epidemic developed in the twentieth-century context.

"The recent increase in the number of suicides has attracted general attention. The present year has been exceptional in this regard. It is not only that we observe a considerable number of suicides, but that these suicides display the characteristics of an epidemic," stated Doctor I. Maizel in 1908, writing in the pedagogical journal *Vestnik vospitaniia*.[85] A year later, in the same journal, another author reiterated his point: "It is no exaggeration to say that there has been a suicide 'epidemic' raging in Russia for the last three years."[86] "We are living through an epoch of suicide of every conceivable kind," echoed, in a somewhat mocking tone, A. Peshekhonov, reviewing current literary events in a popular monthly *Russkoe bogatstvo* in 1908.[87] "The presence of the suicide epidemic is obvious," maintained Doctor D. Zhbankov in 1909, in a scholarly article commissioned by the same journal.[88]

Statistics, widely publicized in the periodical press, dated the onset of the epidemic to 1906 and noted a sharp increase in each subsequent year.[89] As in the 1860s, newspaper chronicles provided both journalists and experts with a source of information that seemed as valid as statistical surveys. Moreover, statistics were sometimes compiled on the basis of newspaper chronicles.[90] As in the age of the Great Reforms, in the years following the first Russian revolution, the press enjoyed increased freedom, which prompted an increase in the number of publications and their circulation, as well as in the scope of coverage.

The epidemic of 1906–14 was discussed in language strikingly similar to that used to talk about suicide in the 1860s–80s, but there were few references to the previous suicide epidemic. The memory of the periodical press was surprisingly short: although the data were available (and works devoted to suicide in the 1860s–80s were cited in scholarly and popular publications), the events that had been heralded by the press forty years earlier as the first Russian suicide epidemic did not figure as a reference point for the current situation. At the same time, historical parallels—to the French revolution and the dissolution of the Roman Empire—were frequently drawn.[91] One could speculate that while analogies with paradigmatic historical events endowed the immediate experience with universal significance, direct comparisons with events of the recent past might have robbed this experience of its singular importance.

As in the 1860s, most of the authors (journalists as well as scientists) writing in the liberal press connected the "suicide epidemic" with momentous events: this time, the revolution. Zhbankov arranged the data to show a direct correlation between minute political developments and the suicide rate:

1905—a year of rising hope for a better immediate future—was not a good year for suicide. People valued life: the number of suicides everywhere either remained at its previous level or declined. The press mentioned only eighty-six cases of suicide having taken place in the past seven months of this year. In 1906, when general disillusionment set in, the number of suicides mounted steadily, making a temporary exception only for the months of May and June, when the First Duma was in session and hopes of revival and reform once again were ignited in some places. From July until the end of that year, the number of suicides continued to grow, showing a marked increase in the autumn. In 1907, all hope was completely lost; the number of suicides grew unchecked, making a sudden leap in June after the Second Duma had been dissolved. While there were 93 cases of suicide in January, the year 1907 ended with 216 in December; moreover, the summoning of the Third Duma did not in any way increase the value of human life.[92]

Zhbankov's arrangement and language definitely implied a causal connection.

The language that linked the suicide epidemic with the revolution was widely shared, but this connection failed to satisfy the need to explain suicide completely. A note of bewilderment characterizes many writings on suicide.

The very notion of "epidemic" now received attention from scientists. Read in its direct, not metaphoric, sense, the notion implied a medical explanation. This issue was addressed in an article by Lev Sheinis, "Epidemic Suicides" (*Epidemicheskie samoubiistva*). Some authors, wrote Sheinis, take the epidemic nature of suicide as a confirmation of the old view that suicide is linked, directly and solely, to mental illness. They see "contagion" as a psychological tendency toward imitation, which works by analogy with bacterial infection. (This view went back to the 1830s and was voiced in Prosper Lucas, *De l'imitation contagieuse, ou de la propagation sympathique des névroses et monomanies,* 1832.) From this point of view, "suicide is an infectious, epidemic disease, which most dutifully obeys the law of imitation."[93] Sheinis refuted the medical explanation by shifting the source of infection from the individual to the social body. In the case of an infectious disease, he argued, its epidemic nature stems from the (contagious) properties of the common agent in a person's body. In the case of suicide, its contagious character stems from a common character of forces that are external to the individual, but shared by the members of a social group—the social influences, which create common attitudes.

As an analogy, Sheinis discussed the outbreaks of mass suicides among members of religious sects that have periodically occurred in Russia, beginning with the mass self-immolations of the Old Believers in the late seventeenth century. Such a case occurred in 1897 in southern Russia, in a place called Ternovskie Khutora, where a group of more than twenty Old Believers "took a shortcut to immortality" by burying themselves alive with small children—an act apparently motivated by fear that interference by the authorities into their liturgical practices posed an immediate threat to salvation. The case was analyzed by the distinguished psychiatrist Professor I. A. Sikorsky in a brochure *Epidemic Voluntary Deaths and Murders at Ternovskie Khutora* (Epidemicheskie vol'nye smerti i smertoubiistva v Ternovskikh khutorakh [Kiev, 1897]). Recurring throughout the course of Russian history (Sikorsky claimed), mass suicides among religious groups followed a clear pattern. He interpreted this fact as an indication of the biological nature of the phenomenon, similar to alcoholic delirium or paranoid delusions. Mass suicide, concluded Sikorsky, is a mental illness of epidemic proportions.[94]

Many discussions of the "suicide epidemic" in 1906–14 focused on the Ternovskie Khutora case. Essentially the same observations that guided Sikorsky (that outbreaks of suicides follow an identifiable pattern and recur over time) led authors like Sheinis to a different conclusion: suicide epidemics have social causes. Like Sikorsky, these authors thought in positivistic terms: common causes produce common effects—in ancient Rome, in seventeenth-century Russia, and in contemporary Russia, mass suicides were the result of similar social processes.[95]

There was one author who questioned both medical and social views in favor of a symbolic interpretation of self-immolation by Russian religious zealots. This was Vasilii Rozanov, a religious thinker of deep Christian convictions and shockingly unorthodox views (he modeled himself after Dostoevsky), and a journalist of modernist sensibilities and outright reactionary political judgments (he was a friend and collaborator of A. S. Suvorin). Rozanov reprinted Sikorsky's essay, in its entirety, in his book *The Dark Face. The Metaphysics of Christianity* (Temnyi lik. Metafizika Khristianstva [St. Petersburg,

1911]), adding—in footnotes—his own extensive commentary. (He invented and widely used this peculiar dialogic genre.) In his notes, Rozanov commented both on the events described by Sikorsky and on the scientist's interpretations. Sikorsky ascribed the actions of the religious zealots to (among other factors) the influence of the newspapers, which some of them read. Rozanov retorted: "The usual medical explanation: 'Gogol died* because he read ascetic literature rather than Feuerbach or Moleschott' and so forth. . . . Is there such a wisdom in the newspapers and secular press? Perhaps there is: the newspapers exert an influence even on professors of psychiatry, who sometimes take their ideas entirely from the daily papers."[96]

For Rozanov, the voluntary deaths of Russian peasants were not a medical or social, but a metaphysical fact: a desperate, perhaps misguided, gesture of faith while pursuing the ultimate goal—salvation of the soul. As a paradigmatic example of death aimed at overcoming death, this collective suicide was an act that transcended in meaning and significance the most important events of Russian nineteenth-century history:

> Perhaps this death is the most horrifying and significant event of the nineteenth century, far more important than the Napoleonic wars! Just as the death of Socrates was more *earth-shaking* and more significant than the Peloponnesian War, *more important and more consequential,* the death of the poor peasants of Ternov holds far more meaning than all of nineteenth-century diplomacy, which is *bad taste personified*. This is a people with special abilities of *such perception and such hearing*; if this *holy nation* [*sviatoi narod*] hears the real life-bearing word either from Heaven or man, it will make itself a center around which all the world and world history turn, as the earth rotates around its axis. But *where* is this word? These lamentable deaths convince us beyond a doubt that the "Word" that has been brought to the people, who have accepted it as the "Word of Life," actually is, was, and always will be the "Word of Death"! This evidence, if we had been more attentive to it, proves that the death of the thirty Socrates of Ternov and the death of the Athenian philosopher are events of equal importance.[97]

A symbolic equivalent to the death of Socrates, the deaths of thirty Russian peasants—which stopped short of the ideal realized in the

---

*Some believed that Gogol starved himself to death (in 1852) in emulation of Christian ascetics.

death of Christ, the bearer of the "Word of Life"—stand as a testimony to the tragic historical and religious situation of the Russian people. This "holy nation," forever unable to fulfill its messianic role, fell victim to what Rozanov saw as the "dark face" of Christianity—its fascination with death.

In this chorus of discordant voices, a new, and authoritative voice sounded in 1912, when, fifteen years after its publication in France, Emile Durkheim's *Suicide* appeared in Russian translation (under the editorship of a writer who signed his publications with the name "Bazarov"). The Russian Durkheim was welcomed as an event of great importance (and a source that was not outdated).[98] The introduction, written by the medical doctor G. I. Gordon, opened with the assertion that in the twentieth century suicide remained an enigma: "Suicide is as old as the human race itself. Doctors, statisticians, philosophers, jurists, and pedagogues have studied it, and still the question of what suicide really means has not yet been answered: is it the manifestation of a sick or healthy human spirit, a crime or a person's natural right, the expression of a person's free will or the manifestation of the universal law of causality, and so forth."[99] These words echo the opening words of the (previously quoted) article on suicide that appeared in *Delo* in 1882, in response to Morselli's 1879 treatise, *Il Suicidio*.[100] Much had been written on suicide since that time. Gordon included a bibliography of about two hundred Russian works on suicide, from medical studies and statistical surveys to discussions in the popular press. Most (170) of these works appeared after 1905. But despite all these efforts, this twentieth-century expert was clearly at a loss. He was especially troubled by the unresolved contradiction between the internal and the external, or, in a disciplinary perspective, the psychological and the sociological explanations. Gordon's own inclination was to invest his hopes in psychology and in "introspective analysis," but he could not help admitting that the human soul was an infinitely complex, "multifaceted," phenomenon: "we are not yet able to divide the soul into its composite parts in the way that we can break down a complicated chemical compound into its simplest elements."[101] And he was keenly aware that Durkheim's solution was to substitute one body and soul for another—the individual for the social: "[Durkheim] devises a complete, consistent theory for studying suicide from the point of view of the collective, which he sees as a living body as if possessing its own soul, its own qualities, and so forth."[102]

Durkheim's solution captivated many Russians—if not his theory, then his metaphors. The metaphor "the disease of the social organism," in many cases directly derived from Durkheim's study, was widely applied to specific events in the Russian Revolution. Another reviewer of the Russian Durkheim, Vladimir Volsky, who also presented Durkheim's solution as a shift of focus from the individual to the collective body, extended the metaphor to describe the years immediately preceding and following the events of 1905:

> People marched in a great army with many detachments; they lived on collective feelings. The weak drew strength from the enormous reservoir of collective will, and the electricity of collective faith energized the skeptics. The meaning of life was plain to see; it had become almost palpable. Great objectives, clearly visible on the straight but difficult path ahead, beckoned to the people from on high with an overpowering strength . . . In 1905, Russian society reached the pinnacle of a historical mountain. . . . Society began its descent from a pass into the valley of political and social reaction. The greater its descent, the faster it went. As the pace quickened, the ranks fell into disarray. Thick shadows in the valley enveloped these people, who were now running. The shadows hid them from one another and covered the mountain peaks to which they instinctively continued and still continue to aspire, each on his own, groping in the dark. The number of suicides began to increase with extraordinary rapidity...[103]

Well aware that the increase in suicide was noted not only in Russia, but also in the West, Volsky commented on the difference—the decadent West met its natural death; in Russia, suicide was suicide, a murderous energy turned inward: "There, the energy for life has already dissipated, and the depleted organism will die a natural death. Here, life has lost its collective meaning, and the unexpended energy, because it hasn't found an outlet or a way of being used, has directed itself against its carrier and is killing it."[104] Another author inspired by Durkheim, L. Slonimsky, thought in the same categories: "the spread of suicide, especially among young people, indicates that a serious illness has affected the entire social organism and is sapping the nation of its most vital energy." He concluded: "We must reflect upon the reasons and conditions precipitating the development of the present epidemic."[105] What he meant was, of course, the social situation after the 1905 revolution.

Some of those for whom the "disease of the social body" was not a metaphor, but a medical diagnosis, saw suicide as a symptom of the mental illness that affected the society after the revolution—a post-traumatic stress disorder *avant la lettre*. Doctor Zhbankov suggested the term (accepted by many), "traumatic epidemic" (*travmaticheska-ia epidemiia*), a syndrome that included a predilection to violence (executions perpetrated by government authorites, revolutionary terrorism, pogroms, violent crimes, suicides, and acts of sexual violence), as well as sexual excesses.[106] The latter category extended from sexual orgies to discussions of sexuality in pornographic, hygienic, and high ("decadent") literature. Doctor Zhbankov recommended specific "measures to be taken in the struggle against the traumatic epidemic": his prescription was "social and political activity," a matter of hygienic necessity for the social body. "Without these measures there will be no end to every imaginable kind of violence, sexual Bacchanalia, and suicide—the most dangerous symptom of the devaluation of life and our internal decomposition."[107]

A dangerous symptom, suicide was consistently linked with other signs of decomposition: revolutionary activity, sectarianism, expressions of sexuality, and "decadence" (as literary style and as lifestyle)—all interchangeable manifestations of the same disease.[108] "Revolutionary psychosis has been succeeded by sexual psychosis," wrote the reactionary newspaper *Novoe vremia*.[109] The liberal journal *Obrazovanie* echoed: "the erstwhile revolutionary is wrapped in a decadent cloak."[110] Decadence was associated with sexual depravity, which, in its turn, entailed murder and suicide, occurring either in a work of literature or in real life. In its review "From Life and Literature" (*Iz zhizni i literatury*), *Obrazovanie* painted the following picture: "A half-crazed artist is an absolute slave of his lust... . . . And then... then... murder... suicide... a black hole."[111]

In the early twentieth century, the suicide epidemic hit Russian literature. Fiction and poetry abounded with suicidal heroes—a development that was passionately discussed by literary critics. Mikhail Artsybashev's scandalous novels, the famous *Sanin* (serialized in *Sovremennyi mir* in 1907) and *At the Last Frontier* (U poslednei cherty, 1911), frequently provided a focal point for such discussions.[112] Artsybashev's Nietzschean characters, viewed by some critics as twentieth-century transformations of the nihilist Bazarov or the new "new men," were among those former social revolutionaries who now faced a different challenge: their own bodies and human sexuality. Men and women who lived in a Godless world, a world of flesh and unlimited individual volition, they ranged from the triumphant "superman" Sanin to those who, by the dozen, put an end to their own lives. (According to the slightly exaggerated estimate of one critic, the suicide rate among the characters of *At the Last Frontier* was one hundred percent.)[113]

The public response to writers' involvement with suicide was twofold: literature was seen as a laboratory for the investigation of real-life suicide; and (decadent) literature was blamed for influencing the propensity to suicide. Among the spokesmen for the latter view, was Maxim Gorky, who affirmed unequivocally: "The suicide epidemic among today's youth is closely tied to the prevailing moods in literature, and contemporary literature must share the blame for the loss of young lives. Certain literary events are undoubtedly responsible for the rise in the number of suicides."[114]

Gorky went so far as to campaign against popular theater productions based on Dostoevsky's novels, *The Brothers Karamazov, The Possessed,* and *The Idiot*: "Who knows whether the dramatization of *The Brothers Karamazov* on a Moscow stage led to the increase in the number of suicides in that city?"[115] While some looked to literature for solutions to the enigma of suicide, others held writers accountable for their alleged role in the suicide epidemic and even for their views on suicide.[116]

In 1912 the prominent critic Kornei Chukovsky devoted an entire review of contemporary literature, written for the liberal newspaper *Rech',* to literary treatments of suicide. Entitled "The Suicides. Essays on Contemporary Literature" (Samoubiitsy. Ocherki sovremennoi slovesnosti), the article discussed the behavior of "the people in our books" as a test case for dealing with suicides in real life:

> a suicide epidemic, as in real life, is also raging in contemporary Russian books. People who strangle or drown themselves have become the most contemporary of heroes. But there is a new, heretofore unprecedented feature: there is no reason why these people hang and poison themselves. "For no particular reason." "Without a reason." . . . Unmotivated suicide is the latest discovery of contemporary Russian letters. It is neither out of grief nor despair that the characters in Russian books have started shooting or hanging themselves—they themselves do not know the reason why.

The failure to articulate one's motives clearly distinguished a suicide in contemporary literature from a suicidal literary hero of the past. A contemporary suicide, declared the critic, would make the eloquent Werther blush. But it was not only the hero who would not tell—the writer also failed to provide any explanation. (The situation was quite different in the literature of the 1860s–80s—a matter for further discussion.)

Having found no explanation of suicide in fiction, the critic turned to science: "I have put these books aside, for no understanding can be gained from them, and I take the weighty, scholarly book of the distinguished sociologist Durkheim." Durkheim has confirmed that the picture presented in fiction was true to reality: "It turns out that people actually do take their lives 'for no particular reason,' or almost without any reason at all; moreover, what they hold to be the reason is really only a figment of their imagination, an illusion, a phantom."[117] Accounts left by suicides themselves do not reveal the true reasons: "'The professed self-motivations to suicide,' writes Durkheim, 'do not offer an explanation of this behavior, and actually in most cases these only appear to be the reasons.'" Chukovsky agreed: "I think that Durkheim is correct." The reason lies not in the individual, but in the disintegration of society: "The ghastly and stupendous process that in recent years has been imperceptibly affecting us all can be attributed to the following: the chords formerly binding us into one have broken, and we even rather liked this." An individual is alive as long as he does not possess an autonomous individual body—"until your heart is not yours alone, and your arms are not yours alone, until *we,* instead of *I,* becomes your standard word." The individual is dead "at the very minute he breaks away from the eternal bestower of life—society."

While literature (and the subject himself) could not articulate the reasons for suicide, science made them clear. The metaphoric solution provided by Durkheim impressed the literary critic as an expression of the one and only truth—to the degree that he chanted Durkheim's words as a magical formula which would bring reality into compliance with the laws of science: "Let what Durkheim said come true: 'If the bonds that hold a person to life are disintegrating, it is because the individual is less securely linked to society.' Durkheim, we know, considered all the plausible and implausible reasons for suicide and systematically rejected them all, for he saw the following to be essentially the one and only reason: the sudden deterioration of the cement adhering us to a collective, no matter which collective it might be, so that one is left all alone."[118]

The crowning achievement of nineteenth-century science, Durkheim's treatise gave additional legitimacy to the use of the metaphor of "the social organism" as an implicit and explicit explanation for the causes of suicide (a practice that had been familiar to Russian authors and readers since the middle of the nineteenth century). While the events of the not-so-remote past—the "suicide epidemic" of the 1860s–80s—seemed to have been forgotten, this metaphor pervaded early twen-

tieth-century discourse on suicide. In the new context, specific net-
works of associations arose, enveloping the theme of suicide in a thick
web of symbolic meaning. As a symbol, suicide was a different entity between 1906 and 1914 than it had been in the 1860s–80s. Suicide
was now associated not only with political violence but also with sexuality and the aesthetics of decadence. Atheism was no longer the
central issue; moreover, the excesses of religious sectarianism now
provided a model for the notion of a suicide epidemic. While autopsy still retained its attraction, psychoanalysis moved in.[119] Without a
doubt, detailed analysis of a large corpus of texts would reveal many
other meanings. Possibly, other explanatory models were at work
also. But the old rhetorical moves proved to be remarkably viable
heuristic strategies.

4 Suicide Notes and Diaries

The investigative zeal of newspaper reporters, forensic pathologists, and statisticians seem to have done little to convince the Russian public that the secrets of suicide could be uncovered. There remained, of course, the testimonies of the suicides themselves. Concluding his review of Wagner's magisterial *Statistik der Selbstmorde,* one Russian author commented: "If only each suicide would leave behind a description of his upbringing and education, the philosophy taught him in school and by life, the sanitary conditions in which he lived, the state of his health, and, finally, the unfortunate events that ruined his nervous system and suggested suicide to him, then the many venerable Germans who have been working on the problem of suicide would arrive at more useful conclusions for society and the advancement of human thought than they have until now."[1]

In fact, as a rule, a suicide left far less behind. In the words of one journalist, "he wrote two or three words, placed the pistol barrel against his forehead or temple, and... as if he walked out of one room and into another! There is no doubt that a long inner struggle preceded this last deed, but its secret is usually taken away to the next world, only a dead body remaining in this one..."[2] Nonetheless, some suicides did leave notes, letters, or diaries to which they confided their last thoughts and feelings. Could these intimate documents, written shortly before or even in the course of the suicidal act, reveal the secrets of suicide to the public?

Public and Private

In Russia, as elsewhere in the modern world, suicide notes have usually fallen into the hands of medico-legal authorities. While today authorities routinely withhold suicide notes from the press, in the past they were frequently published or cited in newspapers as part of suicide reports. In Russia, this practice started in the late 1860s and continued, on a limited scale, until 1917. (In England, it was already widespread by the 1730s.)[3] Suicide notes were also published by scientists. On the whole, published sources are scarce, in Russia[4] as well as in the West.[5]

When, in 1882, A. V. Likhachev published personal statements left by suicides in the appendix to his statistical study, *Suicide in Western Europe and European Russia,* he felt that he needed to justify this procedure: "The instinct for self-preservation and the love of life are so deeply rooted in man, and therefore also in the social classes, that suicide is always considered an act against nature, a pathological phenomenon, and a protest against the organization of life in a society. Consequently, suicide letters and notes can no longer be considered private once the suicides express a resolute intention to exclude themselves forever from the society of the living."[6]

The notion that a suicide's last letter was public property was borrowed from pathological anatomy. First, Likhachev identified the moment when a person made a willful decision to die as the time of death. Consequently, the production of the person's mind that came into being after that moment—his letter—was an equivalent of his dead body. As with the body, the suicide's letter was thought to belong to the public domain because it was evidence of pathology, be it physiological or social pathology.

To illustrate the status of the suicide's body, Likhachev related a discussion that took place at the International Congress of Forensic Medicine in Paris in 1878: one participant, a medical doctor, suggested legislating that dissections of suicides' bodies be performed publicly, in anatomical theatres.[7] Speaking for the law, the president and founder of the Société de médecine légale de France, Doctor M.-G.-A. Devergie, objected: "A legislator will never agree to take away from a family the right to the body of a family member who has committed suicide."[8] But the public clearly sided not with the legal but with the scientific point of view. In the early twentieth century, the writer Vasily Rozanov made a point of commenting on the public's desire to appropriate the body and soul of a suicide: "One cannot avoid mentioning this oddity: the 'populace,' the impersonal 'crowd,' the strangers feel a special right, and a moral right no less, to the 'body of the suicide' and always surround it fervidly, and with a terrifying power they draw the soul of the suicide closer to themselves or they move closer to his soul . . . What's more, it's as if they feel that both the soul, which has been pulled from the body, and the body itself have been removed from the hands of people who are close to the suicide, especially the relatives."[9] Like his body, a suicide's last letter became an object for public viewing and "dissection."

Although publication of suicide notes infringed on the individual's privacy, it also gave considerable power to the average person, who thereby got access to newspapers, and became the author of a public text.[10] In Russia in the 1860s–80s, relatively few suicides addressed their last words to the public. The press did not encourage such communications: journalists took a critical, and at times ironic, attitude toward suicides and suicide notes. One journalist, in an anonymous essay "Suicides (an Essay in Social Pathology)," proclaimed: "not all suicide notes engender feelings of anguish or make one ponder the unfortunate fate of these victims of social conditions. Some suicide notes can elicit only an unpleasant malicious feeling, others—an unintentional smile, and yet others—a feeling bordering upon disdain."[11]

Only those who qualified as victims of society (mostly, victims of poverty) were granted a degree of sympathy. Reproduced verbatim in this essay was a note left by a former student in the town of Vitebsk (identified as B.). Seeing science as his vocation, he sought a higher education. Struck by poverty and disease, and a sole provider for a sick mother, B. was unable to fulfill his dream. After many tribulations, deranged, destitute, and homeless, he took his life, leaving a desperate and articulate note:

> I would have written "no one is to blame for my death," but I feel that this stock phrase does not befit me. And in fact, who is in need of my death? Certainly not thieves nor heirs, for I have nothing aside from my repulsive rags, which out on the street become the plaything of the wind, and of an inexpressible despair. I haven't even pen and ink to express my thoughts on paper for the last time a little more coherently... So then, my biography in two words: I wanted to become a professor but instead became a scarecrow scaring little children, and a suicide. Nekrasov says: "to extol one person, a battle carries off thousands of weak people, for nothing is given without a price: fate requires expiatory offerings." This is true, but where is the justice in it? Please tell me how I am worse than Ivan or Peter? They eat bread and butter, but fate throws me stones instead of bread!.. No, we do die in vain: society is obliged to facilitate our access to higher learning, but it offers us little support! I die like a dog because it's not pleasant or interesting to live nowadays... Oh, how I pity my mother—beyond words!.."[12]

For this unfortunate man, who strove, but failed, to gain a position of authority and a public voice by becoming a professor, this tragic letter—which showed a keen awareness of the literary resources available for such a statement—was his only chance to gain access to the public tribune. The journalist from the liberal *Nedelia* undercut the pathos, however, by classifying this document as one of "the notes of the unlucky ones who were unable to overcome external, financial difficulties."[13]

The following case illustrates the ambivalent status of suicide as a private act which, with the help of the press, could be turned into a public statement and spectacle. On October 17, 1873, *Sankt-Peterburgskie vedomosti* reported a suicide attempt made by twenty-two-year-old Olga Shchavinskaia, the wife of a medical student. The newspaper claimed that the young woman, who suffered from a serious illness, took poison to end her misery, but was discovered by family members and saved. The next day, the newspaper published the disclaimer that Shchavinskaia made upon reading the report of her act:

> Dear Sir,
> The news of my poisoning was reported in today's issue of your newspaper and it was stated that a horrible inner suffering caused by an illness was what led me to resort to suicide. Actually, the poisoning was a mistake. I did not intend to kill myself at all. I took a large dose of opium while suffering from an acute stomach disorder. . . . Thanks to the efforts of doctors Ekk, Kozyrev, Vege, and Dvorianin, I have now almost completely recuperated.
> Please place my notice in the next issue of your newspaper.
> Olga Shchavinskaia[14]

Several days later, the woman made another statement, which was also promptly published:

> I request that my notice printed in no. 287 of *Sankt-Peterburgskie vedomosti* and reprinted in no. 285 of the *Peterburgskii listok,* be considered invalid.
> Olga Shchavinskaia[15]

Having first attempted to counteract unwanted publicity, she now used the newspaper to make her intentions a matter of public knowledge—probably an instrument of power in her private life. The process as a whole attracted the attention of the press: all three reports were reprinted in the October 28 issue of the weekly *Nedelia*. In the end, the press got the better of the individual by revealing the workings of the mechanism by which a private person interacted with the public domain.

By the end of the century, even children seem to have expected that their last notes would reach the reading public. A gymnasium student who shot himself in 1892 (in the public garden of Kiev University) after failing his final examinations left three notes. One of them was addressed to his parents; it required no explanation: "Farewell, dear parents! You know the reason for my death; I couldn't bear it. Good tidings, and most importantly—may you enjoy good health. My regards to all of our relatives and friends." Another, meant for a friend, briefly stated the reason in a sentence that (perhaps unintentionally) rhymed: "Farewell, dear Vanya! I shot myself (*zastrelilsia*) after I failed (*provalilsia*)." In the third note, the longest, the schoolboy bade farewell to "dear readers": "Farewell, dear readers! My annals are short. I am a schoolboy punished by fate. There were people worse off than me and they went up in the world! Oh well, not everyone enjoys equal luck! I couldn't bear living because I felt I would suffer without reason. Better to suffer once and be done with it. Although it's difficult to part with life, what am I supposed to do? I am not the first and I won't be the last. Once again, forgive me."

This schoolboy wrote his explanations in the full awareness that his death had a public dimension and social meaning. The note addressed to the "readers" presented the boy's story as one of many, that is, as a social fact. The boy's expectations for publicity were met—all three notes appeared in the newspapers, which found them to be "very interesting in many respects." But, as in many other cases, the editors who published these notes refused to accept the reason stated by the subject as a valid explanation of his suicide. There had to be another, general cause—a social law of some sort.[16]

In the course of the "suicide epidemic" that followed the 1905 revolution, on the pages of the much freer press, Russian suicides frequently used their last notes as a public forum. One famous case is that of Maria Ogunlukh, a student who drowned herself in Kiev in October 1909. She left a letter addressed "To the Young Women of Russia" (*k russkim devushkam*). A victim of student poverty like B., who died in Vitebsk in 1886, this young woman presented herself as an "expiatory offering" on behalf of many: "My words to you: I am one of many, and I die a victim for many. My last words are a curse on the rich, on poverty and indifference."[17] Much publicized, this document evoked many responses from readers. Another student, A. Krapukhin in St. Petersburg, addressed his parting words to the editors of the liberal newspaper *Rech'*, and sent his suicide note to the editorial office. Although he was also poor, in his letter he rejected the standard interpretation, emphatically claiming: "Financial difficulties were not the reason for my fateful end. I was always able to earn a living." He insisted that an ideological issue caused his death—oppression on a national, not individual, scale: "It is hard to live in Russia when all truly principled, popular, and cultural expressions are ruthlessly destroyed." Krapukhin then thanked the newspaper for its "ideological stand." The newspaper's editor, who published Krapukhin's letter, commented: "What did the unknown man Aleksandr Krapukhin experience before formulating the entire experience of his young life in the words: it's hard to live in Russia. What has poisoned his soul? Who prepared this poison? What? There is no answer."[18]

Threatened by a conventional wisdom which routinely asserted its interpretative authority through newspapers, this young man used the newspaper to regain control over the meaning of his death. The newspaper cooperated with the suicide but stopped short of accepting his letter as the definitive explanation of his act.

A Special Window into the Act?

To some scholars, suicide notes promised access, if not to the cause of the act, then to the experience of dying. Quite recently, the American suicidologist Edwin Shneidman argued: "It would seem that suicide notes, written as they are in the very context of the suicidal act, often within a few minutes of the death-producing deed, would offer a special window into the thinking and the feeling of the act itself. In no other segment of human behavior is there such a close relationship of document to deed."[19]

In 1949 Shneidman unexpectedly came across several hundred suicide notes locked in the vault of a coroner's office in Los Angeles. He saw an opportunity "to unlock the mysteries of suicidal phenomena by using the notes as the keys."[20] But—like other psychologists—he was profoundly disappointed.

According to current data, only 12 percent to 30 percent of suicides leave notes.[21] There is no significant difference in terms of the main demographic variables—sex, age, race, social status, and history of mental illness.[22] In the eyes of readers, only a few are able to state a plausible cause or communicate the essence of their experience. Shneidman found suicide notes to be encumbered by trivia, such as instructions, admonitions, and lists of things to do.[23] (The same could be said about the sample from the 1980s published by Leenaars.) Other psychologists were struck by the highly conventional nature of the genre. As Shneidman put it, "Suicide notes often seem like parodies of the postcards sent home from the Grand Canyon, the catacombs or the pyramids—essentially *pro forma,* not at all reflecting the grandeur of the scene being described or the depth of human emotion that one might expect to be engendered by the situation."[24]

Soviet suicidologists, whose material came from Moscow in the late 1970s and early 1980s, commented: "Sometimes the notes remind one of variations, developed by various people, on a single theme. The very same verbal expressions, style, and logical train of thought are repeated."[25] These twentieth-century scientists saw a discrepancy between the document and the situation. In the nineteenth century, many came to a similar conclusion: in the eyes of their publishers and readers, the suicides' last words carried little weight. Some were shocked to discover that the suicide's last letters were mostly steeped in the mundane.

Indeed, in Russian suicide notes from the 1870s, as in the notes from Los Angeles in the 1940s and 1980s, considerable attention is given to disposition of personal possessions, including articles of clothing, pocket money, and schoolbooks. Very often the suicide is also concerned with the disposition of his body. Quite typical is the letter left by a young newspaper man who shot himself in the 1870s: "All my belongings—outer garments, not excluding what I am presently wearing, undergarments, my papers and the revolver with which I had the good fortune of shooting myself, I leave to my friends, the students N. and NN. There are no reasons for my death: I am simply tired of living. I ask that my body, even though it isn't very tasty, be thrown to hungry dogs. Let the poor beasts eat their fill."[26]

In another such letter, his contemporary, a twenty-five-year-old midwife Nadezhda Pisareva, specified:

Don't forget to have them pull off my new blouse and stockings; I have some old ones on my night table. Have them dress me in those.

I'd rather peasant women bought these things, but if this is not possible, it makes no difference—let anyone who wants buy them.

Please, Lipareva, the twenty-five rubles and the jacket that the Chechotkins gave me for the road, give these back to them; after all, I'm not going where they intended me to. . . . As it may be impossible to sell all of my things quickly, for the time being, the Chechotkins' money may be kept to pay for my funeral, but please, as soon as my rubbish is sold, the very first thing will be to give back the twenty-five rubles to the Chechotkins. *Remember this.* I ask you once again to bury me as inexpensively as possible. It's better to leave something for the living than to bury it in the earth to rot.

While the young man explicitly insisted that there was no reason for his suicide, Pisareva alluded to the reason amid apologies for the inconvenience that her death caused the two friends (Lipareva and Petrova) in whose apartment she took morphine. But first, she made sure her list of things to do was complete:

It seems I've said everything. But here's one more thing: all the rest of my rubbish not mentioned in the list, give to Nastas'ia Moiseeva, the attendant's mother, as she will probably want to dress the deceased, or to someone you find appropriate; give the bonnets, the saltshaker, the spoon, the small coffee-pot, and the icon (it's still at Lizan'ka's) to my sister Maria, Lizan'ka knows her address. If you have to waste money on cabs to settle my affairs, then this needs to be deducted from my money.

Now, Lipareva, forgive me, and let Petrova forgive me too, especially Petrova. I am playing a trick, a dirty trick—moreover, given that she is in bad health, I am simply cruel to her, but I cannot act otherwise: I am tired, terribly tired, and the shooting sound in my head and ears, which can be quite bad sometimes at night, I'm fed up with it. Oh, how tired I am! Where better to rest than in the grave?[27]

This is what this educated and articulate young woman who took her own life chose to say in her last letter.

Published in its entirety in the newspaper *Novoe vremia* (on May 26, 1876), this letter attracted much attention. Dostoevsky found it indicative of the "talentless" suicides of the day and discussed it at length in his *Diary of a Writer*. What struck him was the young woman's preoccupation with trivial material details: "It is truly strange how concerned she is with the arrangements for the disposing of the meager sum of money she left."[28] Like Shneidman, Dostoevsky was struck and disappointed by the discrepancy between the sublime nature of the situation and the trivial character of the record of experience. (Dostoevsky's reading of this letter is discussed in detail in chapter 6.)

Readers who hoped to find in suicide notes a window into the most important human experience, dying, were equally disappointed by those suicides who seemed to have risen above the trivia by leaving a note in verse. (These suicides usually borrowed forms of self-expression from conventional genres of pulp literature.) Likhachev's collection contains one such note, left by a twenty-two-year-old factory apprentice:

Oh happiness, oh reverie,
I bid farewell forever.
I am dying like a rose
in a stormy wind.

Простите на вечно
О счастье мечтанье
Я гибну, как роза
От бури дыханья.[29]

The scientist obviously did not find this text illuminating: he reproduced only part of it, interrupting the verse after the fifth stanza. A similar note, from an eighteen-year-old merchant's son from Voronezh who shot himself because of unrequited love, was reproduced—and ridiculed—in an essay that appeared in the newspaper *Nedelia*:

And so, having decided to shoot himself, he sits down and toils for a long time over a very long and quite ungainly poem:

You deceived me, oh life, you deceived me,
You crushed me and fell asleep,
Fornicatress of savage strength, a bondmaid,
The battle against you is useless.

Обманула ты, жизнь, обманула,
задавила меня и заснула,
Дикой силы блудница—раба,
И бессильна с тобою борьба.[30]

Such notes point to a failure of communication inherent in the act of suicide. In poetic notes, both the desire to convey a profound message which befits the experience, and the inability to do so, are conspicuously present. Found on the dead body, such letters seem to tell us that the human experience remains inaccessible to the subject.

The subjects themselves often expressed their disappointment in their last communications. A thirty-five-year-old retired officer (who shot himself at a cemetery) organized his letter around the theme of the inadequacy of conventional suicide notes, ridiculing the vain expectations of those of his readers who might look for the cause:

I am retired Second Lieutenant N. N., I live in . . . A worn-out phrase: No one is to blame for my death. I departed for the next world of my own accord.

If someone starts trying to find out the reasons or decides that it was on account of love—meaning an unhappy love—he is a fool, and may god [sic] remember him in his kingdom.

Greetings to everyone, except [my] brothers.

If our learned doctors decide that I kicked the bucket on account of drunkenness or insanity, then he is a rascal and a fool, because he tries to please the bosses.

May either God or conscience be above you, those who are in power over the Whole society.

N. N.[31]

Rather than giving a cause, this suicide rejects the causes assigned by conventional wisdom and medical science. (There is, however, a vague implication that society is somehow to blame.)

Another suicide recorded both his last thoughts and his awareness of their inadequacy. On August 24, 1874, the newspaper *Golos* reported the following case: "In the first days of August a poorly dressed young man aged twenty-six or twenty-seven entered a tavern in the village of Moskovskaia Izhora in the Tsarskoe Selo region. He ordered tea and ham, locked himself into one of the rooms, and killed himself with a table knife." He left two notes. One said: "The image of my dear A. does not leave me for a minute; farewell, my darling!" On another piece of paper, the young suicide wrote: "I used to think that in the minute before suicide a multitude of useful thoughts are in a person's mind, but I was mistaken. My head is surprisingly empty. Where has fate led me to end my life?"[32]

In 1909 a note striking in its self-awareness was left by a secondary-school student:

I hung myself. I do not know why. I have done nothing bad, but it seems I had to hang myself. Farewell my dear mommy, [man's name in the diminutive], Auntie [woman's name in the diminutive], [man's name in the diminutive]. Let the merchant [address—street, house number, last name] know that I won't be coming anymore.

Farewell my loved ones.

Living is still better than dying.[33]

This young boy was aware that he had no access to the cause and meaning of his act.

If the secret of suicide was not known to the subject, minutes before death, how then could it be uncovered? If the subject could not convey the meaning of his experience, then who could? For many suicides in the late nineteenth- and early twentieth-centuries, as for many students of suicide, the testimony bequeathed to the world was not the note, but the body. Many notes suggest that the view of man as the body was internalized. Some hoped that opening up the body would reveal the secret of death; others were consumed by the thought of themselves as flesh. The young newspaper man who asked his body to be thrown to hungry dogs expressed this feeling with desperate directness. No less poignant was the message contained in the following note (also from the 1870s), left by a (male) kitchen aide:

> You, N. N., what do you think about a calf's head with a spicy sauce.
> I was yours, and you were mine. Iagor.
> They'll be cutting me up tomorrow.[34]

Both notes, the rational one, left by an intellectual, and the irrational one, left by peasant, equated the self with flesh, reduced at death to food.

In his last note, a suicide often requested that his body be subject to autopsy. The following note from the 1870s (cited below in its entirety) makes such a request—in deference to science and in defiance of state and family authority—its focal point:

> I make the following statement to the authorities who have arrived to draw up the report of my death and are obliged to know everything that happens in life: This evening, on Friday, Nov. 10 of the present year 18—, in a local hotel room, at my own wish, but absolutely without any special reasons, only that I am quite fed up with life, which is nobody's fault, and which I decided long ago, I put an end to my existence by shooting myself and, at the same time, by taking a dose of Cyanur de Potassium (I do not feel any obligation to report where I found these weapons), and I appeal to the above-mentioned individuals with the most humble request that they take measures to carry out my instructions, if it be possible on their part, or, if it not lie within their power, to render assistance in facilitating my last wishes, which consist of the following: after drawing up the report of my death and sending off my corpse, as probably is the accepted procedure, to the nearest mortuary, do not on any account commit my dead body to the earth, despite any protestations my relatives may raise against this, but immediately have it, my corpse, that is, although it surely is not very interesting, sent away for scientific dissection, to be the sole property and at the complete dis-

posal of the Medical–Surgical Academy, or the so-called Clinic. So this is my request, and I flatter myself with the hope that, since the last wishes of a dying person are always fulfilled, this request will be respected and punctually carried out.* I reiterate, no one is to blame for my death, and I ask forgiveness of those people whom I have wronged during my life. There is some money on my person to pay for the hotel room, but in case the room attendant finds this sum inadequate, I suggest he apply for the additional amount at the place of my residence [address and signature].[35]

Minutes before his death, this man sees himself as a body, which is essentially an object for science and properly belongs to its domain, to be removed from the hands of his family. If his act (he claims it to have been committed without any reason) and his person have any value, it can only be confirmed in the "scientific" dissection of his body, on which he insists with such urgency.

One suicide, a criminal investigator, left a letter claiming that his suicide was caused by mental illness. In a separate note, he requested that his body be dissected by "psychiatrists." Likhachev, who published this note, commented: "Evidently, as a criminal investigator, he picked up the idea of the close connection between mental illness and organic changes in the brain; therefore, his wish to be of posthumous use to science and by the same token to humanity, is a most natural one."[36]

Another young man, who claimed that his suicide was caused by unrequited love, concluded by saying: "I want them to natomize [sic] me and look at my chest."[37] The implication is that his heart might show the traces of his emotional affliction. A seventy-year-old retired official, who found himself in extreme financial difficulties, claimed impending eviction as the cause of his suicide and laid the blame on his landlord. He wrote: "I most humbly ask the police not to conduct investigations or inquiries concerning my death, except perhaps for the dissection of my corpse. I have said everything frankly."[38] Although the cause was clear to the subject, he apparently still hoped that opening up his body might reveal secrets that would transcend his frank testimony—something that was not accessible to a criminal investigator (and did not have to be protected from his prying eye).

People of the positivist age thought that the "natural" text of the

*The suicide was mistaken. In the words of the jurist Koni, "most of those who left notes were not aware of the cruel requirements of the old law, according to which the will and testament of a suicide was invalid" (A. F. Koni, *Samoubiistvo v zakone i zhizni* [Moscow, 1923], p. 19).

body, and not the deliberately constructed text of the suicide's final note, held the key to the meaning and cause of this fatal act, an access to which was denied to the subject himself.

By way of last notes, some suicides left records of their experience at the approach of death, couched in the terms of laboratory reports on scientific experiments. The midwife Nadezhda Pisareva ended her letter and her life with "An observation of the effect of morphine":

> An observation of the effect of morphine: at five minutes after twelve, I began taking the morphine that I had taken from the pharmacy, in fifteen minutes I have already finished taking it, threw the empty phial into the loo and went into Petrova's room, they were not sleeping yet. Twenty minutes after twelve—I feel a little nauseous and my head is spinning... half past twelve—I vomited... my head is spinning a lot... I cannot stand... it's hard to see the clock, and writing has become difficult... everything is flashing before my eyes... the nausea has passed... I'm sleepy... I cannot see the minute hand... I don't see what I am writing...[39]

Her record was interrupted by death itself.

Like bequeathing one's body to an anatomical theater, such gestures were meant as a service to science. In drafts of *The Diary of a Writer,* Dostoevsky commented: "perhaps the poor woman really thought her death would 'be of a scientific use.'" Unsympathetic to the cause, he added: "But what nonsense!" (23:231).

Another document of this kind, written by a suicide in Piatigorsk (identified as A. Ts—v), appeared in the newspaper *Grazhdanin* on November 18, 1874. (This case also attracted Dostoevsky's attention.) The dead man was found in bed, in a sitting position, with an open book in his left hand, a pencil in his right; a watch and a sheet of paper were lying nearby. The paper contained the suicide's observations on his condition, made at regular intervals after he took a fatal dose of opium:

> At 12:30, I took the poison. 12:55—I am starting to hear a noise in my ears and feeling light-headed... (I preferred opium to a revolver because I wanted to record insofar as possible the sensations experienced at the approach of death.) 1:00—I can't see clearly, and it's hard to write; I'm trembling nervously; I'm still collected; I have no desire to live. 1:10—My eyes are closing; I feel a little nauseous. 1:20—A strange thing: my nose itches terribly. 1:30—I'm losing my voice—instead of the usual sounds, indistinct, wheezy sounds are now coming out with difficulty. My thoughts are getting confused; my

eyes are closing; I am getting delirious; my ears are ringing. 1:35—
I light a cigarette; the nausea is getting worse; I cannot read what I
have written because it's like writing letters in a fog. 1:45—Time
moves at a crawl's pace, so it seems to me, it passes extraordinari-
ly slowly. I'm writing by memory, and in case I become paralyzed or
forget to blow out the candle, and thus start a fire, I am blowing out
the candle.—I have double vision; my memory, hands, and eyes are
failing me. 1:55—

The publisher concluded the record: "The next two lines are illegible."
The editor from *Grazhdanin* who published the record accompanied
it with the remark: "For what reason did he find it necessary to record
these observations? Why did a person who wanted to die . . . also
want "to record insofar as possible the sensations experienced at the
approach of death"? Perhaps he wanted to do his fellow human beings the great favor of leaving them as an inheritance his experiment
which could serve as a scientific source?"[40] For readers at the time,
even those who, like Dostoevsky and the journalists from the conservative *Grazhdanin,** took an ironic view, the source of the desire
to document the act of dying was clear: it was the positivistic cult of
science.

Those who staged their own suicides as a scientific experiment
strove to resolve the mystery of death. Self-inflicted death allowed the
subject, if not to control, at least to monitor the process. Suicide notes
documented it. Just as with the bodies of suicides, these records were
bequeathed to the authorities in the interest of knowledge. Together,
the dead body and the diary of the experience provided a text in which
"nature" overwrote the suicide's record with its own. In deferring to
science, these people of the 1870s seemed to have acknowledged that
death had no subjective character, but instead fell entirely within the
category of objective events.[41]

Writing in "thick journals," under the same cover as publicists and
scientists, writers laid their claims to reveal the hidden truth about
suicide. The prominent literary critic and publicist Nikolai Mikhailovsky, reflecting on the "suicide epidemic" in his essay "Real-life and
Literary Dramas" (Zhiteiskie i khudozhestvennye dramy) written for
Otechestvennye zapiski in 1879, expressed his disappointment with
the newspaper reports. They usually concluded with "the cause of sui-

*From 1873 through March 1874, *Grazhdanin* was edited by Dostoevsky; by November, someone else was probably in charge of editorial commentaries.

cide is unknown."[42] He turned to suicides themselves—to suicide notes—but found little illumination: "While surveying the long series of suicides of every kind that occurred last summer, one unwittingly encounters reticence as the most common, typical feature of Russian suicides. . . . Of course, there are talkative, even garrulous, Russian suicides. But in their suicide notes, which are often very sincere and touching, the motives behind the decisions to put an end to their lives nearly always remain in a kind of fog through which a stranger cannot discern anything." Assuming this to be a specifically Russian problem, he concluded: "The voluntary or involuntary reticence of Russian suicides becomes especially clear when comparing them to European suicides, at least in some cases."[43]

One Russian suicide had left the following note: "I am poisoning myself with acid because of my unhappy life; I am fed up with life. Maksim." Mikhailovsky commented: "Reticent Maksim left an explanatory suicide note, and still he said nothing." The situation was different in the West. The Swiss writer F.-W. Rustow, in explaining his suicide to his young daughter, left "an entire physiology of contemporary society, an entire treatise that was concise, forceful, and clear. And in Russia, Maksim dies simply because of his unhappy life, or even leaves absolutely nothing for the edification of his contemporaries and descendants." The critic concluded that Russian suicides, unlike their Western counterparts, were simply not capable of "publicly baring their souls."[44]

Likhachev's publication of suicide notes contains one document that I believe to be the reader's response to the writer's reproach. A seventeen-year-old gymnasium student, before shooting himself, left the following letter:

Today I will fulfill a long-cherished dream. But before leaving for the land where Pluto reigns, I will write down what motivated me to commit suicide, because in contemporary journalism one often hears the complaint that suicides in Holy Russia differ from those of Western Europe, where, if someone decides to kill himself, he usually leaves behind clearly stated reasons... Whereas Russian suicides perish without a word (of course, I don't mean those who swiped state monies, but young suicides who took their lives without any apparent reasons). If you look more profoundly into these people who allegedly committed three sins, you will find souls that are pure and responsive to good, who more or less lucidly acknowledge their need to break free from the horrible slime that surrounds them, who understand very well that one may vindicate himself only before others, but not before his own conscience, with the saying "who lives with wolves."*

And so, what ought such a person to do? Perhaps you will say that he should become involved in activities that are useful for the future development of humanity. I am in complete agreement with you, but nevertheless I do not have enough willpower to follow this advice, and I am even less confident in my abilities to carry out the mission, for I myself am in need of missionaries. To continue living at the expense of the common people, while complaining about their vulgarity; that is, to turn into a so-called liberal... God forbid, there are now enough people like that without me. At the same time, you don't see anyone around who will show the way...[45]

Although this youth, as if competing with Rustow's "physiology of society," employed a full arsenal of contemporary social rhetoric, he can hardly be said to have given "clearly stated reasons."

This was probably no surprise to Mikhailovsky. According to him, the victims themselves did not know what led them to suicide. Moreover, "they were unable to explain even to themselves, if only in more or less broad terms, the psychological process that led them to suicidal thoughts." While, in Europe, "the realm of the unconscious is generally more narrow," the Russian suicide "himself does not know . . . vaguely, in the depths of his soul, something is stirring, but he possesses neither completely conscious thought, nor, therefore, words . . . "[46]

If the subject himself does not know, where, then, is the answer to be found? Mikhailovsky turned to science (statistics), and showed it to be of little use. Statistics established correlations between the number of suicides and external factors, but it could not trace the mediating links between the two events—thus (argued Mikhailovsky) statistics failed to uncover the workings of internal mechanisms. It was the artist—the writer—who had the power to penetrate the hidden depths of the human soul: "Where is one to find skillful people? Of course, among artists. Nowhere else. One must still await the successes of scientific psychology."[47] In the rest of the essay, Mikhailovsky looked for the causes of suicide (in his words) on the mournful pages not of Russian life, but of Russian literature. Reviewing literary representations of suicide, this literary critic was able to find much more meaning than in the artless writings of the subjects themselves.

*A reference to the proverb *"S volkami zhit', po-volch'iu vyt'"* ("If you live with wolves, you howl like a wolf").

Coda: In the Twentieth Century

In the twentieth century, psychoanalysis offered a new hope of penetrating the inaccessible. In 1912, the proceedings of a session on suicide at the Vienna Psychoanalytic Society (held in 1910) appeared in a Russian translation, amid discussions of another "suicide epidemic." The introduction said:

It (the book) contains summarized and scientifically reported data that have been drawn not only from books and written documents, in the form of letters, diaries, and so forth (all of which are almost always insincere, manifest an element of posing, or conceal the truth, whether consciously or unconsciously), but the data based on the uncompromisingly candid testimony given by sick people and attempted suicides to medical specialists. Many things in this book are dictated by direct experiences within the depths of the unconscious psychic life of the suicide—those hidden depths where the main impulses of life and death arise and develop. In this book, the secret, backstage side of psychic life is reflected and illuminated in the endeavor of a science, a science, it is true, that is still in its infancy—psychoanalysis.[48]

This description of psychoanalysis—like the descriptions of autopsy that appeared about a century earlier—emphasizes its power to penetrate hidden depths of meaning. Unlike suicide notes and diaries, psychoanalysis reveals the truth of the unintended and unconscious, a truth accessible only to a medical scientist. Psychoanalysis is an autopsy of the soul.

There is a curious analogy: in a book published the same year, a famous spiritualist presented a "revelation" concerning the nature of suicide. According to this medium, who communicated with the spirits of the dead, a suicide reached full awareness of the causes for his suicide only after death. Communication with the dead also revealed the fate of suicides in the other world. The medium summoned the spirit of a suicide, "Alexander," who, surrounded by the heavy smell of decomposition, announced that the sufferings of suicides in the other world were compounded by the fact that they were not capable of separating from their bodies:

While in realms closest to the earth, like a ball attached to a string, we want to dart upward, into the higher realms. But the ball is held on a taut string—this is the bodily connection that always joins us to the earth.

. . . These magic chains absolutely force us to return to the place where we threw our earthly body in cowardice and remind us of all the horrors of suicide.

—Oh, what torture, what a horrible punishment!

—Wait, he said in a muffled voice, that's not all.[49]

And yet, in spite of all the promise held by the disciplines of the spirit—the nascent science of psychoanalysis and the age-old art of spiritualism, which appealed to postpositivist minds—in the twentieth century, as in the nineteenth, the problem of suicide remained unresolved.

5   Dostoevsky's Fiction: The Metaphysics
of Suicide

In the 1860s–80s, the problem of suicide, debated in science and the press, attracted the attention of many Russian writers.[1] Dostoevsky, in particular, seems to have been preoccupied by the issue.[2] Yet in his ruminations on suicide, the writer formulated the problem differently from scientists and journalists. Dostoevsky's heroes met their deaths as the result of the existential dilemma that faced a whole generation of Russians, not because of a medical or social disorder.

In *The Possessed* (Besy, 1871–72), the hero, Kirillov, is caught up in a conflict between two apparently reasonable but mutually exclusive propositions (expounded in his dialogue with Petr Verkhovensky):

—God is necessary, and therefore must exist.
—Well, that's wonderful.
—But I know that He does not and cannot exist.
—That's more like it.
—Don't you understand that a man with these two thoughts cannot
   go on living?
—Must shoot himself, you mean?
—Don't you understand that a man can shoot himself for that alone?
                                                    (10:469/615–16)[3]

In the end, Kirillov commits suicide while Verkhovensky, an atheist, commits murder. As Nietzsche noted in his synopsis of *The Possessed,* this syllogism also "devoured" Stavrogin.[4] After Stavrogin's suicide, his body was subjected to a postmortem examination, but "our medical men, after the autopsy, completely and emphatically ruled out insanity" (these words conclude the novel; 10:516/678). Clearly, medicine could not detect the problem.

The existential dilemma that killed Dostoevsky's heroes had tormented Russian intellectuals since the 1840s. In his memoirs, *My Past and Thoughts* (Byloe i dumy, 1852–68), Alexander Herzen describes a "historical" conversation with a friend (Timofei Granovsky, professor of philosophy at Moscow University) in the summer of 1846:

> I observed that the development of science, its contemporary condition, *obliges us* to accept certain truths apart from whether we like them or not; that, once recognized, they cease to be historical problems and become simply irrefutable facts of knowledge like the theories of Euclid, like the laws of Kepler, like the connection of cause and effect and the indivisibility of spirit and matter.
>
> "All that is so far from being obligatory," answered Granovsky with a slight change in his face, "that I never shall accept your dry, cold idea of the unity of soul and body; with it the immortality of the soul disappears. You may not need it, but I have buried too much to give up that belief. Personal immortality is essential for me."[5]

Dostoevsky (in Kirillov) and Herzen present the conflict as a clash between two types of knowledge—positively-established, scientific facts, on the one hand, and personal convictions, drawn from experience or dictated by a moral imperative, on the other.

This dilemma had received a philosophical formulation in Kant's *Critique of Pure Reason* (1781): it is a perpetual contradiction between two heuristic principles, "dogmatism" and "empiricism," which is inherent in the very nature of human reason. Dogmatism affirms a set of transcendental ideas: the existence of God, a being from whom everything receives origin and unity; the immortality of the soul, which is indivisible and therefore indestructible; and free will, "raised above the compulsion of nature."[6] Pure empiricism, explaining phenomena, denies these postulates. Thus, claims Kant, empiricism robs us, or seems to rob us, of moral principles and ideas: "If there is no original Being, different from the world; . . . if our will is not free, and our soul shares the same divisibility and perishableness with matter, *moral ideas* and principles lose all validity."[7] Although his personal sympathies lay on the side of dogmatism and its transcendental truths, Kant warned that taking one side and ignoring the other presents mortal dangers: "[reason] is tempted . . . either to abandon itself to skeptical despair, or to assume a dogmatic obstinacy, taking its stand on certain assertions, without granting a hearing and doing justice to the arguments of the opponent. In both cases, a death-blow is dealt to sound philosophy, although in the former we might speak of the *Euthanasia* of pure reason."[8]

In Dostoevsky's age, the conflict received special poignancy: developments in positivistic science presented a powerful threat to transcendental truths. Kant's antinomies of pure reason became topical. (Dostoevsky's contemporary and friend, A. F. Koni, cites the case of an eighty-two-year-old learned Jew, Schwartz, who was found dead from an overdose of morphine with an open volume of Kant's *Critique of Pure Reason*.)[9] In his writings, Dostoevsky presented Kant's "scenes of discord and confusion"—dramas created by the conflict of the laws (antinomies) of pure reason.[10] Dostoevsky himself was clearly among those for whom the immortality of the soul was a personal necessity. Keeping vigil by his wife's dead body (on April 16, 1864), he jotted down in his notebook: "Masha is lying on the table. Will I see Masha again?" He continued to reflect on the immortality of the soul and concluded by condemning materialism as a doctrine of death: "The materialist doctrine—universal inertia and the mechanism of matter; this means death" (20:173, 175).[11] But, as Kant admonished, Dostoevsky "granted a hearing" to the arguments of his opponents, the materialists and atheists, in his writings.

Thus, in addressing the common problem of suicide, the writer asked not "what is suicide?" but "what if there is no God and no immortality of the soul?" "Then, everything is permitted, even murder and suicide," concluded some of Dostoevsky's heroes. In his writings, suicide is the answer to these questions, an end point of a syllogism. The high incidence of suicide and murder among those of his characters who espoused atheism suggests that, for Dostoevsky, belief in God and immortality was a necessary condition of human existence.

The Method

Roaming the streets of Petersburg, Raskolnikov, the hero of *Crime and Punishment* (Prestuplenie i nakazanie, 1866), encounters drunks, prostitutes, and would-be suicides. He laments the fate of society's outcasts and the possible fate of his sister, Dunia: "They say that's just how it ought to be. Every year, they say, a certain percentage has to go... somewhere... to the devil, it must be, so as to freshen up the rest and not interfere with them. A percentage! Nice little words they have, really: so reassuring, so scientific. A certain percentage, they say, meaning there's nothing to worry about. Now, if it was some other word... well, then maybe it would be more worrisome... And what if Dunechka somehow gets into the percentage!... If not that one, then some other?.." (6:43).[12]

This is a retort to Russian positivists, who thought that moral statistics proved that a natural law doomed a percentage of the population to moral decay, crime, and suicide.[13] (Adolphe Quétclet's *Treatise on Man* appeared in Russian translation in 1865 and provoked heated discussions.)[14] One of the novel's heroes, Lebeziatnikov, promotes a popular anthology of Western European studies on social statistics and physiology, *A General Conclusion Concerning the Positive Method* (Obshchii vyvod polozhitel'nogo metoda, 1866),[15] as a book containing answers to such problems. It might seem that in his novel, which features a murderer, a prostitute, and a suicide, Dostoevsky offers an alternative to the positive method; unlike the social scientists of his day, he deals not with statistics but with individual cases; unlike medical men, he works not with the body but with human consciousness and ideas.

As Mikhail Bakhtin claimed, Dostoevsky's hero "is merely the career of an independently valid idea."[16] What Dostoevsky does, I believe, is to show how a given idea might be developed and realized in action by an empirical, historically specific individual. The main project of his post-Siberian years is to test the atheist worldview. Each character (the Underground Man, Raskolnikov, Ippolit, Kirillov, Ivan Karamazov, Smerdiakov) represents a model of the "new man," who is "infected with atheism" (10:269); each model tests the initial hypothesis that "there is no God and no immortality of the soul." Thus Dostoevsky proceeds by a method borrowed from positivist science: human consciousness serves as the nutrient medium in which an idea is allowed to grow—the writer stages a scientific experiment.[17] In this way, Dostoevsky anticipated Emile Zola, who suggested in his essay "The Experimental Novel" (Le roman expérimental, 1879) that the experimental method advocated in Claude Bernard's *Introduction to the Study of Experimental Medicine* (Introduction à la médecine expérimentale, 1865) could be practiced by writers in novels.[18] But while Dostoevsky's method is similar to Zola's and to the method used by positivist scientists, his object is different. Zola justified using the experimental method in literature by announcing that "the metaphysical man is dead." "Our whole territory," he claimed, "is transformed by the advent of the physiological man"—a new object of literature.[19] In his novels, Dostoevsky applied the experimental method to the metaphysical man, whose death he refused to certify.

Aside: The Genealogy of the Method

Far from being solely a product of the positivism of the 1860s, Dostoevsky's experimental model has Romantic roots. Among its direct sources is Vladimir Odoevsky's *Russian Nights* (Russkie nochi, 1844), a book that introduced Russians to Romantic epistemology.[20] The work features several experiments staged by characters whom the author calls "experimental spiritualists" (*dukhoispytateli*). An inserted story, "The Last Suicide" (Poslednee samoubiistvo), composed by a young man in the grip of an "all-consuming dialectical doubt," presents a "symbolic vision" of what the future would be if society were to develop according to Malthusian ideas (and these ideas alone); non-being would become a desired state and mass suicide would put an end to humankind. Odoevsky presents his hero's vision of mankind's collective suicide as a "monstrous" creation of "purely experimental knowledge," a worldview untouched by faith.[21] Believing that empiricism and materialism ("forms of old and new paganism") were "highly inadequate means for the cognition of truth,"[22] Odoevsky advocated Schelling's mystical idealism, which opened "the still unexplored part of the world: the human soul."[23] In the words of one of his characters, nineteenth-century science, because it focused on "crude matter," failed to grasp the essence of life; its object is dead. Thus, in vain medicine "puts questions to the cadaver . . . the cadaver is silent or provides answers that only make one more uncertain about the workings of life." In vain scientists strive to define the laws of society; in their social investigations they limited themselves "to an invention of a phantom that they dared to call 'human society'"; their object "remained a phantom," or "merely a word."[24] Knowledge of organic life is tainted because the concepts applied to inorganic bodies were transferred to organic bodies: "Recall the words of Bichat, the great experimenter and laboratory physicist who was killed by his anatomical experiments. . . . Bichat had to admit that 'we need to invent a new language for organic bodies, because all the words that have been taken from the physical sciences and applied to animal and plant economies, invoke concepts which do not at all correspond to physiological phenomena.' With each word we speak, we exhale the remains of a thousand ideas that have been conferred upon this word by the centuries, by various nations, and even by individual people."[25] Language failed scientists. It was the poet who had the privilege of bringing to knowledge the first hope of attaining positive truth.

In the light of this history, one can better understand Dostoevsky's use of experimental models. Dostoevsky shared Odoevsky's concern with the nature of knowledge, also drawing on the opposition between the truth of science—which is dependent on the investigation of matter, verbal mediation, and logical reasoning—and the truth of faith, which is directly apprehended. The latter found its clearest expression in Schelling's *Naturphilosophie* and his philosophy of revelation, which attempted to synthesize science and art. Dostoevsky followed the "Russian Schelling," Odoevsky, in his choice of an object: he worked not with the body, but with the soul. But, unlike Odoevsky and his hero (the author of the story "The Last Suicide"), Dostoevsky had no qualms about reverting to experimental models. Romantic ideas reemerged within the new context, reinforced by scientific positivism. Striving to surpass the scientist, the writer took upon himself the role of experimenter.

Experimental Design: *Le Dernier jour d'un condamné*

The young would-be suicide Ippolit is a crucial figure in the novel *The Idiot* (1868).* An eighteen-year-old youth dying from consumption, he decides to commit suicide before his life runs its natural course, and to shoot himself publicly after reading to the assembled guests a document entitled "My Necessary Explanation" (*Moe neobkhodimoe ob"iasnenie*): "My 'Explanation' would explain everything sufficiently to the police. Those who are keen on psychology and anyone else who likes are at liberty to deduce anything they will from it. I would, however, like my manuscript to be published [*chtob eta rukopis' predana byla glasnosti*]. . . . I bequeath my skeleton to the Medical Academy for the benefit of science" (8:342/422).[26] The youth "bares" both his soul and his body for "science."

Ippolit describes himself as "the one condemned to death." The sentence was handed down by nature, in accordance with the law of physical decay and death, and announced by a medical student, "a materialist, atheist, and nihilist," who declared that Ippolit had several weeks left to live (8:323). In this situation, Ippolit, who (in Dostoevsky's words) refuses to recognize any jurisdiction over himself, asks himself: Is it worthwhile to do good deeds? Why refrain from crime and murder? Ultimately, he asks whether there is any reason for him to wait patiently for the death sentence to be executed: "Finally, there's the temptation: nature has so limited my activities by its

*According to the early plans, "Ippolit is the main axis of the novel" (9:277).

three weeks' sentence that suicide is perhaps the only thing I have still time to begin and end of my own free will. Well, perhaps I want to take advantage of the last possibility of *action*. A protest is sometimes no small matter..." (8:344/425). Having read his confession, Ippolit pulls the trigger. But he survives the attempt, much to his own embarrassment, and soon dies a natural death. The "deed" remains undone, but the word has been spoken.

The story of Ippolit is an emblem of the human predicament in the age of positivism and atheism: if the soul is not immortal, then time is measured for every human being.[27] In a godless world, every man is condemned to death. A "nihilist," Ippolit constructs his argument as if the laws of nature were the sole ordering force in the universe. He is suffering not only from consumption but also from a lack of belief.

Dostoevsky used the situation of a man condemned to death (whether by medicine, in accordance with the law of nature, or in a court of law) as an experimental investigation into the effect of man's awareness of his finitude. One specimen, Ippolit, found life itself pointless: his thoughts turned to suicide. In Dostoevsky's fiction this experiment was repeated several times, most notably with Kirillov and Ivan Karamazov as alternative subjects, under slightly different conditions. On the whole, the experiment proved Kant's deductions to be true: for the possibility of moral existence we must believe we each have something like an infinite amount of time; that is, we must believe in the immortality of the soul.[28]

By using an experimental model, Dostoevsky beat the positivists at their own game. He demonstrated that their project of removing God from human consciousness would result in the collapse of morality and, ultimately, in the annihilation of humankind through suicide and murder. Contrary to the opinion voiced by Zola, it was not the metaphysical man who was dead, but the atheist—dead by his own hand.

Throughout his experiment, Dostoevsky was interested in determining not only the final outcome of the situation but also the psychological condition of his subject. As he commented in his prison memoir, *Notes from the Dead House* (Zapiski iz mertvogo doma, 1861), "I tried to imagine the psychological state of a person being led to his execution" (4:152). Time and again, Dostoevsky attempted to reconstruct the experience of a man facing death. In *The Idiot*, Myshkin, who speaks repeatedly of the torments of a condemned man, forms a hypothesis that pain comes primarily from the awareness that death is certain: "Yet the chief and the worst pain is perhaps not inflicted by wounds, but by your certain knowledge that in an hour, in ten minutes, in half a minute, now, this moment your soul will fly out of your body, and that you will be a human being no longer, and that that's certain—the main thing is that it is *certain*" (8:20/46). (Like an experimental scientist, Myshkin recorded the subject's reactions at regular intervals.)

It was Voltaire (in *Dictionnaire philosophique*) who said that the real content of the experience of dying is not the fact of dying, but the certainty that we have to die.[29] This idea is developed by Victor Hugo. His famous *Le Dernier jour d'un condamné* recreates the diary of a condemned man, who recorded his experience during the last day of his life, up to the very last minute. The certainty of death drives Hugo's character to suicidal despair.[30] Dostoevsky probably borrowed the thought expressed by Myshkin from Hugo, but Myshkin also seeks confirmation of his hypothesis in real-life experience: "Possibly there is a man who has had a death sentence read out to him and has been given time to go through this torture, and has then been told, You can go now, you've been reprieved. Such a man could perhaps tell us" (8:21/46).[31] Such a man was Dostoevsky himself.

Arrested in the spring of 1849 (at the age of twenty-seven) for his participation in the meetings of the Petrashevsky circle (where he discussed socialist and materialist ideas, from Fourier's to Feuerbach's), he was, along with several other members of what was deemed to be a subversive secret society, sentenced to death. Although the original sentence was commuted to penal servitude, it was read to the prisoners, assembled in a public square in Petersburg to face a firing squad; minutes later a retreat was sounded and a commuted sentence was read. In a letter to his brother Mikhail written on the same day (December 22, 1849), Dostoevsky described the events: "they read us all our death sentence, allowed us to kiss the cross, broke a sword over each of our heads, and attired us for execution (white shirts). Then three of us were placed at the post for the execution to be carried out. They were calling three names at a time. I was in the second group and so I had no more than one minute left to live" (28/I:161).[32] A fellow prisoner described Dostoevsky's reaction to the death sentence: "Dostoevsky was quite excited, he recalled *Le Dernier jour d'un condamné* of Victor Hugo, and, going up to Speshnev, said: 'Nous serons avec le Christ' [We shall be with Christ]. 'Un peu de poussière' [A speck of dust]—the latter answered with a twisted smile."[33]

This "experiment," staged by Emperor Nicholas I, could have taught Dostoevsky that a believer, who expected "to be with Christ," and an atheist, who anticipated solely the disintegration of matter, experienced "le dernier jour" differently. In this case, Dostoevsky himself was the control subject; the variable was faith.

Death of an Atheist

In Dostoevsky's life and works the experimental and experiential went hand in hand with the symbolic, which provided access to the metaphysical meaning of death and endowed individual experience with a paradigmatic quality.* Judging by his writings, Dostoevsky interpreted his own experience of facing execution as a "parable, with the death sentence representing man's mortality and the reprieve, resurrection into eternal life."[34] He wrote to his brother Mikhail: "Why, didn't I face death today, live with this thought for three-quarters of an hour, live through my last moment, and now I am living once again!" (28/I:163–64).

One paradigm for such an experience was to be found in the crucifixion and resurrection of Christ. In *The Idiot,* speaking of the pain of a prisoner awaiting execution, Myshkin evoked Christ's torment: "It was of agony like this and of such horror that Christ spoke" (8:21/46). But in the age in which man was viewed primarily as a material being, that is, as a body liable to physical decay, the interpretation of Christ's death and resurrection was subject to revision. Dostoevsky addressed this issue in Ippolit's reflections on Hans Holbein's painting of the dead Christ (1521), an "icon" from the age of humanism:

> The picture depicted Christ, who just been taken from the cross. . . .
> It was a faithful representation of the dead body of a man who has
> undergone unbearable torments. . . . The face has not been spared
> in the least; it is nature itself, and, indeed, any man's corpse would
> look like that after such suffering. I know that the Christian Church
> laid it down in the first few centuries of its existence that Christ re-
> ally did suffer and that the passion was not symbolical. His body on

---

*His contemporaries also thought in terms of shared cultural paradigms. Thus Apollon Maikov described Dostoevsky the revolutionary as a dying Socrates. He recalled how, in January 1849, Dostoevsky paid him a visit (and stayed to spend the night) in an effort to recruit him into a secret society: "I recall how Dostoevsky, sitting like the dying Socrates before his friends, wearing a night shirt with the collar unbuttoned, exerted all his rhetorical eloquence in telling me about the sanctity of this cause, about our duty to save the fatherland, and so forth" (Letter of A. N. Maikov to P. A. Viskovatov, 1885; quote from Dostoevskii 18:191).

the cross was therefore fully and entirely subject to the laws of nature. In the picture the face is terribly smashed with blows, swollen,
covered with terrible, swollen, and bloodstained bruises, the eyes
open and squinting; the large, open whites of the eyes have a sort of
dead and glassy glint. But, strange to say, as one looks at the dead
body of this tortured man, one cannot help asking oneself the peculiar and interesting question: if such a corpse (and it must have been
just like that) was seen by all His disciples, by His future chief apostles, by the women who followed Him and stood by the cross, by all
who believed in Him and worshipped Him, then how could they possibly have believed, as they looked at the corpse, that that martyr
would rise again? Here one cannot help being struck with the idea
that if death is so horrible and if the laws of nature are so powerful,
then how can they be overcome? . . . The people surrounding the
dead man, none of whom is shown in the picture, must have been
overwhelmed by a feeling of terrible anguish and dismay on that
evening which had shattered all their hopes and almost all their beliefs at one fell blow. . . . And if, on the eve of the crucifixion, the
Master could have seen what He would look like when taken from
the cross, would he have mounted the cross and died as he did? This
question, too, you can't help asking yourself as you look at the picture. (8:338–39/418–20)

The experience of contemplating Holbein's dead Christ represents the
trial facing faith in the age of positivism. In its effect on believers, this
"quasi-anatomical vision of the dead Christ" (Holbein is believed to
have found his model—a body recovered from the Rhine, possibly a
suicide—in an anatomical theater)[35] is like positivist science, which
revealed the perishable, bodily side of man's nature. Ippolit placed the
God-man, Christ, in this situation. What if Christ could see himself
as a decomposing body? One thing is clear: in the age of positivism,
man was no longer capable of submitting to execution like Christ. Incapable of joining Christ in the Gethsemane prayer, "Let Thy will be
done," modern man died by his own will—by suicide.

The significance of Ippolit's suicide attempt lies not in the individual,
but in the symbolic dimension of experience. It is Dostoevsky's first
attempt to modify the classic paradigms of voluntary death; most importantly, the death of Socrates and the death of Christ.[36] Dostoevsky
reinterpreted elements of the paradigms and rearranged them into a
new pattern. Like Socrates, Ippolit is a man condemned to death who
chooses to die before the appointed time, by his own hand. He does
not, however, accept his sentence gracefully. Unlike Socrates, Ippolit

does not see death as liberation of the soul from the prison house of the body. His death resembles Seneca's, who took his life in anticipation of Nero's death sentence (and struck a clumsy blow), or Petronius's, who died in the midst of a feast, having chosen to preempt the vengeful death sentence imposed by a despot. In Seneca's words, they renounced nature and flung her gift back in her face.[37] In death (said Lucretius), they closed their eyes to the sun and returned to eternal night. As if following their example, Ippolit chose a classical setting for his suicide, which he saw as a rejection of nature's gift: he planned to die at sunrise, after a "feast" (a celebration of Prince Myshkin's birthday), with a glass of champagne in his hand. Thus, with Ippolit's death, Dostoevsky abandoned the tradition that led from the death of Plato's Socrates to the death of Christ as well as the view of voluntary death as a royal road to immortality. The writer pursued a side line of cultural evolution: the neo-pagan overrode the Christian.

The pattern was also embodied in Dostoevsky's plans for the story "Death of the Poet" (Smert' poeta, contained in his notebook for 1869–70 along with the plans for *The Idiot*). An Atheist, a Priest (*Popik*), an Old Believer (*Raskol'nik*), a nihilist Doctor (*Doktor-nigilist*), and a Poet gather to converse "about liberty and liberated man (N.B. according to the apostle Paul.)" (9:120). In the end, the Poet reads his "last confession" (a confession of nonbelief), drinks champagne, and shoots himself.

According to St. Paul, man had a choice between two ways of life— "after the flesh [and] after the Spirit." The first leads to death; the second to life eternal.[38] Through participation in the life of the spirit, following the example of Christ, "the creature . . . shall be delivered from the bondage of corruption into the glorious liberty of the children of God" (Rom. 8:21). In Dostoevsky's fragment, the Poet rejects this Christian view of life and the example of Christ in favor of the paganism of classical antiquity: "The poet [speaks about] the deification of nature, [he is] a pagan. . . . Delirium, his last moments, 'Götter Griechenlands.' Death" (9:120).[39] Deaths like Ippolit's in *The Idiot* and the Poet's in Dostoevsky's unwritten story befit the age of the new paganism—mid-nineteenth-century materialism.

Le Dernier jour of a Nation

If an individual needs to believe that he has an unlimited amount of time, a nation needs to believe that it has a historical future. This conclusion follows from the case of Kraft, a hero of *The Adolescent* (*Po-*

drostok, 1875): "He [Kraft] has deduced that the Russians are a second-rate people . . . destined to serve as raw material for a nobler race, and not to play an independent part in the history of humanity. In view of this theory of his, which is perhaps correct, Kraft has come to the conclusion that the activity of every Russian must in the future be paralyzed by this idea, that all, so to speak, will fold their hands and . . . " (13:44/47).[40] And he committed suicide.

The idea itself had a firm scientific foundation: "Kraft himself conceived of his death as a logical conclusion. . . . He left behind him a manuscript book full of abtruse theories, proving by phrenology, by craniology, and even by mathematics, that the Russians are a second-rate race, and that therefore, since he was a Russian, life was not worth living for him" (13:134–35/159–60).

Kraft had a real-life prototype in the lawyer Kramer, who died in the early 1870s, having committed ideologically motivated suicide. Students of Dostoevsky surmised that the writer learned the story from the jurist A. F. Koni, who was involved in the investigation of Kramer's death. Years later, Koni described the case in his memoirs and provided extensive quotes from Kramer's diary.[41] A different version of the same document (a short diary, started several days before the suicide and completed at the time of death; ostensibly, moments before the shot was fired) can be found in the appendix to A. V. Likhachev's 1882 statistical treatise, *Suicide in Western Europe and European Russia,* a publication that seems to have so far escaped the attention of Dostoevsky scholars. In this document the suicide explains his beliefs:

I am not an atheist, nor am I a theist—for me there is no life after death; I acknowledge only the life of atoms which manifests itself in the various combinations produced by the force of mutual attraction. As a person, I am composed of a certain mass today, which, after my death, disbands and forms other organisms without ever vanishing, and for this reason I find it of no consequence whether I live in my present form or assume another. Probably as a result of a particular mold of the brain (I do not acknowledge the existence of convictions, and that which others call convictions I consider to be an act predicated upon a given mold of the brain), I have reached the conclusion that the human race is just as transient as all other things and that even the earth itself is not eternal. Only atoms, with their mutual attraction, are eternal. But it's not this that compels me to raise a hand against myself—these thoughts only give me the strength to bid farewell to my life.[42]

(These notions are informed by Büchner's theory of the immortality of matter—a positivistic replacement for the immortality of the soul.) The suicide then elaborated on his motivations, maintaining that it was not a lack of faith in the individual's future life that led him to kill himself, but an awareness that Russia had no future. Like the individual organism, the social organism was destined to decomposition: "I am convinced that . . . its [Russia's] only purpose is to preserve and fertilize the land they now live on for another nation [to come]."[43]

What struck Dostoevsky was that this idea (which echoed Chaadaev's famous "Philosophical Letter" of 1829)[44] found its realization in the actual act of suicide (13:135). He connected the ease with which the word became deed with that particular moment in Russian history when science proved that life was naturally limited (13:171). Whereas in Ippolit's case it was the individual body that was condemned to death or corruption, in Kraft's case it was the social body—the body of the nation.

Suicide Diaries in Life and Fiction

Dostoevsky's character Kraft recorded his experience of dying in his diary: "The last entry in the diary was made just before the fatal shot, and in it he mentioned that he was writing almost in the dark and hardly able to distinguish the letters; that he did not want to light a candle for fear that it should set fire to something when he was dead. 'And I don't want to light it and then, before shooting, put it out like my life,' he added strangely, almost his last words" (13:134/158).

What is the significance of documents that record the suicide's final thoughts and sensations? Two characters (the narrator, the Adolescent, and his friend Vasin) discuss this issue:

I expressed aloud my surprise that although Vasin had had this diary so long in his hands (it had been given him to read), he had not made a copy of it, especially as it was not more than a sheet or so and all the entries were short. "You might at least have copied the last page!" Vasin observed with a smile that he remembered it as it was; moreover, that the entries were quite unsystematic, about anything that came into his mind. I was about to protest that this was just what was precious in this case, but without going into that I began instead insisting on his recalling some of it, and he did recall a few sentences—for instance, an hour before he shot himself, "That he was chilly," "That he thought of drinking a shot to warm himself,

135

but had been deterred by the idea that it might cause an increase in the flow of blood." "It was almost all that sort of thing," Vasin remarked in conclusion. . . .

"But the last thoughts, the last thoughts!"

"The last thoughts sometimes are extremely insignificant. One such suicide complained, in fact, in a similar diary that not one lofty idea visited him at that important hour, nothing but futile and petty thoughts." (13:134/159)

Like his hero, Dostoevsky was intensely interested in the experience of apprehending death directly, an experience he himself had at the time of his mock execution. What could such a man tell? Curiously enough, in a letter to his brother Mikhail written on his execution day, Dostoevsky said little about his actual experience during those minutes he spent face-to-face with death.* Indeed, he had much more to say about the experience of awakening to a new life after the retreat was sounded. But the focal point of the letter is the symbolic potential of the situation, which resembles the death and resurrection of Christ.

What could be learned from the experience of others? Among reports on the last moments, in which death becomes a matter of direct experience, the suicide's report carries special weight: as the person who wills, controls, and monitors death, the suicide is seen as having a better chance of gaining access to the most inaccessible of all human experiences.[45] Dostoevsky had always been fascinated by the disorderly narratives of minds laying themselves bare. There is evidence that he had access to such documents.** In his depiction of Kraft's death in *The Adolescent,* Dostoevsky was guided by two genuine suicide records. In both cases, the suicide recorded his experience at regular intervals, in the format of an experimenter's log. The last-minute thoughts that the writer found in these documents were as trivial as those that his character Vasin found in Kraft's diary.

One of the documents used by Dostoevsky was Kramer's diary. Ac-

---

*All Dostoevsky said was: "I had no more than a minute to live. I remembered you, brother, and your whole family; at that last moment you, only you, was [sic] in my thoughts" (28/1:161).

**In a December 1876 issue of *The Diary of a Writer* Dostoevsky mentioned that "A year and a half ago, one highly talented and competent member of our judicial system showed me a bundle of letters and notes he had collected that were written by suicides, in their own hand, immediately before they took their lives, i.e., five minutes before death" (24:54) (English from Fyodor Dostoevsky, *A Writer's Diary,* trans. Kenneth Lantz [Evanston, 1993], vol. 1, p. 742). According to commentators, the jurist was A. F. Koni.

cording to Koni, who quoted Kramer's diary in his memoirs (published in the 1920s), the last entry read: "It will soon be twelve o'clock! Everything is ready. I am slightly shivering from the cold and yawning a bit, but I am absolutely calm. I wanted to drink some cognac, but they say that alcohol intensifies bleeding—and I am already going to leave a mess here. What an awful book Donders's *Anatomy* is! Two large volumes of small print, and one still can't learn how to find the exact location of the heart."[46]

Likhachev gives a more extensive version of the diary, one strikingly different from Koni's. In Likhachev's publication, the last entry reads:

Thursday 1:45 A.M.

I don't feel the least bit nervous or afraid. It's as if I am getting ready to lie down to sleep. I actually rather feel like sleeping. But I don't know why I am shivering so much, I have had the chills for a month now. To warm myself up, I drank several shots of rum; I know that rum also intensifies bleeding, like all hard alcohol, and this is also why I am drinking it—I am certainly not getting drunk to make it easier to shoot myself. I feel so much unflagging determination within me that I could stand in front of the barrels of dozens of rifles pointed directly at me and not bat an eyelash. But I really don't care what people will think of me.

The more hardened my heart becomes, the more respect I begin to have for myself. I now understand how Christ felt on the cross...

2:45 A.M.

I am surprised at Draper's physiology textbook: in three volumes there is not even an indication of where the heart is located. What a misfortune to have left my anatomy book in Moscow! Three o'clock is approaching, I beg the pardon of the landlord for disturbing the peace in his house.[47]

A man of the positivist age, this suicide staged his death as a scientific experiment—a textbook on physiology and a logbook in hand. But he was also guided by another paradigm: the experience of Christ on the cross which he relived in his suicide.

A note is due on the relationship between the document, in its two versions, and Dostoevsky's fiction. Kraft's diary in *The Adolescent* is closer to Koni's version. For instance, Dostoevsky's character was concerned about leaving a bloody mess—a detail present in Koni's version, but absent from Likhachev's. In fact, according to Likhachev's text, the suicide wanted to increase the flow of blood (and thus ensure death). Likhachev's scholarly publication is obviously more reliable than Koni's memoirs. But which version did Dostoevsky read? One may speculate that it was Koni's and that Koni told Kramer's story to Dostoevsky in a conversation—just like Vasin in *The Adolescent*—quoting the diary from memory (as he later did in his memoirs).

Dostoevsky also used the last letter of the suicide A. Ts—v published in the newspaper *Grazhdanin* on November 18, 1874. Like Kramer, Ts—v viewed his own death as a scientific experiment. His diary, in which he wanted to record "insofar as possible the sensations experienced at the approach of death," ended with the following detail: "I'm writing by memory, and in case I grow numb or forget to blow out the candle and start a fire, I am blowing it out now."[48]

What was to be done with this material? The scientists who published Kramer's diary[49] offered a medical reading: "The oppressed state of his mind, caused by a self-awareness of the insignificance of his social value and an unwillingness to part with his fictitious grandeur, produced a pathological condition in his brain functions. Chills, appearing already for a month, as the author points out, and the treatment by rum on the day of the suicide allow us to conclude that the psychological disorder already had a real organic basis."[50] What scientists saw in this document were clear signs of organic cerebral pathology.

What the writer saw in these accounts, couched in the language of science and filled with trivia, were potential symbols. Dostoevsky's hero, who does not want to leave a bloody "mess" after him (a remark from Koni's account of Kramer's diary), is also concerned about starting a fire (a remark made by Ts—v). Dostoevsky developed the symbolic potential contained in the idea of leaving a fire and in the image of the extinguished candle. In a conversation with the Adolescent, shortly before his suicide, Kraft describes a special quality of contemporary life: "Nowadays they are stripping Russia of her forests, and exhausting her soil. . . . It's as though they were all in a hotel and were leaving Russia tomorrow" (13:54). In his preliminary notes for the novel, Dostoevsky connected this attitude to his central argument—"if there is no immortality of the soul, then everything is permitted": "there is no other life, I am on the earth for one moment, why bother? . . . 'What do I care if they disappear not just in the future, but at this very minute, and I along with them; après moi, le déluge.' A parallel: the extent to which the soil is becoming exhausted and the forests destroyed in Russia" (16:8–9). In this context, Kraft's precautions against starting a fire become a symbolic gesture:

they are a rejection of the "après moi, le déluge" attitude. He also rejected the gesture of extinguishing a candle: "And I don't want to light it and then, before shooting, put it out like my life" (13:134). A common metaphor for death, the extinguished candle has a specific meaning in the Russian Orthodox service for the dead, known to every Russian. At the end of the funeral mass, candles are extinguished as a sign that earthly life has come to an end and the soul has departed to join God, the source of light.[51] Kraft refuses to enact this symbolic confirmation of the immortality of the soul; he also rejects the act of symbolizing itself. Thus the symbol is both present and absent in the scene of Kraft's death.

According to the notes for *The Adolescent,* Dostoevsky planned to address the question of "the reasons that compel almost everyone (or very many people) to write a *confession* before the final moment (N.B. with the means at their disposal, perhaps everyone would write confessions)" (16:68). His conclusion is that suicide, although it is an act motivated by specific biographical reasons, is a metaphysical quest:

> People kill themselves for a host of reasons; they also write confessions for complicated reasons, not out of vanity alone. But one can also find common features, for example, that at such a moment everyone feels the need to write. *Golos*: a man who killed himself with a knife in a tavern: "The image of dear K. is continually before me." . . . But here again is a common feature: right here, in the note that he left (*despite his dear K.,* whose image, *of course,* would not leave him if he killed himself on her account)—right here, he makes the comment: "My head is surprisingly empty. I used to think that at this moment there would be special thoughts."[52] Whether such a remark is intelligent or stupid, it's important that they are all looking for something, that they are asking questions about something to which they can't find an answer, that they are interested in something that resides completely outside their personal interests. In some kind of general and everlasting concern, even in spite of the image of dear K., which, without a doubt, could have warded off any general idea and the necessity to delve deep into the self and could have turned this deed *into a completely personal one.* (16:68–69)

Convinced that the supra-individual is present in every individual act, Dostoevsky ascribed metaphysical meaning to his hero's last-minute entry by turning a practical detail from the suicide's record into a symbol. Symbolic interpretation lent meaning and significance to personal experience, which seemed to have been inaccessible to the subject.

In conclusion, let us reexamine the relationship between the documents and Dostoevsky's fiction. By the time Koni quoted Kramer's diary in his memoirs, he had, without a doubt, read *The Adolescent*. This might explain the discrepancy between the version of the document in Likhachev's publication and the one cited by Koni. Koni *remembered* that the suicide expressed concern about making a mess because Dostoevsky had made this detail into a symbol. It is quite likely that fiction created this document.

The Law of Corruption

The world of Dostoevsky's novel *Adolescent* is ravaged by a suicide epidemic.[53] At early stages of his work on the novel Dostoevsky planned to dispose of almost all of his heroes by suicide. This suicide epidemic is a consequence of the "corruption" that plagues Russian society. Planning his novel in his notebook, Dostoevsky elaborated: "The idea of corruption pervades everything, because everyone has been *separated* and there are no ties left—not only in the Russian family, but not even human ties among people. . . . *Corruption* is the main visible idea of the novel" (16:16–7). The word "*razlozhenie*" (corruption or decomposition) was immediately identifiable to the reader of the "thick journals" as a common element in public discourse, usually applied to the condition of postreform Russia. Widely used in the press, it acquired distinct symbolic connotations: the disintegration of the social body.[54] To these generally accepted connotations, Dostoevsky adds a layer of meaning that draws on the theological concept of "corruption" prominent in the writings of St. Paul and the fathers of the Eastern church.

According to the theological tradition of Eastern Orthodoxy, it was through original sin that man, created in the image and likeness of God, forfeited his divine attributes and, like the rest of physical matter, became subject to natural laws—that is, to corruption, decay, and death. "Corruption," that is, mortality, or (in a personalized sense) simply death, has been viewed as a "cosmic disease" which holds humanity under its sway, both spiritually and physically, and is controlled by the devil, "the murderer from the beginning" (John 8:44).[55] In Gregory Palamas's words, with the mind's submission to the flesh, "we ourselves are dead and, before the death of the body, we suffer the death of the soul; that is to say, the separation of the soul from God."[56] The death and resurrection of Christ will bring every man deliverance from the "bondage of corruption" (Rom. 8:21). This promise is tied to the Christian conception of man: "man is truly man because he is the image of God" (and not an autonomous being). Thus, man is exempt from the law of corruption "if he preserves in himself the image of God."[57]

These notions, familiar to any well-read Christian of Dostoevsky's generation, offered themselves for reinterpretation in the positivist context: Feuerbach's anthropotheism was the modern equivalent of the serpent's "you shall be as gods" and materialism was the new form of subjection to the law of the flesh. Like original sin, these transgressions led to corruption (in its broad metaphorical meaning) and death.

Underlying corruption as the novel's "visible" idea, or its social theme, is a metaphysical and theological one. It is especially prominent in the phraseology and imagery of Dostoevsky's early plans. Consider the following succinct note: "Society decomposes chemically. . . . all of these families and the entire nation [*narodnost'*] decompose; even an image of them will not remain" (16:16). The use of "obraz" (image) is far from accidental. "Obraz" reappears in his plans (and in the novel) as the holy image, the Orthodox icon: the main character, an atheist, "slashed icons," "can't stand *icons* . . . he shoots himself" (16:42, 43).[58] The implication is that the loss of God's image in man leads to disintegration and self-imposed death.[59]

Another entry in Dostoevky's notebook offers a model of the world defined in spatial terms: "Planet earth is in contact with God, the whole, and immortality (the family is being destroyed, and ancestors, and personality (without God); the human race remains; things are restricted, therefore, to earth, and at the resurrection a meeting, knowledge)" (16:170). The starting point is the image of the planet earth in (physical) contact with God. Two notions follow: the whole and immortality. A statement in parentheses refers to the destruction of the family and personality (*lichnost'*, from the root *lik,* face, or image), and "without God" points to the cause. The conclusion is that, with nothing but a succession of generations left, human existence is reduced to its earthly form. These cryptic notes seem to contain a condensed theory of man and the world that is informed by patristic thought.

The novel also questions the integrity of the family. The main heroes form "a type of accidental family, in opposition to an ancestral family" (16:434). The elder hero, Versilov, a gentry intellectual and a European wanderer, formed a ménage with a married peasant woman, Sofia, his former serf (clearly, a symbol of Russia). The couple has two children: a son Arkady (the Adolescent), and a daughter

Liza. By the end of the novel, Liza is pregnant by the young prince Sokolsky, an aristocrat who forges bonds. Versilov attempts to kill a woman he passionately (and hopelessly) loves (Akhmakova), and then shoots and wounds himself. (Completed suicide was planned in the drafts.)* Prince Sokolsky is arrested and dies before the trial (in the drafts, he dies by his own hand), while Liza suffers a miscarriage (according to earlier drafts, she was to commit suicide). Clearly, this is a picture of "corruption"—disintegration of the family unit, disruption of the succession of generations (*rod*), and moral disintegration and decay of the individual.

In early drafts, "atheism" figured as the core of Versilov's personality and an explanation for his family drama: "HIS entire misfortune is that HE is an atheist and does not believe in *resurrection*" (16:15). In the final text, the theme of atheism culminates in Versilov's vision of a future in which God and immortality are absent: "The great idea of immortality would have vanished, and they would have to fill its place; and all the wealth of love lavished of old upon Him who was immortal would be turned upon the whole of nature, on the world, on men, on every blade of grass. They would inevitably grow to love the earth and life as they gradually became aware of their own transitory and finite nature, and with a special love, not as of old, they would begin to observe and could discover in nature phenomena and secrets which they had not suspected before, for they would look on nature with new eyes, as a lover looking on his beloved (13:379/466)." This vision of earthly paradise, an echo of socialist utopias, remains incomplete. In his heart, Versilov feels that such a utopia, if at all possible, will be temporary. The completion of this vision was always an image of the second coming of Christ.

The question arises: what comes in between? In his novel, Dostoevsky refrained from giving an explicit answer. He did, however, supply one missing piece in *The Diary of a Writer* (January 1876 issue), making a clear connection between the loss of faith in immortality and the suicide epidemic (a matter for later comment). The social reality presented in *The Adolescent* prefigures a world disrupted by the

---

*This episode had a real-life basis in the famous hotel Belle Vue case (September 19, 1873), involving the wife of A. S. Suvorin, Anna Suvorina. Dostoevsky's plans for this episode contain direct references to the case: "I . . . I . . . I will destroy you, that's what I'll do (he stood up from his seat, pale). Belle vue" (16:374). "N.B. N.B. About shooting the woman if she does not agree, Suvorin's feuilleton of November 3, No. 303" (16:195). A. S. Dolinin discussed this connection in *Poslednie romany Dostoevskogo* (Moscow–Leningrad, 1963, pp. 141–42); he misquoted Suvorin's feuilleton.

rebellion against God, a world populated by men who fail to preserve the image of God in themselves. Ruled by him who is "the murderer from the beginning," this world is subject to the law of corruption.

It can safely be assumed that the disintegration of individual and social bodies in Dostoevsky's novel is governed not only by the laws of contemporary social and natural science which informed the discourse of the press, but also by the principles of patristic theology. Relying on an additional source, Dostoevsky revealed the metaphysical meaning of individual acts and social events. In this, Dostoevsky's fiction differs from the writings of contemporary scientists and journalists, frequently printed under the same cover with Dostoevsky's novels in the "thick journals." (*The Adolescent,* for example, was serialized in *Otechestvennye zapiski* in 1875.)

To conclude, in dealing with suicide, Dostoevsky used the same language as scientists and journalists—a discourse built from a specific set of metaphors. As scientists and journalists of his time, he described pursuit of knowledge as an experiment—an observation that intervened at the point where life and death converged. In picturing the world, the writer operated with the same spatial model defining the relationship of part and whole (in his case, not the individual and society but the individual and God). And yet, using the same categories and the same words, the discourse of science, the press, and fiction created different meanings.

The Death of Kirillov

In the suicide of Kirillov in *The Possessed* (Besy, 1871–72) Dostoevsky created a paradigm of death for the age of atheism, which informed philosophical notions for years to come (most notably Nietzsche's and Camus's—see below).

Kirillov is an ideologue and proponent of suicide. He preaches that anyone would kill himself were it not for two "prejudices": fear of pain* and "the other world." But the "new man," free of these prejudices, is coming: "There will be a new man, happy and proud. He for

---

*Kirillov's assertion "if it were not . . . for the fear of pain," probably comes from Schopenhauer, whose outlook captured the imagination of Russians in the 1870s and 1880s: "Perhaps there is no one alive who would not already have put an end to his life if this end were something purely negative, a sudden cessation of existence. But there is something positive in it as well; the destruction of the body. This is a deterrent" ("On Suicide," from *Parerga and Paralipomena* [1851]; quoted from Arthur Schopenhauer, *Essays and Aphorisms,* London, 1970, p. 79).

whom it will make no difference whether he lives or does not live, he will be the new man. He who overcomes pain and fear will himself be a god. And this God will not be" (10:93–94/115). The capacity for voluntary death transforms man into god.

The argument unfolds over a series of dialogues. One of Kirillov's interlocutors (the narrator) comes up with a medical explanation of his ideas: the man is clearly insane (10:95). A better-educated listener, Stavrogin, has another explanation:

"Old philosophical places, the same since the beginning of the ages," Stavrogin muttered with a certain squeamish regret.

"The same! The same since the beginning of the ages, and no others, ever!" Kirillov picked up with flashing eyes, as if this idea held nothing short of victory.

(10:188/237)

Indeed, in the death of Kirillov, Dostoevsky combined diverse philosophical commonplaces into a single, seemingly coherent pattern.* The organizing principle, which gives unity and meaning to the whole, comes from Plato's *Phaedo*—a dialogue on death and immortality that ends with a suicide. As Plato was said to have done, Dostoevsky seeks "living words, which are planted and grow in living minds."[60] The argument emerges in the interaction between the philosopher and his interlocuters. The dialogue unfolds in a situation of impending death, which elevates the spoken word to the status of truth. Moreover, as with Socrates, who takes poison at the close of the argument, this truth is ultimately tested in the act itself.[61]

Kirillov's death reenacts the deaths of both Socrates and Christ, conflating the two patterns. For one, Kirillov is unable to tolerate (or even to imagine) the fact of Christ's death: "There was one day on earth, and in the middle of the earth stood three crosses. One on a cross believed so much that he said to another: 'This day you will be with me in paradise.' The day ended, they both died, went, and did not find either paradise or resurrection. . . . And if so, if the laws of nature did not pity even *This One* . . . why live then?" (10:471/618).

Indeed, for nineteenth-century man, Christ's death had a tragic

---

*Contemporary readers had reactions similar to Stavrogin's. One reader recognized Hegel in the statement on the equivalence of being and nonbeing: "In his own original way, this insane man merely reproduces the well-known Hegelian tenet: being and nonbeing are one and the same (Sein und Nichtsein ist dasselbe)" (E. Markov, "Kriticheskie besedy," *Russkaia rech'*, 1879, no. 6: 197; quoted in Dostoevskii 12:268).

meaning. The idea was introduced by Hegel: *"God has died, God is dead*—this is the most frightful of all thoughts."[62] The tragedy was rooted in the disintegration of the relationship between man and God established in the doctrine of God-manhood. For nonbelievers, Hegel claimed, the history of Christ is just what the history of Socrates is "for us": the death of a human being who showed humanity what must constitute the basis of human consciousness. Viewed as a human being, Christ has died a death that implies absolute finitude. And the thought of the death of God might just be more that a man can endure.[63]

Caught up in the Kantian antinomy between the moral necessity for God's existence and the empirical knowledge of God's absence, Kirillov attempts to resolve it by fulfilling God's role: "If there is no God, then I am God" (10:469–70/617). His attempts to explain this transfiguration logically take the individual will as a starting point: "If there is God, then the will is all his, and I cannot get out of his will. If not, the will is all mine, and it is my duty to proclaim self-will. . . . It is my duty to shoot myself because the fullest point of my self-will is—for me to kill myself" (10:470/617).

Kirillov's argument on the new terrible freedom of the individual echoes Hegel's reflections on "absolute freedom and terror"[64]—a state of consciousness brought about by the Enlightenment and the French revolution, which marks the beginning of the end of history. The essence of this new mode of consciousness is disharmony in the relationship between individual will and universal will. In Hegel's view, "universal freedom can produce neither positive achievement nor a deed; there is left for it only negative action; it is merely the rage and fury of destruction." Therefore, the realization of this terrible freedom is death, and "the most cold-blooded and meaningless death of all." Moreover, death is the only deed that an absolutely free individual can accomplish, and the terror of death is the individual's absolute lord and master.[65] People of Dostoevsky's generation applied their readings of Hegelian concepts to a variety of contemporary problems. Dostoevsky apparently found in Hegel a model of nihilistic death—death brought about by absolute atheistic freedom which freed the individual will from subjection to the universal will.

For Dostoevsky and his contemporaries, the will (a notion derived from various sources, from Hegel to the Orthodox catechism) was central in mapping the changing relations between man and God. Christian anthropology regarded free will as the cornerstone of the model of man: the exercise of free will is checked by man's responsibility for his own sins and ultimately rests on a faith in the existence of God and the immortality of the soul. Positivists, having abandoned God and rejected the idea of immortality, replaced the notion of free will with determinism. But Dostoevsky arrived at a different conclusion. His heroes who live in a godless world exhibit a malignant hypertrophy of individual volition, or Hegelian absolute freedom of self-will, not a subjection to determinism. For Dostoevsky, self-will finds its ultimate expression in self-murder (murder of another, suggested by Verkhovensky, is an inferior form of self-willfulness) (10:470). But what is ultimately at stake is God-manhood—with an act of willful death, Kirillov hopes to establish his credentials as the new Savior: "I will begin, and end, and open the door. And save. Only this one thing will save all men and in the next generation transform them physically" (10:472/619). Thus Kirillov becomes God because, in choosing to die a voluntary death for the salvation of humankind, he identifies himself with Christ. (Like Christ, Kirillov—who plans to work on the construction of a new railroad bridge—is a mediator between God and man, or heaven and earth, a pontifex.)

With Kirillov's death, Dostoevsky joined the centuries-long theological debate on whether Christ can be considered a suicide.[66] The location of the will was a pivotal issue in this controversy: those who argued that Christ's voluntary death cannot be considered a suicide, pointed to Christ's appeal in the Gethsemane prayer, "Let *Thy* will be done." Kirillov, who emphatically asserts "Let *my* will be done," clearly commits suicide. A self-willed Christ, Christ the suicide, he is the *new* god.

Kirillov's dialogue with Stavrogin indicates the philosophical source of his idea of the new Savior:

"He will come and his name is the man-god."
"The God-man?"
"The man-god—that's the whole difference."

(10:189/238)

The concept of a "man-god" was favored by the followers of Ludwig Feuerbach, who was immensely popular in Russia. On the surface, Feuerbach, who proclaimed Kant's postulates of faith (the existence of God, the immortality of the soul, and the freedom of the will) to be completely unnecessary, was a positivist. Make do with this world—he insisted—the world given in sensory experience; God is nothing but a mental projection of an object in empirical reality—man. In giving primacy to God, religion "preferred the sign to the thing signified, the copy to the original, fancy to reality."[67] By contrast, Feuerbach thought of himself as a "realist" in the positivist, not scholastic sense: in "deciphering" the Christian doctrine, he read statements about God as statements about man, and statements about a future, heavenly life as statements about earthly life. As a result, in Feuerbach's representation, this world acquired obvious similarities to the other world. In the end, he identified the divine with the human subject, and Christian religion with atheism: "It is not I, an insignificant individual, but religion itself that says: God is man, man is God. . . . I have only found the key to the cipher of Christian religion, only extricated its true meaning. . . . If therefore my work is negative, irreligious, atheistic, let it be remembered that atheism— at least in the sense of this work—is the secret of religion itself."[68] Thus Feuerbach presented his revolutionary conclusions as the result of a rereading of Christian doctrine—a rereading that by reversing the relationship between the sign and the thing revealed its hidden meaning.

Feuerbach's Russian follower Nikolai Speshnev used his doctrine ("the main principle of the new time") as license to reject any higher authority and to posit self-will as the only law. (A member of the Petrashevsky cicle and Dostoevsky's mentor in radicalism, Speshnev is believed to have served as a prototype for Stavrogin.)[69] This is how Speshnev interpreted Feuerbach's teaching: "I now understand that all this means only that no authority, creator, or god exists for mankind—and concerning the philosophical god, mankind is the highest and most genuine incarnation of this god; therefore, there can exist no other god for it, other than mankind itself: like any god, mankind doesn't take orders from others; its own voluntary determination, its own will, its own desire—this is the only law. I am avoiding here . . . [the manuscript breaks off]."[70]

In spite of its far-reaching consequences, Feuerbach's Russian readers, like Feuerbach himself, saw the revolution in the relationship between God and man as a mere linguistic operation. In the words of Speshnev, "Instead of the god-man we now have the man-god. Only the word order has changed. Is the difference between the god-man and the man-god really all that great?"[71] In Kirillov, Dostoevsky demonstrated that a change of word order had the most important consequences: the difference was a matter of life and death.

Among the main implications of this revolution was the new status afforded the body. Feuerbach affirmed that the "identity [between God and man] at last extends even to the flesh, even to the body."[72] At the same time, he insisted that his man was a "positive" and "real" being, that is, man as Matter (with a capital M). This implied a promise that the body would be immortal. Kirillov, as he explains to Stavrogin, believes in physical immortality "not in a future eternal life, but in eternal life here [on earth]" (10:188). Accordingly, he sees the physical transformation of man as a matter of necessity: "in the present physical form . . . it is in no way possible for man to be without the former God" (10:472/619). (Indeed, without the old God, man will find his ultimate end in the body's corruption.) Kirillov explains the mechanism of such transformation to his interlocutors. In a conversation with Stavrogin, he claims:

> "There are moments, you reach moments, and time suddenly stops, and will be eternal."
> "You hope to reach such a moment?"
> "Yes."
> "It's hardly possible in our time. . . . In the Apocalypse the angel swears that time will be no more."
> "I know. It's quite correct; clear and precise."

Kirillov's belief rests on his trust in the absolute reality of philosophical categories:

> "And where are they going to hide it?" [asks Stavrogin]
> "Nowhere. Time isn't an object, it's an idea. It will die out in the mind." (10:188/236–37)

From a philosophical perspective, this is a moment in which the St. John of Revelation joins hands with Immanuel Kant. But, as Kirillov elaborates (in a conversation with Shatov), these moments of personal apocalypse are given in direct sensory experience; ultimately, this experience results in the transformation of the flesh:[73] "There are seconds, they come only five or six at a time, and you suddenly feel the presence of eternal harmony, fully achieved. It is nothing earthly; not that it's heavenly, but man cannot endure it in his earthly state. One must change physically or die" (10:450/590). Kirillov clearly sees such a transformation as a guarantee of physical immortality on earth, for this new condition makes procreation unnecessary: "Why children, why development, if the goal has been achieved?" (10:450–51/591). His interlocutor, Shatov, viewing it from a medical perspective, describes Kirillov's experience as the sensation that precedes an epileptic attack—a condition Dostoevsky knew from personal experience.[74]

Logical proof for the new, positive immortality was obtained by reversing Plato's famous argument in *Phaedo* that death is the separation of the soul from the body:

—Do we believe that there is such a thing as death?

—Most certainly, said Simmias, taking up the role of answering.

—Is it simply the release of the soul from the body? Is death nothing more or less than this, the separate condition of the body by itself when it is released from the soul, and the separate condition by itself of the soul when released from the body? Is death anything else than this?

—No, just that.*

This argument served as the basis for the Christian conception of immortality. In the nineteenth century, Feuerbach described this conception in the following way: "[in the conception of God] the mind is occupied with the separation of the soul from the body . . . with the separation of the essence from the individual;—the individual dies a spiritual death, the dead body which remains behind is the human individual; the soul which has departed from it is God." He then suggested that, in the age of positivism, it was imperative to invert this pattern, restoring the initial wholeness: "But the separation of the soul from the body, of the essence from the individual, of God from man, must be abolished again. Every separation of beings essentially allied is painful. The soul yearns after its lost half, after its body; as God, the departed soul yearns after the real man. As, therefore, God becomes man again, so the soul returns to its body, and the perfect identity of this world and the other is now restored."[75] In reversing Platonic and Christian death, Feuerbachian death fuses the body with the soul, reuniting them after centuries of separation. Clearly, it is Feuerbach's notion of immortality—the immortality in this world— that Kirillov strives to achieve.

Combining and reinterpreting existing philosophical paradigms, most importantly, the death of Socrates and the death of Christ, Dos-

---

*Plato, *The Collected Dialogues*, p. 47. Dostoevsky used a similar narrative pattern; cf. Kirillov's conversation with the narrator:

"But aren't there ways of dying without pain?"

"Imagine," he stopped in front of me, "imagine a stone the size of a big house; it's hanging there, and you are under it; if it falls on you, on your head—will it be painful?"

"A stone as big as a house? Naturally, it's frightening."

"Fright is not the point; will it be painful?"

"A stone as big as a mountain, millions of pounds? Of course, it wouldn't be painful at all." (10:93/114)

toevsky created in Kirillov's suicide a new paradigm of death, one be-
fitting the age of positivism and atheism.

For Dostoevsky, attention to the metaphysical and symbolic meanings of death went hand in hand with his interest in psychology. Guided by his life-long fascination with the direct apprehension of death,
the writer offered his readers voyeuristic glimpses of Kirillov's last
moments, presented through the eyes of an onlooker, Petr
Stepanovich Verkhovensky. This is what Verkhovensky witnessed
when, impatient to see Kirillov dead, he entered the room to which
Kirillov had disappeared with a revolver:

> to the right of the wardrobe, in the corner formed by the wardrobe
> and the wall, Kirillov was standing, and standing very strangely—
> motionless, drawn up, his arms flat at his sides, his head raised, the
> back of his head pressed hard to the wall. . . . Pyotr Stepanovich . . .
> could observe only the protruding parts of the figure. . . . What
> struck him above all was that the figure, despite his shout and furi-
> ous lunge, did not even move, did not even stir one of its members—
> as if it were made of stone or wax. The pallor of its face was
> unnatural, the black eyes were completely immobile, staring at some
> point in space. Pyotr Stepanovich moved the candle from up to down
> and up again, lighting it from all points and studying this face. He
> suddenly noticed that, although Kirillov was staring somewhere
> ahead, he could see him out of the corner of his eye, and was per-
> haps even watching him. Then it occurred to him to bring the flame
> right up to the face of "this blackguard," to burn it and see what he
> would do. . . . The moment he touched Kirillov, the man quickly
> bent his head down, and with his head knocked the candle from his
> hands; the candlestick fell to the floor with a clang, and the candle
> went out. At the same instant he felt a terrible pain in the little fin-
> ger of his left hand . . . he had struck . . . with the revolver on the
> head of Kirillov, who had leaned to him and bitten his finger. He fi-
> nally tore the finger and rushed headlong to get out of the house,
> feeling his way in the darkness. Terrible shouts came flying after him
> from the room:
> "Now, now, now, now . . . "
> Ten times or so. But he kept running and had already reached
> the front hall when there sudddenly came a loud shot.
> (10:475–76/624–25)

This description shocked some readers. One of them was Dmitry
Merezhkovsky: "The description of Kirillov's suicide is one of Dostoevsky's creations in which he steps beyond the boundaries of art; it

is something that one should not write about, one should not even talk about. It is cynical, terrible, perhaps criminal—artistically as well as morally criminal. It is a kind of vivisection, an anatomical dissection of a living soul. Gazing at the gaping wound and the bloody guts of the human soul, we watch their final shudderings with disgust and horrible curiosity."[76] In Merezhkovsky's words, Kirillov in his last moments is not the man-god, but a mental patient. It appears that, at the last moment, Dostoevsky switched from the metaphysical frame of reference to the medical one. Yet, as we know, Dostoevsky borrowed details for this scene from Hugo's *Le Dernier jour d'un condamné*.[77] And contrary to Merezhkovsky's impression, the writer refrained from depicting the very moment of suicide: the shot is fired behind the scenes. Artistic vivisection failed to capture the moment of death itself. The experience of dying remained inaccessible even to the artist.

The Real Kirillov

The relationship of art to reality was crucially important for Dostoevsky, who, like an experimental scientist, took pride in his ability not only to represent, but also to anticipate, life.[78] In Kirillov, he saw his intuition confirmed. Soon after completing the novel, Dostoevsky encountered his character in real life: his name was Alexander Malikov. Dostoevsky referred to this event in his notebooks for 1876 (misspelling Malikov's name): "I have been told *that Kirillov* is unclear. I should have told you about Mal'kov" (24:163) and (earlier) "I heard about Mal'kov".[79] A "nihilist," Malikov participated in the revolutionary movement and was arrested in 1866 in connection with the Karakozov affair. Living in exile, this renegade revolutionary turned to preaching the religion of god-men (*bogocheloveki*). A fellow revolutionary, A. I. Faresov, described his conversion. One day in March 1874, Malikov greeted him declaring: "In your absence I stopped being an 'old' man. Listen . . . you too must open up [*vskroite*] the 'godly soul' in yourself. Become a Christian. Rebuke the thought that violence is abolished by violence."[80] Every man, he elaborated, is made in the image and likeness of God; therefore, every man is a god-man; "he breathed out his soul into us and made us god-men."[81] Another fellow revolutionary learned of the event from Malikov's son: "Malikov's little son, while hopping on one leg, reported this news to him: Daddy is god! Daddy is god! . ."[82]

Malikov's belief in the divine nature of man was founded on the notion of the unity of human beings treated collectively as a single body. Following organic models in social science, he called the body "the social organism"; following physical theories, he pictured the individual as an "atom" of this organism. He identified the social organism with the body of Christ, which, following Christian theology, he saw as a corruptible, yet immortal, entity. The social organism was to become an object of worship in the revolutionary milieu: "A Christian regards even an evil person as an imperfection in his own body, understanding that they both are part of one mankind, that all people are atoms of the social organism that I now worship. I am convinced that many Russian revolutionaries will be reborn, if they see and talk to me!"[83] This sequence of reasoning, propelled by the power of metaphors, seemed to ensure personal immortality.

Malikov's proselytizing did not fall on deaf ears: several well-known members of the revolutionary movement were influenced by his ideas, among them Nikolai Chaikovsky, a leader of the important populist circle, and O. I. Kablits, author of the influential *Foundations of Populism* (*Osnovy narodnichestva*). When Malikov was arrested (the same year), he preached the religion of the social body to the police. Faresov mentions the following episode, ostensibly related to him by an officer of the gendarmes: "When they brought him to us, he started talking about God, about the social organism that needs the great and the little men alike, just as each of us needs not only a brain, but each of our fingers . . . He was immediately set free."[84] In influencing his jailers, Malikov met with more success than Christ.

Personal—physical—immortality was a crucial part of these beliefs. According to another contemporary, the writer Nikolai Korolenko, Malikov and his followers actually hoped that the human spirit would overcome the corruptibility of the flesh. Korolenko once heard them discussing the fate of the early Christian martyrs who chose voluntary death in imitation of Christ. Their argument went as follows. Metaphorically speaking, the martyrs' spirit triumphed over the flesh: their faces bore expressions of delight as their flesh burned, although their bodies were consumed by flame. Malikov reasoned: "Yes, the body burned . . . But must this always be the case?. . Can you imagine one more step in this direction: an even larger exertion of faith and fire will lose its power to burn the body." (Examples were then quoted from Holy Writ that allowed for such an interpretation.) Bewildered, Korolenko asked Malikov's followers: "Do you really think that the human body can become inflammable as a result of purely nervous functions?" One of them, an "old materialist," answered unequivocally: "Yes, I do."[85] It appears that these materialists believed that metaphors could be transformed into physical reality.

Malikov was not a suicide; the quest that took him from atheism to anthropotheism ended happily with his return to the Orthodox faith.* And yet, in the course of his personal evolution, the idea of voluntary death in *imitatio mortis Christi* did arise for him and his followers. On the whole, the story of Malikov seems to show that, as Dostoevsky hoped, his fiction could transcend the limits of empirical reality and reveal a possible future reality. In the long run, Dostoevsky's experiment seems to have worked: it showed that when men lived in the consciousness that there was no God and no immortality of the soul, self-annihilation seemed to be permitted and even desirable, both to those who, like Kramer, believed in the eternal life of atoms and to those who, like Malikov, believed that the social organism was God.

Thus suicide was a test case in Dostoevsky's investigation of the consequences of atheism. Dostoevsky also made use of suicide for a scientific project of a different order: for transgressive, voyeuristic penetration into the very process of dying. What the writer performed was, in Merezhkovsky's words, a vivisection of the soul. This enterprise, which shocked Merezhkovsky, would have won the approval of Claude Bernard, who insisted on the scientific value of vivisection ("an autopsy of the living"), citing examples of "experiments and vivisections" performed on men condemned to death.[86]

But what did Dostoevsky learn? Reports of those who faced death, be they Dostoevsky's own letter to his brother or the last-minute diaries of suicides, offered disappointingly little. Was the experience itself inherently meaningless? Or was it forever inaccessible to the subject as well as to the external observer?

In an effort to make individual experience significant, the writer read it as a metaphor that had a long tradition and far-reaching symbolic resonance: suicide was seen as an act of *imitatio Christi* performed by an atheist—the predicament of humankind in a faithless world. By infusing it with symbolism, which turned an individual act into a cultural paradigm, the writer gave meaning to the meaningless.

*Desire to realize his teachings in real life brought Malikov to America, where he organized a commune, but the enterprise met with little success. Toward the end of his life, Malikov (who died in 1904) was close to Tolstoy and the Tolstoyans; in the end, he returned to Orthodoxy.

Coda: From Dostoevsky through Nietzsche to the Twentieth Century

For many philosophers, Kirillov's suicide, like that of Socrates, became a paradigm. It was the model death of a modern man. Several reread Kirillov's death from a modernist perspective; moreover, viewing them through Dostoevsky, they reread the philosophical sources that informed Dostoevsky's image of Kirillov.

One of the first to do so was Friedrich Nietzsche, for whom Dostoevsky's novels seem to have colored his reading of the Gospel and image of Christ: "That strange and sick world to which the Gospels introduce us—a world like that of a Russian novel, in which the refuse of society, neurosis and 'childlike' idiocy seem to make a rendezvous. . . . One has to regret that no Dostoevsky lived in the neighbourhood of this most interesting *décadent* [Christ]."[87] Nietzsche was keenly appreciative of the fact that Dostoevsky lived in the neighborhood of the man-god—the nineteenth-century nihilist. In his notebooks for 1887–88, Nietzsche made summaries of selected passages from *The Possessed*,[88] which most likely belonged to his plans for *The Will to Power* (Der Wille zur Macht), a book that was to be largely devoted to the theoretical and practical advent of nihilism. The greatest event in Nietzsche's history of nihilism was man's recognition that "God is dead."[89]

Nietzsche's summaries of Dostoevsky's novel are preceded by his sketch "The Diary of the Nihilist" which describes the spiritual "catastrophe" of modern man: the "nihilist" suspects, as does Nietzsche himself, that the origin of meaning—otherwise called God—lies in human interpretation and that meaning is nothing more than a fiction.[90] "The Diary of the Nihilist" is followed by a summary of the letter Stavrogin wrote to Dasha shortly before his death. Thus Nietzsche's genre of choice in presenting the advent of nihilism is a personal document—as Dostoevsky before him, he presented disbelief as an inner experience. But rather than summarizing Stavrogin's letter, Nietzsche rewrote it in the form of a suicide note. In Dostoevsky's version, the letter cannot be understood as such: reiterating his inability to kill himself, Stavrogin invites Dasha to join him in an escape to Switzerland. In Nietzsche's notebook, Stavrogin's letter opens with what could be the literal translation of a conventional Russian formula used in suicide notes (*nikogo ne vinit'*): "No one is to blame—[*Niemanden anklagen*]."[91] His version of the letter, furthermore, omits all references to Stavrogin's future plans and ends by confirming his intention to commit suicide: "I know that I should kill myself, that I should clean the earth of myself, like a miserable insect."* Thus Nietzsche confirms and reinforces the importance that Dostoevsky accorded to suicide in his analysis of nihilism: suicide is the inevitable psychological consequence of disbelief.

Further in his notes, Nietzsche meticulously records the main points of Kirillov's theory of suicide: suicide is "the most perfect way to prove one's independence [from God]"; "if nature has not spared its masterpiece [Jesus], then the planet rests on a lie"; "fear is the curse of humanity"; "five, six seconds of eternal harmony . . . in order to endure this longer one would have to transform oneself physically"; and "why have children if the goal is attained?" But what seems to fascinate him especially in Dostoevsky's novel is how the philosophical, or logical, development of atheistic principles converges with the psychological process at work in the mind of a man possessed by these ideas. Two sections of Nietzsche's notes are subtitled "Toward the Psychology of a Nihilist" and "The Logic of Atheism." In "The Logic of Atheism," Nietzsche quotes almost verbatim from Kirillov's classical formula defining emotional consequences of denying God's existence: "To feel that God does not exist, and not to feel at the same time that one therefore has become God, is an absurdity: otherwise one would not fail to kill oneself. If you feel this, you are a tsar, and far from killing yourself, you will live at the height of glory."[92] Nietzsche then rephrases Kirillov's antinomical argument on the existence of God in the form of a syllogism:

God is necessary, therefore he must exist
But he doesn't exist
So one can't live anymore.[93]

Thus he juxtaposes a transciption of personal feeling with logical deduction; what Nietzsche saw in Dostoevsky was the psycho-logic of nihilism.[94]

For Nietzsche, taking notes from Dostoevsky's novel was like rewriting a text that he had already written. Indeed, many of these ideas

*Nietzsche, p. 384. In Dostoevsky's novel the letter continues: "I know I ought to kill myself, to sweep myself off the earth like a vile insect, but I'm afraid of suicide, because I'm afraid of showing magnanimity. I know it will be one more deceit—the last deceit in an endless series of deceits. What's the use of deceiving oneself just to play at magnanimity? There never can be indignation and shame in me; and so no despair either" (10:514). English from Fyodor Dostoevsky, *Demons,* trans. Richard Pevear and Larissa Volokhonsky (New York, 1994), p. 676.

had appeared in his own earlier writings.* In his speeches on God and the Superman in *Thus Spoke Zarathustra* (first published in 1883), Nietzsche's prophetic hero deals with concerns similar to Kirillov's; furthermore, Zarathustra's reasoning is grounded in the same logic as Kirillov's. And for Nietzsche, as for Dostoevsky, the conclusion is a psychological state—a desire for annihilation:

> *if* there were gods, how could I endure not to be a god! *Therefore* there are no gods.
>
> I, indeed, drew that conclusion; but now it draws me.
>
> God is a supposition: but who could imbibe all the anguish of this supposition without dying?[95]

These two literary characters share the same view: like Kirillov, Zarathustra envisions two possible outcomes, a negative one (death) and a positive one (the transformation of the ordinary man into the Superman).** But their creators differ on this point: whereas Dostoevsky considers suicide to be the only possible, logical outcome of ni-

---

*The general opinion is that Nietzsche did not know Dostoevsky until 1887. This view is based on Nietzsche's own claim, made in a letter to his Russian-born friend Franz Overbeck, of February 23, 1887: "A few weeks ago, I did not even know Dostoevsky's name. . . . A fortuitous reach in a bookstore. . . ." (Quoted in Kaufmann, who forcefully advanced this view; see Walter Kaufmann, *Nietzsche: Philosopher, Psychologist, Antichrist,* 3d ed. [New York, 1968], p. 318, n. 10. For a detailed review of the connections between Nietzsche and Dostoevsky, see also Wolfgang Gesemann, "Nietzsches Verhältnis zu Dostoevskij auf dem europäischen Hintergrund der 80er Jahre," *Die Welt der Slaven,* 1961, no. 2:129–56.) Nietzsche's assertion may or may not be true. Since there was no translation, he could not have read *The Possessed* at the time when he wrote *Thus Spoke Zarathustra*. There were, however, personal links between Nietzsche and Russian nihilism. Dostoevsky's ideas could have been transmitted orally by two women friends born in Russia and steeped in Russian culture. One of them was Malwida von Meysenbug (a friend of Herzen's family and a tutor to his daughters), whom Nietzsche met in 1872 and on whose advice he contemplated marrying Herzen's daughter Natalie in 1876 ("the best qualified" candidate for matrimony, as he put it in a letter to von Meysenbug; see R. J. Hollingdale, *Nietzsche: The Man and His Philosophy* [London, 1965], p. 133). Another was Lou Andreas-Salome (whom Nietzsche also considered a candidate for matrimony); there is a widespread belief (challenged by some scholars) that she influenced the ideas expressed in *Thus Spoke Zarathustra*.

**It is worth noting that Nietzsche's Christ is a suicide. According to Zarathustra (in "Of Voluntary Death"), "the Hebrew Jesus . . . was seized by the longing for death" (*Thus Spoke Zarathustra,* p. 98). In a section (no. 131) of *The Gay Science,* subtitled "Christianity and Suicide," Nietzsche associated the craving for suicide with the coming of Christianity.

hilistic thought, Nietzsche believes that such thinking can inspire man to overcome the self. In this way, Nietzsche's view coincides not with Dostoevsky's judgement, but that of Dostoevsky's character Kirillov.

The coincidence of some of Dostoevsky's and Nietzsche's ideas is easy to explain. Their thought was informed by the same sources: the precepts of Christian theology as reworked by Hegel and the Hegelians.[96] Hegel had employed the notion of "God is dead" quite frequently—particularly when speaking of the union of God and man in Christ. As Hegel argued, Christ's death is both the death of a man and the death of God. For a Christian, the terrible thought of Christ's death (the death of God) is tolerable because it is inextricably linked to the resurrection, which "belongs just as essentially to faith as the crucifixion."[97] While Hegel affirmed this fairly optimistic view, some of his followers questioned the notion of resurrection. David Strauss and Ludwig Feuerbach replaced divine entities with human ones. Max Stirner, in *The Ego and His Own* (Der Einzige und sein Eigentum, 1845), went still further and maintained that man, who, "in our day," brought the work of the Enlightenment to a victorious end by vanquishing God, has killed God in order now to become the sole God. Later in the nineteenth century, Dostoevsky and Nietzsche, in their reenactments of the death of the God-man, brought the sequence of events known to every Christian to a halt at the moment of Christ's death. The final verdict was "God is dead." As if echoing the words of Dostoevsky's Ippolit, Nietzsche reported in *The Gay Science* (*Die fröhliche Wissenschaft*, 1882): "Do we smell nothing yet of the divine decomposition? Gods, too, decompose. God is dead. God remains dead. And we have killed him."[98] But both Nietzsche and Dostoevsky viewed the declaration that "God is dead" not as a dogmatic statement about supernatural reality, but as a diagnosis of the current psychological state of man.[99] The death of God was an event in the history of human experience, a psychological fact. Both writers portrayed man at the moment when his philosophy, or logic, was translated into experience and became psychology.

What united Dostoevsky and Nietzsche was not only the common sources of their ideas, but also their shared heuristic strategies: they worked not only as epistemologists concerned with the mode of knowledge but also as epidemiologists concerned with the state of the human psyche. In each case, the philosopher assumed the role of doctor.

Some readers found the coincidence of Dostoevsky's and Nietzsche's thought truly miraculous. One such reader, the ideologist of Russian modernism Dmitrii Merezhkovsky, believed that Dostoevsky's Kirillov had prefigured Nietzsche with "mathematical precision" at each and every point of the latter's thought. Merezhkovsky believed, moreover, that the coincidence of these two prophetic visions attested to their divine inspiration.[100] For him, Dostoevsky and Nietzsche were characters in a revelatory text written by a divine hand.

Reading Nietzsche through Dostoevsky (in a work from 1901), Merezhkovsky identified the philosopher with Kirillov. Nietzsche-Kirillov—as the writer called his hero[101]—prefigured the new man, the man-god who overcame death psychologically (by conquering the fear of death) and physically (by having imperishable flesh). But the Russian Nietzsche, Kirillov, went further in his experience, becoming a super-Nietzsche. While both of them understood the theological idea of man's physical transformation in the context of the theory of evolution, only Kirillov combined the sensory with the extrasensory (or mystical) in his thought and experience. For Merezhkovsky, Kirillov's "kingdom of the *Übermensch*" approaches the ideal of the New Jerusalem from the Revelation of St. John; one more step and the teaching of Kirillov—an improved version of Nietzscheanism before Nietzsche—would coincide with the teaching of Christ.[102]

Merezhkovsky was clearly striving for the synthesis of man-god and God-man, an ideal that inspired fin-de-siècle thought in Russia. He had to admit, however, that, in the long run, both Nietzsche and (to a lesser degree) Kirillov fell short of this ideal—for each had failed to attain full religious consciousness. This emotional, or experiential, failure was coupled with an intellectual shortcoming: their denial of the existence of God had been predicated on an error in deductive reasoning. Kirillov and Nietzsche failed to appreciate the Kantian principle: that the notion of God lies beyond the realm of sensory experience. After Kant's *Critique of Pure Reason* (Merezhkovsky claimed), Kirillov's argument ("God is necessary, therefore, he must exist; but I know that he does not exist, therefore, I cannot live") can only be considered a philosophical blunder. Insisting that God could be killed by reason, Kirillov and Nietzsche both made the mistake of ignoring Kant's argument (Nietzsche, according to Merezhkovsky, went so far as to claim that "Kant is an idiot").[103] Along with Büchner and Moleschott, they had replaced God with "a dead frog."[104] (a mistake, one might add, that Turgenev's Bazarov made as well). This mistake in reasoning, moreover, had fatal consequences for their mental health, in Merezhkovsky's words, "from one picayune mistake in the critique of knowledge, all wisdom suddenly becomes madness."[105] Dostoevsky's Kirillov dies not as a man-god but as a madman, howling, kicking, and biting. For Merezhkovsky, Kirillov's death (a clinical phenomenon described by Dostoevsky the vivisectionist) is an analog of Nietzsche's death: "The Superman, the Man-God, has turned into a man-animal. The terrible titan Zarathustra-the-Antichrist has turned into a pitiful cripple, the former German doctor of philology Friedrich Nietzsche who is being kept in a mental hospital."[106]

The coincidence of the two deaths is interpreted by Merezhkovsky as a warning of a future epidemic illness: "The madness of Kirillov and Nietzsche is only the first weak strain of the historic world-wide contagion of insanity."[107] Thus, in the end, by diagnosing the world-wide contagion of insanity, the writer-philosopher assumed the role of doctor.

Another twentieth-century philosopher, Albert Camus, writing in 1940, insisted that suicide, which had been formerly approached solely as a social problem, must be now considered as a phenomenon of individual life and thought. ("Suicide has never been dealt with except as a social phenomenon," Camus claimed arrogantly.)[108] He opened his book on suicide, *The Myth of Sisyphus,* with a statement that has since been quoted by many a scholar of suicide: "There is but one truly serious philosophical problem, and that is suicide. Judging whether life is or is not worth living amounts to answering the fundamental question of philosophy. . . . And if it is true, as Nietzsche claims, that a philosopher, to deserve our respect, must preach by example, you can appreciate the importance of that reply, for it will precede the definitive act."[109] A modern philosopher was put into Socrates' position. But Camus's immediate reference point was Dostoevsky's Kirillov. In *The Myth of Sisyphus* he gave his own account of Kirillov's death, rereading Dostoevsky through Nietzsche.*

Summarizing, retelling, and citing selected passages from *The Possessed,* Camus followed the course of Kirillov's argument, analyzing its "logic." (He also considered Dostoevsky's Stavrogin and Ivan Karamazov, characters in which he saw Kirillov "reappear.") Like Merezhkovsky, Camus identified Dostoevsky's Kirillov with Nietzsche, his thought and his personal fate. Prompted by the knowledge of Nietzsche's death in an insane asylum, he emphasized that the logical outcome of atheism was madness, a condition which ultimately led Kirillov to suicide: "Of course, like Nietzsche, the most famous of

*Camus was primarily inspired by *Thus Spoke Zarathustra*. Nietzsche's notes on *The Possessed* were not published until 1970.

God's assassins, he [Dostoevsky's composite hero] ends in madness."[110] Thus Camus's reflections on the metaphysical condition of modern man, like Merezhkovsky's, end in a medical diagnosis.

Ludwig Wittgenstein was another philosopher who saw in Dostoevsky a paradigm of suicidal logic. For Wittgenstein, suicide was not only a subject for philosophical reflections, but also an intensely personal matter. (Three of Wittgenstein's brothers committed suicide, and he contemplated killing himself at several points throughout his life.) In January 1917, Wittgenstein jotted down the following thoughts in his notebook:

> If suicide is allowed then everything is allowed.
> If anything is not allowed then suicide is not allowed.[111]

This argument is clearly patterned on the statement from *The Brothers Karamazov,* "if there is no God, then everything is permitted." An attentive reader of the novel, Wittgenstein knew that suicide was central among Dostoevsky's "things permitted."[112] In his own philosophical reflections, he took suicide as a point of departure for further development of his ideas on ethics. For Wittgenstein, like for Camus, suicide was a fundamental philosophical problem. Like Nietzsche, Wittgenstein committed his thoughts on suicide to his private notebook:

> This sheds light on the nature of ethics, for suicide is, so to speak, the elementary sin.
> And when one investigates it, it is like investigating mercury vapour in order to comprehend the nature of vapours.
> Or is even suicide in itself neither good nor evil![113]

The wording of his concluding remark clearly evokes Nietzsche. Like other philosophers, Wittgenstein investigated suicide under the dual influence of Dostoevsky and Nietzsche.

And as was the case for other philosophers, metaphysical reflections overlapped psychological ones. In fact, Wittgenstein considered thought a kind of experience, which does not need a subject:

> Is belief a kind of experience?
> Is thought a kind of experience?
> All experience is world and does not need the subject.[114]

The death of Kirillov retroactively influenced the twentieth-century reading of Dostoevsky's main philosophical source—Hegel. Thus reflections on Dostoevsky's Kirillov—read through Nietzsche—affected Alexandre Kojève's influential interpretation of the *Phenomenology of Spirit* (his lectures delivered at the Ecole des Hautes Etudes in 1933–39).[115] Kojève sees notions of "man's faculty of death" and "man's fear of death" as central concerns in Hegel's philosophy; suicide (voluntary death without any vital necessity) is the most obvious manifestation of negativity, or freedom, in Hegel. (Kojève remarked in a footnote that this Hegelian theme was taken up by Dostoevsky in *The Possessed* and dramatized in the death of Kirillov.[116]) According to Kojève, Hegel asserts that one can become a free Christian man only by becoming a man without God, "or, if you will, a God-Man": "[man] must realize *in himself* what at first he thought was realized in his God. To be *really* Christian, he *himself* must become Christ."[117] And if man can kill himself, in emulation of Christ, he can thereby render himself immune to death. Kojève claimed that "Hegel actually asserts this [idea] on several occasions," but he failed to show that Hegel ever posed suicide as a central philosophical issue.[118] In presenting the Hegelian understanding of the Christian world as nothing more than a progression toward the acceptance of death, or an atheistic awareness of man's essential finiteness, he was clearly prompted by Nietzsche. I believe that his understanding of both Hegel and Nietzsche was also influenced by Dostoevsky's Kirillov. Born Aleksandr Kozhevnikov, in Russia in 1902, Kojève reread Hegel through Dostoevsky and Nietzsche, or rather through the thought of a composite philosopher created in the imagination of twentieth-century thinkers—Nietzsche/Kirillov.[119]

To conclude, major twentieth-century philosophers, writing after Nietzsche, saw Kirillov's suicide as a paradigm of death in the godless world. The death of Kirillov played a role similar to the role that the deaths of Socrates and Christ had played in the philosophical thought of the previous centuries. The fictional character, Kirillov, whom modern thinkers, influenced by positivism, tended to view as a clinical case, replaced Socrates and Christ. Inscribed on a palimpsest, Kirillov's image reshaped the images of his predecessors.

6 *Diary of a Writer:* Dostoevsky and His Reader

As if he wondered whether, after all, experience was to be captured in the world of fact, not fiction, Dostoevsky returned to the theme of suicide in his *Diary of a Writer* (Dnevnik pisatelia)—a work in a personally designed genre. This was how he described his publication in a Petersburg newspaper: "In 1876, F. M. Dostoevsky's *Diary of a Writer* will be published in individual monthly installments . . . in the format of our weekly newspapers. But this will not be a newspaper; the twelve installments . . . will constitute a whole—a book written by one hand. This will be a diary in the literal sense of the word, an account of the impressions actually experienced each month, an account of what was seen, heard, and read. Short works of fiction may be incorporated into the diary, but [only] those that tell about actual events" (December 1875; 22:136).[1]

A private diary made public or a journal written by one person, the *Diary of a Writer* contained diverse material: reflections on criminal cases and suicides (mostly those reported in the newspapers),[2] discussions of public issues, such as the Russian family ("father and sons") and the "national question," accounts of Dostoevsky's visits to a foundling hospital and a colony for juvenile delinquents, memories of his childhood, and pieces of fiction that grew out of the writer's impressions of the events he had related in the *Diary*.[3] The publication, issued and distributed by the writer and his wife, was a huge success. It incited the active participation of readers, who reacted to Dostoevsky's personal reflections and shared their own experiences.[4] Dostoevsky occasionally quoted readers' letters in his *Diary*; he also responded to them personally. On several occasions the writer intruded into the situation he described, influencing the course of events. The most dramatic example of this involved the much-discussed case of Ekaterina Kornilova, a woman who threw her young stepdaughter out of a window (miraculously, the girl was unharmed). At first, Dostoevsky was indignant, but when he found out that Kornilova was pregnant at the time, he changed his judgment. His coverage of the case, which included vivid pictures of what *could have* happened (that is, fiction), his personal involvement with the accused (whom he visited in prison), and the participation of the readers touched by Dostoevsky's account helped to bring about the woman's acquittal.

Because he relied on personal experience and on public and private documents (newspaper accounts and readers' letters), the *Diary*—unlike fiction—seemed to allow the artist to establish direct contact with "life." It was Dostoevsky's heroic attempt to transgress the boundaries that separated the writer, the reality that he represented, and the reader.

In this chapter, I explore the discussions of suicide in the *Diary of a Writer* (for 1876 and 1877) and in the letters of Dostoevsky's readers. I examine two incidents in particular. The first begins with Dostoevsky's reaction to the newspaper announcement of the suicide of a young midwife, Nadezhda Pisareva. The second focuses on the suicide of the daughter of a "much too famous Russian émigré." In each case, Dostoevsky took as his starting point a real-life incident described by newspaper reporters or his personal correspondents. Unfolding their meaning was a laborious process, extending over several months. First, Dostoevsky interpreted the suicide (and the suicide note) by reading it as a poetic text—a cluster of metaphors. He then elaborated on his reading in response to the queries and comments of the readers. At the next stage, the writer replaced the real-life case with a fiction constructed along similar lines. The fiction, in turn, evoked responses from the readers, who either validated or challenged the writer's construction, sometimes offering themselves and their experiences as additional evidence.

Death of a Midwife

In May 1876, the newspaper *Novoe vremia* published the last letter of a young midwife who poisoned herself with morphine.[5] Dostoevsky discussed the case at length in the May issue of the *Diary*. He introduced it in the following way: "She was twenty-five, and her name was Pisareva. She was the daughter of landowners who had once been prosperous, but she came to Petersburg and paid her dues to progress by becoming a midwife. She got through the course, passed the examination, and found a position as a *zemstvo* midwife. She herself states that she was never in need and was able to earn a rather good living. But she got *tired,* very tired, so tired that she wanted to rest. 'Where better to rest than in the grave?'" (23:24/1:497).[6]

Dostoevsky went on to give a detailed explication of Pisareva's farewell letter. He focused on the young woman's preoccupation with her possessions: "It is truly strange how concerned she is with the arrangements for disposing of the meager sum of money she left: 'This bit of money must not be taken by my relatives; this bit is to go to Petrova; the twenty-five rubles that the Chechotkins gave me for my trip should be returned to them'" (23:25/1:497). On this basis, the writer drew a far-reaching conclusion: "The importance she attributes to money is, perhaps, the last echo of the main prejudice of her life—'that those stones be made bread.' In sum, one sees here the conviction that guided her whole life, i.e., 'if everyone were provided for, everyone would be happy; there would be no poor people and no crimes. There are no crimes whatsoever. Crime is a pathological condition resulting from poverty and from an unhappy environment,' etc., etc." (23:25/1:497–98).[7] Deeply disturbed by the meaninglessness of both the act and note, Dostoevsky infused them with meaning by interpreting the suicide's concern with material details as an expression of socialist convictions. Describing these convictions, he freely put words into the dead woman's mouth. (As far as psychology is concerned, Dostoevsky was mistaken—preoccupation with such details is judged by present-day psychologists to be typical for suicide notes.)[8]

The victim's very name was read as a symbol: she had the same name as the arch-nihilist Dmitrii Pisarev, the radical critic whose death (by drowning) in 1868 was rumored to have been suicide. The connection does not stop here. A year earlier, in June 1875, the newspapers reported the suicide of Pisarev's twenty-two-year-old sister (Ekaterina Pisareva-Grebnitskaia), a young woman who also studied natural science and held "progressive views," and who also died of *taedium vitae* (she left no note).[9]

The fact that the suicide was a midwife (a popular occupation among emancipated young women) in a *zemstvo* (an institution created by the reforms) imbued the affair with additional symbolic potential. The theme of pregnancy assumed central importance in the symbolism of the case. In the story's opening lines, the writer tells that he thought of this suicide during a visit to a foundling hospital. He muses: "So why was it that in this building I set to thinking about suicides, looking at . . . these infants? (23:24/1:496). The reason is clear to the reader who is attentive to the logic of metaphor. Like the foundlings, young suicides are society's "miscarried children" (23:26). The juxtaposition of the two images creates a metaphor: suicide is a miscarriage suffered by the social body, mother Russia. And a society attended by midwives such as Pisareva is doomed to miscarry. Pisareva is, simultaneously, the child and the midwife, the victim and the perpetrator.[10]

Dialogue on the Immortality of the Soul

The discussion of Pisareva's suicide started an exchange of opinions between Dostoevsky and his readers—a dialogue on the immortality of the soul, in the course of which some participants seemed to have proved the truth of their convictions by committing suicide.

For some readers, the symbolism of Dostoevsky's account of Pisareva's death was bewildering. An orchestra player from the Imperial Opera, V. A. Alekseev, wrote to Dostoevsky on June 3, 1876, asking him to explain a New Testament parable: "Allow me to *ask* you what you meant . . . by the frequent references in your letter to the words of the Gospels concerning the stones turned into bread. The devil proposed this to Christ to tempt him, but the stones were not made into bread and did not turn into food."[11]

Significantly, the reader called Dostoevsky's essay "a letter," treating it as an invitation to a dialogue. Alekseev, who—judging by his writing—was not an educated man, addressed Dostoevsky as an authority of Godlike stature and a mediator between "science" and the general public. "I beg your pardon for troubling you with a such a question, but since the remarks came from you, I considered it best to turn directly to you. I am a man ignorant in this matter; therefore, I ask that you not lead me into temptation. Science has opened many things to you gentlemen—from you the light pours forth onto the unenlightened people."[12]

The parable of the stones turned into bread had already appeared in the *Diary*. In one of the first sections, the author playfully outlined a hypothetical situation—the kingdom of the devil on earth. Devils would overpower man with scientific discoveries, bringing an end to material need. What would happen to people then? Everyone would be in raptures at first: "they would extract fabulous harvests from the earth, create new organisms through chemistry; and there would be beef enough to supply three pounds per person, just as our Russian socialists dreamt—in short, eat, drink, and be merry" (22:33/1:335).

But this socialist paradise would be a temporary stage: "But such rapturous outpourings would scarcely be enough for even one generation! People would suddenly see that they had no more life left, that they had no freedom of spirit, no will, no personality, that someone had stolen all this from them; they would see that their human image had disappeared . . . and humanity would begin to decay; people would be covered in sores and begin to bite their tongues in torment, seeing that their lives had been taken away for the sake of bread, 'for stones turned into bread'" (22:34/1:335).

The culmination would be an epidemic of taedium vitae and suicide: "People would be overcome by boredom and sickness of heart: everything has been done and there is nothing more to do; everything has become known and there is nothing more to discover. There would be crowds of people seeking to end their lives, but not as they do now, in some obscure corner; masses of people would gather, seizing one another's hands, and suddenly destroy themselves by the thousands through some new method that they discovered along with all their other discoveries" (22:33–34/1:335–36).[13] This picture supplied the elements missing from Versilov's vision of the world without God in *The Adolescent* (discussed in the previous chapter). What had been implicit in the novel was now explicit in the *Diary*. The contemporary epidemic of suicides prefigured a socialist utopia, or the kingdom of the devil on earth.

Dostoevsky promptly responded to Alekseev, in a private letter which, as it has been noted, contained the germ of Ivan Karamazov's argument in "The Grand Inquisitor":[14]

There are three colossal, universal ideas blended together in the devil's Temptation of Christ: and now eighteen centuries have gone by and there is nothing more difficult, i.e., more complex, than these ideas, and they have not been worked out even yet.

"Stones and bread" means the social question of the day, a question of *environment*. There is no prophecy here, it has always been this way. "Rather than going to the downtrodden beggars, who, suffering from starvation and oppression, look more like wild beasts than human beings, rather than going to the hungry and preaching abstention from sins and humility and chastity—would it not be better to *feed* them first? . . .

"You are the son of God and are therefore omnipotent. Here, you see these stones, they are legion. You have only to will it and the stones shall be turned into loaves of bread.

"Order things, then, so that henceforth the earth will produce without toil, give people the wisdom or show them the order that will guarantee their welfare. Surely you do not doubt that the vices and miseries that afflict man have come from cold, hunger, and poverty and from all forms of struggle for existence. . . ."

To that Christ answered, "Man does not live by bread alone"—i.e., he gave expression to the axiom that man is spiritual in origin. (29/2:84–85)[15]

By applying the New Testament allegory to contemporary society, Dostoevsky confirmed the validity of the Biblical truth—the old model of man had not lost its explanatory power. What Dostoevsky offered to his reader was a strategy for establishing correspondences between the two languages, Christian and positivist.

Another query came from a member of the opposite ideological camp, P. P. Pototsky, a student who was troubled by the social side of the matter:

Look here, why do you make such attacks, why do you feel such regret about Pisareva, and not just ordinary regret, but apparently some kind of special regret? What's special about her? Perhaps Pisareva is an anomaly to you? Is her condition, suffered by some contemporary women, at all astonishing?

Do you find a large group of women of this kind?!

Why don't you aim at the cause rather than at the effect? As soon as you find the cause, Pisareva will no longer astonish you.

Compared to you, I am your grandson. It would be dishonest on your part to treat my letter too haughtily. Satisfy me in some way, and do it at once (especially if you are able to do so). I implore you.

I trust you will understand why I am making this appeal to you.

P. Pototsky.

I am convinced that you will answer me—you must do this (address me, as I said, on an equal footing. . . .) Don't laugh.[16]

In spite of his arrogant tone and challenge to Dostoevsky's views, the young reader expressed the same sense of urgency in seeking illumination from the writer as had the respectful Alekseev. Dostoevsky responded promptly. Imagining the experience of women and men like Pisareva, he rephrased the argument about "turning stones into bread" in a secular key:

[they] want to lead a *spiritual* life and participate in the affairs of mankind, [are] prepared for heroic action and for acts of magna-

nimity (*velikodushie*). But when they leave their homes, they fall among groups of people who assure them that there is no such thing as a spiritual life, that spiritual life is a fairy tale and not realism; and that there is no such thing as magnanimity either, but only the struggle for existence.

Pisareva asked then, "What am I to do?" "Be a midwife," they answered her. "At least that way you'll be useful to society." She believed them and studied to become a midwife. They were long years of study, without any spiritual food whatever. . . . Finally she is struck by an idea: they have told her that there is no such thing as magnanimity and that, if she wished to be useful, she should become a midwife. But if there is no magnanimity, *there is no need to be useful, either*. Useful to whom, anyway? And complete disillusionment follows. (29/II:86–87)[17]

To his young opponent, Dostoevsky appeals in the language of the "new men": there is not a single reference to God in this discussion. His famous proposition, "if there is no immortality of the soul," is rendered in secular terms: "if there is no magnanimity."

Soon after the appearance of the *Diary* containing the story of Pisareva, Dostoevsky started receiving letters from men who were contemplating suicide.[18] One such letter was signed N. N.; the envelope marked "confessio morituri." In response to Dostoevsky's arguments, this reader explained his credo of nonbelief. His deity is *The Great Mystery*, or "the force of being," to which believers and nonbelievers gave different names:

> what some people call God, others call a cell, and yet others call it an unknowable, inaccessible spirit—in a word, *The Great Mystery*. But once a mystery, always a mystery, and it is in this that the full meaning of our existence lies, the complete cycle of the conditions in which the world subsists. You see, this is atheism (at least, that's what some people understand as atheism), but I ask you not to react to this word with preconceived notions or even feelings, since for you, as a Christian, a profound Christian, feeling always comes first . . . I would only like to ask you whether I am right or not, but first I will say a few preliminary words about myself.

What follows is N. N.'s life story, presented as a typical story of a member of the Russian gentry: "an atrocious upbringing at home," a superficial and unprincipled education, an attempt at government service—all these experiences left N. N. with a sense of the meaninglessness of life. He then settled on his estate and educated himself by reading. His reading, which included the standard positivist classics, made a "new man" out of N. N.:

Renan enticed me, *Mill* was extremely attractive, *Buckle* provided me with the meaning of history, but *Darwin* was the one who overturned everything inside me: my entire system and all my thoughts. I became intoxicated with this new, clear, and most importantly, positively precise picture of the world! I became another person. *Feuerbach* completed in the realm of the spirit that which Darwin had begun in the realm of facts. I have lost feeling (that is, religion), but have acquired thought and convictions. Luck, however, has not spoiled me in my life. After a whole series of unfortunately linked circumstances (of course, not without faults and mistakes on my part)—I found myself in a hopeless situation. Everything had been working so as to convince me that I was a superfluous person; like a nasty weed, I was not a support, but a burden to my family (I have three children—it's a pity to abandon them, but I have to). On the basis of sound reason and mathematically correct calculations, I determined the hopelessness of my situation and the complete harmfulness of my existence—and decided to die. (My family, naturally, is more or less provided for; they will be provided with moral and physical assistance.)

In N. N.'s story, the decision to end his life directly follows from his loss of faith and his newly acquired convictions. Adopting Dostoevsky's metaphors of pregnancy and miscarriage, the would-be suicide also describes himself as "a burden the earth carries." He defends the right to suicide, when it is an act calculated with mathematical precision: "A suicide epidemic can occur only among schoolchildren, pitiable, weak young women, and also among proletarian martyrs,— but suicide as the result of a thorough consideration of all one's chances, of the very meaning of life and of one's own *I*—it is not a crime or even a mistake—it is a right." N. N. then laments the failure of the reforms, adding: "It is not possible to live on Russian Earth." The specific circumstances that led to his decision are not disclosed. He concludes:

Several days remain for the necessary provision of my practical affairs—and if you wish and can find the time, write me a word or two. I have taken a great liking to you and respect you; although a mystic, you are nevertheless an honest soul. Are there many like you? Do what you have to do—mankind will not forget you. Can you be-

lieve that I am on the threshold of the grave—and in my heart all has become calm, peaceful, and clear! I am going to mother nature. I came from her and must return to her. That's the Mystery! Isn't it?
  Respectfully yours,

  N. N.[19]

In conclusion, N. N. urged the writer to reply immediately ("poste restante, to Mr. X. Y. Z., marked 'From belief to nonbelief,' or better yet *an answer to a confession*"). His sense of urgency was even greater than that of Dostoevsky's two other correspondents, for N. N. was living through his last days. There is no evidence that Dostoevsky answered this letter from an atheist.

  In the October issue of the 1876 *Diary,* Dostoevsky published a confessional letter (signed N. N.) which contained the "deductions" of a "materialist" who, through logical reasoning, made the decision to kill himself. This was a work of fiction—Dostoevsky's own reconstruction of an atheist's suicidal mind. Entitled "The Sentence" (Prigovor), this document was written in the form of a protocol of a legal hearing, in which the judge and the defendant were one and the same person.

  Starting in mid-sentence, the "materialist" appeals to mother nature, who brought him forth: "In fact, what right did this nature have to bring me into the world as a result of some eternal laws of hers? I was created with consciousness, and I was *conscious* of this nature: what right did she have to produce me, a conscious being, without my willing it?" (23:146/1:653) He uses his powers of reason to consider whether he would "consent to living," contending that among men with developed intellects the desire for life and happiness is blocked by the realization of life's finitude: "I will not and cannot be happy under the condition of nothingness that threatens tomorrow. This is a feeling, a direct feeling, and I cannot overcome it" (23:147/1:654). Having analyzed logically and consistently his relations with nature, N. N. passed sentence:

  Whereas nature replies through my consciousness to my questions about happiness only by telling me that I can be happy in no other way than through harmony with the whole, which I do not understand and, evidently, never will be capable of understanding;

  And whereas nature not only refuses to recognize my right to receive an account from her and indeed refuses to answer me at all, and not because she doesn't want to answer, but because she cannot answer;

  And whereas I have become convinced that nature, in order to an-

170

swer my questions, has assigned to me (unconsciously) *my own self* and she answers me through my own consciousness (because I am saying all this to myself);

And whereas, finally, under such circumstances I must assume simultaneously the roles of plaintiff and defendant, accused and judge. . . .

Therefore, in my incontrovertible capacity as plaintiff and defendant, judge and accused, I condemn this nature, which has so brazenly and unceremoniously inflicted this suffering, to annihilation along with me. . . . Since I am unable to destroy nature, I am destroying only myself, solely out of the weariness of enduring a tyranny in which there is no guilty party. (23:147–48/1:655–56)

With the wording of his sentence, Dostoevsky seems to respond to his anonymous correspondent, the suicide N. N., who had written: "I am going to mother nature." The nature of suicide contemplated by N. N. in "The Sentence" is different: rather than a return to the mother's womb, it is an act of matricide.

On the whole, in "The Sentence," Dostoevsky seems to have adjusted reality: having ignored the confession of nonbelief sent to him by a real suicide, Dostoevsky wrote one himself, patterned on his own work of fiction—the confession of Ippolit in *The Idiot*.[20]

In emphasizing N. N.'s solipsism, Dostoevsky exposed the structural principles organizing the new model of the world and of man. The removal of God (the external point of reference) disrupted the relationship between the individual and the world (between the part and the whole). The result was confusion between "I" and the other or "I" and the world. Images of pregnancy, which played an important role in the *Diary,* exemplify this fusion of the part and whole. The situation of N. N. in "The Sentence" is analogous to that of Kornilova (discussed in the same issue of the *Diary*). The pregnant woman (as Dostoevsky stressed) was tried and sentenced together with her unborn child (23:140). In "The Sentence," the mother (nature) is condemned together with her son, who, although not unwanted—as are the children in the foundling hospital—is unwilling to live.

Explicit as it was, "The Sentence" bewildered Dostoevsky's readers: "As soon as my article appeared I was overwhelmed by inquiries—by letter and in person—about what I meant in my 'Sentence.' 'What are you trying to say here?' people ask; 'Aren't you justifying suicide?'" (24:45/1:731). The form—"the confession of a suicide, his last words written . . . before he put the gun to his head" (24:44/1:729)—obscured the intended authorial message. Some readers even felt that

Dostoevsky's essay might tempt potential suicides to translate the writer's words into action and carry out the "sentence" by committing suicide. They argued that the article should have been followed by "a clear and simple explanation from the author of his intent in writing it, and even that a clear moral should be added" (24:44/1:729). In the December issue Dostoevsky offered a clarification to "each and every reader" (section "Unsubstantiated Assertions [*Goloslovnye utverzh-deniia*]"): "My article 'The Sentence' concerns the fundamental and the loftiest idea of the human existence: the necessity and the inevitability of the conviction that the human soul is immortal. Underlying this confession of a man who is going to die 'by logical suicide' is the necessity of the immediate conclusion, here and now, that without faith in one's soul and its immortality, human existence is unnatural, unthinkable, and unbearable" (24:46/1:733).

Given the initial premise, claims Dostoevsky, suicide is a logical conclusion. The mistake is in the premise itself—in abandoning the idea of the soul and its immortality. Socialists offered men a substitute: "Those who deprived humanity of its faith in its own immortality want to replace that faith, in the sense of the highest purpose of existence, by 'love for humanity'" (24:49/1:736). Abandoning logical reasoning, Dostoevsky maintains, "without substantiation," that love for humanity is *utterly impossible without faith in the immortality of the human soul to go along with it*"[21]—

love for humanity *in general, as an idea,* is one of the most difficult ideas for the human mind to comprehend. Precisely as an idea. Feeling alone can justify it. But such a feeling is possible only with the conviction of the immortality of the human soul to accompany it. (Again, an unsubstantiated assertion.)

The result, clearly, is that when the idea of immortality is lost, suicide becomes an absolute and inescapable necessity for any person who has developed even slightly above the animal level. On the other hand, immortality, promising eternal life, binds people all the more firmly to earth. . . . Without the conviction of his immortality, the links between the person and the earth are broken; they grow more fragile, they decay, and the loss of a higher meaning in life (experienced at least in the form of unconscious anguish) surely brings suicide in its wake. (24:49/1:736)

The writer built his model with the help of the same categories as his opponents, the positivists. In both models, suicide was the inevitable result of the disintegration of the whole. But while for positivists the individual was viable as long as he was embedded in the social body, for Dostoevsky it was the connection to God, established through the human soul, that kept the individual alive.

In the next section, "Something About Our Youth" (Koe-chto o molodezhi, December 1876), Dostoevsky addressed those readers who sent him accounts of suicides: "I receive many letters setting forth the facts of suicide and asking me what I think about these suicides and how I explain them (24:50)."[22] He adopted the commonly accepted language, calling suicide an epidemic illness. It is a disease, however, of the soul, not the body: "these suicides killed themselves from one and the same spiritual illness [*ot dukhovnoi bolezni*]: from the absence of any higher ideal of existence in the souls of these people" (24:50/1:737). (A standard phrase connoting mental illness, *"dushevnaia bolezn'"* is replaced with *"dukhovnaia bolezn',"* "spiritual illness.") Common phraseology highlights the difference: for Dostoevsky, neither the individual man nor society is the body.

What Dostoevsky did not mention was that he also received letters from readers who challenged his interpretations and his emphasis on the soul's immortality, and did so on the basis of personal experience. One reader, S. Iaroshevsky, wrote to him on January 5, 1877:

> The suicide question has also interested me for quite some time. It began to occupy my interest when I learned of the existence of the theory that claims all suicides to be mentally ill. This seemed rather odd to me. Are all suicides really mentally ill people? . . . This question, as I have said, greatly interested me and I began to look for other reasons that cause such an anomaly in social life. Two years ago I heard, by chance, the story of the death of a certain Kievan student who killed himself only because he could not make himself perfectly honest. At least that is the sense of the note he left. Being myself in a mood closely approximating that of this unfortunate student, I decided to analyze logically and consistently such a state of mind in order to arrive at a result, to reach some kind of conclusion. This was easy for me to do, because, as I said, I was in the exactly the same mood, though in a more general sense. I did the following: I chose the form of a story in which my main character, after intense moral sufferings, in the end stands on objective soil and logically and consistently proves that he must kill himself: neither love, the feeling of duty, nor affection were able to hold him back...

Dostoevsky's reconstructions of a suicide's consciousness in "The Sentence" provided a reference point in relation to which Iaroshevsky judged his own conclusions: "Having just read your arguments about suicide and your conclusion, I must confess that, on the one hand, I am overjoyed that there is a person (and what a person!) who is also asking these preposterous questions; on the other hand, I started thinking and thinking hard. I wasn't looking in the right place for the reasons, I thought: I should have taken it a bit higher . . . Your conclusion about the immortality of the soul completely baffled me." Although he took Dostoevsky's analysis as a validation of his own deductions, Iaroshevsky differed from Dostoevsky on one point—the immortality of the soul:

> You say that the love of one's fellow man is a feeling and not an idea. In my opinion, this is an enormous mistake. Were the love of man not an idea, the liberation of the slaves (the liberation of our Russian peasants) would not yet have occurred... This is the most real, the most positive of all ideas, and it is accessible to anyone who engages in a conscious relationship with his physical surroundings... . . . Russian suicides with an education suffer from precisely this idea, and not from a lack of faith in the immortality of the soul... Isn't this idea higher than the idea of the immortality of the soul, isn't it more real, isn't it more accessible to every mortal, doesn't it alone suffice to fill the world with harmony?..

In conclusion, the reader offered the writer some advice: "Frankly, your talent would be put to a thousand times better use if you would propagandize the idea of love of one's fellow man in the way that the latest findings of science address it, rather than developing the idea of the immortality of the soul..."[23] Dostoevsky did not mention Iaroshevsky's letter in the *Diary* and there is no evidence that he responded.

Dostoevsky and the Diary of a Reader

Dostoevsky's deductions were also challenged by a believer. A would-be suicide and aspiring writer (aged twenty-two), Alexander Voevodin, wrote to him on March 16, 1878:

> I would like to talk to you about suicide. I uphold that:
> (1) Every person has a right to suicide.
> (2) In certain circumstances, every person must commit suicide.
> (3) A person may commit suicide while professing faith in God and life after death.

Why did I arrive at these convictions—it would take a long time to explain. The enclosed notebook, perhaps, will provide the answer.

In addition to what I have written about the suicide question, I wanted to present you with a short story (it's in the notebook) and ask you whether you think I should continue writing. . . .

If you would be so kind, answer me either in your *Diary of a Writer* or—I realize this may be a bold request on my part—write to me at the address . . . Answer categorically "yes" or "no": I have nothing to lose.[24]

The thick notebook that arrived with Voevodin's letter was his diary—a disorganized text which contained accounts of intimate experiences, pieces of autobiographical fiction ("Schoolboy's Notes" [Zapiski gimnazista], letters he had received (and letters he had written to himself), articles copied from newspapers (mostly, suicide reports), poems (especially those touching on the themes of despair and suicide, like Lermontov's "I skuchno i grustno" [I am sad and bored]), etc.[25] With this gesture, the reader responded in kind to the author of the *Diary of a Writer*. A very special communication took place: writer and reader exchanged diaries. Both of them were on the verge of insanity. In his second letter to Dostoevsky, Voevodin mentioned that his famous reader had reasons to consider him "somewhat insane." As Voevodin probably knew, Dostoevsky's readers—his fellow journalists—frequently intimated that they found the *Diary of a Writer* to be a product of a "sickly" mind, "bordering on insanity."[26]

In his writings Voevodin presents himself as a man irresistibly drawn to suicide. In the two letters he addressed to Dostoevsky (the second followed on April 26), he reiterated: "This is the fourth year that I have been feeling the urge to kill myself, and I have given my word to several people that I will not do it earlier than 1880; I am afraid that I will not keep my promise."[27] For Voevodin, preoccupation with suicide became a life-long project of self-examination, self-improvement and social affirmation, aimed at benefiting himself and society. (Voevodin died in 1903 at the age of forty-six; the cause of his death is not known.) The heavily edited published version of Voevodin's diary, which appeared in 1901, offered an extensive explanation:

That I will commit suicide I know for sure. This thought has long been coming to me, and I will carry it out. Or my name isn't Voevodin!

I am interested in my suicide for many reasons. I want this suicide to demonstrate many things to society; moreover, I can use the bloodletting. This—to be of use to myself and to society—I vaguely understand, but I can't make all of this entirely clear. It infuriates me; in my thinking, I hover around and nearby these two motives without ever completely grasping them and solving this problem. You'll understand that my mind is in a kind of fog, I cannot grasp and destroy myself... But the suicide will come, it will come...[28]

What remained a puzzle to the would-be suicide was the same problem that troubled scientists and social thinkers of the time: the relationship between the individual and the social in suicide. In Voevodin's experience, the individual and the social were intertwined. Preoccupied with his own impending death, he followed suicide statistics from government publications. He remarked: "Of course, these statistics do not provide absolutely accurate data and do not explain the reasons for the suicides."[29] He found newspaper reports of suicide cases more revealing and collected newspaper clippings of the most interesting cases. (Among his treasures was the last letter of Nadezhda Pisareva from *Novoe vremia,* copied, almost word for word, in his diary.)[30]

According to Voevodin, his pious father saw his son's suicidal inclinations as a product of nihilism and atheism.[31] But, much like Dostoevsky, the elder Voevodin missed the point. A member of the young generation who held progressive views, the younger Voevodin insisted that the right to suicide was compatible with belief. It was not God but life that he refused to accept: "I do not accept life as it is. I cannot tolerate many things about it, many things about it make me nauseous. Spite, indignation, and hate are suffocating me . . . I have based my *rejection* of life on countless sources around you and me: my own life, the life of my relatives and good friends, and the life that I have encountered . . . and finally on the mound of books I have read, on the works of sociology."[32] This confession of "faith" (Voevodin's word) resembled Ivan Karamazov's famous argument: it is not God but his world that I refuse to accept (14:214).[33]

Voevodin's dialogue with Dostoevsky was central to his preoccupation with suicide. Planning the details of his future suicide, he responded to Dostoevsky's disappointment with contemporary youth. The first issue of Dostoevsky's *Diary of a Writer,* in January 1876, opened with the writer's appeal to readers: "Haven't you heard about notes like this: 'Dear Papa, I am twenty-three years old and I still have accomplished nothing. I am certain that I will never amount to anything, so I have decided to end my life....'" (22:5/1:299). Furthermore, Dostoevsky lamented that present-day Russian suicides did not follow in the footsteps of Hamlet or Werther. Their last messages did not contain Hamlet's hope "of something after death" or Werther's farewell appeal to the stars of eternal heaven (Dostoevsky's "the beautiful constellation, the Great Bear"; 22:6). The details that Dostoevsky found lacking were scattered through Voevodin's diary (they are especially prominent in the published version of the diary). Contemplating suicide, he seeks inspiration in the stars of eternal heaven: "It was a dark night, not a star in the sky . . . the Great Bear constellation did not shine."[34] In a moment of suicidal temptation, at the verge of death, he asks himself in the words of Dostoevsky's Hamlet about the world beyond (*tam*) and hopes that his notes might serve as material for some writer to create a "new Hamlet on the Neva shore."[35]

Well-read, articulate, and exalted, this young man was imbued with a sense of the cultural significance of his suicidal wish and of his private writings.* He felt that he was not only Dostoevsky's reader but also a potential character. As living material, he offered his confessions to the writer and, with the insolence of Ippolit from *The Idiot*, demanded an immediate, decisive answer to his existential dilemma. In his second letter to Dostoevsky, Voevodin described his previous attempt at such a communication: in 1876, at the age of nineteen, he had sent his fiction, and expressed his intention to commit suicide, to a prominent member of the press, A. S. Suvorin. The journalist had commented: "it is just such schoolchildren who shoot themselves"; nevertheless, he refused to see the young man.[36]

Dostoevsky promptly responded to Voevodin's letter. He stated that he was profoundly confused by this communication:

> in your letter there were quite a few things that I did not understand. You write: "answer categorically: yes or no" and then you add: "I have nothing to lose." But what is the question I am supposed to answer? The points you make about suicide? I don't think, however, that you expect to receive an answer from me in a letter. It's not at all possible to write letters on these subjects, especially when I do not know you personally and do not know your thoughts. On the basis of your notebook, it is very difficult to get any idea of who you are. . . . Moreover, although I have read more than half of your notebook, it is so

---

*Introducing the publication of his diary in 1901, Voevodin mused: "the autobiography of the most insignificant person . . . may be entertaining, and how so! . . . So what if it's incoherent, awkward, and absurd. . . . Anyone, I believe, can be the writer of an autobiography" (Galitsky, *Na beregakh Nevy,* pp. 5–6 and 8).

disorderly and written so intimately (that is, written for you alone), that I must admit that it was a great labor to read and provided me with few explanations.

Finally, does your question "yes or no" have to do with your "Schoolboy's Notes"? (April 24, 1878; 30/1:26)

Dostoevsky was not only perplexed by the "disorderly" and much too "intimate" character of his reader's diary, but also found it difficult to separate Voevodin's concern with matters of life and death from his concern with the value of the literature he produced in the course of his life struggle. What was it that the reader demanded from the writer: "yes or no" to the question "to be or not to be," or "yes or no" to the question of whether the diary of a suicide was of publishable quality? Confused by the disorganized writings of his troubled correspondent, Dostoevsky invited him for a personal interview. According to Voevodin, the meeting took place, but we do not know what passed between them.[37] In maintaining this laborious communication with a disturbed youth, Dostoevsky was probably pursuing the goal that motivated the whole enterprise of the *Diary of a Writer*—he was trying to establish intimate contact with his object ("reality") and his reader.

Daughter of an Emigré

In the October 1876 issue (following his analysis of the Kornilova case), Dostoevsky discussed two suicides, both involving women ("Two Suicides [Dva samoubiistva]"). One of them, the young daughter of "a much-too-famous Russian émigré," killed herself without "material, visible, external reasons" (23:145/1:652). (Dostoevsky did not know, or chose to ignore, the newspaper report stating that the young girl's suicide was provoked by unrequited love.) She died in Florence, by inhaling chloroform. Another young woman, a Petersburg seamstress Maria Borisova, killed herself "because she was absolutely unable to find enough work to make a living" (23:146/1:653). She threw herself out of a window, "and fell to the ground *holding an icon in her hands*":

This icon in the hands is a strange and unprecedented feature in suicides! This, now, is a meek and a humble suicide. Here, apparently, there was no grumbling or reproach: it was simply a matter of being unable to live any longer—"God did not wish it"—and so she died having said her prayers. . . . This meek soul who destroyed herself torments one's mind despite oneself. It was this latter death that reminded me of the suicide of the émigré's daughter I had heard about last summer. But how different these two creatures are—just as if they had come from two different planets! And how different the two deaths are! (23:146/1:653)[38]

The icon (of the Mother of God) indicated that the woman was not an atheist—in the very act of suicide, the victim affirmed her faith.

"The daughter of a famous émigré," whom Dostoevsky did not identify by name, left the following note, reproduced in the *Diary* in the original French and Russian translation:

Je m'en vais entreprendre un long voyage. Si cela ne réussit pas qu'on se rassemble pour fêter ma résurrection avec du Cliquot. *Si cela réussit*, je prie qu'on ne me laisse enterrer que tout à fait morte, puisqu'il est très désagréable de se réveiller dans un cercueil sous terre. *Ce n'est pas chic!* [sic]

Which, translated, is: I am setting off on a long journey. If the suicide should not succeed, then let everyone gather to celebrate my resurrection from the dead with glasses of Cliquot. *If I do succeed,* I ask only that you not bury me until you have determined that I am completely dead, because it is most unpleasant to awaken in a coffin underground. *That would not be chic at all!* (23:145/1:652)[39]

The girl was seventeen-year-old Liza Herzen, the illegitimate daughter of Alexander Herzen, born of his affair with N. A. Tuchkova-Ogareva, the wife of his best friend and collaborator Nikolai Ogarev. For Dostoevsky, she was the epitome of "an accidental child of an accidental family," or society's miscarried child. Born and raised outside of Russia, in the "accidental" family of an atheist and socialist, she had no connections to faith and to the native soil. Konstantin Pobedonostsev, from whose letter Dostoevsky learned about the case,[40] described life in the family: "The daughter and the mother hated each other and bickered from sunrise to sunset. Since childhood, of course, the daughter was brought up in an atmosphere of complete materialism and nonbelief."[41] Dostoevsky clearly took these circumstances as a clue to this case: Liza Herzen was the victim of atheism, a disease contracted at birth. Nonetheless, there was a significant difference between Herzen and his daughter—a historical, generational difference. Herzen's socialist and atheist convictions were a matter of ardent belief and replaced the Christian faith of his early years. The next generation, brought up in atheism, was altogether deprived of spirituality. In his plans for the *Diary,* Dostoevsky elaborated: "She certainly never possessed, and never could, the convictions of her late father and his aspiring faith in these convictions; otherwise she wouldn't have killed herself. . . . On the other hand, there is no doubt that she grew up without ever questioning God's existence but fully convinced of materialism; perhaps even questions of the spiritual origin of the soul and the immortality of the spirit did not agitate her soul or mind during her whole life. . . . What for her father was life—or the source of life, thought, and consciousness—for the daughter turned into death" (23:324–25).

From her suicide note, Liza Herzen appeared to be a person for whom resurrection was nothing but a metaphor, life after death was waking up in a coffin (the result of being buried alive), and "spirit" was a bottle of champagne.[42] This is how, in the *Diary of a Writer,* Dostoevsky read the note:

> In this nasty, vulgar *chic* I think I hear a challenge—indignation, perhaps, or anger—but about what? . . . What could she be angry about? About the simplicity of the things she saw around her? About the lack of any meaningful content in life? Was she one of those very well-known judges and negators of life who are angry at the "stupidity" of man's presence on earth, at the senseless unintentionality of his apperance here, at the tyranny of brute causality with which they cannot reconcile themselves? Here we have a soul of one who has rebelled against the "linearity" of things, of one who could not tolerate this linearity, which was passed on to her from childhood in her father's house. (23:145/1:652)

In Liza Herzen, Dostoevsky found the real-life embodiment of the consciousness he portrayed through Ippolit's confession in *The Idiot.* In the *Diary,* her story is immediately followed by "The Sentence." Indeed, "The Sentence" can be seen as an elaboration of the note left by Liza Herzen, who, Dostoevsky claimed, was herself not fully conscious of her motivations (she died "in animal, so to say, and unaccountable suffering"; 23:146/1:653).

Documents about Herzen's family confirm Dostoevsky's intuition about the centrality of suicide in an "accidental family." After Herzen's death in 1870, his family led a nomadic existence in Europe. Correspondence among Liza Herzen, a family friend named Charles Letourneau, Liza's mother (N. A. Tuchkova-Ogareva), and Liza's half-siblings, Natalia and Alexander Herzen (the latter was a physiologist of a materialist bent, a friend of Carl Vogt, and the author of *The Physiology of Will*) portrays the family circle as a veritable suicide club. In her passionate and impatient letters to the object of her unrequitted love—French sociologist Charles Letourneau, the author of *La Physiologie des passions* (forty-four at the time and happily married), Liza contemplated suicide in terms offered by the classic works of Russian literature. In one of her letters she used (without reference) a prose rendition of Lermontov's "I skuchno i grustno" (the allusion probably escaped Letourneau): "I'm sad and bored and no one offers a hand during moments of indecision and despair! What's there to do on earth? Desire? Why should one eternally desire in vain? It's true, this kills time, but desire carries away our best years. Love? But whom? It isn't worth the trouble for just a minute, and to love forever is impossible."[43]* In response, the famous expert on the physiology of passion gently reproached his "baby" for her "funereal fantasies."[44] Yet he shared with her his own suicidal moods: his experience of a "strong attraction to death."[45] In a letter to Tuchkova-Ogareva (assuring the alarmed mother that he was neither tempting Liza nor being tempted by her), he described the usual condition of his own soul: "weariness, at times bordering on aversion to life."[46] In the meantime, in her correspondence with the anarchist Elisé Reclus, Liza's mother debated whether to live or not to live (she cited as reasons for suicide her difficult relationship with Liza, and her feeling that Liza was not a worthy daughter of the "great Herzen"). Reclus, speaking as one "philosopher" to another (and inviting the "good, honest Spinoza," along with Schopenhauer, to participate in their dialogue), affirmed his theoretical approval of suicide, but offered specific reasons why Madame Tuchkova-Ogareva should not kill herself. His main argument was that the public would use her suicide to create "a whole monstrous novel" directed against Herzen's family.[47] (After Liza's death, her mother did attempt suicide, but survived.)

Dostoevsky's interest in Herzen and his family predated his 1876 essay on the death of Herzen's daughter. A Russian leading the life of

---

*Cf. the first stanza of the poem:
> И скучно и грустно, и некому руку подать
> В минуту душевной невзгоды . . .
> Желанья! . . что пользы напрасно и вечно желать?
> А годы проходят—все лучшие годы!
> Любить . . . но кого же?.. на время—не стоит труда,
> А вечно любить невозможно.

Known to every Russian, these lines—written in 1840—are considered to be the classic statement of Romantic pessimism in Russian culture.

a European wanderer, tormented by his love for the country he abandoned and by his loss of faith, Herzen played an important (though not exclusive) role in the literary genealogy of the main hero of *The Adolescent,* Versilov.[48] It is quite likely that Herzen's family was on Dostoevsky's mind when he created Versilov's confused family. In his plans for the novel, Dostoevsky described the family as an unruly crowd of stepchildren (*svedennye deti*). The girl Liza, the Adolescent's half-sister, is pictured as a bright, capricious, and unbalanced adolescent, prone to outbursts of emotion, from poignant spite to loving joy (see 16:32 and 60–61). Planning Liza's death by suicide, Dostoevsky tried out different motivations. One variation connected the girl's suicide to her tormented relationship with her mother (16:9); another version—to passionate and unruly love for an older man (16:61). After Liza Herzen's suicide in December 1875, Dostoevsky's treatment of the suicide of his heroine Liza in his plans for *The Adolescent* (drafted in 1874) seemed to have been prophetic.[49] Suicide, which had remained unrealized in the novel, was realized in life. Dostoevsky's novel proved to be a working model of reality.[50]

The Artist and Reality

Throughout the *Diary of a Writer,* Dostoevsky fluctuated between "reality" as it appeared in newspaper accounts or personal experiences and "reality" as depicted in a work of art. The first of the two suicides, that of a humble seamstress, had a counterpart in the story "The Meek One" (Krotkaia),[51] subtitled "A Fantastic Story" (Fantasticheskii rasskaz), which appeared in the November 1876 issue. Dostoevsky took only one detail from the real-life case: the heroine throws herself from the window with an icon in her hands. He offered a complex motivation for the young woman's suicide—an emotional entanglement, for which poverty (a factor that motivated Maria Borisova's suicide) was only a starting point. Throughout the narrative, Dostoevsky continued to weave a web of metaphors that connected materialism and death.[52] But he devoted the most attention to the narrative form: the whole story of "the meek one" and her suicide is presented through her husband's inner monologue. In the introductory paragraphs, Dostoevsky explained: "Imagine a husband whose wife only a few hours earlier has killed herself by jumping out a window; her body now lies on the table before him. He is in a state of bewilderment and still has not managed to collect his thoughts. He paces through the apartment, trying to make sense of what has happened, to 'focus his thoughts'" (24:5/1:677). The narrative imitates this thought process. (As Dostoevsky noted in the introduction, the form was inspired by Victor Hugo's *Le Dernier jour d'un condamné*.) Thus Dostoevsky chose to focus not on the person who faced death, but on the one who was faced with the other's death and had to comprehend its meaning. As a "realist," he had no other choice. The suicide left no note; there was only the body, marked by nothing more than "a handful of blood." (The husband desperately wants to keep the body at home.) The act itself was probably the result of an impulse, a momentary whim: "The moment lasted no more than ten minutes, perhaps; the decision was made just while she was standing by the wall, her head resting against her arm, and smiling. The thought flew into her head, made her dizzy and—and she couldn't resist it" (24:34/1:716). What Dostoevsky's story communicated was that the act itself was inaccessible. Limited access to it could be gained through the interpretive efforts of another, which were presented by the artist in a seemingly raw form—as a stream of consciousness. And this, implied Dostoevsky, was as close as one could get to "reality."

"Two Suicides" started with a dialogue between the author and a fellow writer on the relationship of art to reality. The fellow writer (M. E. Saltykov-Shchedrin, a radical realist) advanced the idea of the superiority of reality over art: "whatever you write or portray, whatever you set down in a work of art, you can never match real life. It doesn't matter what you depict—it will always come out weaker than real life" (23:144/1:651).* Dostoevsky readily agreed (and, moreover, strove to establish his precedence): "I had known this ever since 1846, when I began writing, and perhaps even earlier, and this fact has struck me more than once and has caused me no small bewilderment: what is the use of art when we can see it so lacking in power? In truth, if you investigate some fact of real life—even one that at first glance is not so vivid—you'll find in it, if you have the capacity and the vision, a depth that you won't find even in Shakespeare. But here, you see, is the whole point: *whose vision and whose capacity?*" (23:144/1:651).

In his private notebook, planning the *Diary,* Dostoevsky clearly answered the last question: "But it is the poet who sees the real life, while others see nothing" (23:191). He retorted: "He (Shchedrin) forgot that reality is defined by poets" (23:190). While agreeing, in print,

---

*This statement clearly echoes Chernyshevsky's famous treatise *Aesthetic Relations of Art to Reality* (Esteticheskie otnosheniia iskusstva k deistvitel'nosti, 1853), a manifesto of materialist aesthetics.

that art was impotent, in private he insisted on the power of the artist to establish "reality."

These reflections illuminate the purpose and meaning of the *Diary of a Writer*. This text was designed to offer the reader not fiction but facts of reality, which were deeper than a work of fiction—reality as seen through the eyes of the artist. It is from this position that Dostoevsky explored the enigma of suicide in his *Diary*.

7 Portrait of a Journalist: Albert Kovner

From newspaper reporters to scientists and writers, many different individuals participated in the construction of the meaning of suicide. The question arises: Who is speaking? And does it matter who is speaking? In the case of the great writer, Dostoevsky, we know how his personality, which was in the spotlight throughout his career, informed his interpretations and legitimized them in the eyes of others. But what about the anonymous authors of articles that appeared in newspapers and journals? What about those who worked in genres that called for the effacement of the author? Throughout this study, we have had glimpses of the people behind the writings. In conclusion, I would like to present the complete story of one such anonymous journalist. It is no accident that my choice fell on the feuilletonist from *Golos,* the author of the popular weekly feature "Literary and Social Curiosities," who signed himself "—r" In this one case, the life story of a newspaper man proved accessible to a historian: due to a peculiar set of circumstances, —r received public notoriety and scholarly attention.[1]

The author of "Literary and Social Curiosities" (Literaturnye i obshchestvennye kur'ezy, 1872–73) was among those newspaper writers who considered it their duty to chart the course of the suicide epidemic. His column in *Golos* usually listed recent suicides:

Let's take, say, the last week: in the Znamenskaya Hotel, a middle-aged woman named Mrs. Pazh hanged herself; in the bathhouse at the Vyazemsky house, a young woman hanged herself in a private bathroom; several days later, the retired regional doctor Meigrov killed himself with a knife; in Tsarskoe Selo, a certain Mr. R.—who, according to the newspapers, belongs to a rather high social circle—shot his wife with a revolver (although the wound was not fatal, the unfortunate spouse was missing several teeth after the shot); in an isolated spot selected for the purpose, a retired soldier inflicted two

185

wounds to his throat . . . The list is composed of events occurring only in St. Petersburg. The number of similar events in the provinces is countless, and no one even bothers to count them.[2]

In accordance with the conventions of the feuilleton, —r colored his accounts with a tone of bitter mockery, transforming grave social issues into manifestations of the absurd. His sarcasm was frequently aimed at the explanations that the public received from his fellow members of the press, especially those who spoke for science. In one of his feuilletons, he ridiculed attempts to explain suicide within the positivistic notion of determinism, conflating in his mock explanation scientific laws and legal prescription: "On the basis of the general suicide trend, a scientist might deduce the existence of a law: all people are equal before this law and, therefore, are indispensably subject to it when it approaches with its demands! Well, what then?"

The feuilletonist rejected outright the public's desire to find order in the chaos captured by the newspaper reporter:

> Look over the mournful list of suicides and attempted suicides for the last few days—well, where do you find a system here? Tikhon Gerasimov, twenty-four years old, drowned himself; the kitchen maid Firsova hanged herself; a midwife jumped off a bridge, and of course she is not at fault for being saved from drowning; Belov wounded himself in the chest; a student wanted to shoot himself on the street in broad daylight, but again, through no fault of his own, remains alive; Vedernikov, a petit bourgeois [*meshchanin*], shot himself in a cabana just as a prostitute accompanying him went into the water; a clerk about forty years of age jumped off the Nikolaevskii Bridge into the Neva River and was saved despite his original intention. Where can one find a system in this chaos of suicides?[3]

This mockery of science could be read as a direct response to the social interpretation of suicide statistics that had appeared in *Golos* several months earlier, in the same issue as —r's feuilleton. The (anonymous) author of the chronicle of current events classified and tabulated the "rich statistical data that can be derived from the diary of events," arranging it by sex, age, occupation, social class, and means of suicide. Having noted a preference for drowning and hanging in the Petersburg population, he drew a significant social conclusion, claiming a correlation between the means of suicide and the social class: "The number of suicides by drowning this year considerably exceeded the number by hanging, while in the previous years the opposite was the case. The reason why simple methods of suicide (by rope and water) are more often selected will be better understood if we relate the following fact: 70 percent of the Petersburg residents who commit suicide come from the lower classes and only 30 percent from the upper classes."[4]

Reflecting on recent cases reported in newspaper chronicles, —r ridiculed the scientific explanations of his colleague: "The kitchen maid lost five rubles of her pay and decided that she no longer had any reason to live; the midwife was probably led to suicide by a more significant reason than that. However, the kitchen maid hanged herself, and the midwife threw herself into the water."[5] Early in 1873, another journalist, Dostoevsky, while gathering material for the newspaper *Grazhdanin,* reflected on the same event in his notebook: "What is there for a man to desire [*chego emu zhelat'*]? What does one live for? The kitchen maid lost five rubles. What a meaningless and silly joke [*kakaia pustaia i glupaia shutka*]!"[6] The writer read the newspaper report on the kitchen maid's suicide as a metaphysical poem on the meaninglessness of life (Dostoevsky's phrasing echoes the concluding line of Lermontov's "I skuchno i grustno" [I am sad and bored]). The feuilletonist expressed the same idea literally: both life and death appeared to —r as a joke—a "curiosity."

The author of "Literary and Social Curiosities" also reviewed suicides that occurred within literature, paying particular attention to Dostoevsky. What he found lacking in the novel *The Possessed* was that which science offered too much of—explanations of madness and suicide:

> Mr. Dostoevsky takes actual, living people and turns them into idiots and maniacs and has them rant and rage deliriously. He does not explain the causes that influence their inexperienced heads or push them to madness and death; instead, he only mocks his characters, making them slaughter and hang one another without any basis for doing so. The principal "curiosity" of the novel is that almost all of Dostoevsky's characters go out of their minds, or act like plain idiots, or kill each other, or, finally, shoot or hang themselves. . . . All the same, it seems that Mr. Dostoevsky has been laboring just for me, so that I could include yet one more curiosity in my "literary curiosities"...[7]

In the long run, the feuilletonist questioned not only the validity of scientific or literary interpretations of suicide, but the very reality of the events, suggesting that the suicide epidemic was created by the media itself—by extensive coverage of the events that had been previously hidden from public view: "the thoughtful police used to conceal these 'horrors,' but now the press reports them on a daily basis to the reader. . . . Formerly, if a person killed himself, it was the business of no one but the police, and now? You need only unfold the newspaper—a dazzling sight: a person has drowned himself, another killed himself with a knife, and yet another hanged himself. Most likely suicide was an even more frequent phenomenon in the past than it is now, but people spoke about it less, because they didn't know, so the issue of suicide has become so very fashionable without any legitimate reason."[8]

On the whole, the feuilletonist moved in a circle: from reiterating the lists of suicides that appeared in the same newspaper to rejecting existing interpretations to maintaining that the whole issue was only a product of the journalist's pen.

The feuilletonist's anonymity ended when, in May 1875, he was arrested and tried for embezzlement. His name was Albert Kovner.[9] The circumstances of the case were widely reported and discussed in the press, giving an obscure journalist scandalous notoriety. Addressing the jury during the trial, the prosecutor lamented: "on newspaper and journal pages, this man instructed us on the norms of social morality and then, with this criminal act, proceeded to trample upon these very norms. Poor, poor printed word!"[10] So, who was speaking about crime and suicide in the daily newspapers?

Who, However, Is This "I"?

From prison, on the eve of his deportation to Siberia (on January 26, 1877), Kovner addressed Dostoevsky:

Dear Fyodor Mikhailovich,
   The strange idea of writing this letter occurred to me. Despite the fact that you receive letters from all corners of Russia—and among them undoubtedly rather ridiculous and odd ones—you never could count on letters from me.
   Who, however, is this "I"?
   First of all, I am a Jew—and you are not overly fond of Jews (I will speak about this later, however). Second, I was one of the journalists whom you despise, who often vehemently and maliciously criticized you (that is, your literary works). (If I am not mistaken, in one article during your tenure as the editor of *Grazhdanin,* you spoke of

me—without mentioning my literary pseudonym, however—in remarkably accurate terms as a person who did all in his power to try
to engage you in a personal polemic and challenge you to a battle,
but you silently ignored all my outbursts and refused to satisfy my
ambition.)*

Third, and finally, I am a criminal and write you these lines from
prison.

Since you have long been following all the more or less prominent
events in public life, and particularly the criminal trials, I think you
have guessed that I am Kovner, the one who wrote feuilletons in *Golos* in the column "Literary and Social Curiosities," who was later
employed by the Petersburg Accounting and Lending Bank, who, on
April 28, 1875, stole 168,000 rubles by forgery from the Moscow
Merchant Bank, disappeared, was detained in Kiev with all the money, sent to Moscow, tried, and sentenced to four years of penal servitude.[11]

---

*Attacks on Dostoevsky can be found in —r's feuilletons on January 18 and 25 and
March 1, 1873. Dostoevsky responded in "Dve zametki redaktora" in *Grazhdanin*
on July 2, 1873:

> we will answer only the question that has been asked of us several times: Why
> do we seldom or even never answer the criticisms, charges, and abuses that are
> constantly leveled against us? . . .
>
> Why don't we answer? First of all, and the main reason: Is there an answer for
> every clown?
>
> Undoubtedly there are people who are not clowns. There are intelligent peo-
> ple, and sometimes astute people, and there are also people who are educated
> in literature, which is a rare thing nowadays and something to be valued. But it
> is absolutely impossible to answer some of them, even though on occasion one
> wants to—it is impossible because in the final analysis you do not know what they
> want. You do not understand why they act against their consciences that way, why
> they contradict themselves so much, what their goal is, what they are after, what
> their history is, what the future holds for them? . . .

> But there are also people whom it is in no way possible to answer. . . . There
> is an entire mob-like literary brotherhood that some time ago inherited several
> liberal ideas from their ancesors, but naively stripped them bare, depriving them
> of development and all sense. . . . They certainly do not know what to make of
> the facts concerning the increase of suicides or the terrible state of drunkenness
> today. He will not be so bold as to risk writing about these things with aversion
> and dread, for it might come out sounding illiberal, and at this point he resorts
> to mockery, to be on the safe side. . . . Must one really answer these people and
> stoop to their level by engaging in a polemic with them? Stepping on an ant hill
> only brings trouble! Moreover, for them, apparently, it is pleasant to get into a
> squabble—many things have made me aware of this. And how they tried to pick
> a quarrel! (21:156–57)

(On this exchange, see Grossman, *Ispoved'*, p. 66, and Dostoevskii 21:466.)

It was Kovner's status as a criminal that justified his appeal to Dostoevsky the author of *Crime and Punishment*. But it was Dostoevsky's status as the publisher of *The Diary of a Writer* that invited the personal communication from Kovner the reader: "What exactly is the intent of my letter? As a profound psychologist, you will believe me when I say that I cannot myself explain the intent, and perhaps I don't have any intent. What inspired me to write you was your publication *Diary of a Writer,* which I have been reading with the utmost attention, and each installment of which greatly inspires me to praise and to censure you at one and the same time, to refute the paradoxes that appear to me, and to marvel at the genius of your analysis."[12] In his last letter to Dostoevsky, on January 21, 1878, Kovner lamented: "By suspending publication of *The Diary of a Writer,* you ceased being public property to whom everyone has the right to address his letters, doubts, sorrows, and even personal interests. Now you are a private person not to be probed by the public."[13] (Kovner also wrote to another literary authority, the journalist A. S. Suvorin, who did not respond.)

As a reader, Kovner highly praised Dostoevsky's later novels. He delighted in the writer's depiction of his "sickly" characters and in his analysis of their motivations. His letter continued:

> I must confess to you that although I used to mock and scoff at you in all sincerity, I have read your writings with more pleasure than I do all other Russian writers. . . . I regard *The Idiot* as your chef d'oeuvre. I have read *The Possessed* many times, and I went into raptures over *The Adolescent.* And in your recent writings I love those sickly creatures, the life and actions of which you have drawn with such inimitable mastery and, one could say, genius. At a time when others have been finding your recent works boring, I, on the other hand, literally cannot tear myself away from the pages of your books. Almost each section I read several times and am startled by the lively analysis of all the actions of your characters.[14]

Ironically, these "others" who did not appreciate Dostoevsky's recent novels included —r, the author of "Literary and Social Curiosities."

Kovner addressed Dostoevsky not only as his reader and critic but also as his character. By way of introduction, he identified himself—emphatically and totally—with the protagonist of "The Sentence," the atheist suicide from *The Diary of a Writer:* "With regard to my *profession de foi,* I *completely* share *all* the thoughts uttered by the suicide N (in your *Diary* for October), and *all* the conclusions arising therefrom; for this reason, I will not elaborate on this."[15]

In conclusion, Kovner offered Dostoevsky an excerpt from his own private diary,[16] his reflections on writers' attitudes toward their characters and toward living people:

> You know, while I was recently reading the eleventh installment of the *Diary*, that is, "The Meek One" [*Krotkaia*], and I was thinking of writing to you, several thoughts occurred to me, which I have written in my own "diary" and which I cite here word for word. Judge for yourself whether I am right or not.
>
>   This is what is written in my "diary":
> "I am certain that the greatest psychological novelists, who create the most truthful character types of vice and base instincts, analyze all their actions and spiritual strivings, find in them the spark of God, sympathize with them, believe in and desire their conversion, and elevate them to the level of the "Prodigal Son" in the Gospel, these same great writers, however, upon meeting a real-life criminal under lock and key in a prison, would turn away from him if he began to ask them for help, advice, and consolation, even though he isn't at all the type of inveterate criminal that these writers so often depict in their literary works. They will look upon him with astonishment and be nonplussed. "What could my moral purity possibly have in common with this genuine dirt who has been disgraced by the court, prison, exile, and public opinion?" This may be explained, in part: while creating artistically negative types . . . our writers look at them as their own masterpieces, as one's own dear child. And the writers love them, that is, love themselves in their ability to faithfully capture a character type from life and form it artistically. . . . But what business of theirs is a living being, a stranger who has sullied himself with crime, even if he is yearning for God's world, seeking salvation, and holding out his hands to them?"[17]

Here Kovner was trying to manipulate the writer into advancing to a real-life person the same understanding and forgiveness that he extended to a character in his novels. The reader, who eagerly identified himself with the character, claimed his right to the writer's attention, demanding recognition and judgement as well as intervention in his fate. In this and other letters, Kovner appealed to Dostoevsky for practical assistance, begging him to arrange for the publication of his manuscripts and to supply him with letters of recommendation (facilitating his settling in Siberian exile), as well as money.[18] The reader took upon himself the role of the writer's "prodigal son."

Kovner's claim to the status of Dostoevsky's character rested on more than his eagerness to see himself in the protagonist of "The Sentence"—it also lay in the nature of his crime. But before speaking of his crime, he found it necessary to reveal his background.

The Jewish Pisarev

First of all, I am a Jew—and you are not overly fond of Jews.

This is how, writing to the Russian writer, Kovner described his background: "I was born [in 1842] into a large, destitute Jewish family in Vilnius, in which—I mean in the family—people cursed each other over a piece of bread. I received an exclusively Talmudic education, and, according to Jewish custom, I wandered until seventeen years of age from one small Jewish town to another, living at the expense of others." In his other writings Kovner described Jewish theological education in more detail. Wandering from seminary (*yeshiva*) to seminary, in search of religious wisdom as well as scarce bread (given in charity), a student lived an ascetic life, in which "the material played no role." This tradition, Kovner maintained, went back to early Christian times—a suggestion rich in symbolic implications.[19]

Talmudic studies involved learning the intricate art of Biblical exegesis. This is how Kovner described the hermeneutical process:

> the preacher would usually start with a biblical text and crowd it with a multitude of questions, then he would turn to another text apparently having no relation to the first, and he would pepper this one as well with various questions to prove that it possessed neither logic nor sound reason. After doing this, he would dwell on a third text, in which he would find an array of contradictions, misunderstandings, and so forth. Then suddenly, citing some saying from the Talmud, he would pronounce some pointed syllogism, and after a little intellectual maneuvering, you would see that all the texts seem to agree with each other, all the contradictions disappeared, all the questions were clarified, and the explanations of the preacher made the dictums of the Bible and the Talmud shine brighter than the sun.[20]

The interrogation of the original text led to negation of its meaning. From this negation, and from the juxtaposition of the text with other, seemingly unrelated, texts, in the end meaning emerged.

Further on in his letter, Kovner related how he entered Russian society:

> At seventeen, I was married off to a girl much older than I. At eighteen, I ran away from my wife and went to Kiev, where I began studying Russian, foreign languages, and elementary subjects starting with the ABCs. I possessed an unwavering intention to enter university. This was at the beginning of the 1860s, when Russian literature and young people were enjoying the heyday of progress. Having soon mastered Russian thanks to my not inconsiderable talents, I got carried away, as other people had, with Dobroliubov, Chernyshevsky, Sovremennik, Buckle, Mills, Moleschott, and the other leading figures of authority reigning then. I grew to hate classical education and therefore did not enter university. Having a sound knowledge of the Hebrew language and Talmudic literature, I conceived the idea of becoming the reformer of my unfortunate people. I wrote several books in which, on the basis of European science, I proved the absurdity of Jewish superstitions—but Jews burned my books, and cursed me. Then I fell into the arms of Russian literature. . . . In 1871, I arrived at St. Petersburg. Here I began working for *Delo, Biblioteka, Vsemirnyi trud, Peterburgskie vedomosti,* and then I became a full-time writer for *Golos.* After taking my leave of Kraevsky [the editor of *Golos*] . . . I was employed by the Accounting Bank.[21]

Addressing Dostoevsky, Kovner presented himself as a convert: an orthodox Jew well versed in Biblical exegesis who, as a Russian literary critic, became an ardent proponent of the "new word"—an atheistic, positivist, or "nihilist" doctrine.

A "traitor to the Jewish people," as he was known among Jewish intellectuals, Kovner abhorred anti-semitism. He bitterly reproached Dostoevsky for his "hatred of the Jew," revealed in almost every issue of the *Diary*: "Can you really not bring yourself to recognize the basic law of any social life, which holds that *all* citizens of a given state, without exception, must enjoy *all* the rights and advantages occasioned by it, if they uphold all the obligations necessary for the existence of that state?"[22] For Kovner, unlike Dostoevsky, there was neither Russian nor Jew.

A Russian critic who inspired Kovner was Dmitrii Pisarev.[23] He followed Pisarev in his militant posture, caustic and arrogant style, and, most importantly, in promoting the cult of man based on the materialistic physiology of Moleschott, Vogt, and Büchner, the ethics of rational egoism (with its roots in Chernyshevsky's versions of English utilitarianism), and the rejection of any higher authority. Kovner's ideal was not only Pisarev but also Pisarev's Bazarov: "He does not recognize any regulating authority, any moral law, or any principle—neither above nor outside or inside himself. A lofty goal does not drive him forward, he has no lofty thought in his head, and despite all this, he possesses enormous power."[24] Addressing another Jewish critic of Russian literature, who was known as "the Jewish Belinsky," Kovner described himself as "the Jewish Pisarev." Many of his contemporaries agreed; others compared him to Chernyshevsky.[25] The Jewish Belinsky's real name was A. I. Paperna.[26] In the end, the critic's identity was mediated by a chain of images in which real-life figures stood side by side with their literary creations. A bridge between the Jewish *shtetl* and the Russian culture was built by merging life and literature.

The Jewish Raskolnikov

Third, and finally, I am a criminal and write you these lines
from prison.

In his letter to Dostoevsky, Kovner gave the following account of his crime:

I began working at the Accounting Bank. . . .* And I was infected by a new line of work antithetical to my education, habits, and convictions. While observing the operations of the bank over two years, I became convinced that all banks are founded on deception and fraudulent practices. I saw how people make millions and became tempted, deciding to steal a sum comparable to 3 percent of one year's *net profit* by the shareholders of the richest bank in Russia. This 3 percent amounted to 168,000 rubles.

This was the first (and last) blot on my conscience and it destroyed me. My love for an honest girl from an honest family played the major role in the crime I committed. Being passionate by nature, enjoying good health, and distinguished by an ugly appearance, I had not known the love of a good woman. In Petersburg, a pure and nice girl fell in love with me selflessly, deeply, and passionately (yes, passionately). She loved me, of course, not for my appearance, but for my spiritual qualities, for my little mind, for my heartfelt kindness,

---

*Kovner's status as a writer helped to make this possible: a Jewish writer, G. I. Bogrov, introduced Kovner to the Bank's Jewish Director, A. Zak, who held men of letters in high esteem (see Tsinberg, "A. Kovner," p. 152, and Grossman, *Ispoved'*, p.73). Kovner's position was that of "Russian correspondent."

for my willingness to render anyone a good turn, and so forth. She was very poor, she had only a mother (her father had died long ago) and three sisters. I wanted to marry her, but I did not have a *reliable* source of income because I worked in the bank without a written contract, and the director could dismiss me at a moment's notice. Moreover, I had debts. . . .

After all this, isn't it natural that I infringed upon the above-mentioned 3 percent? With this 3 percent, I would have provided for my elderly parents, my large, indigent family, the small children from my first marriage, my beloved and loving young woman, her family, and a host of the "insulted and injured," without causing anyone *substantial* harm by doing so. These are the real motives of my crime.

I am not trying to vindicate myself, but I boldly declare even before you that I do not and did not feel any pangs of conscience after committing this crime.[27]

Addressed to the author of *Crime and Punishment,* this account clearly drew an analogy between Kovner's crime and Raskolnikov's. Kovner's motivations echoed those that impressed Dostoevsky's hero: "On the one hand, you have a stupid, meaningless, worthless, wicked, sick old crone. . . . On the other hand, you have fresh, young forces that are being wasted for lack of support, and that by the thousands and that's everywhere! . . . Kill her and take her money, so that afterwards with its help you can devote yourself to the service of all mankind and the common cause. . . . At the cost of one life, thousands of lives are saved from decay and decomposition. One death for hundreds of lives—it's simple arithmetic" (6:54).[28] What Kovner did was to take *literally* the metaphor "that's arithmetic." The carefully calculated scheme of embezzling money from a lending bank replaced the murder and robbery of a pawnbroker.[29] (He definitely thought that such an act was morally justified: in his feuilletons he attacked the new, capitalistic financial institutions, which "perform the operation of 'unloading the pockets' of the trusting public so flawlessly and so carefully, that you can't sue them in any court.")[30]

Kovner's legal deposition also contained details that suggested a parallel with *Crime and Punishment.* As he told Dostoevsky, his love for a woman and desire to save her played a major role in his crime. The woman was the sickly daughter of Kovner's poverty-stricken landlady, a widow by the name of Kangisser. By an uncanny coincidence, the young woman's name was Sofia. For Kovner, two images from *Crime and Punishment* converged in Sofia Kangisser: Raskolnikov's fiancée, the sickly daughter of his landlady, and Sofia Marmeladova. This is how he presented the situation to the judge and jury:

In Petersburg I rented a room from a certain family, the impover-
ished Kangisser family. . . . The family was composed of the mother (a poor widow), the eldest daughter—there she is (pointing to his
wife)—two younger daughters, and a son who was employed in a
glove shop. When I found out they were Jews, I wanted to move, but
because they were so poor and honest and I was providing them with
some income, I stayed with them out of a feeling of pity. . . . Their
poverty was dreadful. They lived without any means . . . (The defendant Kangisser is crying.)* I did all in my power to try to help
them the best I could. Sofia Kangisser didn't know how to read or
write yet, and asked me to teach her. In her gratitude she became
attached to me—until that time she did not have any acquaintances.
In short, she fell in love with me . . . She was sick, ailing constantly from a catarrh in the lungs, and had to get fresh air, but this was
not possible in the apartment. She did not recover, even though I
brought her various medicines ... In short, she lived by my labor.[31]

The labor that supported the "eternal Sonia" was the source of intense anxiety and humiliation. The bank director A. Zak regarded
Kovner's appointment as an act of charity. The arrangement was informal and Kovner was paid only a token salary; his request for a
salary increase was denied. It was under these circumstances that
Kovner conceived and executed his embezzlement scheme. Taking off
with the money, he addressed a letter to the bank director; it opened
with the dramatic "I am avenged! [ia otomshchen]" and continued:
"Now I will tell you the motive that led me to commit this act. You are
guilty of this, and no one else! In my soul, I am an honest person. I
never committed anything remotely resembling a crime. Having de-
meaned myself to ask you for a position, I thought that you would understand the difference between an ordinary hired hand, who
understands nothing beyond his desk, and a person like me, who has
ascended to the pinnacle of European education. But you didn't pay
any attention to this, and I became your most vindictive personal enemy. . . . I decided to avenge myself on you, and did it!"[32]

It appears that Kovner's crime was motivated not only by the urge
to save the other Sofia, but also by his belief in Raskolnikov's division
of men into two categories: the "ordinary" and the "extraordinary."
The Jewish Pisarev clearly regarded himself as belonging to the latter category, while his antagonist, the bank director, was endowed
with the qualities of the old pawnbroker from *Crime and Punishment*.
He wrote to Zak: "You will now be a laughing-stock, and I rejoice when

*Remark in the protocol.

196

I see that an atrocious egoist like you—a heartless, conceited, uneducated, half-crazed Jew cut off from his own people and all humanity—has been shamed and cast down from his imaginary pedestal; this is a great victory for the many people who truly think." At the conclusion of his letter, Kovner divulged his plan: an escape to America and a new life, and in case of failure—suicide. He signed it: "Despisingly yours [*preziraiushchii vas*], A. Kovner."[33]

The plan failed. With the money, Kovner started on a journey south, hoping to leave the country. He was accompanied by Sofia, who knew nothing of his crime. They were married en route, not legally, but in accordance with an ancient Jewish rite. The couple was arrested in Kiev, about two weeks after their disappearance. Kovner knew what should be done: he promptly confessed to embezzlement, and insisted on his wife's innocence; having then distracted the attention of policemen, he pulled out a revolver and, aiming at his forehead, fired three shots. Only one bullet hit his head, inflicting a superficial wound. The newspaper *Golos* described its former correspondent's attempt in minute detail.[34] Kovner was in despair: "What a nuisance! Three shots, and not one to the mark; I will not live, I cannot live!"[35]

But he did live to stand trial, and Sofia was tried as his accomplice. Kovner's trial, in Moscow, in September 1875, was covered by all the major newspapers and attracted considerable public attention. Literature was heavily implicated in this event. The defendant's speech—an account of his whole life, which ended dramatically with Kovner bursting into tears, was a tour de force of literary skill. (His narrative served as the basis for subsequent historical accounts.)[36] But what seems to have impressed the public most was the straightforward deposition by Kovner's landlady, the widow Kanigisser: "Kovner lived with us for three-and-a-half years and behaved like a real gentleman. My daughter was frequently sick, and he helped her. . . . He helped us a lot, he helped us very much. He took pity on me and on my small girls. 'Momma,' said one of them, 'this is our papa arisen from the grave.' I said, 'No, he is not our family, but he is a very good person, he pities us.'"[37]

The state prosecutor, N. V. Murav'ev, future Minister of Justice, tried to make Kovner's case less glamorous. (In his view, the perpetrator's literary reputation and the attention of the press made it dangerously appealing.)[38] And yet he too took a literary approach: like Porfiry Petrovich, the investigator in Dostoevsky's novel, he read the defendant's published work: he requested that *Golos* send him a complete set of Kovner's feuilletons and familiarized himself with his literary productions.[39] Although he did not name Kovner's literary source, Murav'ev apparently saw his crime as an application of Raskolnikov's philosophy to real life. Attempting to separate life from literature, he pointed to the base self-interest behind the "sublime" motive: "Before us unfolds the picture of a mercenary crime, an infringement of another person's property, an unceremonious appropriation. But they say that all this was done on account of high-minded and honest moral objectives."[40] He then described Kovner's utilitarian calculations of social benefits, in terms suggested by radical social theories:

> Kovner's argument is highly original and unique. The Moscow Merchant Bank, he reasons, receives an enormous interest rate on its fixed capital. The sum of 168,000 rubles means nothing to the bank. The bank, moreover, does not make favorable or productive use of its capital. He, Kovner, would manage it much better, and in his hands capital in the amount of 168,000 rubles would receive the most efficient use. Why, then, doesn't he—this is his logic—take this capital out of the bank and use it as he sees fit? And he considers himself in the right for doing so, as you have seen, and is unashamed of his methods. And why be ashamed? By stealing 168,000 rubles from a bank, after all, he has satisfied the economic precept of the most efficient productivity of capital by putting it to better use; in sum, he has performed a socially useful act. . . . When one contemplates the results and conclusions to which this kind of reasoning could have led, had it been further developed, one realizes the terrifying prospects.[41]

The prosecutor did not need to say any more—to those who had read *Crime and Punishment,* it was clear where Kovner's train of thought could have led. The prosecutor could only hope that the jury would reestablish the primacy of reality over literature, and rule that Raskolnikov's ideal of the extraordinary man was merely an illusion: "Perhaps he considers himself some kind of extraordinary person who has not been properly acknowledged by others and for whom the forgery itself is an act of heroism, the swindling scheme is lit with halo of valor and honor? . . . Let your stern verdict show that there are no such people in this world or, better yet, that society repudiates them and juries prosecute them."[42] For their foreman, the jury elected Professor N. S. Tikhonravov of Moscow University (the future rector), a reputable literary scholar.

The jury found Kovner guilty, but recommended mercy; Sofia

Kangisser was acquitted. Shortly after the trial she died of consumption. Kovner did not serve all of his four-year sentence: in 1877, he was transported to Siberia, where, like Dostoevsky, he lived as an exile in Tobolsk, Tomsk, and Omsk, enjoying the protection of Murav'ev, to whom, remembering the prosecutor's appraisal of his literary talent, he had appealed for help.[43]

A Dialogue on the Immortality of the Soul

With regard to my *profession de foi*, I *completely* share *all* the thoughts uttered by the suicide N (in your *Diary* for October), and *all* of the conclusions arising therefrom.

Before Dostoevsky had time to respond to Kovner's letter of January 26, 1877, Kovner received in his prison cell the December 1876 issue of the *Diary,* in which he found a response to some of the concerns expressed in his letter. Having read Dostoevsky's account of his visit to Kornilova (incarcerated for the attempted murder of her stepdaughter), Kovner no longer felt that the writer was incapable of dealing with a real-life criminal. The December issue of the *Diary* also contained Dostoevsky's clarification of his position on the atheist suicide N. N. from "The Sentence," with whom Kovner so eagerly and fully identified. Kovner was taken aback by the forceful rebuttal of N. N.'s views that Dostoevsky offered in his follow-up essay, "Unsubstantiated Assertions"—a passionate defense of the necessity of faith in God and immortality.[44] In response, Kovner wrote Dostoevsky another letter (January 28, 1877), in which he spoke as if on behalf of N. N.: "[your 'Unsubstantiated Assertions'] cannot convince anyone who has been "touched" by the ideas of N. Of course, this subject is so profound and so vast that hundreds of volumes would not suffice to resolve this universal problem about which so many minds and geniuses have written *pro and contra* over many centuries. . . . Be that as it may, I cannot restrain myself from making a few comments, which, however, I hope will allow you to understand the grounds on which the opponents of your 'Assertions' stand. And I would like for you to refute them soundly."[45] Hoping to involve Dostoevsky in a dialogue on the immortality of the soul, he offered counterarguments. Writing from a scientific perspective, Kovner challenged the epistemological premises of the idea of God:

I fully acknowledge the existence of some kind of "power" (you may call it God, if you wish) that created the universe, that creates *eter-*

nally, and that cannot *ever* be comprehended by the human mind. But I cannot tolerate the idea that this "power" takes an interest in the life and actions of its creations and *consciously* controls them, no matter who or what these creations are.

I won't tolerate this idea because I *know* that the entire world—I mean by this the earth—is only one atom in the solar system, that the sun is one atom among the heavenly bodies, that the Milky Way comprises myriad suns (science tells us all this, and no thinking person can negate science), that the universe is infinite, that the earth has been around for a relatively small number of years, that geology testifies to the infinite number of cataclysms on the earth, that Darwin's hypothesis about the origin of the species and of man is highly probable (in any case, it explains the origin of life on the earth more reasonably than all the religious and philosophical treatises taken together), that protozoa, of which there are millions in every droplet of water, little flies, fish, birds—in short, all living things— have the same right to existence as man, that up to this day there have been millions, hundreds of millions, of people who do not substantially differ from animals, that our civilization spans merely some four thousand years, that there is an infinite number of religions of every imaginable kind (and one contradicts the other), that the idea of monotheism arose relatively recently, and so on, and so forth.[46]

Kovner also challenged the role of Christianity in Russia: "You will say that man has the spark of God, and therefore he is higher than all others. But how many people are like this? Literally a drop in the sea. You must admit that of the eighty million Russian people chosen by you, and in whom you claim to have found the cure . . . indeed, sixty million live like animals, having no reasonable understanding of God, Christ, the soul, or the soul's immortality..."[47]

In his conclusion, the former Talmudic scholar, admirer of Moses Mendelssohn, (whom he called "a Jewish Socrates"),[48] and a follower of Pisarev, demanded from the Russian writer positive proof of the existence of God and of the immortality of the soul: "In any event, I should like to see the day that your 'assertions' are no longer 'unsubstantiated.' Oh, how I would like to be convinced of these 'assertions'! Believe me, I will be the first to bow down before your 'truths,' when it is proven that they are 'truths.' But I am afraid that you will never be able to prove these things."[49]

Dostoevsky responded to Kovner in a long, somewhat irate, letter (dated February 14, 1877): "I haven't answered you for such a long time because I am a sick person and have been writing my monthly publication with extreme difficulty. Moreover, every month I must answer dozens of letters. Finally, I have a family and other affairs and obligations. There is absolutely no time left for living and it's impossible to enter into a long correspondence. Especially with you." He continued on a different note: "I have seldom read anything more intelligent than your first letter to me (your second letter is another matter). I completely believe everything you say about yourself. About the crime you once committed, you expressed yourself so lucidly and intelligibly (for me at least) that not knowing your case *in detail,* I now at least look upon it as you yourself regard it." But on one point Dostoevsky challenged Kovner: "N. B. I did not take to heart the two lines in your letter in which you say that you do not feel any remorse for the act you perpetrated at the bank. There is something higher than conclusions based on reason and any and all circumstances—and every person is obliged to subject himself to it." Apparently, in the writer's eyes, the unrepentant Kovner was not a true Raskolnikov: as a Jew, Kovner was not subject to "something higher."

Dostoevsky then turned to another topic raised by Kovner—the Russian Jews: "How can they not fall into discord, at least *in part,* with the root of the nation, with the Russian tribe? . . . look how you hate Russians, and precisely and *only because you are a Jew,* albeit an intellectual. In your second letter, there are several lines about the moral and religious consciousness of sixty million Russian people. These are words of appalling hate, yes, hate, because as intelligent a person as you must himself understand that on this point (that is, regarding the question of the degree to which the common Russian man is a Christian), you are a highly incompetent judge."*

Finally, the writer firmly refused to enter into a dialogue on the immortality of the soul with the young Jewish atheist: "I will not even speak to you about your ideas on God and immortality. I swear to you, I already knew these objections (i.e., all of yours) before I had reached twenty years of age."[50] Scientific atheism was something from his own, much repented, past.

---

*In his response on February 22, 1877, Kovner corrected Dostoevsky: "I am utterly bewildered, where did you get it into your head that I 'hate' Russians and moreover '*precisely because I am a Jew*'? Oh God, how you are mistaken! Could you really have derived such a conviction from my letter?" He affirmed his right to make judgements about Christianity and the Russian people: "why do you suppose that, as a Jew, I 'am an exceedingly incompetent judge . . . of the degree to which the common Russian man is a Christian'? I know the history of Christianity very well, I am so bold to think that I understand its spirit, and I know Russian history, and I am also rather closely acquainted with the life of the Russian people. Why, then, am I incompetent?" (GBL, f. 93.II.5.82).

Dostoevsky did, however, engage in a polemic with Kovner on another matter: the Jewish question. The March 1877 issue of the *Diary* featured an extensive discussion of the issue, presented as a dialogue with the reader, whose letters the writer quoted at length; at Kovner's request, Dostoevsky's correspondent remained unnamed. (Sections on "The Jewish Question [Evreiskii vopros]," "Status in statu," "Pro i contra," etc.)

Several years later, Dostoevsky returned to the theme of the immortality of the soul in *The Brothers Karamazov,* in terms that were very close to those he used in his exchange with Kovner. His presentation of the theme culminated in Part Five (containing the legend of the Grand Inquisitor), entitled "Pro and contra," and took the form of a dialogue, initiated by Ivan Karamazov, who contemplated returning his "ticket" to his Creator.[51]

The Dialogue Continues in the Twentieth Century

A quarter of a century later, in 1901, Kovner addressed a letter to Vasily Rozanov, an author who strongly identified with Dostoevsky in matters of ideology and in his personal life. (Rozanov, whose first important book was a study of the legend of the Grand Inquisitor, went so far as to marry Dostoevsky's former mistress, Apollinaria Suslova, which resulted in a personal tragedy.) "I want to talk to you as I once talked with Dostoevsky," declared Kovner.[52] The main topic was the Jewish question: shaken by the pogroms, he argued in favor of granting full civil rights to Russian Jews. (At the end of 1897, Kovner addressed a memorandum on the Jewish question to the minister of justice, Murav'ev, the man who had prosecuted him for embezzlement.) Once again, he bitterly reproached a Russian writer for his anti-Semitism, but, before long, the letter turned to the "eternal question"—the immortality of the soul. (By this time, Kovner was at least nominally a Christian, but, as he explained, he accepted baptism purely pro forma, so that he could marry a Russian woman.)[53]

In a long letter of December 31, 1902, Kovner offered his second confession of nonbelief, a small treatise entitled "Why I Do Not Believe" (Pochemu ia ne veriu), which developed and refined the theses advanced in his 1877 letters to Dostoevsky. Rozanov published this document (calling it "Credo [Ispovedanie]") in his book *By the Church Walls* (Okolo tserkovnykh sten, 1906), complete with his commentaries, placed in footnotes. The result was a peculiar dialogue on the immortality of the soul.

In twenty-five years, Kovner had not found positive proof for the "Unsubstantiated Assertions," about which he had appealed to Dostoevsky in 1877. In 1902, his argument, colored by the legend of the Grand Inquisitor,[54] focused on the issue of the moral necessity of Christian faith. Although he did not rule out the possibility of immortality, Kovner emptied this factor of all moral consequences: "The possible continuation of man's existence in any form after death does not bind man in any way." (This notion echoes Spinoza's thesis that belief in an afterlife, the possibility of which he did not deny, is not a necessary condition for ethical conduct.) He stated that the regulation of human conduct was the task of physiology and sociology, not religion. Moreover, "with regard to the positive good" (such as the establishment of hospitals, orphanages, and asylums for the sick), he claimed that "when one builds a society on the basis of reason and justice, it can be realized without religious impulses."[55] Rozanov responded to this assertion in a footnote:

> I profoundly agree with all this. It was Dostoevsky who calumniated man: "without God and faith in the afterlife, people will devour one another." First of all, people burned each other while professing "faith" in both "God" and the "afterlife." This is hardly better than devouring; and they have been burning for centuries, not on a personal basis but on behalf of the Church. But let us leave these old stories. It is completely self-evident to me and known from immediate facts that those who do not at all believe in God or the afterlife are also the people who lead astoundingly clean lives full of love and kindness toward others; they are simple, not oversensitive, and unenvious people. It is awfully sad for me to have to say this, because it is a dreadful ordeal for any faith: the especially pure, good, righteous, kind people I have met are almost exclusively atheists. This is so dreadful and incomprehensible that I am confused, but I have to say what I have seen.[56]

In 1906, Rozanov, a believer and self-professed heir of Dostoevsky, sided with the atheist Kovner, a Jew, criminal, and attempted suicide. Although in the twentieth century the individual might have retained personal faith, the issue of immortality of the soul lost, if not its poignancy, then its ability to organize human thought about morality, crime, and suicide. It seemed that Dostoevsky had been wrong: life went on after the death of God.

Conclusion

In conclusion, let us return to the question "who is speaking?"—the Nietzschean question dramatized by Foucault.[57] And does it matter who is speaking? Is it not man but the word itself that speaks?

In this study, I have followed the process of interpretation from newspaper chronicles and feuilletons to social commentary and scientific analysis, from suicide notes to literary representations and writers' reflections. My survey took me from *dnevnik proisshestvii,* a daily record of events in society's life compiled by an anonymous newspaper reporter, to the diary of a great writer, Dostoevsky, published as a journal for public use. I then tried to reveal the identity of an anonymous newspaper writer. The result is intriguing: the personality of this journalist—the one journalist whose life proved accessible to a historian one hundred years later—turns out to have been Dostoevsky's creation. Indeed, in Kovner we see a man who rejected his roots to recreate himself in the image and likeness of a Dostoevskian character, an atheist, criminal, and suicide; a man who owes his very presence in historical records to his connection with the great writer.* The "great writer" assumes a special role in the cultural construction of human experience in nineteenth-century Russia. Taking his material from the newspapers, Dostoevsky strove to transcend the fleeting reality of the everyday, as well as the purportedly positive truth of science, and to reveal the true reality in his artistic visions. Thus the writer aspired to bring the process which had its starting point in the newspaper to conclusion. But the fact that an anonymous newspaperman was a product of Dostoevsky's fiction locks the hermeneutical process into a circle, effacing human agency.

And yet, as Hans-Georg Gadamer put it, "the genuine reality of the hermeneutical process seems to me to encompass the self-understanding of the interpreter as well as what is interpreted."[58] This seems to be true for the writer. As I have tried to show, Dostoevsky found the words that made the act of suicide comprehensible to him

---

*Kovner's correspondence with Dostoevsky and the fact that their dialogue reflects on the Jewish question assured Kovner a long life. In 1927, a revised edition of Leonid Grossman's book on Kovner was published in German (in Munich) under the title *Die Beichte eines Juden in Briefen an Dostojewski.* Freud, who at the time was working on his essay "Dostoevsky and Parricide," had a copy of this book in his library. James L. Rice, in his *Freud's Russia: National Identity in the Evolution of Psychoanalysis* (New Brunswick, 1993), speculates about Freud's reactions, making him "a presumed reader of the exchange between Kovner and Dostoevsky" (pp. 211–17).

at the intersection of his personal experience and the experience of his age. Such was the metaphor of *le dernier jour d'un condamné,* applied to an individual, to a nation, and to all mankind living in the age of atheism. But what about the journalist, Kovner—a precarious by-product of the great writer's fiction, did he bring his personal experience to his interpretations? It seems that he did. The experience of conversion, from the Old Testament of traditional Judaic wisdom to the "new word" of Russian atheism, formed Kovner's vision. The old pattern was transferred to new material: the intricate syllogisms of the Talmudic biblical exegesis are recognizable in the rhetorical devices Kovner used to interpret current events in his feuilletons. First, the feuilletonist interrogated the event, reducing it to an absurdity, then, abruptly shifted to another, seemingly unrelated event. But, in keeping with the nihilist spirit of the age, in the end, rather than the total clarity achieved by an explicator of the Bible, Kovner's interpretations achieved nothing. The journalist even suggested that the suicide epidemic was an illusion created by media coverage. Method prevailed over truth.

In my study, the interpreter—the journalist Kovner and the scientist Virchow[59]—appears as a living metaphor, embodying the convergence of different trends of his age. Moreover, Kovner's life experience exemplifies the notion of metaphor itself, that is, the idea of transference, or conversion—from the old to the new, from the religious presumption of meaning to the nihilistic acceptance of meaninglessness. His life also exemplifies the contingencies of the critic's cultural role: the mutual dependence of literature and real life, interpreter and interpretation, man and method. The man is a living metaphor—and because he is a living, bodily being, that is, a unity, however precarious, the man connects the themes and trends that torment his age. In this limited, sense, it does make a difference who is speaking—at least throughout the nineteenth century, when man, his body, the locus of his actions, his divergence from God, and his finitude became central questions.

Notes

Introduction

1. Suicide also defies definition. Reviewing sociological investigations of suicide, the contemporary sociologist Jack D. Douglas remarked that "concrete suicidal phenomena do not have clear and sufficient cultural definition in the Western world" (*The Social Meanings of Suicide* [Princeton, 1967], p. 81). For psychologists' attempts, see Edwin S. Shneidman, *Definition of Suicide* (New York, 1985), and the recent review article by Jean-Pierre Soubrier, "Definitions of Suicide," in *Suicidology: Essays in Honor of Edwin S. Shneidman,* ed. Antoon A. Leenaars (Northvale, N.J., 1993). For a linguistic perspective, see D. Daube, "The Linguistics of Suicide," *Philosophy and Public Affairs* 1 (1972).

2. Suicidology took shape as a field in the mid-1950s in the United States. For the state of the field, see three landmark collections: Edwin S. Shneidman and Norman L. Farberow, eds., *Clues to Suicide* (New York, 1957); Edwin S. Shneidman, Norman L. Farberow, and Robert E. Litman, eds., *The Psychology of Suicide* (New York, 1970); and Leenaars, *Suicidology.*

3. Sigmund Freud, "Contributions to a Discussion on Suicide," *Standard Edition of the Complete Psychological Works,* 24 vols. (London, 1953–65), 11:232.

4. Gregory Zilboorg, "Differential Diagnostic Types of Suicide," *Archives of Neurology and Psychiatry* 35 (1936): 271. A major authority on suicide, Zilboorg helped to organize in 1936 the Committee for the Study of Suicide, the first such organization in the world. Born and educated in Russia, Zilboorg was a distinguished psychiatrist, political activist (a cabinet member in the government of Alexander Kerensky), and, in the United States, translator of Russian literature into English.

5. Edwin S. Shneidman, "Suicide," *Encyclopaedia Britannica,* 1973, 21:383.

6. Antoon Leenaars, *Suicide Notes: Predictive Clues and Patterns* (New York, 1988), p. 17.

7. Emblematic of the status of suicide in the popular imagination is the following poem, which belongs to a productive genre. The text depicts the body of a young suicide and, next to it, a bewildered witness; the theme is the enigma, its symbol—"a black hole":

On the side of his head the accursed black hole!..
He has departed with the fateful mystery
of his last days and last thoughts...
And what has ruined this young life
Has remained an enigma.

Чернеет на виске проклятое пятно!...
Унес с собой он тайну роковую
Последних дум своих, последних дней...
И что сгубило жизнь его младую,—
Осталося загадкой для людей.

(Ivan Iakunin, "Samoubiitsa," *Delo,* 1875, no. 11).

8. The view of suicide as a meaningful action constructed by the individual on the basis of shared (cultural) patterns of meaning was advanced by the sociologist Jack D. Douglas in *Social Meanings of Suicide.* Douglas challenged the "positivist" Durkheimian approaches to the investigation of suicide, which rely on statistical data and strive to investigate the behavior itself and its causes; he advocated focusing on how the act is understood by suicides themselves, by their contemporaries, and by society at large. In recent years, historians have started investigating the meanings assigned by culture. Michael MacDonald and Terence R. Murphy produced a comprehensive, sophisticated historical study of this type, *Sleepless Souls: Suicide in Early Modern England* (Oxford, 1990), which uses English material for the period from 1500 to 1800. Olive Anderson's *Suicide in Victorian and Edwardian England* (Oxford, 1987), although it focuses on the behavior itself, includes a historical interpretation of statistical data. Barbara T. Gates's *Victorian Suicide: Mad Crimes and Sad Histories* (Princeton, 1988) is a study of Victorian attitudes toward suicide written by a literary scholar. To this day, there has been no history of suicide in Russia.

9. Paul Ricoeur wrote of "the process by which human action becomes social action when written down in the archives of history. Thanks to this sedimentation in social time, human deeds become 'institutions,' in the sense that their meaning no longer coincides with the logical intentions of the actors" ("The Model of the Text: Meaningful Action Considered as a Text" [1971], in *Interpretive Social Science,* ed. Paul Rabinow and William M. Sullivan [Berkeley, 1979], p. 85).

10. A study of suicide in early twentieth-century Russia is being prepared by Susan Morrissey. For some preliminary results, see chapter 5, "The Epidemic of Student Suicides: Debates on the Death of the *Studenchestvo,*" in her Ph.D. dissertation, "More 'Stories about the New People': Student Radicalism, Higher Education, and Social Identity in Russia, 1899–1921" (University of California, Berkeley, 1993), and "Suicide and Civilization in Late Imperial Russia," *Jahrbücher für Geschichte Osteuropas* 43 (1995).

11. Wolfgang Iser, *The Act of Reading* (Baltimore, 1978), p. 6. Iser offers an explanation of the special status of fiction: "In contrast to previous eras, when there had been a more or less stable hierarchy of thought systems, the nineteenth century was lacking in any such stability, owing to the increasing complexity and number of such systems and the resultant clashes between

them. These conflicting systems, ranging from theological to scientific, continually encroached on one another's claim to validity, and the importance of fiction as a counterbalance grew in proportion to the deficiencies arising from such conflicts."

12. Histories of suicide—constructed as surveys of celebrated cases and popular views—date back to the eighteenth century. One of the earliest (perhaps the first) is *Istoria critica e filosofica del suicidio* by Tito Benvenuto Buonafede, published (under the name Agatopisto Cromaziano) in Lucca, Italy, in 1761 (reissued in 1784 and 1788). A historical survey of this type was included in many studies of suicide written in the eighteenth, nineteenth, and early twentieth centuries (such studies usually combined history with views from medicine, philosophy, and ethics and with statistical information). Among the most popular ones are: A. Brierre de Boismont, *Du suicide et de la folie suicide* (Paris, 1856); P. E. Lisle, *Du suicide, statistique, médicine, histoire, et législation* (Paris, 1856); A. Legoyt, *Le suicide ancien et moderne: Etude historique, philosophique, morale et statistique* (Paris, 1881); A. Bayet, *Le suicide et la morale* (Paris, 1922); H. W. Heller, *Über den Selbstmord in Deutschland* (Frankfurt, 1787); C. F. Stäudlin, *Geschichte der Vorstellungen und Lehren vom Selbstmorde* (Göttingen, 1824); Charles Moore, *A Full Inquiry into the Subject of Suicide*, 2 vols. (London, 1790); Forbes Winslow, *The Anatomy of Suicide* (London, 1840); W. W. Westcott, *Suicide: Its History, Literature, Jurisprudence, Causation, and Prevention* (London, 1885); and James O'Dea, *Suicide: Study on Its Philosophy, Causes, and Prevention* (New York, 1882). The last (and most comprehensive) historical survey of this type is Henry Romilly Fedden's *Suicide: A Social and Historical Study* (London, 1938). For an extensive annotated bibliography, see Hans Rost, *Bibliographie des Selbstmords* (Augsburg, 1927). The historical survey in A. Alvarez's invaluable study, *The Savage God: A Study of Suicide* (New York, 1971), deserves a special mention.

13. Plato's words (*Phaedo*), quote from *The Collected Dialogues of Plato,* ed. Edith Hamilton and Huntington Cairns (Princeton, 1961), p. 64.

14. In my interpretation of the death of Socrates, I rely on the work of Nicole Loraux, "Therefore, Socrates Is Immortal," in *Fragments for a History of the Human Body,* Part Two, ed. Michel Feher with Ramona Naddaff and Nadia Tazi (New York, 1989), pp. 13–45.

15. Loraux, "Therefore," p. 36.

16. Anthropologists have suggested that Athenian execution through self-administered poison was seen at the time as a "controlled suicide." See Louis Gernet, *The Anthropology of Ancient Greece* (Baltimore, 1981), p. 255, and R. Hackforth, *Plato's Phaedo* (Cambridge, 1955), p. 36, n. 4.

17. Friedrich Nietzsche, *Twilight of the Idols,* p. 44 (the closing argument of "The Problem of Socrates").

18. See, for example, a recent exchange of views: R. G. Frey, "Did Socrates Commit Suicide?" *Philosophy* 53 (1978): 106–8; Michael Smith, "Did Socrates Kill Himself Intentionally?" *Philosophy* 55 (1980): 253–54; Harry Lesser, "Suicide and Self-murder," *Philosophy* 55 (1980): 255–57; William E. Tolhurst, "Suicide, Self-Sacrifice, and Coercion," *Southern Journal of Philosophy* 21 (1983): 109–21; and Suzanne Stern-Gillet, "The Rhetoric of Suicide,"

Philosophy and Rhetoric 20, 3 (1987): 160–70. See also Jerome Eckstein's strong argument for suicide in his *The Deathday of Socrates* (Frenchtown, N.J., 1981), p. 48.

19. The case was mentioned by Cicero. See W. E. H. Lecky, *History of European Morals,* 2 vols. (New York, 1955), 1: 212, n. 2; and Henry Romilly Fedden, *Suicide: A Social and Historical Study* (New York, 1972), p. 72. R. Hackforth cites several authors who draw an inference that reading the dialogue inspired Cleombrotus's suicide (*Plato's Phaedo,* pp. 30–31).

20. Augustine, as cited by Donne, end of Part 3 of *Biathanatos.*

21. This is, of course, a liberal reworking of the well-known Aristotelian syllogism,

All men are mortal.
Socrates is a man.
Therefore, Socrates is mortal.

I took a cue from Loraux ("Therefore," p. 20).

22. In dealing with the early Christian interpretations of the deaths of Christ and Socrates, I used Arthur J. Droge and James D. Tabor, *A Noble Death: Suicide and Martyrdom among Christians and Jews in Antiquity* (San Francisco, 1992). Justin (in the *Second Apology*), John Chrysostom (in *Homilies on 1 Corinthians*) and Clement of Alexandria (who made frequent allusions to *Phaedo* in his writings) were among those who drew the analogy explicitly, claiming Christ (and the Christian martyrs) as enacting a superior variant of the death of Socrates (see Droge and Tabor, pp. 139 and 142). So did Augustine, in a different context, condemning voluntary martyrdom and suicide. Origen was among those who discussed Christ's (and Christian) death in Platonic terms, as a separation of the soul from the body. In the words of a contemporary philosopher, Suzanne Stern-Gillet, "the claims that Socrates as well as Jesus committed suicide are either to stand or to fall together" ("Rhetoric of Suicide," p. 97).

23. The formulation belongs to Droge and Tabor, *Noble Death,* p. 129.

24. Pointed out by Droge and Tabor (ibid., pp. 150–51), in reference to Origen's "exegesis of the cup." In his exegesis of the Gethsemane prayer (*Exhortation to Martyrdom,* p. 28), Origen merged Jesus's almost too human appeal "Father, if it be possible, let this cup pass from me" (Matt. 26:39) with the Old Testament promise "I will take the cup of salvation and call on the name of the Lord" (Ps. 116:13). Here and further translations from the Bible are taken from the King James version.

25. Tertullian, Origen, St. Jerome, the Venerable Bede, and John Donne were among those who discussed Christ's death as a suicide. (Their arguments convinced some modern historians of suicide; see Fedden, *Suicide,* pp. 10 and 143; Alvarez, *Savage God,* p. 67.) In John Donne's words, Christ "chose" to sacrifice his life and shed his blood (*Biathanatos,* Part 1, Distinction 3, Section 2). A counterargument was offered by De Quincey (in his essay "On Suicide"): the charge rests on a false definition of suicide (not explicitly stated, but assumed), a definition that draws no distinction between self-homicide and self-murder.

26. In modern times, this view was upheld by authors as diverse as Buon-afede (a monk of the Celestino Order), in his *Istoria critica* and Madame de Stäel in her *Réflexions sur le suicide* (1813).

27. Gadamer comments that the view that Socrates' proof of immortality in *Phaedo* is a counterpart to the Christian overcoming of death is a mis-conception, which "nonetheless has been a productive misconception for the eighteenth century in particular" (Hans-Georg Gadamer, *Dialogue and Dialectic: Eight Hermeneutical Studies on Plato* [New Haven, 1980], p. 21).

28. On the Socrates and Christ of the philosophes, see John McManners, *Death and the Enlightenment* (Oxford, 1981), p. 416.

29. From *Hegel's Lectures on the Philosophy of Religion,* ed. Peter C. Hodgson (Berkeley, 1988), p. 463, n. 196.

30. See Gregory Zilboorg, "Suicide among Civilized and Primitive Races," *American Journal of Psychiatry* 92, 6 (1936): 1368; Shneidman and Far-berow, "The Logic of Suicide," in Shneidman and Farberow, eds., *Clues to Suicide,* pp. 31–41; Charles W. Wahl, "Suicide as a Magical Act," in *Clues to Suicide,* pp. 22–30; Herbert Hendin, "Psychodymanics of Suicide," in his *Suicide and Scandinavia* (New York, 1964), p. 22. Hendin reports a contempo-rary case (from Scandinavia) of identification with Christ in a female suicide; Forbes Winslow reports a case of suicide by self-crucifixion in 1803 in Italy (*Anatomy of Suicide,* pp. 329–33).

31. Douglas, *The Social Meanings of Suicide,* pp. 284–300.

32. See Helen Silving, "Suicide and Law," in Shneidman and Farberow, eds., *Clues to Suicide,* pp. 80–82.

33. The idea goes back to Freud's "Mourning and Melancholia" (1915). It also appears in Karl Menninger's *Man against Himself* (New York, 1938). For a contemporary view, see John T. Maltsberger, "Confusion of the Body, the Self, and the Others in Suicidal States," in Leenaars, ed., *Suicidology.*

34. See Shneidman and Farberow, "The Logic of Suicide," pp. 31–41.

35. Plato, *Phaedo,* p. 45.

36. The subject received comprehensive treatment in Ian Donaldson's *The Rapes of Lucretia: A Myth and Its Transformations* (Oxford, 1982), which traces the transformations of the story from antiquity to the Enlightenment. Donaldson showed that the image of Lucretia had Christian connotations, with some visual representations arranged to remind us of the crucified Christ (pp. 26–27). The image of Lucretia was important in the French Revolution-ary culture (see also Dorinda Outram, *The Body and the French Revolution* [New Haven, 1989], pp. 85–86).

37. Plutarch, *The Lives of the Noble Grecians and Romans,* the Dryden translation (Chicago, 1952), pp. 645–46.

38. J. M. Rist, *Stoic Philosophy* (Cambridge, 1969), p. 233.

39. For a brief survey, see Donaldson, *Rapes of Lucretia,* pp. 147–55.

40. On Addison's *Cato,* see S. E. Sprott, *The English Debate on Suicide* (La Salle, Ill., 1961), pp. 113–16, and Donaldson, *Rapes of Lucretia,* pp. 150–66. On the use of Cato in the moral debates of French Enlightenment, see Lester G. Crocker, "The Discussion of Suicide in the Eighteenth Centu-ry," *Journal of the History of Ideas* 13, 1 (January 1952). See also Roland

Bartel, "Suicide in Eighteenth-Century England: The Myth of a Reputation," *Huntington Library Quarterly* 20, 3 (1960).

41. From the author's introduction to *La Mort de Caton* by H. Panckoucke (1768); quote from McManners, *Death and the Enlightenment,* p. 415.

42. McManners, *Death and the Enlightenment,* p. 415.

43. In my discussion of the Stoic suicide and its appropriation in Revolutionary culture, I am indebted to Dorinda Outram (chapters 5 and 6 of her *The Body and the French Revolution* deal with neo-Stoicism and heroic suicide).

44. See R. Trousson, *Socrates devant Voltaire, Diderot, et Rousseau* (Paris, 1967); quote from McManners, *Death and the Enlightenment,* p. 416.

45. See Outram, *The Body and the French Revolution,* p. 94.

46. *Hegel's Lectures,* p. 463.

47. Outram, *The Body and the French Revolution,* p. 101.

48. J. Dulaure; quote from Outram, ibid., p. 78 (where the quote appeared in the original French). According to Outram, the image of Socratic death was widespread in French revolutionary culture.

49. Outram, ibid., p. 72.

50. Maurice R. Funke, *From Saint to Psychotic: The Crisis of Human Identity in the Late Eighteenth Century* (New York, 1983), pp. 174–75.

51. The idea is associated with Albrecht von Haller and P.-J. Cabanis. See L. J. Jordanova, "Naturalizing the Family: Literature and the Bio-Medical Sciences in the Late Eighteenth Century," in *Languages of Nature: Critical Essays on Science and Literature,* ed. L. J. Jordanova (New Brunswick, N.J., 1986), pp. 98–99.

52. Karl M. Figlio, "Perception and the Physiology of Mind," *History of Science* 13, pt. 3, 21 (September 1975): 186–87.

53. Johann Wolfgang von Goethe, *The Sorrows of Young Werther,* trans. Michael Hulse (London, 1989), p. 134.

54. *Goethe's Autobiography: Poetry and Truth,* trans. R. O. Moon (Washington, D.C., 1949), p. 509 (Book XIII).

55. Funke, p. 126.

56. Goethe himself participated in the perpetuation of this myth. He lamented in *Dichtung und Wahrheit* that readers thought that "one ought to change poetry into reality, and that they must imitate such a romance, and in any case blow their brains out. What thus in the beginning took place among a few, afterward happened with the great public" (*Goethe's Autobiography,* p. 519; from Book XIII, published in 1814). His belief in the power of literature was shared by his fellow Romantics. In a dedication of *Marino Faliero* addressed to Goethe, Byron wrote: "I rather suspect that, by one single work of *prose, you* yourself have excited a greater contempt for life, than all the English volumes of poesy that ever were written. Madame de Staël says, that 'Werther has occasioned more suicides than the most beautiful woman'; and I really believe that he has put more individuals out of this world than Napoleon himself,—except in the way of his profession" (*The Poetical Works of Lord Byron* [London, 1866], 6:51; quoted by Stuart Pratt Atkins, *The Testament of Werther in Poetry and Drama* [Cambridge, Mass., 1949],

p. 210). Even Doctor Esquirol, the author of the authoritative *Des maladies mentales* (1838), who considered suicide to be evidence of mental illness, took for granted Madame de Staël's assurance that *Werther* produced suicides (*Mental Maladies,* trans. E. K. Hunt [Philadelphia, 1845], p. 280).

57. Martin Swales, *Goethe, The Sorrows of Young Werther* (Cambridge, 1987), p. 94.

58. The opinion that *Werther* provoked a suicide epidemic has often been repeated by literary critics and by students of suicide. Two or three cases have usually been cited as evidence. See, for example, William Rose, *Men, Myth, and Movements in German Literature* (London, 1931), pp. 147 and 150. An annotated bibliography of literature pertaining to the "Werther fever," compiled by a believer in the suicide epidemic, appears in Hans Rost's *Bibliographie des Selbstmords,* pp. 316–26. There are, however, sober voices who point out that there is no evidence that such an epidemic occurred. In addition to Swales, see Atkins, *Testament of Werther,* pp. 210–11, and Jacques Choron, *Suicide* (New York, 1972), p. 31.

59. The first translation, *Strasti molodogo Vertera* (St. Petersburg, 1781; 2d ed., 1794) (trans. F. Galchenkov), was followed by *Strasti molodogo Vertera, soch, g. Gete* (St. Petersburg, 1796; 2d ed., 1816) (trans. I. Vinogradov, who seems to have adapted Galchenkov's translation). On Russian translations of *Werther,* see V. Zhirmunskii, "Gete v russkoi poezii," *Literaturnoe nasledstvo,* 4–6 (1932): 514–15.

60. Modern Russian distinguishes between *strasti* (indicating passion, this word is applied to the agony of Christ) and *stradaniia* (suffering), a dichotomy similar to *das Leiden–die Leiden.* Modern Russian translations of Goethe's novel use *Stradaniia molodogo Vertera* (this title first appeared in the 1829 translation by N. Rozhalin, published in Moscow). In the late eighteenth century, the semantic difference between *strasti* and *stradaniia* was not as clearcut as it was by the 1820s. Moreover, the word *strasti* could be interpreted in two ways, depending on how one viewed its origin: as a Church Slavonic word, it carried obvious Christological connotations; as a possible calque from French, it meant *"passion"* (a strong [sexual] emotion). And yet Goethe's first translator already had the word *stradaniia,* with its purely human connotations, at his disposal. Thus, another Russian translator of Goethe, O. Kozodavlev, in the introduction to his 1780 translation of the drama "Clavigo," spoke of *Stradaniia mladogo Vertera.* I am indebted to Joachim Klein for the explication of the meanings of *strasti/Leiden.*

61. His novel was published posthumously as *Rossiiskii Verter, poluspravedlivaia povest', original'noe sochinenie M.S. molodogo, chuvstvitel'nogo cheloveka, neschastnym obrazom samoizvol'no prekrativshego svoiu zhizn'* (St. Petersburg, 1801). The work was part of a large set of literary imitations of *Werther.* See V. V. Sipovskii, "Vliianie 'Vertera' na russkii roman XVIII veka," *Zhurnal Ministerstva narodnogo prosveshcheniia,* January 1906, V. Zhirmunskii, "Gete v russkoi poezii," Wolfram Eggeling and Martin Schneider, *Der russische Werther* (Munich, 1988). The best source on Sushkov is Maarten Fraanje, "Proshchal'nye pis'ma M. S. Sushkova (O probleme samoubiistva v russkoi kul'ture kontsa XVIII veka)" (*XVIII vek,* no. 19 [St.

Petersburg, 1995]); I am much indebted to Maarten Fraanje's archival findings and penetrating analysis and grateful to him for allowing me to see his article before it was published.

62. For an analysis of Sushkov's rendition of Cato's monologue, see Fraanje, "Proshchal'nye pis'ma," pp. 160–63.

63. *Rossiiskii Verter,* pp. 85–86 (these words conclude the novel).

64. Sushkov's letter to his uncle, M. V. Khrapovitskii, July 15, 1792 (archival copy). Quote from Fraanje, "Proshchal'nye pis'ma," p. 155. The importance of merging Voltairean freethinking with Sentimentalism was noted by Zhirmunskii, "Gete v russkoi poezii," p. 524.

65. Fraanje advances a different interpretation: he distinguishes between two different types of suicide in late-eighteenth-century Russia: death in imitation of Werther (the Sentimentalist death) and death in imitation of Cato (the rationalist death). The first prevailed in literature; the second in real-life behavior. Fraanje treats Sushkov's suicide as an example of the second type, downplaying its connection to Werther ("Proshchal'nye pis'ma," pp. 166–67).

66. Ivan Opochinin's last letter was published (by L. N. Trefolev) in 1883: "Predsmertnoe zaveshchanie russkogo ateista," *Istoricheskii vestnik* 11 (January 1883): 224–26. In the 1880s it sounded topical. Fraanje writes of a hand-written collection from the early nineteenth century that included Sushkov's and Opochinin's letter.

67. In my treatment of Radishchev, I rely on Iurii Lotman's analysis in "Poetika bytovogo povedeniia v russkoi kul'ture XVIII veka," *Trudy po znakovym sistemam* 8 (Tartu, 1977), published in English as "The Poetics of Everyday Behavior in Eighteenth-Century Russian Culture," in *The Semiotics of Russian Cultural History,* ed. Alexander D. Nakhimovsky and Alice Stone Nakhimovsky (Ithaca, 1985), pp. 87–94.

68. A. N. Radishchev, *Polnoe sobranie sochinenii,* 2 vols. (Moscow, 1907), 1:131; English translation from Nakhimovsky and Nakhimovsky, *Semiotics,* p. 91.

69. On Radishchev's treatise, see G. A. Gukovsky's commentaries to Radishchev, *Polnoe sobranie sochinenii,* 2:370–75.

70. This attitude is documented in Louis Maigron's *Le Romantisme et les moeurs* (Paris, 1910), a book that holds Romanticism responsible for causing a suicide "epidemic" (see chapter "Le Romantisme et le suicide"). See also Lisa Lieberman, "Romanticism and the Culture of Suicide in Nineteenth-Century France," *Comparative Studies in Society and History* 33, 3 (July 1991): 611–29, and, on nineteenth-century England, Gates, *Victorian Suicide.* Gender is an important issue in dealing with nineteenth-century suicide. See Margaret Higonnet, "Suicide: Representations of the Feminine in the Nineteenth Century," *Poetics Today* 6, 1–2 (1985): 103–18; and Howard I. Kushner, "Suicide, Gender, and the Fear of Modernity in Nineteenth-Century Medical and Social Thought," *Journal of Social History* 26, 3 (Spring 1993): 461–90.

71. Michel Foucault, *The Order of Things: The Archaeology of Human Sciences* (New York, 1970), pp. xxiii, 317, 319, and passim.

72. Michel Foucault, *The Birth of the Clinic: An Archaeology of Medical Perception* (New York, 1975), p. 197.

73. Rist, *Stoic Philosophy*, p. 233.

74. C. E. Bourdin, *Du suicide considéré comme maladie* (Batignolles, 1845), pp. 78–79. His opinion is quoted by Lisle in *Du suicide*, pp. 142–45.

Notes to Chapter 1

1. Emile Durkheim, *Suicide: A Study in Sociology*, trans. John A. Spaulding and George Simpson (New York, 1951), p. 38.

2. Esquirol, *Mental Maladies*, pp. 301 and 312.

3. Ian Hacking claims in *The Taming of Chance* (Cambridge, 1990), "He had a not very hidden agenda. [. . .] Esquirol lived during one of the great periods of imperial expansion of his profession" (p. 65). On "medicalization" of suicide in England, see Michael MacDonald, "The Medicalization of Suicide in England: Laymen, Physicians, and Cultural Change, 1500–1870," *The Milbank Quarterly* 67, suppl. 1 (1989); reprinted in *Framing Disease: Studies in Cultural History*, ed. Charles E. Rosenberg and Janet Golden (New Brunswick, N.J.), 1992.

4. Ian Hacking traces these developments. One of the first to question the identity of suicide and insanity was G. F. Etoc-Demazy in *Recherches statistiques sur le suicide, appliquées à hygiène publique et à la médecine légale* (Paris, 1844). (To whom Bourdin responded in his *Du suicide considéré comme maladie*.) Etoc-Demazy was followed by the "alienist" Francois Leuret, in *Traitement moral de la folie* (Paris, 1848), whose assertion that "suicide is not always an instance of madness" was quoted on the title page of Lisle's widely acclaimed *Du suicide;* later he deleted the word "always" (Hacking, *Taming of Chance*, pp. 70–71).

5. Esquirol, *Mental Maladies*, p. 307.

6. Ibid.

7. Winslow, *Anatomy of Suicide*, p. v.

8. Ibid., pp. 280–82.

9. Ibid., p. 282.

10. Ibid., pp. 227–28.

11. Hacking, *Taming of Chance*, p. 70, quoting G. M. Burrows, *Commentaries on the Causes, Forms, Symptoms, and Treatment, Moral and Medical, of Insanity* (London, 1828), p. 416.

12. Ivan Gvozdev, *O samoubiistve s sotsial'noi i meditsinskoi tochki zreniia* (Kazan, 1889), p. 30 (emphasis added).

13. Reviewed for the Russian reader by Doctor G. Gordon, in "Sovremennye samoubiistva," *Russkaia mysl'*, 1912, no. 5, p. 79.

14. Claude Bernard, *An Introduction to the Study of Experimental Medicine*, trans. Henry Copley Greene (New York, 1927), p. 113.

15. Ludwig Büchner, *Force and Matter*, trans. Louis Buchner (London, 1870), p. 120.

16. Ibid., pp. 113–14.

17. Ian Hacking provides a sophisticated treatment of moral statistics and

its epistemological implications in *The Taming of Chance;* see chapters 9, 13, 14, 15.

18. F. A. Lange, *The History of Materialism* [1865], 3 vols. (London, 1925), 3:194.

19. Henry Morselli, *Suicide: An Essay on Comparative Moral Statistics* (New York, 1882), p. 4.

20. D. K., "Tendentsioznoe samoubiistvo," *Russkoe bogatstvo,* 1880, no. 12, p. 43 (emphasis added).

21. On the connection between statistical regularity and the postulation of causality, see also Hacking, *Taming of Chance,* pp. 129–31.

22. L. Adolphe Quételet's *Sur l'homme et le développement de ses facultés, ou Essai de physique sociale,* 2 vols. (Paris, 1835) is considered to be the first comprehensive statement of the principles of the new discipline. The term "moral statistics" first appeared in A. M. Guerry's *La statistique morale de la France* (Paris, 1833). Quételet called his system "social physics" (he borrowed the phrase from Comte).

23. Regularity in human action was also interpreted as a reflection of the divine order of things. This argument goes back to the eighteenth-century author (whom Durkheim named as "the true founder of moral statistics") Pastor Süssmilch, in his *Die göttliche Ordnung in den Veränderungen des menschlichen Geschlechts, aus der Geburt, dem Tode und der Fortpflanzung desselben erwiesen* (1742) (see Durkheim, *Suicide,* p. 300, n. 1). A late nineteenth-century attempt to view moral statistics in a Christian context is Alexander von Oettingen's *Die Moralstatistik in ihrer Bedeutung für eine Christliche Socialethik* (1874). Quételet and Adolph Wagner, in his *Die Gesetzmässigkeit in den scheinbar willkürlichen menschlichen Handlungen vom Standpunkte der Statistik. Statistik der Selbstmorde* (Hamburg, 1864), only gradually came to the rejection of free will; Morselli, who wrote in the 1870s, appeared on the scene as a radical opponent of free will.

24. Henry Thomas Buckle, *History of Civilization in England,* 2 vols. (London, 1873), 1:19–27.

25. Morselli, *Suicide,* p. 16. Moritz Wilhelm Drobisch is the author of *Die moralische Statistik und die menschliche Willensfreiheit* (Leipzig, 1867).

26. Morselli, *Suicide,* p. 187.

27. Ibid., p. 3.

28. Ibid., pp. 6–7 and 9.

29. Ibid., p. 10.

30. In Hacking's words, Quételet "transformed the mean into a real quantity" (*Taming of Chance,* p. 107).

31. Quételet, *Sur l'homme;* quote from the 1842 English translation, *A Treatise on Man and the Development of His Faculties,* ed. Solomon Diamond (Gainesville, 1969). In the text, the first page number refers to the English translation; the second to the French original.

32. On Quételet's cultural background, see Diamond's introduction to *A Treatise on Man,* pp. vi–vii.

33. Durkheim, *Suicide,* pp. 317–18.

34. Ibid., p. 300.

35. The first page number refers to the English translation of Morselli's treatise; the second to the Italian original.

36. Ernst H. Kantorowicz, *The King's Two Bodies: A Study in Medieval Political Theology* (Princeton, 1957).

37. Ibid., p. 201.

38. Outram, *The Body and the French Revolution,* p. 66.

39. Büchner, *Force and Matter,* pp. 12–13.

40. Ibid.

41. On this issue, see Erwin H. Ackerknecht, *Rudolf Virchow* (New York, 1981), p. 71.

42. Rudolf Virchow, *Cellular Pathology,* trans. Frank Chance (Philadelphia, 1863), p. 40.

43. Ibid.

44. Rudolf Virchow, "Atoms and Individuals," in his *Disease, Life, and Man,* trans. Lelland J. Rather (Stanford, 1958), p. 130.

45. Ackerknecht, *Rudolf Virchow,* p. 45 (all terms are Virchow's). Owsei Temkin analyzes Virchow's use of social metaphors in "Metaphor of Human Biology," *Science and Civilization,* ed. Robert C. Stauffer (Madison, Wisc., 1949). Ernst Hirschfeld first noted a parallel between Virchow's biological views and his liberal political opinions in "Virchow," *Kyklos* (1929) 2:106–16.

46. Virchow, "Atoms and Individuals"; all quotes are on p. 139.

47. Ibid.

48. Ackerknecht, *Rudolf Virchow,* p. 153.

49. Paraphrasing Virchow, "Atoms and Individuals," p. 120.

50. Ackerknecht, *Rudolf Virchow,* p. 154.

51. On the image of the social organism in Romantic mythology, see A. J. L. Busst, "The Image of the Androgyne in the Nineteenth Century," in *Romantic Mythologies,* ed. Ian Fletcher (London, 1967), especially pp. 12–13, 24, 28–29.

52. This argument was made by Pitirim Sorokin, *Contemporary Sociological Theories* (New York, 1928), p. 200, and David G. Hale, "Analogy of the Body Politic," *Dictionary of the History of Ideas,* ed. P. Weiner (New York, 1973), p. 67.

53. See John Theodore Merz, *History of European Thought in the Nineteenth Century,* 4 vols. (Edinburgh, 1914), 4:518.

54. On this subject, see Judith E. Schlanger, *Les métaphores de l'organisme* (Paris, 1971), p. 168 (see also bibliography in n. 97 on p. 168); F. W. Coker, *Organismic Theories of the State* (New York, 1910); D. C. Phillips, "Organicism in the Late Nineteenth and Early Twentieth Centuries," *Journal of the History of Ideas* 31 (1970): 413–22; and Sorokin, *Contemporary Sociological Theories,* pp. 200–207.

55. "La condition *sine qua non* pour que la sociologie puisse être élevée au rang d'une science positive et que la méthode d'induction puisse lui être appliquée, c'est . . . la conception de la société humaine en sa qualité d'organisme vivant réel, composé de cellules à l'égal des organismes individuels de la nature" Paul von Lilienfeld, *La pathologie sociale* (Paris, 1896), p. xxii.

56. Paraphrasing Büchner, *Force and Matter,* p. xii.

57. Bernard, *Introduction to Experimental Medicine*, p. 60.

58. Quoted from Merz, *History of European Thought*, 2:600.

59. Maxwell, from a paper entitled "Does the Progress of Physical Science Tend to Give Any Advantage to the Opinion of Necessity (or Determinism) over That of the Contingency of Events and the Freedom of the Will?" quoted from Merz, *History of European Thought*, 2:600–601.

60. Ibid.

61. Virchow, "Atoms and Individuals," p. 127; this statement was used by Lange in his famous *History of Materialism*, 2:39.

62. Maxwell's words; quoted from Merz, *History of European Thought*, 2:602.

63. Foucault, *Birth of the Clinic*, p. 124; the comment concerns early-nineteenth-century medicine. Foucault points out that the view that post-Enlightenment medicine was connected to the *discovery* of pathological anatomy is historically false. Yet, as a myth surrounding such eighteenth- and nineteenth-century scientists as Cabanis, Bichat, Claude Bernard, and Virchow, it has a "reality" of its own. Since Foucault, anatomy as an instrument of knowledge has become a popular theme. Important insights are offered by, among others, Ludmilla Jordanova, *Sexual Visions: Images of Gender in Science and Medicine between the Eighteenth and Twentieth Centuries* (London, 1989), and Barbara Stafford, *Body Criticism: Imaging the Unseen in Enlightenment Art and Medicine* (Cambridge, Mass., 1991).

64. The metaphors are Foucault's (*Birth of the Clinic*, pp. 134 and 135).

65. Bernard, *Introduction to Experimental Medicine*, p. 104.

66. Ibid., p. 99.

67. See Ackerknecht, *Rudolf Virchow*, p. 48 (emphasis added).

68. Quoted from Rudolf Virchow, *Post-mortem Examinations with Especial Reference to Medico-Legal Practice*, trans. T. P. Smith (Philadelphia, 1896), p. 42. A Russian translation, *"Tekhnika vskrytiia trupa, s osobennym primeneniem k sudebno-meditsinskoi praktike,"* appeared in *Sbornik sochinenii po sudebnoi meditsine* (St. Petersburg, 1876).

69. Virchow, *Post-mortem*, p. 45.

70. Cf. the argument in Ackerknecht, *Rudolf Virchow*, pp. 241–42.

71. Morselli, *Il suicidio*, p. 18. The part that contained this statement was omitted from the English translation of 1882.

72. A. V. Likhachev, *Samoubiistvo v Zapadnoi Evrope i Evropeiskoi Rossii. Opyt sravnitel'no-statisticheskogo issledovaniia* (St. Petersburg, 1882), p. 6.

73. Paraphrasing Douglas, *Social Meanings of Suicide*, p. 15.

74. All English-language quotations are taken from Durkheim, *Suicide: A Study in Sociology* (New York, 1951).

75. In bilingual quotes, the first page number refers to the English translation, the second to the French original, quoted from the Emile Durkheim, *Le suicide* (Paris, 1912). *L'âme* is translated as "mind."

76. The issue of Durkheim's use of metaphors has been raised before. Henri Peyre, "Durkheim: The Man, His Time, and His Intellectual Background," in *Emile Durkheim, 1858–1917*, ed. Kurt H. Wolff (New York, 1964), notes Durkheim's frequent recourse to biological metaphors, which

he attributes to the influence of Herbert Spencer's organicism. (On this issue, see also Harry Alpert, *Emile Durkheim and His Sociology* [New York,
1939], pp. 32–33.) Dominick LaCapra comments on Durkheim's "fascination
with medical metaphors" (*Emile Durkheim: Sociologist and Philosopher*
[Ithaca, 1972], p. 7). Robert A. Nye points out that Durkheim, despite his
well-deserved reputation for separating the science of sociology from psychology and biology, "was dependent on a medical model of social analysis"
(among other medical models, he used the theory of degeneration) and used
biological metaphors (*Crime, Madness, and Politics in Modern France: The
Medical Concept of National Decline* [Princeton, 1984], pp. 145, 147). Jack
Douglas suggests that Durkheim's "power to convince has been more the result of the *rhetoric* of the work" (*Social Meanings of Suicide,* p. 22). The importance of metaphors in sociological knowledge is emphasized by Robert A.
Nisbet ("Sociology as an Art Form") and Morris R. Stein ("The Poetic
Metaphors of Sociology"), in *Sociology on Trial,* ed. Maurice Stein and Arthur
Vidich (Englewood Cliffs, N.J., 1963).

77. The explanatory power of metaphors has been acknowledged by historians, philosophers, scientists, cognitive linguists, and literary scholars. On
metaphor in science, see, for example, Max Black, *Models and Metaphors*
(Ithaca, 1962); Richard Boyd, "Metaphor and Theory Change: What Is
'Metaphor' a Metaphor For?" and Thomas S. Kuhn, "Metaphor in Science,"
in *Metaphor and Thought,* ed. Andrew Ortony, 2d ed. (Cambridge, 1993).

78. Hacking comments that in Durkheim's *Suicide* "a medical notion
(pathology) was transferred to the body politic on the back of statistics" (*Taming of Chance,* p. 64).

79. See Virchow, "Atoms and Individuals," p. 139; Bernard, *Introduction
to Experimental Medicine,* p. 60 (quoted earlier in this chapter).

80. The metaphor of circulation in application to the body social is developed by Spencer (in volume 1, part 2, of his *Principles of Sociology,*
1878–80).

81. A similar argument was made earlier by Lilienfeld, who attacked those
who, in discussing analogies between nature and society, conceive of them
only as rhetorical figures (*Gedanken über die Socialwissenschaft der Zukunft,*
5 vols. [Mitau, 1873–81], 1:26 and 28).

82. Douglas offers the following arguments: "Durkheim's philosophical realism is evident in two aspects of his theory of suicide: (1) his tendency to
draw conclusions about the nature of reality from his conceptual analysis; and
(2) his tendency to go from the general or universal to the particulars rather
than from the particulars to the general" (*Social Meanings of Suicide,* p. 22).
I would add that Durkheim's reliance on metaphors as a major instrument of
knowledge and his insistence that his metaphors of collective personality are
"things" (or "forces") sui generis, rather than mere verbal entities, also establish him as a philosophical realist. A different view is expressed by Harry
Alpert, who argues that "social realism" and "social nominalism" should not
be confused with philosophical or ontological realism/nominalism, adding
that, even within the latter, Durkheim was not a realist (*Emile Durkheim,*
pp. 146–63). He admits nevertheless that Durkheim's "phraseology is, in fact,

decidedly that of the realist" (p. 150). For a different interpretation of Durkheim's notion of "reality," see Hacking, *Taming of Chance,* especially chapter 20, "As Real as Cosmic Forces."

83. For instance, Catherine Gallagher demonstrated that the relationship between the individual and social organisms, expressed rhetorically, structured population theory. See her "The Body versus the Social Body in the Works of Thomas Malthus and Henry Mayhew," in *The Making of the Modern Body: Sexuality and Society in the Nineteenth Century,* ed. Catherine Gallagher and Thomas Laqueur (Berkeley, 1987).

84. Morselli, *Suicide,* p. 114.

Notes to Chapter 2

1. K. Lizin [K. Arkadaksky], "Samoubiistvo i tsivilizatsiia," *Delo,* 1882, no. 7:285.

2. Paraphrasing W. Bruce Lincoln, *The Great Reforms: Autocracy, Bureaucracy, and the Politics of Change in Imperial Russia* (De Kalb, Ill., 1990), p. 143.

3. From E. Likhacheva, "O samoubiistve," *Otechestvennye zapiski,* 1881, no. 7:22.

4. From the review of suicides in N. A. Demert's chronicle "Nashi obshchestvennye dela" in *Otechestvennye zapiski,* 1872, no. 7:83, and Likhacheva, "O samoubiistve," p. 31.

5. Anonymous review of A. V. Likhachev's *Samoubiistvo v Zapadnoi Evrope i Evropeiskoi Rossii* (St. Petersburg, 1882), in *Otechestvennye zapiski,* 1882, no. 9:133.

6. Büchner, *Force and Matter,* p. 226.

7. A. Klitin, *Nashe vremia i samoubiistvo* (Kiev, 1890), pp. 3–6. Klitin relied on a popular antinihilist pamphlet by P. P. Tsitovich, *Khrestomatiia novogo slova,* 3d ed. (Odessa, 1879).

8. It was Ivan Turgenev who called Bazarov, the main character of his *Fathers and Sons* (*Ottsy i deti,* 1862), "a *new* man" (in the essay "Po povodu 'Ottsov i detei'," 1869) and brought the term "nihilism" into common currency. Pisarev's main work on Bazarov is the essay "Bazarov" (1862).

9. D. I. Pisarev, "Motivy russkoi dramy," in his *Sochineniia,* 4 vols. (Moscow, 1955–56), 2:392. For a discussion of these metaphors, see Michael Holquist, "Bazarov and Sechenov: The Role of Scientific Metaphor in *Fathers and Sons,*" *Russian Literature* 16 (1984), and Irina Paperno, *Chernyshevsky and the Age of Realism: A Study in the Semiotics of Behavior* (Stanford, 1988), pp. 12–15, 17, and 272–73 (n. 27).

10. Richard Wortman, *The Crisis of Russian Populism* (Cambridge, 1967), p. 28. On the study of statistics in Russia, see also Alexander Vucinich, *Science in Russian Culture,* 2 vols. (Stanford, 1970), 2:89.

11. From "Pessimizm nashei intelligentsii" (published anonymously) in *Nedelia,* 1880, no. 42:1337–38 (among other topics, the essay discussed the prevalence of suicide). The author is I. Kablitz [I. Iuzov], whose *Osnovy narodnichestva* (1882) is a compendium of populist phraseology.

12. The metaphor of the collective organism has a Russian lineage. Two major representatives of social organicism, who were mostly known as Western authors, Paul von Lilienfeld and J. Novicow, were of Russian origin. Lilienfeld articulated the analogy between the individual and social body in his *Osnovnye nachala politicheskoi ekonomii* published in St. Petersburg in 1860 (under the penname Liliev). His *Mysli o sotsial'noi nauke budushchego* appeared in a St. Petersburg edition in 1872. The German edition of his works, widely read in the West, followed in the years 1873–81. Spencer, by whose authority this metaphor gained high currency, introduced it in his *Principles of Sociology,* published in 1878–80.

13. "Pessimizm nashei intelligentsii," p. 1338.

14. Likhacheva, "O samoubiistve," p. 23.

15. On suicide in Western European canon law, see Dublin, *Suicide,* pp. 139–40, and Fedden, *Suicide,* pp. 133–35; a useful early source is R. S. Guernsey, *Suicide: History of the Penal Laws* (New York, 1883).

16. MacDonald and Murphy, *Sleepless Souls,* p. 2.

17. Quote from N. S. Tagantsev's *O prestupleniiakh protiv zhizni po russkomu pravu,* 2d ed., 2 vols. (St. Petersburg, 1873), 2:408. (The eighteen canons of Timothy of Alexandria are found in the second volume of the Pandects, and in volume 1 of the Conciliar Records.)

18. See E. Golubinskii, *Istoriia russkoi tserkvi,* 2d ed., 2 vols. (Moscow, 1901), 1, 1:650, n. 4, and 657. There were also prescriptive documents compiled by local church hierarchs, such as the "Ustav" or "Zapoved' sviatykh otets k ispoveduiushchim synom i dshcherem" ascribed to Metropolitan Georgii (1073–1074) and the so-called "Voprashanie Kirikovo" (answers collected from the bishops of Novgorod in the early twelfth century). Rule 93 of the "Ustav" of Metropolitan Georgii prescribed: "If a man not possessed by a demon kills himself, do not chant over him, but lay down his body without burying him" (Golubinsky, 1, 2:542). According to church historians, however, this document was hardly known even to the bishops (see Golubinsky, 1, 1:437).

19. Ibid., p. 430.

20. N. Suvorov, *Uchebnik tserkovnogo prava,* 5th ed. (Moscow, 1913), p. 185.

21. It is believed that the article on denial of Christian burial was borrowed from a Roman prayer book. See Metropolitan Makarii, *Istoriia russkoi tserkvi,* 12 vols. (St. Petersburg, 1882), 11:608, n. 485. Funeral rites were also denied to those who died of intoxication. The latter category was exempted from the category of suicides in the decree of the Holy Synod of July 10, 1881 (*Tserkovnyi vestnik,* 1881, no. 41; see S. V. Bulgakov, ed., *Nastol'-naia kniga dlia sviashchenno-tserkovno-sluzhitelei* [1892], 2d ed. [Kharkov, 1900], p. 1250).

22. *Nomokanon pri Bol'shom Trebnike,* ed. A. Pavlov (Odessa, 1872), article 178.

23. "Gramota pskovskomu dukhovenstvu s resheniiami po nekotorym voprosam tserkovnoi distsipliny mitropolita Fotiia," *Russkaia istoricheskaia biblioteka* 6 (St. Petersburg, 1880), p. 379. Quoted (with omission of the last

phrase) in A. Chebyshev-Dmitriev, *O prestupnom deistvii po russkomu do-Petrovskomu pravu* (Kazan, 1862), pp. 230–31, where the date is given as 1416, and in Tagantsev, *O prestupleniiakh,* 2:407.

24. *Polnoe sobranie zakonov Rossiiskoi Imperii* (St. Petersburg, 1835), vol. 3, no. 1612. Tagantsev, *O prestupleniiakh,* 2:407–8.

25. Quote from *Russko-amerikanskii pravoslavnyi vestnik,* September 1951, p. 144. (Unfortunately, I could not find the original.) This is a rare example of Satan being mentioned as an instigator for suicide in a document written by a Russian churchman.

26. Bulgakov, *Nastol'naia kniga,* p. 1250, n. 2, quoting the proceedings of the Third All-Russian Congress of Missionaries; see also p. 1252, n. 2.

27. Ibid., p. 1249, n. 3.

28. Fedden, *Suicide,* p. 117.

29. S. V. Maksimov, *Nechistaia, nevedomaia i krestnaia sila* (St. Petersburg, 1903), pp. 17–18. Suicide sometimes appears as a means of transportation (horse, ram) used by evil forces; see D. N. Sadovnikov, *Skazki i predaniia Samarskogo kraia* (Samara, 1993), 2:23–24 (no. 77), and O. P. Semenova, "Smert' i dusha v pover'iakh i rasskazakh krest'ian . . . Riazanskoi gubernii," *Zhivaia starina,* 1898, no. 2:233.

30. D. K. Zelenin, *Ocherki russkoi mifologii. Vypusk pervyi: Umershie neestestvennoi smert'iu i rusalki* (Petrograd, 1916). The study is based on extensive data collected in different parts of rural Russia, Ukraine, and Belorussia in the second half of the nineteenth and the early twentieth centuries.

31. See, for example, the classic studies of A. Van Gennep, *The Rites of Passage,* trans. M. B. Vizedom and G. L. Caffee (Chicago, 1960); and Victor Turner, *The Ritual Process* (Ithaca, 1969) and *The Forest of Symbols* (Ithaca, 1967), which informed the views of historians of suicide in early modern England Michael MacDonald and Terence R. Murphy (see *Sleepless Souls,* pp. 18–19 and 45–47).

32. Zelenin gives a variety of concrete examples, see pp. 9–11 and 14–22. Other sources include V. N. Perets, "Derevnia Budogoshcha i ee predaniia," *Zhivaia starina,* 1894, no. 1:12, and O. P. Semenova, "Smert' i dusha," pp. 232–34.

33. See Perets, "Derevnia Budogoshcha," p. 12, Maksimov, *Nachistaia, nevedomaia i krestnaia sila,* pp. 17–18, and V. Dobrovol'skii, "Narodnye skazaniia o samoubiitsakh," *Zhivaia starina,* 1894, no. 2:204.

34. On *rusalki,* see Zelenin, *Ocherki,* pp. 123–52.

35. According to the folklorist V. Dobrovol'sky, "that a person does not take his own life, but is led to suicide, and sometimes even directly murdered or drowned by a devil or wood-goblin, is a characteristic belief of the Russian people." As evidence he cites five stories from village life, in three of which the devil (*chort*) or demon (*bes*) makes a brief appearance (in the phraseology chosen to describe the event) ("Narodnye skazaniia o samoubiitsakh," p. 204). The ethnographer S. V. Maksimov records two stories involving the devil's intervention in suicide (*Nechistaia, nevedomaia, i krestnaia sila,* pp. 15–17). At the end of the nineteenth century, the ethnographer V. N. Tenishev included the following question in his comprehensive survey: "Do

the people think that suicide is instigated by the devil?" He recorded only two answers, neither of which mentioned the devil. (See *Byt velikorusskikh krest'ian-zemlepashtsev [opisanie materialov etnograficheskogo biuro knizia V. N. Tenisheva]*, comp. B. M. Firsov and I. G. Kiselev [St. Petersburg, 1993], pp. 279 and 462).

Making a parallel between the situations in Russia and in England, Louise McReynolds, who discussed the newspaper coverage of suicide in the 1870s in her *The News under Russia's Old Regime: The Development of a Mass-Circulation Press* (Princeton, 1991), claimed: "In the newspaper, melancholia, alcoholism, or an impossibly hard life, not the devil induced the deed. Reports of suicide provide one more example of how newspapers could undermine the authority of the Orthodox church without challenging it directly" (p. 66). I see no basis for this conclusion. The Russian situation differed from the English one: the view of suicide as an act instigated by the devil seldom appeared in religious writings.

36. The idea seems to have been especially popular in England, emphasized in the wording of the early canon law codes (see Dublin, *Suicide,* p. 139); "the instigation of the devil" continued to figure not only in popular imagination, but also in the language of canon law well into the eighteenth century (see MacDonald and Murphy, *Sleepless Souls,* pp. 42–76).

37. See MacDonald and Murphy, *Sleepless Souls,* pp. 34–39 and chapter 2.

38. For documentation, see Zelenin, *Ocherki,* pp. 57–59.

39. Citing the thirteenth-century epistle of Bishop Serapion of Vladimir, the 1416 instruction of Metropolitan Fotii, and the writings of Maxim the Greek from the early sixteenth century, Zelenin emphasizes this point (ibid., pp. 58–59).

40. For documentation, see ibid., pp. 74–75 and 86–88.

41. For examples, see ibid., pp. 5, 13, 14, 30, 54, 55. Custom also prescribed burying the suicide at the site of the act (ibid., pp. 12, 13, 53).

42. Zelenin cites several examples of using stakes (ibid., pp. 15 and 17). Stakes were a preferred method of fixing the spirit of the suicide to its grave in medieval England, and was occasionally used even in modern times (see MacDonald and Murphy, *Sleepless Souls,* pp. 19, 47–48, and passim).

43. Zelenin, *Ocherki,* pp. 29–30.

44. There are several sources of Russian law: *Polnoe sobranie zakonov Rossiiskoi Imperii* listed all laws (canon and secular) ever enacted in chronological order. *Svod zakonov Rossiiskoi Imperii* (henceforth *Svod;* different versions appeared in 1835, 1842, and 1857) listed all currently active laws by topic. (Vol. 15 contained criminal laws, and vol. 10 civil laws; regulations of police and medical–legal authorities were in vol. 13.) Penal practice was primarily guided by another edition, which contained not only the text of the laws, but also commentaries intended to guide lawyers and judges: *Ulozhenie o nakazaniiakh ugolovnykh i ispravitel'nykh* (henceforth *Ulozhenie,* first issued in 1845). (Subsequent revised and amended editions included those of 1857, 1866, 1873, and 1885.) The last edition of *Svod,* which was in effect until the revolution of 1917, contained sixteen volumes published at different times (some volumes were from the 1857 edition; other volumes belonged to

a new, incomplete edition begun in 1876 and published between 1876 and 1897). Volume 16 contained *Ustav ugolovnogo sudoproizvodstva,* adopted in 1864 in the course of the Great Reforms.

45. The development of secular law with regard to suicide in Western Europe is difficult to trace (see Fedden, *Suicide,* 136–37). Dublin sees evidence that *felo de se* first appeared in a secular statute (introduced by the Danes after their invasion of Britain) as early as the tenth century (*Suicide,* p. 140). According to Fedden, the crystallization of suicide procedure in secular law, based on canon law and custom, occurred chiefly between the thirteenth and fifteenth centuries (p. 141). In Helen Silving's study, the earliest example is from thirteenth-century France. Silving concluded that secular laws in continental European countries were influenced by canon law (Silving, "Suicide and Law," p. 82). Clearly, from the Middle ages to the nineteenth century, both church and secular authorities concerned themselves with suicide.

46. See Donald W. Treadgold, "Russian Orthodoxy and Society," in *Russian Orthodoxy under the Old Regime,* ed. Robert L. Nichols and Theofanis George Stavrou (Minneapolis, 1978), p. 23.

47. Quoted in Tagantsev, *O prestupleniiakh,* 2:409. Verified with *Ustav voennyi: voinskie artikuly,* chapter 19, article 164 as published in *Polnoe sobranie zakonov Rossiiskoi Imperii* (St. Petersburg, 1835), vol. 5.

48. Quoted in Tagantsev, *O prestupleniiakh,* 2:409–10.

49. Ibid. On Roman law, see Silving, "Suicide and Law," p. 80, who cites Justinian's *Digest* (533 A.D.), article 48.19.38.12. The *Digest* specified that the exemption from punishment was allowed when suicide was caused by "impatience or pain or sickness, some grief, or by another cause" or by "lunacy, or fear of dishonor"; it also listed taedium vitae as a legitimate cause—a clause omitted by all Christian legislations.

50. The clause on expelling attempted suicides from the regiment was replaced with one expelling them from civil service. See Tagantsev, *O prestupleniiakh,* 2:410.

51. Quoted in ibid., p. 410, n. 14.

52. As its foundation, the code cited article 164 of *Voinskii artikul* of 1716 and article 117 of *Morskoi ustav* of 1720 as well as the Senate decree of November 10, 1766, in connection with the case of the princes Shakhovskoi, which dealt with the validity of a suicide's will (No. 12779 in *Polnoe sobranie zakonov*). On this decree, see Tagantsev, *O prestupleniiakh,* 2:411.

53. The new code was published as *Ulozhenie o nakazaniiakh ugolovnykh i ispravitel'nykh* (1845), which replaced vol. 15 of *Svod* of 1835; it was reprinted, without changes, in 1857, as vol. 15 of the new *Svod* and as subsequent editions of *Ulozhenie.*

54. Tagantsev, *O prestupleniiakh,* 2:423.

55. I am indebted to Laura Engelstein for this argument.

56. The case of women killing themselves to avoid violation was addressed by Augustine in his *City of God;* he unequivocally condemned this practice as "pagan" and incompatible with Christian precepts.

57. It appears that cases in which someone was driven to suicide through cruel treatment were not common in Russian courts. For the period of the

Great Reforms, Tagantsev cited the case of the peasant Ozersky, who was accused of driving his wife to suicide by severe beatings (he was acquitted because the prosecution failed to prove the causal connection between the beatings and the suicide; see Taganstev, *O prestupleniiakh,* 2:445, n. 29, and *Sudebnyi vestnik,* 1868, no. 143) and that of the Umetskie (*Sudebnyi vestnik,* 1868, no. 160). The latter case, involving a fifteen-year-old, Olga Umetskaia, driven to arson and a suicide attempt by cruel treatment at the hands of her parents, was covered in the press and attracted wide attention; Dostoevsky planned to use it in the *Idiot* (see F. M. Dostoevskii, *Polnoe sobranie sochinenii,* 30 vols. [Leningrad, 1972–90], 9:340–42).

58. *Proekt ulozheniia o nakazaniiakh ugolovnykh i ispravitel'nykh, vnesennyi v 1844 godu v Gosudarstvennyi Sovet, s podrobnym oznacheniem osnovanii kazhdogo iz vnesennykh v sei proekt postanovlenii* (St. Petersburg, 1871), pp. 623–24. Tagantsev, *O prestupleniiakh,* 2:417, quotes this commentary with some inaccuracies.

59. *Proekt,* p. 623.

60. Russian lawyers were in error: in the nineteenth century at least one code, the Sardinian Code of 1839, rendered a suicide's testament invalid (Silving, "Suicide and Law," p. 83). On the will, see also Guernsey, *Suicide,* pp. 32–33.

61. Ibid., p. 623.

62. Quote from the 1857 edition of *Svod.*

63. *Proekt,* p. 623. The authors of *proekt* may have been in error. Though I found no evidence that attempted suicides were sentenced to penal servitude (the usual punishment for attempted murder), there is evidence that they were exiled to Siberia. According to the ethnographer S. V. Maksimov, whose data came from *"Tobol'skie tabeli"* (the local registers), between 1838 and 1843, there were 347 male and 134 female attempted suicides, from different parts of the empire. In terms of social class, the largest number were serfs, with sixty-three cases in twelve years; there were thirty-six cases among the state peasants, twelve cases among the military and four cases among the *meshchanstvo* [petit bourgeoisie]. Maksimov found no record of exiled attempted suicides from the clergy, merchant, and gentry classes and suggested that members of the upper classes had means to avoid such punishment. (S. V. Maksimov, *Sibir' i katorga,* 2 vols. [St. Petersburg, 1871], 2:74–75.)

64. See Silving, "Suicide and Law," pp. 82–83; Dublin, *Suicide,* pp. 140–43.

65. See Silving, "Suicide and Law," pp. 82–84.

66. Dublin, *Suicide,* p. 144.

67. Fedden, *Suicide,* p. 210.

68. See Silving, "Suicide and Law," pp. 87–89. Selections from Ferri's treatise (concerning murder legislation) appeared in *Iuridicheskii vestnik* in 1888 and 1889.

69. Michael Foucault, "The Discourse on Language," in his *The Archaeology of Knowledge* (New York, 1972), p. 219.

70. On the confusion between administrative and judicial authorities, see Engelstein, *The Keys to Happiness: Sex and Search for Modernity in Fin-de-Siècle Russia* [Ithaca, 1992], pp. 18 and 20.

71. On legal reform, see Richard S. Wortman, *The Development of a Russian Legal Consciousness* (Chicago, 1976).

72. Holbach, Montesquieu, Rousseau, and Hume were among those philosophers who articulated a philosophical and moral opposition to the prejudice surrounding suicide and to the legal punishment of the act. (See Fedden, *Suicide,* chapter 7, and McManners, *Death and the Enlightenment,* chapter 12.) But it was the Italian criminologist Beccaria who first advanced legal arguments against punishing suicide. In his discussion of suicide in his *Essay on Crimes and Punishments* (*Trattato dei delitti e delle pene,* 1764) Beccaria deliberately ignored the Christian principle of the sanctity of human life. He argued that suicide was a crime that did not allow for a punishment: "Suicide is a crime, which seems not to admit of punishment; for it cannot be inflicted on the innocent [the suicide's family and heirs], or upon an insensible dead body. . . . The laws are obeyed through fear of punishment, but death destroys all sensibility" (*An Essay on Crimes and Punishments by the Marquis Beccaria of Milan with a Commentary by M. de Voltaire* [Albany, 1872], p. 121). His other argument was utilitarian: comparing the right to suicide with the right to emigration, Beccaria pointed out that "he who kills himself does a less injury to society, than he who quits his country forever, for the other leaves his property behind him" (ibid., pp. 121–22). I believe that in *Crime and Punishment* (1866), Dostoevsky made an ironic reference to Beccaria's argument: Svidrigailov, who shoots himself in the presence of an "official witness" (a Jewish fireman standing guard in front of a fire station), tells him as he prepares to pull the trigger that he is leaving for America. (A Russian translation of Beccaria, complete with commentaries comparing it to Catherine the Great's *Nakaz* and contemporary Russian laws, appeared in the postreform age: S. Zarudnyi, *Bekkaria o prestupleniiakh i nakazaniiakh* [St. Petersburg, 1879].)

73. See Tagantsev's comment, *O prestupleniiakh,* 2:412, n. 12.

74. Ibid., p. 415.

75. See C. G. Wächter's "Revision der Lehre von dem Selbstmord," *Neues Archiv des Criminalrechts* 10 (1828). Tagantsev discussed Wächter's argument in *O prestupleniiakh,* 2:413–16.

76. Another jurist, A. Kopei, discussed this issue in detail in "Dukhovnye zaveshchaniia samoubiits," *Iuridicheskii vestnik,* 1875, no. 4/6. According to Kopei, legal practice followed criminal law: "and if it is proven that a person committed suicide in a state of mental disturbance, his will remains valid. If the person committed suicide otherwise, his will is null and void" (p. 135). The problem was later addressed by P. F. Bulatsel' in *Issledovaniia o samovol'noi smerti* (Revel, 1894), pp. 162–67.

77. Tagantsev, p. 425. Laura Engelstein, in her penetrating analysis of the legal regulation of family and sexual life, ran up against what she described as "the awkward combination of religious values and secular regular principles," which characterized Russian law in the mid-nineteenth century, as well as the European legislation that "served Russians as a guide" (*The Keys to Happiness,* p. 36).

78. The first article on suicide to appear in the course of this debate, "O

samoubiistve" by Mikhail Bul'mering (*Iuridicheskii vestnik,* 1860, no. 5), was untouched by the reform spirit. Conflating moral, legal, and psychological points of view, the author asserted his personal condemnation of suicide as "unconditionally criminal." He argued, however, for repealing the denial of Christian burial, based on the argument that suicide is always insane in at least one point—the idea that man has a right to his life; therefore, the suicide cannot be held fully responsible for his actions (p. 45).

79. P. Obninskii, "Ob ugolovnom presledovanii pokusivshikhsia na samoubiistvo," *Iuridicheskii vestnik,* 1871, no. 6:3.

80. Obninsky himself was Jewish (for this information I am indebted to Laura Engelstein).

81. Obninskii, "Ob ugolovnom presledovanii," p. 7, citing commentary on article 1016 of *Ustav ugolovnogo sudoproizvodstva.*

82. Ibid., p. 4.

83. I. N. Shestakov, "Po povodu stat'i P. N. Obninskogo 'Ob ugolovnom presledovanii pokusivshikhsia na samoubiistvo'," *Iuridicheskii vestnik,* 1872, no. 1:134–35; Obninsky and Shestakov continued their polemic: see Obninsky's comment in no. 9 for 1871 and Shestakov's response in no. 4/5 for 1872.

84. His comments appeared in "Iuridicheskie zametki" section of nos. 9 and 10/11 of *Iuridicheskii vestnik* for 1873; see no. 10/11: 45.

85. "Iuridicheskie zametki," *Iuridicheskii vestnik,* 1873, no. 9: 52.

86. Ibid., no. 10/11:59.

87. Burial was regulated by article 704 of *Ustav meditsinskoi politsii,* book 2 of *Ustav vrachebnyi* (vol. 13 of *Svod*). Bulgakov's advice on procedure was based on article 752 of *Svod gubernskikh uchrezhdenii* in the 1892 edition of *Svod,* which concerned cases of "apparent [vidimye] and unquestionable causes of death." In cases where the suicide was known to have suffered from a mental disorder, a police officer (*stanovoi pristav*), without a medical expert, had the authority to determine the cause of death (suicide as a result of insanity) as "apparent and doubtless," thus permitting Christian burial. In other cases, medical examination was required by law (Bulgakov, *Nastol'naia kniga,* p. 1251).

88. Ibid., p. 1251.

89. Ibid., p. 1249, n. 5, and p. 1251, citing an earlier manual, *Prakticheskoe rukovodstvo dlia sviashchennosluzhitelei,* comp. P. I. Nechaev (St. Petersburg, 1890), pp. 277–78.

90. In the words of Nancy Mandelker Frieden, *Russian Physicians in an Era of Reform and Revolution, 1856–1905* (Princeton, 1981), p. 68; see also pp. 60–61 and 73.

91. Article 370 of the 1835 edition of *Svod* (it lists the Petrine *Voinskii ustav* of 1716 as its source); article 710 in the later editions. Bulgakov reiterated this rule, without a commentary, in his 1892/1900 manual for parish priests.

92. Bulgakov discussed this issue at length in *Nastol'naia kniga,* p. 1252, n. 2, citing *Tobol'skie eparkhial'nye vedomosti,* 1895, no. 6, and *Tserkovnye vedomosti* 1895, no. 29.

93. Ibid., p. 1252, n. 1, citing *Kishinevskie eparkhial'nye vedomosti,* 1894, no. 10.

94. The manual warned the parish priests that breaking the law on the obligatory medico-police investigation of suicide was punishable by article 860 of *Ulozhenie* and that according to article 708 of *Ustav meditsinskoi politsii,* "a priest may not avoid burying the dead without special legal reasons for doing so." (See Bulgakov, *Nastol'naia kniga,* pp. 1251–53, ns. 1 and 2.) The manual specified: "there is no civil law which gives the priest the right to deny a suicide a Christian burial upon receiving certification from the police (after the forensic medical examination) that a funeral will not be obstructed" (Bulgakov, p. 1252, referring to *Tserkovnye vedomosti,* 1898, no. 23).

95. Laura Engelstein made a similar argument about sexual behavior; see *Keys to Happiness,* p. 18.

96. Mainly based on Esquirol, the book also surveyed other studies that followed Esquirol's view: Winslow's *Anatomy of Suicide,* A. Brierre de Boismont's *Du suicide,* Louis Bertrand's *Traité du suicide considéré dans ses rapports avec la philosophie, la théologie, la médicine et la jurisprudence* (Paris, 1857), and Lisle's popular *Du suicide.*

97. From "Vnutrennee obozrenie," *Delo,* 1868, no. 10:82.

98. A. Ketle, *Chelovek i razvitie ego sposobnostei. Opyt obshchestvennoi fiziki* (St. Petersburg, 1865) and *Sotsial'naia sistema i zakony eiu upravliaiushchie* (St. Petersburg, 1866). Among the main participants of the polemic were the radical journalist V. A. Zaitsev, a proponent of Quételet, and his opponent, the criminologist and statistician N. Nekliudov, the author of *Ugolovno-statisticheskie etiudy. Etiud pervyi* (St. Petersburg, 1865).

99. *Otechestvennye zapiski,* 1868, no. 1:76. A review of *Nravstvennaia statistika v sviazi s istorieiu prilozheniia chisel k naukam nravstvennym,* published by N. I. Lamanskii (St. Petersburg, 1867).

100. By the early 1860s, Buckle's book had appeared in two Russian translations. See Alexander Vucinich, *Darwin in Russian Thought* (Berkeley, 1988), p. 10.

101. V. A. Zaitsev, in "Bibliograficheskii listok," *Russkoe slovo,* no. 3:83–85, 1865. Quote from V. A. Zaitsev, *Izbrannye sochineniia,* 2 vols. (Moscow, 1934), 1:154–55.

102. Ibid., p. 78. This essay, which appeared in *Russkoe slovo* in 1863 (no. 7), was the first exposition of Quételet's views in the Russian press (see commentaries on p. 469); the statement echoes Buckle.

103. Ibid., pp. 72 and 83. In the May 1863 issue of *Russkoe slovo,* Zaitsev reviewed the Russian translation of Vogt: K. Fogt, *Estestvennaia istoriia mirozdaniia* (Moscow, 1863).

104. See Vucinich, *Science in Russian Culture,* 2:7.

105. N. Radiukin [N. Shelgunov], "Statistika samoubiistva (po povodu sochineniia Vagner'a "Statistik der Selbstmorde")," *Delo,* 1866, no. 1:312–13. On Shelgunov's authorship, see N. I. Sokolov, "'Delo'," *Ocherki po istorii russkoi zhurnalistiki i kritiki,* 2 vols. (Leningrad, 1965), 2:311.

106. Censor F. P. Elenev; quoted in Sokolov, "'Delo'," p. 315.

107. On these developments, see V. I. Etov, *Dostoevskii* (Moscow, 1968), p. 221.

108. Reactions to Morselli's treatise include E. Likhacheva, "O samoubiistve," *Otechestvennye zapiski,* 1881, no. 7; Lizin, "Samoubiistvo i tsivilizatsiia"; B. S., "O samoubiistve v tsivilizovannykh stranakh (po Morselli)," *Russkoe bogatsvo,* 1885, no. 10.

109. From Likhacheva, "O samoubiistve," pp. 22–23.

110. For reviews of available sources of statistical data see Likhachev, *Samoubiistvo,* pp. 12–20; M. N. Gernet, *Moral'naia statistika* (Moscow, 1922); and D. Rodin, "O postanovke statistiki samoubiistva," *Vestnik statistika,* 1921, no. 5–8. A bibliography of statistical studies can be found in M. N. Gernet, *Ukazatel' russkoi i inostrannoi literatury po statistike prestuplenii, nakazanii i samoubiistv* (Moscow, 1924).

111. M. Sukhomlinov, "Materialy dlia istorii prosveshcheniia v Rossii v tsarstvovanie imperatora Aleksandra I," *Zhurnal Ministerstva narodnogo prosveshcheniia,* 1866, no. 11:26–27.

112. Ch.-Th. Herrmann, "Recherches sur le nombre des suicides et des homicides commis en Russie pendant les années 1819 et 1820," *Mémoires de l'Académie impériale des sciences de St. Petersbourg,* 6th series, vol. 1: Sciences politiques, histoire, et philologie (St. Petersburg, 1832).

113. Quételet, *Sur l'homme,* 2:157.

114. *Zhurnal ministerstva vnutrennikh del,* part 18 (1847).

115. Iu. Gübner's "Samoubiistva v St. Peterburge s 1858 po 1867 god," *Arkhiv sudebnoi meditsiny i obshchestvennoi gigieny* 3 (1868). The journal, published since 1865, was probably modeled on the French *Annales d'hygiène publique et de la médicine légale* (started in 1829).

116. Gübner had at his disposal Ia. Chistovich, "Perechen' sudebno-meditsinskikh vskrytii" (*Voenno-meditsinskii zhurnal,* 67 [1856], 70 [1857], 72 [1858], 78 [1860]) which included 149 cases of suicide for the years 1838–60. See his criticism of the government data (which was available in reports issued by statistical committees, both the *Tsentral'nyi statisticheskii komitet* and the provincial committees) and his comments on the newspaper data on pp. 90–94. For a critical analysis of data from the police newspaper, see Likhachev, *Samoubiistvo,* pp. 18–19. Gübner estimated that his figures, which were much higher than official statistics, reflected about one-third of the actual suicides (p. 92).

117. I. Pasternatskii, "Statisticheskoe issledovanie samoubiistv v Peterburge za 1870, 1871 i 1872 gody," *Meditsinskii vestnik,* 1872, nos. 34, 36, 38; and 1873, no. 41.

118. The first issue to include suicide statistics, *Russkii kalendar' na 1873 god,* published data for 1858–1871 (there were no data for 1869) collected by Gübner from *Vedomosti Sankt-Peterburgskoi gorodskoi politsii.* In subsequent publications, the years 1877 and 1878 remained undocumented.

119. "*neprigodna dlia raboty*" (Gernet, *Moral'naia statistika,* p. 228).

120. N. V. Ponomarev, "Samoubiistvo v Zapadnoi Evrope i Rossii v sviazi s razvitiem umopomeshatel'stva," *Sbornik sochinenii po sudebnoi meditsine* (St. Petersburg, 1880), vol. 3.

121. Ponomarev's study was discussed, along with Morselli's, by E. Likhacheva in her "O samoubiistve"; reviews of Likhachev's book appeared in

Otechestvennye zapiski, 1882, no. 9; *Nedelia,* 1882, no. 40; and *Vestnik Evropy* for September 1882.

122. Listed below are the nineteenth-century studies other than those reviewed in this section. Medical studies (besides Ponomarev's) include two brochures by I. P. Lebedev, *O samoubiistve v normal'nom i boleznennom sostoianii* (St. Petersburg, 1888); *O samoubiistve s meditsinskoi tochki zreniia* (St. Petersburg, 1897); and his article "O samoubiistve s meditsinskoi tochki zreniia," *Arkhiv psikhiatrii, nevrologii, i sudebnoi psikhopatologii,* 1896, no. 2: and a brochure by Ivan Gvozdev, *O samoubiistve s sotsial'noi i meditsinskoi tochki zreniia* (Kazan, 1889). None of these Russian studies offered original interpretations. There was a book for a popular audience, which approached suicide from a historical (mostly anecdotal) and legal perspective: P. F. Bulatsel''s *Issledovaniia o samovol'noi smerti* (reprinted as *Samoubiistvo s drevneishikh vremen do nashikh dnei* [St. Petersburg, 1900]), which relied heavily on earlier studies, among them Brierre de Boismont, Lisle, and Legoyt as well as their Russian popularizer Ol'khin. He also used a Polish study, M. Dzedushitskii's *Samoubiistvo,* published in Russian in Kiev in 1877 and 1878. A rare attempt to deal with the provincial material is I. S. Fal'kner's brochure *Samoubiistva v Odesse (Statisticheskii ocherk)* (Odessa, 1890). In the twentieth century, abundant, though far from original, literature dealing with suicide was published in two waves—between 1906 and 1914, mainly in the periodical press, and in the 1920s. Book-length studies include: V. A. Bernatskii, *Samoubiistva sredi vospitannikov voenno-uchebnykh zavedenii* (St. Petersburg, 1911); V. M. Bekhterev, *O prichinakh samoubiistva* (St. Petersburg, 1912); M. Ia. Fenomenov, *Prichiny samoubiistv v russkoi shkole* (Moscow, 1914); A. F. Koni, *Samoubiistvo v zakone i zhizni* (Moscow, 1923); Ia. L. Leibovich, *1,000 sovremennykh samoubiistv* (Moscow, 1923); and M. N. Gernet, *Moral'naia statistika,* 2 vols. (Moscow, 1922, 1927). A useful, though not complete, bibliography of Russian studies on suicide is M. Teodorovich, *Samoubiistvo (Ukazatel' literatury na russkom iazyke)* (Moscow, 1928) (published as a supplement to *Sotsial'naia gigiena,* 1928, no. 2–3 [12–13]). A bibliography of statistical studies can be also found in M. N. Gernet, *Ukazatel' russkoi i inostrannoi literatury po statistike prestuplenii, nakazanii i samoubiistv* (Moscow, 1924). Very little work was done in the Soviet period after the 1920s. See review articles by A. G. Ambrumova and S. V. Borodin, "Suitsidologicheskie issledovaniia v SSSR: sostoianie i problemy," in *Aktual'nye problemy suitsidologii, Trudy Moskovskogo nauchno-issledovatel'skogo instituta psikhiatrii* (Moscow, 1981), 92:6–25; and Martin Miller, "Suicide and Suicidology in the Soviet Union," *Suicide and Life Threatening Behavior* 18, 4 (1988): 303–21. A recent *Estetika samoubiistva* by L. Tregubov and Iu. Vagin (Perm, 1993) is aimed at a popular audience of the present day.

123. Likhachev, *Samoubiistvo,* pp. 4 and 6.

124. This notion, advanced by nineteenth-century statisticians such as Wagner, Oettingen, and Morselli, did not remain unchallenged: some Western authors argued that factors inherent in the very process of gathering data, such as the increasing tendency to register suicides, accounted for the in-

crease in figures. Likhachev gave a summary of such views (p. 41). However, the idea that, beginning with the nineteenth century, suicide rates progressively increased has clearly predominated until this day.

125. St. Petersburg was believed to be different, since it was catching up—in terms not only of its growth rate, but also of absolute figures—with cities like Paris. According to A. S. Suvorin's *Russkii kalendar' na 1875 g.*, which featured the article "Samoubiistva v Peterburge," the increase started in 1864 (the data were provided by A. F. Koni). In the 1880s, suicide was seen as an integral part of urban horrors: V. Mikhnevich's popular *The Sores of Petersburg* (Iazvy Peterburga. Opyt istoriko-statisticheskogo issledovaniia nravstvennosti stolichnogo naseleniia [St. Petersburg, 1886]) includes a chapter on suicide. Following Morselli, many Russian authors tied the increase in the incidence of suicide to the development of civilization. Some took seriously Morselli's Darwinian argument: suicide is an effect of the struggle for existence and of natural selection, which works among the civilized nations. Thus, E. Likhacheva, in her 1881 essay "O samoubiistve," discussed Morselli's Darwinian argument at great length. (It is remarkable that E. Likhacheva introduced T. G. Masaryk's *Der Selbstmord als sociale Massenerscheinung der modernen Civilisation* [Vienna, 1881], which also drew a connection between suicide and civilization, as a work that had little to offer, because Masaryk saw the cause of the suicide epidemic in the decline of religion [p. 23, n. 1].) On the whole, ideology prevailed over all other considerations. To give one example, the author of one essay, "Samoubiitsvo i tsivilizatsiia" (signed K. Lizin, it was written by the radical activist Konstantin Arkadaksky), rearranged Likhachev's statistical data to show that the development of industry caused the increase in suicide; capitalism was the invisible killer plaguing Russian cities and villages. (On Arkadaksky, see *Russkie vedomosti, 1863–1913: Sbornik statei* [Moscow, 1913] p. 15.)

Notes to Chapter 3

1. See chapter 9 of MacDonald and Murphy, *Sleepless Souls.*

2. According to a nineteenth-century student of suicide, until the mid-1870s *Vedomosti* suppressed suicide reports at the request of relatives and friends of the victims. (A. V. Likhachev's *Samoubiistvo*, p. 18.)

3. Organs aimed at the popular reader (*malaia pressa*), which appeared in Russia for the first time in the mid-1860s, devoted much attention to crime and suicide. (See McReynolds, *The News Under Russia's Old Regime.*) *Peterburgskii listok* (published from 1864) was known for capitalizing on sensational criminal and suicide cases; *Peterburgskaia gazeta* (from 1867), according to McReynolds, outnumbered other newspapers in its coverage of suicide cases (McReynolds, p. 66, n. 59). *Novosti* (from 1871) presented selected suicide cases in extended, fictionalized scenes, with dialogue and vivid detail (for example, see "Facts and Rumors: A New Suicide!" [*Fakty i slukhi: novoe samoubiistvo!*] in the September 20, 1873, issue).

4. See, for example, *Golos,* 1872, no. 215, and *Vedomosti Sankt-Peterburgskoi politsii,* 1870, no. 7; 1873, nos. 43, 44, and 118.

5. For coverage of suicide in *Grazhdanin,* see 1873, nos. 2, 13, 18, 19, 21, 23, 38–40, 43, and 49; 1874, nos. 1, 2, 11, and 12. In 1874, *Grazhdanin* featured a debate on nihilism between Meshchersky and Ia. P. Polonsky (both wrote under pseudonyms), in which suicide played a prominent part. (*Grazhdanin,* 1874, nos. 4, 7, 9–11, 13, and 14 ("Pis'ma khoroshen'koi zhenshchiny" and responses by "Olits").

6. A *cause célèbre* covered in *Moskovskie vedomosti* involved the double suicide of two sisters, Praskov'ia Goncharova, 22, and Alexandra Lavrova, 19, in 1872 and 1873 respectively, which followed a duel between the well-known lawyer E. Utin and the journalist A. Zhokhov (who was loved by the older sister). On April 28, 1873, *Moskovskie vedomosti* published an epitaph written by the grieving father of the two young suicides, who he said "fell victim to the school of nihilism." Meshchersky responded in *Grazhdanin,* treating the epitaph as "a curse on nihilism" ("Mysli vslukh," *Grazhdanin,* 1873, no. 19 [May 7]).

7. *Golos* (first published in 1863) was closed in 1881; *Sankt-Peterburgskie vedomosti* abandoned its liberal position in 1875, *Otechestvennye zapiski* (which changed hands in 1867) and *Delo* (created in 1866) were closed in 1884, *Nedelia* (begun in 1866) had abandoned its oppositional orientation by the late 1880s.

8. From Orest Miller, "Samoubiistvo ot ekzamena," *Zaria,* 1870, no. 6:178.

9. For a comparative perspective, one could draw on Western material. It was in the eighteenth century, when England saw the rapid growth of the periodical press, that the public concluded that suicide was a common (and specifically English) phenomenon. See Michael McDonald, "Suicide and the Rise of the Popular Press in England," and the response by Reginald Zelnik in *Representations,* 1988, no. 22 (Spring).

10. From the section "Vnutrenniaia khronika," *Otechestvennye zapiski,* March 1871, pp. 171 and 174; signed D. [N. A. Demert].

11. From the section "Nashi obshchestvennye dela," *Otechestvennye zapiski,* 1873, no. 10:261; signed D. [N. A. Demert]. In this review Demert used material not only from the popular *Golos, Birzhevye vedomosti, Peterburgskaia gazeta* and *Peterburgskii listok* (all published in Petersburg), but also from *Moskovkaia politseiskaia gazeta* and the little-known provincial organs, *Kamsko-volzhskaia gazeta* and *Akmolinskie oblastnye vedomosti.*

12. See, for example, the June 3, 1873, issue of *Nedelia.*

13. "Maniia samoubiistv," *Nedelia,* 1884, no. 22:733.

14. See the following articles in *Nedelia:* "Po povodu samoubiistva detei," 1884, no. 18; "Maniia samoubiistv," 1884, no. 22; "Nash pessimizm," 1888, no. 24; "Otorvannost' ot zhizni," 1888, no. 47.

15. "Samoubiistva (Etiud po obshchestvennoi patologii)," *Nedelia,* 1886, no. 18 [May 4]: 621.

16. [N. V. Shelgunov], "Ocherki russkoi zhizni," *Russkaia mysl',* 1889, no. 1; quoted from N. V. Shelgunov, *Ocherki russkoi zhizni* (St. Petersburg, 1895), p. 654.

17. See, for example, the section "Nashi obshchestvennye dela" in the October (no. 10) 1873 issue of *Otechestvennye zapiski* (written by N. A. Demert).

18. E. K., "Glasnye dramy intimnoi zhizni," *Nedelia,* 1873, no. 39:1415.

19. Details of the case were elaborated in the September 22, 1873, issue of the "small press" organ *Peterburgskaia gazeta* ("Peterburgskie otgoloski: Ubiistvo g—zhi Suvorinoi i samoubiistvo").

20. *Novosti,* September 21, 1873.

21. *Golos,* September 21, 1873.

22. *Sankt-Peterburgskie vedomosti,* October 4, 1873.

23. B. Ongirskii, "Statisticheskie itogi samoubiistv," *Delo,* 1873, no. 11:1.

24. *Novosti,* September 22, 1873.

25. E. K., "Glasnye dramy," p. 1419; *Delo* also indignantly commented on the indiscretion of "literary trash" (*literaturnaia shval'*) from *Novosti* (B. Ongirskii, "Statisticheskie itogi," p. 58). *Otechestvennye zapiski* opened the October chronicle of current events with a discussion not of the case, but of the fact that the public vigorously discussed it.

26. *Novosti,* September 21, 1873.

27. E. K., "Glasnye dramy," p. 1419.

28. Ongirskii, "Statisticheskie itogi," p. 1. A brief report of the suicide of the peasant (Avdot'ia Nikiforova) appeared in *Vedomosti Sankt-Peterburgskoi gorodskoi politsii* on September 27, 1873; on September 22, the police paper printed an equally brief report on the Belle Vue case, entitled "Murder and Suicide" (*Ubiistvo i samoubiistvo*).

29. E. K., "Glasnye dramy," p. 1416.

30. Neznakomets, "Nedel'nye ocherki i kartinki," *Sankt-Peterburgskie vedomosti,* November 3, 1874. The discussion of these cases was reprinted in the edition of Suvorin's feuilletons, as a separate piece, entitled "Murderers-Suicides" (*Ubiitsy-samoubiitsy*); see A. S. Suvorin, *Ocherki i kartinki,* vol. 2 (St. Petersburg, 1875).

31. A direct heir to the radicalism of the 1860s, *Delo* was actively involved in propaganda of positivistic and materialistic science. The populist *Nedelia* took a liberal stance and treated science with a degree of skepticism.

32. Ongirskii, "Statisticheskie itogi," pp. 1–2.

33. According to this source, poverty (combined with drunkenness) constituted 53 percent of the cases known for 1870, 1871, and 1872. (See I. Pasternatskii, "Statisticheskoe issledovanie samoubiistv v Peterburge za 1870, 1871 i 1872 gody," *Meditsinskii vestnik,* 1873, nos. 34, 36, 38 and 41.) Ongirsky ignored the fact that Pasternatsky used information from *Vedomosti Sankt-Peterburgskoi politsii,* which had access mostly to suicides among the low classes.

34. E. K., "Urok nekoemu publitsistu 'Dela'," *Nedelia,* 1873, no. 49:1801, 1803.

35. Quoted from P. L. Lavrov, *Istoricheskie pis'ma* (St. Petersburg, 1917), p. 45.

36. "Nashi obshchestvennye dela," *Otechestvennye zapiski,* 1872, no. 7:83–84.

37. E. K., "Glasnye dramy," p. 1414. The picture agrees with the views of contemporary physiology. In Büchner's words, electricity "plays, according to modern investigations, a very essential part in the physiological functions of

the whole nervous system": electric currents constantly surround the nerves (*Force and Matter,* p. 138).

38. E. K., "Glasnye dramy," p. 1414.

39. From the review of A. V. Likhachev's study on suicide published in *Otechestvennye zapiski,* 1882, no. 9:131.

40. D. Kulikovskii, "Samoubiitsy i nirvana," *Slovo,* 1880, no. 11:178.

41. Ibid.

42. A. Klitin, *Nashe vremia i samoubiistvo* (Kiev, 1890), p. 3.

43. Vera N. [V. P. Meshcherskii], "Pis'ma khoroshen'koi zhenshchiny," *Grazhdanin,* 1874, no. 7:208.

44. "Mysli vslukh": *Grazhdanin,* 1873, no. 19:557 and 559.

45. Peter Pozefsky makes insightful observations about the representation of the nihilist's body in the writings of the anti-nihilists, noting the predominance of images of rape, incest, and suicide. Guided by the idea, formulated by Mary Douglas (*Natural Symbols: Explorations in Cosmology* [New York, 1970]), that the human body is often used as a metaphor for society as a whole and that certain social situations engender certain types of body imagery, Pozefsky interprets these images as a metaphor of the disintegration of society as a whole. See Peter C. Pozefsky, "Dmitrii Pisarev and the Nihilist Imagination: Social and Psychological Origins of Russian Radicalism (1860–1868)," Ph.D. Dissertation, University of California, Los Angeles, 1993, pp. 293–322.

46. M. [V. P. Meshcherskii], "Dve Rossii," *Grazhdanin,* 1874, no. 1:7.

47. All quotes are from section "Nashi obshchestvennye dela," *Otechestvennye zapiski,* 1873, no. 10:261–62 (written by N. A. Demert).

48. Ibid., p. 264.

49. *Golos,* September 1, 1873.

50. "Po povodu odnoi smerti," *Ustoi,* July 1882. The case involved the double suicide of two young officers, Schultz and Khrzhanovsky. Suspected of being "politically disloyal," they were put under arrest. Although nine months later the investigation determined that the accusation was groundless, both chose to resign from the military and retired to their estates. Khrzhanovsky soon shot himself; his friend committed suicide several months later. (Some letters pertaining to the case were published in *Nedelia,* 1882, no. 33.)

51. "Po povodu odnoi smerti," p. 43.

52. Ibid., pp. 43–44.

53. "Vnutrennee obozrenie," *Delo,* 1868, no. 10:82–83.

54. The (anonymous) journalist used Iu. Iu. Gübner's study of suicide in Petersburg for 1858–67, published in *Arkhiv sudebnoi meditsiny i obshchestvennoi gigieny,* 1868, vol. 3.

55. "Vnutrennee obozrenie," *Delo,* 1868, no. 10:84.

56. Ibid., p. 88–89.

57. Ibid., p. 90.

58. Ibid., p. 85; reiterated on p. 91.

59. Alain Corbin, *The Foul and the Fragrant: Odor and the French Social Imagination* (Cambridge, Mass., 1986), p. 29; chapter 2 treats the mythology of "miasmic soil."

60. Ibid., pp. 27 and 24.

61. I. Gvozdev, *O samoubiistve s sotsial'noi i meditsinskoi tochki zreniia* (Kazan, 1889), p. 5.

62. Ibid.

63. Ibid., p. 42.

64. In his view of the brain, Gvozdev was guided by Wilhelm Griesinger, the author of a standard work on mental pathology (1845), translated into Russian in the 1860s.

65. Ibid., pp. 42–43.

66. Büchner, *Force and Matter,* p. 120.

67. Gvozdev, *O samoubiistve,* p. 21.

68. Ibid., p. 23.

69. Ibid., p. 25.

70. "Donesenie popechitelia Kazanskogo uchebnogo okruga P. D. Shestakova g. Ministru narodnogo prosveshcheniia ot 27 ianvaria, za N 31, otnositel'no samoubiistva gotovivshegosia k postupleniiu vo 2-iu Kazanskuiu gimnaziiu Platona Demerta," *Zhurnal Ministerstva narodnogo prosveshcheniia,* February 1871:181.

71. Ibid., p. 180.

72. Ibid., p. 183.

73. See *Otechestvennye zapiski,* 1871, no. 3:175, and 1872, no. 7:92 ("Nashi obshchestvennye dela," also signed D. and written by N. A. Demert).

74. An account of N. A. Demert's activities can be found in *Russkie pisateli, 1800–1917. Biograficheskii slovar',* ed. P. A. Nikolaev (Moscow, 1992), 2:104–5 (prepared by N. P. Emel'ianov). See also B. I. Esin, *Russkaia zhurnalistika 70–80-kh godov XIX veka* (Moscow, 1963), p. 68; N. Emel'ianov, *"Otechestvennye zapiski" (1868–1884)* (Leningrad, 1986), pp. 41–44; and B. Agafonov, "Kazanskie poety," *Istoricheskii vestnik,* 1900, vol. 81, no. 8: 597–98.

75. Gleb Uspenskii, "Nikolai Aleksandrovich Demert," *Polnoe sobranie sochinenii,* 6 vols. (St. Petersburg, 1908) 6:505.

76. Ibid.

77. A. M. Skabichevskii, *Literaturnye vospominaniia* (Moscow–Leningrad, 1928), pp. 293–94.

78. Ibid., p. 293.

79. Uspenskii, "Nikolai Aleksandrovich Demert," p. 506.

80. Ibid.

81. Skabichevskii, *Literaturnye vospominaniia,* p. 292. Skabichevsky writes of two suicides in Demert's family (p. 292); Mikhailovsky, in his memoirs *Literatura i zhizn'* (1891), mentions three deaths that followed one another: the death of Demert's brother, his nephew's suicide, and the death of his mother (*Polnoe sobranie sochinenii* [St. Petersburg, 1909], 7:23).

82. "Vnutrenniaia khronika," *Otechestvennye zapiski,* 1871, no. 3:175 (signed D.).

83. Skabichevskii, *Literaturnye vospominaniia,* p. 294.

84. I am paraphrasing Clifford Geertz's famous formula, inspired by Max Weber: "man is an animal suspended in webs of significance he himself has spun." Clifford Geertz, *The Interpretation of Cultures* (New York, 1973), p. 5.

85. I. Maizel, "O samoubiistvakh sredi uchashchikhsia," *Vestnik vospitaniia*, 1908, no. 8:158.

86. Lev Sheinis, "Epidemicheskie samoubiistva," *Vestnik vospitaniia*, 1909, no. 1:130. Since it was believed that the suicide epidemic had special relevance for the young, pedagogical journals paid particular attention to the issue.

87. A. Peshekhonov, "Na ocherednye temy," *Russkoe bogatstvo*, 1908, no. 5:126.

88. D. Zhbankov, "O samoubiistvakh v poslednie gody (Statisticheskii ocherk)," *Russkoe bogatstvo*, 1909, no. 4:28. He was proud to have noted an increase and predicted an epidemic as early as 1906 in an article published in the medical newspaper *Prakticheskii vrach*, 1906, nos. 26–29.

89. A bibliography of statistical surveys can be found in M. N. Gernet, *Ukazatel' russkoi i inostrannoi literatury po statistike prestuplenii, nakazanii i samoubiistv* (Moscow, 1924). Statistical data on students were collected and published by the Ministry of Education. See the series *Samoubiistva, pokusheniia na samoubiistva i neschastnye sluchai sredi uchashchikhsia uchebnykh zavedenii Ministerstva Narodnogo Prosveshcheniia* for the years 1905–1913 (St. Petersburg, 1906–1915), ed. G. V. Khlopin (1906–1909), N. G. Ushinskii (1910), and E. A. Neznamov (1911–1913). For a discussion of statistical data, see G. I. Gordon, "Sovremennye samoubiistva," *Russkaia mysl'*, May 1912; D. Zhbankov, "O samoubiistvakh v poslednie gody (statisticheskii ocherk)"; L. Slonimskii, "Samoubiistvo s obshchestvennoi i nravstvennoi tochek zreniia," *Vestnik Evropy*, January and February 1914. Since the authors, mostly liberal and radical, who wrote about the suicide epidemic were suspicious of official government statistics, they resorted to newspaper chronicles and to privately compiled statistical surveys. A much-quoted source of the latter type is N. I. Grigor'ev's "Samoubiistva i pokusheniia na samoubiistva v Peterburge za piatiletie s 1906–1910 gg. Doklad chitannyi v psikhich. sektsii Psikho-Nevrologicheskogo Instituta 10 marta 1911 g." Grigor'ev's figures were almost double the official figures, thus placing Petersburg first among major cities of the Western world. Having compared the two sets of figures, Gordon commented, not without satisfaction: "Hence, we Peterburgers hold the first place in the world for the number of annual suicides" (Gordon, "Sovremennye samoubiistva," p. 75).

90. In his 1909 article "O samoubiistvakh v poslednie gody," subtitled "A statistical survey," Zhbankov (a *zemstvo* doctor and prominent social activist with leftist sympathies) combined data derived from official statistical bulletins (his source for Petersburg), the annals of the medical first-aid service (his main source for Odessa), and information from newspaper chronicles (the sole source of his Moscow data). Zhbankov's statistical data was used by many other authors.

91. See, for example, L. Slonimsky, "Samoubiistvo," *Vestnik Evropy*, January 1914, p. 255.

92. Zhbankov, "O samoubiistvakh v poslednie gody," p. 29.

93. See Sheinis, "Epidimicheskie samoubiistva," pp. 131–32.

94. Sikorsky's view was a polemic response to left-wing historians, such

as Aleksandr Pypin, who, writing in the 1860s, when this topic attracted considerable attention, presented self-immolation by the Old Believers as a direct result of the government's repressive measures—as a simple means to avoid inevitable punishment (analogous to the heroic suicides of those French revolutionaries who faced a death sentence). For a survey of views on the cause of religious suicides, see D. I. Sapozhnikov, *Samosozhzhenie v russkom raskole (so vtoroi poloviny XVII veka do kontsa XVIII)* (St. Petersburg, 1891). (Sapozhnikov was one of the few authors who saw self-immolations as an act aimed at the salvation of the soul.) Another author, A. S. Prugavin, in "Samoistréblenie (Proevlenie asketizma i fanatizma v raskole)," subtitled "Ocherki, analogii i paralleli," drew a thinly disguised analogy between the "suicide epidemic" of the 1860s–80s and the mass suicides among Russian Old Believers and sectarians, whom he called "religious nihilists." First published in *Russkaia mysl'* in 1885 (nos. 1, 2, and 7), the work was reissued as a book when another "suicide epidemic" hit Russia (*Religioznye otshchepentsy. Ocherki sovremennogo sektantstva* [Moscow, 1906]).

95. Sheinis, *Epidemicheskie samoubiistva,* p. 149.

96. Vasilii Rozanov, *Temnyi lik. Metafizika Khristianstva* (St. Petersburg, 1911), p. 126, n. 2.

97. Ibid., p. 136, n. 1.

98. See reviews of the Russian translation: V. Bazarov, "Samoubiistvo kak sotsial'noe iavlenie," *Zaprosy zhizni,* 1912, no. 19; V. Vol'skii, "Traurnyi progress," *Sovremennyi mir,* 1912, no. 6; V. Iakovenko, "E. Durkgeim, 'Samoubiistvo,'" *Vestnik vospitaniia,* 1912, no. 6. Several reviews of the original French edition had appeared at the time of its publication: A. N. Ostrogorsky, "Samoubiistva i ikh prichiny," *Severnyi vestnik,* 1898, no. 5; N. K., "Samoubiistvo i ego prichiny (pis'mo iz Frantsii)," *Russkoe bogatstvo,* 1898, no. 4; A. R., "O samoubiistve. (Sotsiologicheskii etiud Durkgeima)," *Obrazovanie,* 1898, no. 5/6.

99. G. I. Gordon, "Predislovie," E. Diurkgeim [Durkheim], *Samoubiistvo. Sotsiologicheskii etiud,* trans. A. N. Il'inskii, ed. V. A. Bazarov (St. Petersburg, 1912), p. xv.

100. Lizin, "Samoubiistvo i tsivilizatsiia," p. 265; cited above.

101. Gordon, "Predislovie," p. xviii.

102. Ibid., p. xxiii.

103. Vol'skii, "Traurnyi progress," p. 289.

104. Ibid., p. 290.

105. Slonimskii, "Samoubiistvo," *Vestnik Evropy,* January 1914, p. 256. For Slonimskii's review of Durkheim's treatise, see the conclusion to his essay in the February issue of *Vestnik Evropy,* pp. 212–19.

106. For a definition, see Zhbankov, "Sovremennye samoubiistva," *Sovremennyi mir,* 1910, no. 3:40.

107. Zhbankov's "Polovaia prestupnost'," *Sovremennyi mir,* 1909, no. 7:90–91.

108. In discussing the various manifestations of the "morbid development" of the social body responsible for the increase in the incidence of suicide, Durkheim placed "the anarchist, the aesthete, the mystic, the socialist revo-

lutionary" side by side (*Suicide,* p. 370). The themes of sexuality and suicide intersected in discussions of Otto Weininger's *Geschlecht und Charakter* or, rather, of the author's suicide, which occurred shortly after the book was published in Vienna in 1903. Weininger's book came out in Russian in 1908, at the height of the "suicide epidemic" (three more Russian translations, all entitled *Pol i kharakter,* appeared by 1912, followed by the translation of Swoboda's book on Weininger's death, *Smert' Otto Veiningera* [Simferopol, 1912]). The Weininger case was widely discussed in the press.

109. "Malen'kii fel'eton," *Novoe vremia,* April 22, 1908.

110. V. L'vov, "Iz zhizni i literatury (okonchanie)," *Obrazovanie,* 1908, no. 4:45.

111. L'vov, "Iz zhizni i literatury," *Obrazovanie,* 1908, no. 1:57.

112. For a bibliography, see S. O'Dell and N. J. L. Luker, *Mikhail Artsybashev: A Comprehensive Bibliography* (Nottingham, 1983).

113. Kornei Chukovskii, "Samoubiitsy (Ocherki sovremennoi slovesnosti)," *Rech',* 1912, no. 352 (December 23).

114. Maxim Gorky, "O sovremennosti" [1912], *Stat'i (1915–1916)* (Petrograd, 1918), p. 103.

115. Gorky, "O 'Karamazovshchine,'" ibid., p. 162.

116. In 1912 the journal *Novoe slovo* asked major Russian writers to express publicly their views on suicide ("Samoubiistvo [Nasha anketa]," *Novoe slovo,* 1912, no. 6). Leonid Andreev, Mikhail Artsybashev, Viacheslav Ivanov, Mikhail Kuzmin, Aleksandr Kuprin, and Fedor Sologub (all of whom portrayed suicide in their fiction) were among the eleven writers who responded to the questionnaire. Discussing the writers' responses, some authors directly blamed the writers for the increase in suicide. See, for example, Maxim Gorky, "Izdaleka," *Zaprosy zhizni,* 1912, no. 7, and A. Gladkii, "Vzgliad khudozhnikov na zhizn' i samoubiistvo," *Vestnik vospitaniia,* 1913, no. 6. Such accusations were especially frequent in the discussions of Artsybashev's novels. For his response, see "Epidemiia samoubiistv" (chapter 8 of Artsybashev's *Zapiski pisatelia,* in his *Sobranie sochinenii* [Moscow, 1914]), vol. 3.)

117. All preceding quotes are from Chukovskii, "Samoubiitsy (Ocherki sovremennoi slovesnosti)," *Rech',* no. 352 (December 23, 1912).

118. All preceding quotes are from the second part of Chukovsky's essay, published in *Rech'* on December 24, 1912 (no. 353).

119. For example, in 1909 in Vienna, the physician Anton Brosch, following in the footsteps of the nineteenth-century alienists Falret and Bourdin, performed 371 autopsies to search for physical manifestations of the causes of suicide (he found definite traces of mental abnormality in 7.6 percent of cases; very probable, in 23.4 percent; probable, in 57.6 percent; and no evidence of abnormality, in 11.4 percent of cases). These and other anatomical investigations were reviewed for the Russian reader by Doctor G. Gordon, in "Sovremennye samoubiistva" (*Russkaia mysl',* 1912, no. 5:79). In 1912 the proceedings of the 1910 session of the Vienna Psychoanalytic Society on suicide appeared in a Russian translation, *Samoubiistva sredi uchashchikhsia. Diskussii Venskogo psikhoanaliticheskogo fereina,* trans. M. Bikerman, ed. M. V. Vul'f (Odessa, 1912).

Notes to Chapter 4

1. Radiukin, "Statistika samoubiistva," p. 347.
2. "Maniia samoubiistv," p. 733.
3. See MacDonald and Murphy, *Sleepless Souls,* pp. 324–34.
4. A. V. Likhachev published thirty-six suicide notes from the 1870s in the appendix to his *Samoubiistvo.* (In preparing this appendix, which he deemed to have "required special medical knowledge," Likhachev sought assistance from a medical doctor, G. I. Arkhangel'sky.) Another major publication of this sort, containing 128 notes left by secondary school and university students, appeared in the early twentieth century—as an addendum to statistical brochures issued by the Ministry of Public Education (*Samoubiistva, pokusheniia na samoubiistva i neschastnye sluchai*); among the annual issues edited by Khlopin, the ones for 1907, 1908, and 1909 contained suicide notes. Some suicide notes are reviewed in Koni's *Samoubiistvo v zakone i zhizni.* For a later period, we have a review of an unspecified number of suicide notes (with extensive quotations) left by Moscow suicides in 1979 and 1982, in A. G. Ambrumova and L. I. Postovlova, "Analiz predsmertnykh zapisok suitsidentov," in *Nauchnye i organizatsionnye problemy suitsidologii* (Moscow, 1983).
5. A comprehensive annotated bibliography of publications of and research on suicide notes, relating to Western material, can be found in Leenaars, *Suicide Notes.* The first source in Leenaars's bibliography is Brierre de Boismont's *Du suicide et de la folie suicide,* which contains a brief review of 1,328 suicide notes (some of them are paraphrased and cited, but none is reproduced verbatim). Leenaars lists no other nineteenth-century publication; my own research also yielded no other sources. For the twentieth century, the most extensive scholarly source listed by Leenaars is W. Morgenthaler's *Letzte Aufzerchnungen von Selbstmorten* (Bun, 1945), which contains forty-seven notes from Berne from 1928 to 1935. It was Erwin Shneidman who drew the attention of clinicians to suicide notes. His *Clues to Suicide* presented thirty-three notes selected from a collection of 721 from Los Angeles in 1945–54. Leenaars' *Suicide Notes* contains fifty-three notes from 1983–84 (also taken from Shneidman's source, the Los Angeles County Coroner's Office). Historians Michael MacDonald and Terence R. Murphy, for their *Sleepless Souls,* assembled over seventy eighteenth-century notes from press reports and archival sources (some of them are cited in the section "Suicide Notes").
6. Likhachev, *Samoubiistvo,* p. 233.
7. There were precedents. In England, in 1751, a correspondent of *Gentleman's Magazine* suggested that the bodies of all suicides be publicly dissected on a stage erected in a public place, both to express a condemnation of suicide as a crime and to provide badly needed cadavers for the medical profession (21:504). From Roland Bartel, "Suicide in Eighteenth-century England: The Myth of a Reputation," *Huntington Library Quarterly* 23 (1960): 150.
8. *Comptes rendus sténographiques. Congrès international de médecine légale,* no. 14 (Paris, 1879); quoted in Likhachev, *Samoubiistvo,* p. 170.

9. Rozanov's essay appeared in the collection *Samoubiistvo* (Moscow, 1911); see p. 48.

10. Michael MacDonald and Terence R. Murphy, writing about eighteenth-century England, assert that "access to the papers and the capacity to write suicide notes . . . enabled men and women to lend complex meanings to their own deaths. . . . All men and women were potentially makers of texts that might move the hearts and engage the minds of a multitude of others." Through the press, "they had gained access to a powerful new way to create images of themselves, even to make history" (*Sleepless Souls,* pp. 327 and 337).

11. "Samoubiistva (etiud po obshchestvennoi patologii)," *Nedelia,* May 11, 1886, p. 649. This is the conclusion of the essay published in the May 4 issue.

12. Ibid., p. 623.

13. Ibid., p. 649.

14. *Sankt-Peterburgskie vedomosti,* October 18, 1873.

15. Ibid., October 24, 1873.

16. All quotes are from *Russkie vedomosti,* July 11, 1892; this Moscow newspaper reprinted the notes from *Kievlianin.*

17. Quote from *Na pomoshch' molodezhi. Sbornik statei, pisem, i zametok o studencheskikh nuzhdakh i samoubiistvakh uchashchikhsia,* comp. T. Krivonosov (Kiev, 1910), p. 1.

18. *Rech',* January 17, 1910; the case is discussed in Susan K. Morrissey, "More 'Stories about the New People': Student Radicalism, Higher Education, and Social Identity in Russia, 1899–1921," Ph.D. Dissertation, University of California, Berkeley, 1993, p. 302.

19. Edwin S. Shneidman, *Voices of Death* (New York, 1980), p. 42.

20. Ibid., p. 42.

21. See Shneidman, ibid., p. 58, and Leenaars, *Suicide Notes,* p. 35.

22. Shneidman, *Voices of Death,* p. 44. In the words of psychologist Erwin Stengel, "the writers of suicide notes . . . differ from the majority only in being good correspondents" (Erwin Stengel, *Suicide and Attempted Suicide* [Baltimore, 1964], pp. 44–45).

23. Shneidman, *Clues to Suicide,* p. 7.

24. Shneidman, *Voices of Death,* p. 58. At the same time, Shneidman admired Dostoevsky's letter to his brother written on the day of his mock execution—evidence of "the nobility to which the human spirit is capable of rising." His explanation was that "when put to the ultimate test of a direct threat of death, the human spirit, *as victim,* does not fail"; as perpetrators, suicides fail to rise to the occasion in their last letters (pp. 102–3). The dean of American suicidology, Shneidman dedicated his *Voices of Death* to his late parents, who created a "bridge" from a czarist *shtetl* to an American university.

25. They continued: "One finds absolutely original explanations for the act of suicide only in two cases: these were sick people who killed themselves in a psychotic state" (Ambrumova and Postovalova, "Analiz," p. 60).

26. Likhachev, *Samoubiistvo,* p. 236 (no. 3). Marked "The note of an ed-

ucated young man who was formerly a translator in the editorial office of one of the newspapers." In this and other notes published by Likhachev, in compliance with medical ethics, all personal names and other identifying information has been replaced by such conventional signs as "N." Brackets indicate omitted personal information.

27. L. W., "Iz zhizni i sudebnoi praktiki."

28. Dostoevskii, *Polnoe sobranie sochinenii,* 30 vols., 23:25. In the rest of the chapter, references to this edition are given in the text. (The English translation of this sentence is from Fyodor Dostoevsky, *A Writer's Diary,* 2 vols., trans. Kenneth Lantz [Evanston, Ill., 1993], 1:497.)

29. Likhachev, *Samoubiistvo,* p. 248 (no. 27).

30. "Samoubiistva," *Nedelia,* May 11, 1886, p. 650.

31. Likhachev, *Samoubiistvo,* p. 245 (no. 13).

32. Dostoevsky discussed this case in the notes for *Podrostok.* See more in the chapter that follows. Quote from the commentaries to Dostoevskii, 17:405–6.

33. From Khlopin, ed., *Samoubiistva, pokusheniia na samoubiistva i neschastnye sluchai,* p. 73 (no. 3). Khlopin's brackets.

34. Likhachev, *Samoubiistvo,* p. 236 (no. 4). Marked "The note of a kitchen aide who hanged himself."

35. Ibid., (no. 2). The suicide is presented as an "honorary citizen" of his town (*lichnyi pochetnyi grazhdanin*).

36. Ibid., p. 238. Likhachev did not publish the text of the note.

37. Ibid., p. 245 (no. 14).

38. Ibid., p. 247 (no. 21).

39. L. W., "Iz zhizni i sudebnoi praktiki."

40. All quotes are from *Grazhdanin,* November 18, 1874.

41. Paraphrasing Thomas Mann, in *The Magic Mountain.*

42. Nikolai Mikhailovsky, "Zhiteiskie i khudozhestvennye dramy," *Otechestvennye zapiski,* 1879, nos. 1 and 2; quoted from *Sochineniia N. K. Mikhailovskogo* (St. Petersburg, 1897), 4:641.

43. Ibid., pp. 643–44.

44. Ibid.

45. Likhachev, *Samoubiistvo,* pp. 237–38 (no. 7). It is unclear whether the ellipsis is the author's or the publisher's.

46. Mikhailovsky, "Zhiteiskie i khudozhestvennye dramy," p. 644.

47. Ibid.

48. *Samoubiistva sredi uchashchikhsia,* pp. 6–7.

49. *Stradaniia samoubiitsy v potustoronnem mire. Magicheskoe otkrovenie (Punar Bhava) Ch. von Chinskogo. Perevod s frantsuzskogo E. L.* (St. Petersburg, 1910), p. 22.

Notes to Chapter 5

1. For a review of literary texts dealing with suicide, see Ian Lilly, "Imperial Petersburg, Suicide, and Russian Literature," *Slavonic and East European Review* 72, 3 (1995): 401–23.

2. For a list of suicides in Dostoevsky, see N. N. Shneidman, *Dostoevsky and Suicide* (Oakville, Ontario, 1984).

3. All references to the works of Dostoevsky are to Dostoevskii, *Polnoe sobranie sochinenii,* 30 vols. The second page number refers to the English translation. This and subsequent English translations of *Besy* are taken from: Fyodor Dostoevsky, *Demons,* trans. Richard Pevear and Larissa Volokhonsky (New York, 1994). Capitalization of God follows editions of Dostoevsky's novels that appeared in his lifetime.

4. Friedrich Nietzsche, "Nachgelassene Fragmente Herbst 1887 bis März 1888," *Nietzsche Werke,* ed. Giorgio Colli and Mazzino Montinari, vol. 8, part 2 (Berlin, 1970), p. 386.

5. A. I. Gertsen, *Byloe i dumy,* parts 4–5 (Moscow, 1967), p. 156 (chapter 32); English from *My Past and Thoughts. The Memoirs of Alexander Herzen,* trans. Constance Garnett (London, 1924), p. 349.

6. Immanuel Kant, *Critique of Pure Reason,* trans. F. Max Muller (New York, 1966), p. 332 ("Transcendental Dialectic," book 2, chapter 2: "The Antinomy of Pure Reason").

7. Ibid., p. 333.

8. Ibid., p. 296.

9. Koni, *Samoubiistvo v zakone i zhizni,* p. 20.

10. Kant's formulation; *Critique of Pure Reason* (p. 296). I believe that there is a direct link between Kantian antinomies and Dostoevsky's images. It was Dmitrii Merezhkovsky, in his *L. Tolstoi i Dostoevskii* (part *Religiia*), who first connected Kirillov's dilemma to the Kantian antinomy (*Polnoe sobranie sochinenii,* 24 vols. [Moscow, 1914], 12:192–93). Ia. E. Golosovker, in his *Dostoevskii i Kant* (Moscow, 1963), interpreted the confrontation between the characters in *The Brothers Karamazov* over the issue of faith and atheism as a personification of Kant's thesis and antithesis. This book, written in the genre of "a reader's meditations," has been largely ignored by scholars. The role of Kant in Dostoevsky's thought remains underestimated.

11. For a recent interpretation of this note, see Liza Knapp, *The Annihilation of Inertia: Dostoevsky and Metaphysics* (Evanston, Ill., 1996), pp. 1–2 and passim.

12. English from Fyodor Dostoevsky, *Crime and Punishment,* trans. Richard Pevear and Larissa Volokhonsky (New York, 1992), p. 50.

13. On Raskolnikov's tirade about moral statistics, see Harriet Murav, *Holy Foolishness: Dostoevsky's Novels and the Poetics of Cultural Critique* (Stanford, 1992), pp. 57–59.

14. A. Ketle, *Chelovek i razvitie ego sposobnostei,* t. 1 (St. Petersburg, 1865). On Dostoevsky's connections to Quételet, see G. M. Fridlender, *Realizm Dostoevskogo* (Moscow–Leningrad, 1964), pp. 150–57. On Quételet in the Western European context, see chapter 1.

15. Translated and edited by N. N. Nekliudov (St. Petersburg, 1866). The book included works by Rudolf Virchow, Claude Bernard, Moleschott, Theodor Piderit, and Adolph Wagner. Lebeziatnikov especially recommends Wagner's *Zakonosoobraznost' v, po-vidimomu, proizvol'nykh chelovecheskikh deistviiakh s tochki zreniia statistiki* (an essay based on the 1864 *Die*

Gesetzmässigkeit in den scheinbar willkürlichen menschlichen Handlungen vom Standpunkte der Statistik) and *Mozg i ego deiatel'nost'. Ocherk fiziologicheskoi psikhologii dlia vsekh mysliashchikh chitatelei d[okto]ra Piderita* (from Theodor Piderit's *Gehirn und Geist* [Leipzig, 1863]). On this edition, see Fridlender, p. 151, and Dostoevskii 6:307, 7:391–92.

16. Mikhail Bakhtin, *Problems of Dostoevsky's Poetics,* ed. and trans. Caryl Emerson (Minneapolis, 1984), p. 79.

17. Dmitrii Merezhkovsky, in his *L. Tolstoi i Dostoevskii* (part *Tvorchestvo*), described Dostoevsky's method as a scientific experiment. In his words, Dostoevsky, like an experimental chemist, places "human souls . . . in extraordinary and artificial conditions, not knowing himself, but waiting to see, what will become of them" (Merezhkovskii, *Polnoe sobranie sochinenii,* 10:106–7; English from Dmitri Merejkowski, *Tolstoi as Man and Artist, with an Essay on Dostoevsky* [Westport, Conn.], 1970, pp. 254–55).

18. Zola's essay was first published (through Ivan Turgenev's efforts) in *Vestnik Evropy* in 1880.

19. Emile Zola, *The Experimental Novel and Other Essays* (New York, 1893), p. 54.

20. Similarities between Dostoevsky's method and Odoevsky's were first noted by R. G. Nazirov, in "Vladimir Odoevskii i Dostoevskii," *Russkaia literatura,* 1974, no. 3.

21. Vladimir Odoevskii, *Russkie nochi,* ed. B. F. Egorov et al. (Leningrad, 1975), p. 53.

22. Odoevsky quoted in P. N. Sakulin, *Iz istorii russkogo idealizma. Kniaz' V. F. Odoevskii. Myslitel'. Pisatel',* 2 vols. (Moscow, 1913), 1, 1:483. See also commentaries to *The Russian Nights,* Odoevskii, *Russkie nochi,* p. 281.

23. Odoevskii, *Russkie nochi,* pp. 15–16.

24. Ibid., pp. 19–20.

25. Ibid., pp. 141–42. Odoevsky's quotation is from Bichat, "Recherches physiologiques sur la vie et la mort" (Paris, 1829), p. 108.

26. This and subsequent English translations of *Idiot* are taken from Fyodor Dostoevsky, *The Idiot,* trans. David Magarshak (London, 1955).

27. Noted by A. L. Bem in his "Pered litsom smerti" [1936], in his *O Dostojevskem. Sbornik stati a materialu* (Praha, 1972), pp. 168–69. See also Knapp, *The Annihilation of Inertia,* for an extended analysis of the symbolism of Ippolit's death and the death sentences in *The Idiot* (pp. 67–75, 84–96).

28. Paraphrasing *Critique of Practical Reason;* see J. B. Schneewind, "Autonomy, Obligation, and Virtue: An Overview of Kant's Moral Philosophy," in *The Cambridge Companion to Kant,* ed. Paul Guyer (Cambridge, 1992), p. 332.

29. On Voltaire's idea, see P. L. Landsberg, *The Experience of Death* (London, 1953), pp. 1–3.

30. "Est-il bien vrai que cela ne se peut, qu'il faudra mourir demain, aujourd'hui peut-être, que cela est ainsi? O Dieu! l'horrible idée à se briser la tête au mur de son cachot!" Victor Hugo, *Le Dernier jour d'un condamné,* préface de Roger Borderie (Paris, 1970), p. 287 (end of chapter 7). On Dos-

toevsky and Hugo's story, see V. V. Vinogradov, "Iz biografii odnogo 'neistovogo' proizvedeniia. Poslednii den' prigovorennogo k smerti," in his *Evoliutsiia russkogo naturalizma. Gogol' i Dostoevskii* (Leningrad, 1929); see also Bem, "Pered litsom smerti," passim, and Dostoevskii 9:429–30.

31. The translation has been edited.

32. English from *Selected Letters of Fyodor Dostoevsky,* ed. Joseph Frank and David I. Goldstein, trans. Andrew R. MacAndrew (New Brunswick, 1987), pp. 50–51.

33. F. N. L'vov, "Zapiska o dele Petrashevtsev," *Literaturnoe nasledstvo,* no. 63 (Moscow, 1956), p. 188. English translation from Joseph Frank, *Dostoevsky: The Years of Ordeal* (Princeton, 1982), pp. 57–58. In the letter to his brother, relating the experience, Dostoevsky recalled (and quoted) *Le Dernier jour* again (Dostoevskii 28/I:162).

34. In the words of Liza Knapp; see her introduction to *Dostoevsky as Reformer: The Petrashevsky Case,* ed. and trans. Liza Knapp (Ann Arbor, 1987), p. 26, n. 52.

35. The formula and information are from Julia Kristeva, "Holbein's Dead Christ," in *Fragments for a History of the Human Body,* ed. Michel Feher with Ramona Naddaff and Nadia Tazi (New York, 1989), 1:248.

36. See my Introduction for a discussion of the deaths of Socrates and Christ as cultural paradigms.

37. I am referring to the final paragraph of Seneca's "On Providence."

38. Dostoevsky commentators mistakenly identified the source as St. Paul's First Letter to the Corinthians (9:497); it is clearly the Letter to the Romans, chapter 8 (especially verse 1–21).

39. The reference is to Schiller's poem (1788), translated by Dostoevsky in 1861 (9:497).

40. This and subsequent English translations of *Podrostok* are taken from Fyodor Dostoevsky, *A Raw Youth,* trans. Constance Garnett (London, 1916).

41. A. F. Koni, *Na zhiznennom puti,* (Revel–Berlin, 1924), 3, 1:180–81. The connection between Kraft and Kramer was first established by I. I. Lapshin in "Obrazovanie tipa Krafta v 'Podrostke'," in *O Dostoevskom. Sbornik statei,* ed. A. L. Bem (Prague, 1929), 1. Lapshin compares Kraft's motivation to that of Otto Weininger, who killed himself (in 1903) after having argued, in scientific terms, that Jews were an inferior race (p. 143).

42. Likhachev, *Samoubiistvo,* p. 242.

43. Ibid., p. 243. In his diary, Kramer wrote of his (unrealized) plan to postpone the execution of his death sentence so that he could develop a scientific corroboration of his view on Russia: "I have thought about staying alive for another five or six years to devote myself to the investigation of scientific proofs confirming the truthfulness of my views" (Likhachev, *Samoubiistvo,* p. 243). What remained unrealized by Kramer in real life was fulfilled by Dostoevsky's character, Kraft, who is said to have left a notebook of such scientific deductions.

44. Noted in commentaries to Dostoevskii (17:366). The connection to Chaadaev does not stop here: rumor had it that Chaadaev's death in 1856 was a suicide (see Charles Quénet, *Tchaadaev et les lettres philosophiques* [Paris, 1931], pp. 387–93).

Notes

45. I am indebted to Liza Knapp for this argument.

46. Koni, *Na zhiznennom puti,* p. 180.

47. Likhachev, *Samoubiistvo,* pp. 240–45.

48. *Grazhdanin,* November 18, 1874, p. 1140. It was A. S. Dolinin who established that Dostoevsky used the letter published in *Grazhdanin* for the suicide letter of Kraft in *The Adolescent.* See his *V tvorcheskoi laboratorii Dostoevskogo* (Leningrad, 1947), p. 101, and *Poslednie romany Dostoevskogo* (Moscow–Leningrad, 1963), p. 140. In reproducing the letter, Dolinin made serious mistakes. For example, instead of "self-composure has not left me; I have no desire to live [*zhit'*]," Dolinin has: "self-composure is leaving me; I have no desire to drink [*pit'*]." The suicide figures as A. P., not A. Ts—v.

49. They were A. V. Likhachev, a social scientist, and a medical doctor, G. I. Arkhangel'sky.

50. Likhachev, *Samoubiistvo,* p. 241.

51. The extinguished candle plays a central role in the symbolism of Anna Karenina's suicide. (See a comment by Elisabeth Stenbock-Fermor in her *The Architecture of Anna Karenina* [Lisse, 1975], p. 44) (Dostoevsky's *Adolescent* appeared while Tolstoy was working on *Anna Karenina.*) The image of the candle also plays a significant role in the scene of Kirillov's last minutes in *The Possessed.*

52. Dostoevsky is quoting a newspaper report from *Golos,* August 24, 1874 (see Dostoevskii 17:405–6). This suicide probably inspired Vasin's remark in the novel: "one such suicide complained, in fact, in a similar diary that not one lofty idea visited him at that important hour, nothing but futile and petty thoughts" (13:134/159).

53. The theme of suicide in *Podrostok* was briefly reviewed by A. S. Dolinin in his *V tvorcheskoi laboratorii Dostoevskogo,* pp. 96–104, and *Poslednie romany Dostoevskogo,* pp. 134–42.

54. For discussion of this metaphor, see Chapter 3.

55. As defined by John Meyendorff in *Byzantine Theology: Historical Trends and Doctrinal Themes* (New York, 1979), p. 144. This view was articulated in Gregory of Nyssa's treatise *On the Creation of Man* (see Meyendorff, *Byzantine Theology,* pp. 138–39; Georges Florovsky, *The Eastern Fathers of the Fourth Century* [Vaduz, 1987], p. 193). The patristic roots of the concept of "corruption" are discussed by Knapp in *The Annihilation of Inertia,* pp. 56, 70–71, and passim. I am indebted to Liza Knapp for drawing my attention to this concept.

56. Quoted in Meyendorff, *Byzantine Theology,* p. 141.

57. Ibid., pp. 141 and 143.

58. A reference to "image" appears also in the notes to *The Possessed;* Kirillov is explicating his theory of suicide: "If there is no God (image) [*Esli net Boga (obraz)*]" (inserted on the margin) (11:294).

59. On the connotations of *obraz* in Dostoevsky, see Robert Louis Jackson, *Dostoevsky's Quest for Form: A Study of His Philosophy of Art* (New Haven, 1966), pp. 58–59 and passim.

60. Richard McKeon on Platonic dialogue in "Dialogue and Controversy in Philosophy," in *The Interpretation of Dialogue,* ed. Tullio Maranhao (Chicago, 1990), p. 27.

61. On the genre of Socratic dialogue and its relevance for Dostoevsky, see Bakhtin, *Problems of Dostoevsky's Poetics,* pp. 110–12. Bakhtin did not connect Kirillov's argument to *Phaedo;* he demonstrated that Dostoevsky evoked *Phaedo* in a parodic treatment of the theme of the immortality of the soul, his story "Bobok" (1873) (see pp. 137–41).

62. See Hegel, *Lectures on the Philosophy of Religion* [1827], ed. Peter C. Hodgson (Berkeley, 1988), p. 465, n. 199. The importance for Dostoevsky of Hegel's claim "God is dead," is noted by Knapp in *The Annihilation of Inertia,* p. 223, n. 6. It should be added that the theme first appeared in Hegel's *Phenomenology of Spirit* (1807) (in the conclusion to section C of Chapter 7).

63. Hegel, *Lectures on the Philosophy of Religion,* p. 463, n. 196, and p. 465, n. 199.

64. The title of section 3 of part B in Chapter 6 of *The Phenomenology of Mind.*

65. G. W. F. Hegel, *The Phenomenology of Mind* [*Phänomenologie des Geistes*], trans. J. B. Baillie (London, 1949), pp. 600, 604–5. These ideas were extended in the reading of Hegel advanced by Alexandre Kojève in his *Introduction to the Reading of Hegel,* ed. Allan Bloom, trans. James H. Nichols (Ithaca, 1969), see especially pp. 56–57.

66. For a review of these debates, see my introduction.

67. Ludwig Feuerbach, *The Essence of Christianity,* trans. George Eliot (New York, 1957), p. xxxix. (From the author's preface to the second edition, 1843.)

68. Ibid., p. xxxvi.

69. See chapter 18, "Dostoevsky and Speshnev," of Joseph Frank's *Dostoevsky: The Seeds of Revolt, 1821–1849.*

70. From draft of a letter to a friend, ca. 1847; original in German. Quote from N. A. Speshnev, "Pis'ma k K. E. Khoetskomu," in *Filosofskie i obshchestvenno-politicheskie proizvedeniia Petrashevtsev* (Moscow, 1953), p. 502.

71. Ibid., p. 496. On the connection between Kirillov's theory and interpretations of Feuerbach by Petrashevtsy, see commentaries to Dostoevskii (12:221–22).

72. Feuerbach, *Essence of Christianity,* p. 183.

73. The physical, sensory nature of Kirillov's experience was noted by Dmitry Merezhkovsky, who also commented on the convergence of Apocalypse and Kant in this episode. See Merezhkovskii, *L. Tolstoi i Dostoevskii. Religiia,* in *Polnoe sobranie sochinenii,* 12:188 and 190.

74. On this experience, see James L. Rice, *Dostoevsky and the Healing Art: An Essay in Literary and Medical History* (Ann Arbor, 1985), pp. 77–108.

75. Feuerbach, *Essence of Christianity,* p. 183.

76. Merezhkovskii 12:198 (from *L. Tolstoi i Dostoevskii,* written in 1900–1902).

77. Vinogradov, "Iz biografii," pp. 150–52.

78. This was Dostoevsky's reaction to the case of A. Danilov, a student whose crime, committed after the publication of the first parts of *Crime and Punishment,* resembled Raskol'nikov's. (See Dostoevskii 7:349–50.) One

might recall Claude Bernard's insistence that experimental method permits us to foretell the appearance of phenomena.

79. That "Mal'kov" is A. Malikov is noted in the commentaries for *The Possessed* (Dostoevskii 12:223); commentaries for the notebooks and the name index, however, list "Mal'kov" as an "unidentified person" (22:399; 24:447; 30/II:262).

80. A. I. Faresov, *Semidesiatniki. Ocherki umstvennykh i politicheskikh dvizhenii v Rossii* (St. Petersburg, 1905), p. 297.

81. Ibid., pp. 298–99.

82. V. G. Korolenko, *Istoriia moego sovremennika*, in his *Polnoe sobranie sochinenii* (Moscow, 1955), 7:181.

83. Faresov, *Semidesiatniki,* p. 300.

84. Ibid., p. 302.

85. Korolenko, *Istoriia moego sovremennika,* p. 185.

86. See Bernard, *Introduction to the Study of Experimental Medicine* [1865], pp. 99–104.

87. *Antichrist* (1895), quoted in Friedrich Nietzsche, *Twilight of the Idols and The Anti-Christ,* trans. R. J. Hollingdale (London, 1968), pp. 152–53.

88. The notes, made in German, were taken from the French translation of Dostoevsky's 1872 novel, published in 1886; the title (in Nietzsche's hand) is transliterated Russian, "Besi." The notes were first published in the Giorgio Colli and Mazzino Montinari edition of Nietzsche, "Nachgelassene Fragmente Herbst 1887 bis März 1888," *Werke. Kritische Gesamtausgabe,* (Berlin, 1970) 8, 2. This document was discussed in detail by Iu. Davydov in his *Etika liubvi i metafizika svoevoliia* (Moscow, 1989).

89. Friedrich Nietzsche, *The Will to Power,* trans. Walter Kaufmann and R. J. Hollingdale, ed. Walter Kaufmann (New York, 1967), p. 45, n. 39.

90. Nietzsche, *Werke* 8/2:382. Davydov believes that the diary of Nietzsche's nihilist is based on Stavrogin's last letter (see Davydov, *Etika liubvi,* pp. 167–70).

91. Nietzsche, *Werke* 8/2:383. This and subsequent translations of Nietzsche's notes are by Andreas Johns.

92. Ibid., p. 387. Cf. Dostoevskii 10:471.

93. Ibid., p. 386. Cf. Dostoevskii 10:469.

94. Davydov created the pun *psikho-logika.*

95. Friedrich Nietzsche, *Thus Spoke Zarathustra,* trans. R. J. Hollingdale (London, 1969), p. 110 (Part Two, chapter "On the Blissful Islands").

96. Nietzsche's connection with Hegel and the Hegelian school was discussed, among other authors, by Karl Löwith, *From Hegel to Nietzsche: The Revolution in Nineteenth-Century Thought,* trans. David E. Green (New York, 1964), pp. 181–88; Walter Kaufmann, *Nietzsche,* p. 100; and Hollingdale, *Nietzsche,* p. 40. Dostoevsky's connection to Hegel is a topic that remains to be investigated. D. I. Chizhevsky, in his comprehensive study of Hegel in Russia, *Gegel' v Rossii* (Paris, 1939), failed to find "*visible* traces of familiarity with Hegel" in Dostoevsky's writing (p. 321; see also bibliographic note on p. 353). However, Dostoevsky belonged to a generation and a literary circle who knew Hegel by heart.

97. Hegel, *Lectures on the Philosophy of Religion*, p. 465, n. 199 (from the 1831 lectures).

98. Friedrich Nietzsche, *The Gay Science*, trans. Walter Kaufmann (New York, 1974), p. 181 (section 125).

99. I am paraphrasing and extending Kaufmann: "Nietzsche's pronouncement does not at all purport to be a dogmatic statement about a supernatural reality: it is a declaration of what he takes to be a historical cultural fact. . . . an attempt at a diagnosis of contemporary civilization" (Kaufmann, *Nietzsche*, p. 100).

100. Merezhkovskii, *Polnoe sobranie sochinenii*, 12:184–85 (from part of *L. Tolstoi i Dostoevskii* written in 1901). Merezhkovsky believed that Nietzsche did not know Dostoevsky and could not have been influenced by him (ibid.).

101. Ibid., p. 186.

102. Ibid., pp. 190–91.

103. Ibid., pp. 192–94. For "Kant is an idiot," Merezhkovsky gives a reference to Nietzsche's *Der Wille zur Macht*, published the same year as chapter 4 of *L. Tolstoi i Dostoevskii*, in 1901 (Merezhkovsky mistakenly gives the date as 1899).

104. Ibid., pp. 194–95.

105. Ibid., p. 198.

106. Ibid., p. 199.

107. Ibid., p. 201.

108. Albert Camus, *The Myth of Sisyphus and Other Essays*, trans. Justin O'Brien (New York, 1961), p. 4 (first published in 1942).

109. Ibid., p. 3.

110. Ibid., p. 109.

111. Ludwig Wittgenstein, *Notebooks 1914–1916*, 2d ed., trans. G. E. M. Anscombe (Chicago, 1979), p. 91.

112. According to his biographer, Ray Monk, Wittgenstein knew whole passages of *The Brothers Karamazov* by heart (Ray Monk, *Ludwig Wittgenstein: The Duty of Genius* [London, 1990], p. 136).

113. Wittgenstein, *Notebooks*, p. 91.

114. Ibid., p. 89.

115. Published (from the transcript made by the poet and novelist Raymond Queneau) as Alexandre Kojève, *Introduction à la lecture de Hegel* (Paris, 1947). For a brief discussion of Kojève's role in proselytizing Hegel in twentieth-century France, see Mark Lilla, "The End of Philosophy: How a Russian Emigré Brought Hegel to the French," *Times Literary Supplement* (April 5, 1991), pp. 3–5.

116. Kojève, *Introduction to the Reading of Hegel*, p. 248, n. 33. Kojève thanks Jacob Klein for this interpretation of the Kirillov episode.

117. Ibid., p. 67.

118. Kojève quotes from the essay "Natural Right" (1802): "pure freedom in its appearance is death; and through the faculty of death the subject shows himself as [being] free and absolutely elevated above all constraint" (ibid., p. 247). One other reference (on the same page as the reference to the Kirillov

episode) is to Hegel's *Lectures at Jena* of 1805–1806 (ibid., p. 248, n. 34).

119. The fact that Kojève's Hegel is a blend of the ideas of Hegel, Feuerbach, Marx, Heidegger, and Nietzsche has been noted by many scholars. According to Judith R. Butler, Kojève's commentaries to Hegel "are extensions of the text, they *are* the text in its modern life" (*Subjects of Desire: Hegelian Reflections in Twentieth-Century France* [New York, 1987], p. 63). See also a recent book by Shadia B. Drury, *Alexandre Kojève: The Roots of Postmodern Politics* (New York, 1994), pp. xi and 13. Nobody, however, has seen Dostoevsky in Kojève's Hegel. Consequently, Drury sees no reason why "gratuitous suicide" plays such a large role in Kojève's vision of the end of history (p. 63).

Notes to Chapter 6

1. Here and further references are to Dostoevskii, *Polnoe sobranie sochinenii,* 30 vols.

2. The notebooks in which Dostoevsky recorded his plans for the *Diary* indicate that he took most of his material from the liberal *Golos.* He also regularly used *Birzhevye vedomosti, Novoe vremia, Peterburgskaia gazeta, Sankt-Peterburgskie vedomosti, Russkii mir,* and *Moskovskie vedomosti* (the last he considered to be the best Russian newspaper; 24:163, 259). Dostoevsky took a particular interest in suicide reports; among the notes on suicides that did not find their way into the *Diary* are those in 24:71, 72, 98, 151, 190, 223.

3. For an extensive discussion of the *Diary* as a genre, see Gary Saul Morson, "Introductory Study: Dostoevsky's Great Experiment," in Fyodor Dostoevsky, *A Writer's Diary,* 2 vols., trans. Kenneth Lanz (Evanston, Ill., 1993 and 1994), vol. 1.

4. Dostoevsky's archive contains about two hundred letters from readers of the *Diary* for 1876–77, many more than he received for any of his novels. The number of subscribers was about six thousand (a figure close to the subscription of the main "thick journals"). See Igor Volgin, "Pis'ma chitatelei k F. M. Dostoevskomu," *Voprosy literatury,* 1971, no. 9:173; see also his "Dostoevskii i russkoe obshchestvo ('Dnevnik pisatelia' 1876–1877 godov v otsenkakh sovremennikov)," *Russkaia literatura,* 1976, no. 3.

5. L. W., "Iz zhizni i sudebnoi praktiki."

6. This and subsequent English translations are from Dostoevsky, *A Writer's Diary,* trans. Kenneth Lantz. The first page reference refers to Dostoevskii's *Polnoe sobranie sochinenii;* the second to the English translation.

7. The translation has been edited.

8. See chapter 4 for details and references.

9. See the anonymous article "Skuka zhizn'iu," *Nedelia,* June 29, 1875. A brief note on this suicide appeared in *Golos,* June 18, 1875, and *Novoe vremia,* June 22, 1875 (for this information I am indebted to Peter Pozefsky). On this case, see Peter Pozefsky's Ph.D. dissertation, "Dmitrii Pisarev and the Nihilist Imagination," pp. 303–12. In the words of Pozefsky, "the two incidents blended in Dostoevsky's imagination . . . in his writings the suicide

of Nadezhda Pisareva symbolized the social consequences of the nihilist views shared by [Dmitry] Pisarev and his cohort" (pp. 308–9).

10. The nihilist midwife Virginskaia from *The Possessed* comes to mind as an example from fiction; the child whom she delivers (Stavrogin's child) and his mother (Maria Shatova) both die. In his plans for the *Diary,* Dostoevsky recorded information about another suicide of a young midwife (see 24:72 and 406).

11. This letter is part of Dostoevsky's archive, IRLI (Institut russkoi literatury, or Pushkinskii dom), fond 100, no. 29632. Quote from Dostoevskii 29/II:249.

12. Quoted from F. M. Dostoevsky, *Pis'ma,* 4 vols., ed. and commentary A. S. Dolinin (Moscow–Leningrad, 1934), 3:362.

13. This image is inspired by Vladimir Odoevsky's "Poslednee samoubiistvo," a tale inserted in *Russkie nochi.* See Odoevskii, *Russkie nochi,* p. 58.

14. See commentaries to Dostoevsky's works; Dostoevskii 15:407–9 and 29/II:249–50.

15. English from *Selected Letters of Fyodor Dostoevsky,* ed. Joseph Frank and David I. Goldstein, trans. Andrew MacAndrew (New Brunswick, 1987), p. 420; the translation has been edited.

16. June 6, 1876. Quoted from Dostoevskii 29/II:251; original in IRLI, fond 100, no. 29823.

17. English from *Selected Letters of Fyodor Dostoevsky,* p. 422; the translation has been edited.

18. In addition to the letters discussed below, the Dostoevsky archives contain another letter that appears to be a suicide note addressed to the author of the *Diary of a Writer:*

Dear Sir Fyodor Mikhailovich.
In an hour as measured by the tablespoon
But I will soon be silent! You will go on living for a long time. Do not be surprised by such insolence. Oh God, life is dear to me, each step is dear, when life is visible. And no one has understood *our* life better than you. I have two brothers: one is a European—a practical man; the other is a Russian—a man of theory, a professor, and so forth. And you have explained both of my brothers to me. You must understand that I have the right to love you.

   [Once again,]
     Your Reader
Farewell.

(Mailed on May 17, 1876; IRLI, fond 100, no. 29943)

19. All quotes are from N. N., letter to Dostoevsky of June 9, 1876; IRLI, fond 100, no. 29956.

20. The arguments expounded in "Prigovor" were developed further in Ivan Karamazov's famous monologue on returning one's ticket of entry to the Creator. V. V. Rozanov, in *Legenda o velikom inkvizitore F. M. Dostoevskogo* [1894], was one of the first to note this connection (pp. 261–66 of the Berlin edition of 1924).

21. The idea echoes that of Odoevsky, expressed in the introductory remarks to "Poslednee samoubiistvo" (see Odoevskii, *Russkie nochi,* p. 53).

22. The statement appears to have been an exaggeration. Three such letters are contained in Dostoevsky's archives. M. A. Iurkevich, a teacher from Kishinev, wrote to Dostoevsky on November 11, 1876, describing the suicide of a young boy (IRLI, fond 100, no. 29911). Dostoevsky responded with a brief letter on January 11, 1877 (29/2:134) and discussed the case in the January 1877 issue of the *Diary* (section "Nameday," *Imeninnik*). F. M. Pliusnin, a merchant's son from the Viatka region, on December 10, 1876, described two suicides (IRLI, fond 100, no. 29814). L. P. Bliummer, on December 16, 1876, described two suicides that occurred in his home town, Saratov (IRLI, fond 100, no. 29646).

23. IRLI, fond 100, no. 29919. Commentators on Dostoevsky's works thought that this letter was written on January 6, 1876 (a clear mistake; the date is January 5, 1877) and erroneously interpreted Dostoevsky's reasoning in the January 1876 issue as a response to Iaroshevsky's letter (22:312–13).

24. The original of Voevodin's letter of March 16, 1878, is not known; parts of this letter (including a large part of the passage that I quoted) are reproduced in the second letter Voevodin sent to Dostoevsky, on April 26, 1878 (IRLI, fond 100, no. 29663). The first letter was also reproduced in a published version of Voevodin's diary, N. I. Galitskii, *Na beregakh Nevy* (St. Petersburg, 1901); I quote the letter from Galitskii, p. 103. The introduction to the book stated that the diary of A. D. Voevodin was published posthumously by his friend, N. I. Galitskii. Apparently, *Na beregakh Nevy* contained some of the material from the notebook that Voevodin had sent to Dostoevsky in 1878, but it was heavily edited as well as amended. It was intimated that the author committed suicide. Thus, on the last page of the published diary, he bids farewell to "mother nature." The last entry reads: "*1. avg. 189., O Bozhe moi, Bozhe m*" [O my God, my God] (p. 111). According to I. F. Masanov, Galitskii is a fictitious figure; the publication is Voevodin's (*Slovar' psevdonimov* [Moscow, 1956], 1:285). According to commentators of Dostoevsky's complete works, Voevodin died in 1903 (see Dostoevskii 30/I:422).

25. In spite of inconsistencies in the dates, I believe that a document in the Dostoevsky archive in IRLI is Voevodin's original diary (fond 100, no. 14310).

26. See Volgin, "Dostoevskii i russkoe obshchestvo," pp. 127–28; Morson, "Introductory Study," pp. 10–11.

27. Voevodin's letter to Dostoevsky of April 26, 1878 (IRLI, fond 100, no. 29663); this passage is presented as a quote from his first letter.

28. Galitskii, *Na beregakh Nevy,* p. 10.

29. Ibid., p. 44.

30. On his collection of newspaper clippings, see ibid., pp. 19, 44–45. Pisareva's letter is reproduced on pp. 46–48 (names have been changed).

31. See Galitskii, *Na beregakh Nevy,* p. 61.

32. Ibid., pp. 10–11.

33. Most likely, these reflections, quoted here from *Na beregakh Nevy,* were written after *The Brothers Karamazov;* the text that Voevodin sent to Dostoevsky in 1878 does not seem to contain this passage.

34. Galitskii, *Na beregakh Nevy*, p. 40. A similar experience was related in the original diary; IRLI, fond 100, no. 14310, p. 53.

35. Galitskii, *Na beregakh Nevy*, pp. 91, 93, and 95.

36. See Voevodin's letter to Dostoevsky of April 26, 1878, IRLI, fond 100, no. 29663.

37. See Galitskii, *Na beregakh Nevy*, pp. 104–5n.

38. The case of Maria Borisova was reported in *Novoe vremia*, October 3, 1876, *Golos*, October 2, 1876, and *Birzhevye vedomosti*, October 2, 1876.

39. The translation has been edited.

40. K. P. Pobedonostsev to Dostoevsky on June 3, 1876 (published in *Literaturnoe nasledstvo* 15, pp. 130–31); in his *Diary*, Dostoevsky quoted the letter almost verbatim. The case was briefly (and inaccurately) reported in Russian newspapers, *Kievskii telegraf*, April 25, 1876, and *Golos*, May 3–4, 1876, which listed "hopeless love" as one of the causes (the suicide occurred in December 1875). The circumstances of this suicide are related and documented in *Arkhiv N. A. i N. P. Ogarevykh*, ed. M. Gershenzon (Moscow-Leningrad, 1930) (pp. 6–7 and 129–247). The actual suicide letter is somewhat, but not significantly, different from the version known to Dostoevsky; the statement that so shocked Pobedonostsev and Dostoevsky, "c'est ne pas chic" (as it is reproduced in Dostoevsky's complete works) is phrased differently; in the Russian translation it reads: *"eto budet ochen' nepriiatno"* ("this will be very unpleasant") (*Arkhiv Ogarevykh*, p. 214; French original unknown).

41. *Literaturnoe nasledstvo* 15, p. 130. Pobedonostsev was right: Liza was brought up in atheism. Herzen even took a particular pride in the fact that Liza was not baptized (this could not have happened had she been born in Russia). The accuracy of his description of the "domestic hell" is confirmed by family correspondence. A vivid picture of the family is given in the diary of E. F. Litvinova, who was Liza's tutor; see I., "Nelegal'naia sem'ia (iz zagranichnogo dnevnika 70-kh godov)," *Nabliudatel'*, 1901, no. 9:247–95.

42. In the plans for the *Diary* Dostoevsky gives such a reading: "All the same, Herzen's daughter, it would seem, should have been an inspired being with at least an understanding of something more elevated than a bottle of Cliquot" (23:325).

43. Letter no. 105; *Arkhiv N. A. i N. P. Ogarevykh*, p. 148. The original of this and all other letters quoted below were in French, but they were published only in Russian translation.

44. Letter no. 138; ibid., p. 191.

45. Letter no. 140; ibid., p. 193.

46. Letter no. 136; ibid., p. 187.

47. See Reclus's letter to Ogareva of June 7, 1875 (no. 129), pp. 177–81, which paraphrases Ogareva's letter to her (the original is unknown). Herzen's family was already connected with a scandal involving suicide: in 1867, Charlotta Götson, the mistress of Alexander Herzen junior and mother of his illegitimate son, who lived with the Ogarevs, drowned herself in Lake Geneva (see *Arkhiv Ogarevykh*, pp. 321).

48. Dolinin, who connected Versilov to Herzen, identified specific parallels

and documented their sources; see Dolinin, *V tvorcheskoi laboratorii Dostoevskogo,* pp. 69–76 and *Poslednie romany Dostoevskogo,* pp. 104–12.

49. Cf. the observation by Nina Perlina in "Vozdeistvie Gertsenovskogo zhurnalizma na arkhitektoniku i polifonicheskoe stroenie *Dnevnika pisatelia* Dostoevskogo," *Dostoevsky Studies* 5 (1984): 143–44.

50. Dostoevsky's prediction was based not only on his view of the dangers of atheism for the young, but also on his knowledge of Herzen's family. He saw Herzen's daughters during his European trip of 1863. In his plans for the *Diary,* Dostoevsky related both a long conversation with the elder daughter, Natalia, who later "lost her mind" (Dostoevsky did not know that this was a temporary condition), and his impressions of seeing the second daughter, then a child ("Herzen's second daughter, the suicide"). He ascribed Natalia Herzen's insanity to the atmosphere in the family ("the life of this entire *family* was strange and this young soul was unable to bear it" [23:324]) and depicted the second daughter as a capricious child, the center of the family's attention. Dostoevsky was mistaken; he had actually seen another daughter, Olga; see the commentaries, 23:407.

One uncanny coincidence was that champagne played such a role in Liza Herzen's suicide note. In the plans for *The Adolescent,* the hero's love for champagne marked his connection to Herzen. (Herzen was known as a lover of champagne, which accompanied intellectual discussions in his home.) Dostoevsky made the following "shorthand" notes: "Drinks champagne à la Herzen" (16:50); "Herzen's chitchat over champagne" (16:54); "Let's drink. Like Herzen"; "Long live life—champagne! (16:418, 419).

51. The word "krotkaia" appears in Dostoevsky's description of the case of Maria Borisova (23:146).

52. An interpretation of the story as a variation on the theme of materialism and mortality was offered by Liza Knapp, in her "The Force of Inertia in Dostoevsky's *Krotkaja,*" *Dostoevsky Studies* 6 (1985): 143–56.

Notes to Chapter 7

1. The main work devoted to —r, or Albert Kovner, is Leonid Grossman, *Ispoved' odnogo evreia* (Moscow–Leningrad, 1924); for an English translation see Leonid Grossman, *Confession of a Jew,* trans. Ranne Moab (New York, 1975). See also an earlier essay by S. L. Tsinberg, "A. Kovner (Pisarevshchina v evreiskoi literature)," *Perezhitoe. Sbornik, posviashchennyi obshchestvennoi i kul'turnoi istorii evreev v Rossii* (St. Petersburg, 1910), vol. 2, from which Grossman borrowed some of his material and interpretations. See also Israel Zinberg, "Abraham Uri Kovner," in his *A History of Jewish Literature,* trans. Bernard Martin (New York, 1978), vol. 12. For a bibliography of materials on Kovner, see A. I. Reitblat, "Kovner," *Russkie pisateli 1800–1917. Biograficheskii slovar'* (Moscow, 1992), 2:582–83.

2. *Golos,* June 1, 1873. Occasionally, the feuilletonist would relate a suicide case in detail, complete with suicide note (see *Golos,* July 12, 1873).

3. All quotes are from *Golos,* June 16, 1873.

4. "Peterburgskaia khronika," *Golos,* December 1, 1872.

5. *Golos,* June 16, 1873.

6. Dostoevskii 17:405. In the plans for the *Adolescent,* Dostoevsky alluded to this case again (16:68).

7. *Golos,* January 18, 1873.

8. *Golos,* June 16, 1873.

9. Kovner's real name was Avraam-Uriia; he used the name Albert throughout most of his career in the Russian press.

10. From the coverage of the trial in *Golos,* September 7, 1875.

11. The text of Kovner's letter to Dostoevsky of January 26, 1877, was published (with many minor inaccuracies) in Dostoevskii, *Pis'ma* 3:378–82. This and subsequent citations are from Dolinin's edition of *Pis'ma,* with corrections made from the original (GBL [Gosudarstvennaia biblioteka im, V. I. Lenina], fond 93, II.5.82). For the corrections, I am indebted to K. Rogov. I follow the somewhat idiosyncratic grammar of the original; in Dolinin's publication the text has been edited to adhere to a grammatical standard. Dostoevskii, *Pis'ma,* 3:378.

12. Ibid.

13. GBL, fond 93, II.5.82.

14. Dostoevskii, *Pis'ma,* 3:378.

15. Ibid., 3:380.

16. Kovner hoped that the diary "might some day be published." The material from the diary was later used in Kovner's memoirs: A. K., "Tiuremnye vospominaniia," *Istoricheskii vestnik,* 1897, nos. 1–4.

17. Dostoevskii, *Pis'ma,* 3:381–82.

18. Between January 1877 and January 1878, Kovner addressed at least six letters to Dostoevsky, only two of which have been published; the other four, devoted largely to practical matters, are in GBL, fond 93, II.5.82.

19. From Kovner's article on Jewish theological education, "Eshibotnaia bursa," published in the Odessa newspaper *Den',* June 20, 1869; quote from Grossman, *Ispoved',* pp. 25–28.

20. From Kovner's memoirs, published anonymously: A. G., "Iz zapisok evreia," *Istoricheskii vestnik,* March 1903, p. 996.

21. Letter to Dostoevsky of January 26, 1877; Dostoevskii, *Pis'ma,* 3:379. The account of his literary activities is quite accurate. Among Kovner's works addressed to the Russian Jews are two collections of articles, published in Hebrew, *Cheker Dowar* [The pamphlets, Kiev, 1865] and *Zeror Perachim* [A Wreath of Flowers, Odessa, 1868], which criticize the religious foundations and social conservatism of modern Jewish literature and education. They met with fierce attacks by members of Jewish literary community. In 1872, Kovner published a novel, *Vne kolei* (under the penname, A. Kornev) in *Biblioteka deshevaia–obshchedostupnaiia,* a literary journal for mass readership; a separate edition, entitled *Bez iarlyka,* was banned by censorship. (On the book, see L. M. Dobrovol'skii, *Zapreshchennaia kniga v Rossii* [Moscow, 1962], pp. 97–98.)

22. Dostoevskii, *Pis'ma,* 3:380.

23. The role of Pisarev as Kovner's model was discussed by Tsinberg, "A. Kovner" (p. 139), and Grossman, *Ispoved'* (pp. 51–53).

24. After Pisarev's definition of Bazarov's character; Grossman, *Ispoved'*, p. 52.

25. Vasilii Rozanov, in *Okolo tserkovnykh sten,* vol. 2 (St. Petersburg, 1906), defined Kovner as "'Pisarev' evreistva" (p. 410); S. L. Tsinberg subtitled his 1910 essay on Kovner "Pisarevshchina v evreiskoi literature." The comparison with Chernyshevsky was made by the Jewish critic Gotlober (see Tsinberg, "A. Kovner," p. 144) and by Kovner's critics from *Grazhdanin* (and Kovner himself, see his feuilleton in *Golos,* December 1, 1872).

26. On Kovner and Paperna, see Tsinberg, "A. Kovner," pp. 144–45, based on A. I. Paperna, "Vospominaniia," *Geed Gazman,* no. 132 (1909).

27. Dostoevskii, *Pis'ma,* 3:379–80.

28. English from Fyodor Dostoevsky, *Crime and Punishment,* trans. Richard Peaver and Larissa Volokhonsky (New York, 1992), p. 65.

29. The scheme involved two banks, the St. Petersburg Savings Bank, where Kovner worked, and the Moscow Merchant Bank. For details, see Tsinberg, "A. Kovner," pp. 153–55. Both Tsinberg and Grossman in *Ispoved'* (chapter 3, "Opyt Raskol'nikova") connected Kovner's crime to *Crime and Punishment.*

30. —r, "Literaturnye i obshchestvennye kur'ezy," *Golos,* February 1, 1873. Noted by Tsinberg, p. 149.

31. Kovner's deposition at his trial; "Sudebnaia khronika," *Moskovskie vedomosti,* September 6, 1875 (no. 226); Grossman, *Ispoved',* pp. 72–73, quotes it with minor deviations.

32. "Sudebnaia khronika," *Russkie vedomosti,* September 6, 1875. Grossman does not cite this letter. In his reading of Kovner's crime as an emulation of Raskolnikov's, he emphasized the salvation of Sofia: "'But the main thing is Sonechka, eternal Sonechka,' . . . the courageous transgressor of criminal prohibitions could repeat after the main character of the novel that made such a strong impression on him: 'Sonya! Sonya! Gentle Sonya!'" (Grossman, *Ispoved',* p. 77, quoting Dostoevskii 6:38 and 212).

33. All quotes are from "Sudebnaia khronika," *Russkie vedomosti,* September 6, 1875 (no. 192); Tsinberg, "A. Kovner," p. 154, quotes the letter with minor deviations from this text.

34. See *Golos,* May 15, 1875.

35. Quote from Tsinberg, "A. Kovner," p. 155.

36. Grossman admits this on p. 81 of his *Ispoved'.*

37. "Sudebnaia khronika," *Moskovskie vedomosti,* September 6, 1875 (no. 226); Grossman, *Ispoved',* p. 84, quotes the text with minor deviations.

38. See coverage of the trial in *Golos,* September 7, 1875.

39. Tsinberg, "A. Kovner," p. 156; repeated by Grossman, *Ispoved',* p. 85.

40. "Sudebnaia khronika," *Moskovskie vedomosti,* September 7, 1875 (no. 227).

41. Ibid.; quoted in Grossman, *Ispoved',* pp. 87–88 (with minor deviations).

42. Ibid.

43. Tsinberg, "A. Kovner," p. 157.

44. For a discussion of "Goloslovnye utverzhdeniia" and "Prigovor," see chapter 6.

45. Dostoevskii 29/II:280.

46. Dostoevskii 29/II:280–81.

47. Ibid., p. 281.

48. Grossman, *Ispoved'*, p. 68.

49. Dostoevskii 29/II:281.

50. All quotes are from Dostoevskii 29/II:138–41.

51. Grossman connects the discussion in *The Brothers Karamazov,* and the formula of "pro and contra," with Kovner's letter (p. 116).

52. Quoted in Grossman, *Ispoved'*, p. 136. Originals of Kovner's letters to Rozanov are in GBL, fond 249, M. 3828.

53. Grossman, *Ispoved'*, p. 133.

54. Noted by Grossman, *Ispoved'*, p. 145.

55. Quoted in Rozanov, *Okolo tserkovnykh sten,* 2:428.

56. Ibid., pp. 428–29, Rozanov's note 2.

57. I mean, of course, Michel Foucault's famous discussion of these issues in *The Order of Things: An Archaeology of the Human Sciences* (New York, 1973), pp. 303–7 and passim.

58. Hans-Georg Gadamer, "On the Problem of Self-Understanding" [1962], in his *Philosophical Hermeneutics,* trans. and ed. David E. Linge (Berkeley, 1976), p. 58.

59. Virchow's role is discussed in chapter 1.

Appendix   The Russian Texts

Listed below are the original Russian texts of quotations found in the book in translation. Appendix entries are keyed to endnote numbers or to sources.

Introduction

После него остались многие философические сочинения, которые никогда не были и не могли быть напечатаны. Оставшиеся деньги [. . .] он велел раздать нищим, а попам ничего.[63]

никогда и никто не был столько уверен в небытии души, как я.[64]

После смерти нет ничего!
Сей справедливый и соответствующий наивернейшему правилу резон [. . .] заставил меня взять пистолет в руки. Я никакой причины не имел пресечь свое существование. Будущее, по моему положению, представляло мне *своевольное и приятное* существование. Но сие будущее миновало бы скоропостижно; а напоследок самое отвращение к нашей русской жизни есть то самое побуждение, принудившее меня решить самовольно мою судьбу.

О! Если бы все несчастные имели смелость пользоваться здравым рассудком...[66]

Господа нижние земские судьи! Я оставляю вашей команде мое тело. Я его столько презираю... Будьте в том уверены.[66]

Случается, и много имеем примеров в повествованиях, что человек, коему возвещают, что умерсть ему должно, с презрением и нетрепетно взирает на шествующую к нему смерть во сретение. Много видали и видим людей отъемлющих самих у себя жизнь мужественно. [. . .] Нередко таковый зрит и за предел гроба, и чает возродиться.[68]

Notes to introduction

7.   Чернеет на виске проклятое пятно!..
         Унес с собой он тайну роковую
         Последних дум своих, последних дней...
         И что сгубило жизнь его младую, —
         Осталося загадкой для людей.

Chapter 2

Самоубийство так же старо, как и само человечество. [. . .] Но не в одну эпоху истории человечества оно не было так распространено [. . .] как в наш просвещенный и гуманный XIX век. Теперь самоубийство сделалось какой-то эпидемической болезнью и, притом, болезнью хронической, которая вырывает тысячи жертв из среды населения решительно всех цивилизованных стран Европы. Так говорит статистика, это же может сказать всякий, кто следит за городской хроникой.[1]

переходное время, между ветхим и новым, идеализмом и позитивизмом.[4]

весь прежний психический мир человека рухнул.[5]

Не далеко еще ушло от нас то время, когда нашей молодежи проповедывали, что [. . .] у человека никакой души или духа нет, а есть рефлексы головного мозга; — что душа и дух должны [. . .] исчезнуть из нашего литературного оборота; у человека есть только мозг и «мозги». [. . .] Об ответственности за поступки тут не могло быть и речи; ибо все совершается по неодолимой и независящей от человека силе внешних обстоятельств или под влиянием расстройства «рефлексов мыслящего мозга». Наука объявила [. . .] человек силен только в фактах и опытах. Знай законы, по которым совершаются эти факты и опыты, и человек покорит весь мир. «Вы будете боги», говорит нам наука.[7]

тут-то именно, в самой лягушке-то и заключается спасение и обновление русского народа.[9]

Делалось ясным, что лягушки с пробирками мало подвигают русских людей на действия, имеющие в виду общее благо. Развитые люди задумались на мгновенье и решили изменить систему воспитания. Не естествознание спасет русский народ, а социальные науки [. . .] Оказывалось, что спасение русского народа зависит от распространения социологии. Взялись за нее. Социальные науки толкуют о народе, о его благосостоянии [. . .] Новые люди указали [. . .] на народ.[11]

Рождение, брак, размножение, смерть — таков цикл внешнего существования отдельного человека; но в то время, как люди рождаются, живут и умирают, остается род, человечество, развивающееся в своем целом по определенным, правильным и неизменным законам.[14]

— Аще кто, будучи вне себя, подымет на себя руки, или повержет себя с высоты: за такового должно ли быти приношение, или нет?
— О таковом священнослужитель должен рассудити, подлинно ли, будучи вне ума, соделал сие. Ибо часто близкие к пострадавшему от самого себя, желая достигнути, да будет приношение и молитва за него, неправдуют и глаголют, яко был вне себя. Может же быти, яко соделал сие от обиды человеческия, или по иному какому случаю от малодушия: и о таковом не подобает быти приношение, ибо есть самоубийца. Посему священнослужитель непременно должен со всяким тщанием испытывати, да не подпадает осуждению.[17] [Канонические ответы Тимофея Александрийского, Ответ 14.]

Никто не отрицает обязательной силы канонов церковных; но в практической жизни действуют не они непосредственно, а заведенный на основании их (а отчасти и помимо их и вопреки им) обычай; в практической жизни требуется знание и соблюдение сего последнего и нисколько не первых, знание которых представляется излишним и ненужным и простою ученою роскошью. На этом основании даже в настоящее время мы не найдем ни одного священника, который бы порядочно знал каноны церковные и имел бы сколько-нибудь удовлетворительное понятие о книге, называемой Кормчею (кроме того, что она есть книга весьма толстая).[19]

главным образом, практика церковная определялась не «правилами св. апостолов и св. отец», а обычаем, сложившимся в течении веков.[20]

сами себя убивающие от отчаяния и гнева, разве аще прежде смерти знамения покаяния показаша.[21] [Требник Петра Могилы, 1646.]

А который от своих рук погубится, удавится, или ножем избодется, или в воду себе вв́ержет: ино по святым правилам тех не повелено у церквей хоронити, ни над ними пети, ни поминати, но в пустом месте в яму вложив, закопати; створит же о душах их Господь яко же сам весть, по своим неизреченным судебам, занеже святыи отцы именуют тех самовольною жертвою, даема не Богу.[23] [Послание Митрополита Фотия к псковскому духовенству, 1417.]

А который человек обесится или зарежется, или купаясь и похваляся и играя утонет, или вина опьется или с качели убьется, или иную смерть сам над собою, своими руками учинит или на разбое и на воровстве каком убит будет: и тех умерших тел у церкви Божии не погребать, и над ними отпевать не велеть, а велеть их класть в лесу или на поле, кроме кладбища и убогих домов.[24] [Инструкция патриарха Адриана поповским старостам или благочинным смотрителям, 26 декабря 1697, статья 21.]

Уже сатана раз насмеялся над несчастной. Неужели надо допустить сатане еще раз насмеяться над ней? Похоронить по православному.[25]

Самоубийство, совершенное обдуманно и сознательно, а не в припадке умоиступления, Церковь признает столь же тяжким грехом, как и отнятие жизни у другого (убийство). Жизнь для каждого человека есть драгоценнейший дар Божий — и по естеству, и по благодати искупления. Налагающий на себя убийственную руку христианин вдвойне оскорбляет Бога: и как Творца, и как Искупителя. Само собою понятно, что такое деяние может быть только плодом полного неверия и отчаянья в Божественном Провидении [. . .] А кто чужд веры в Бога и упования на Него, тот чужд и Церкви, Она смотрит на вольного самоубийцу, как на духовного потомка Иуды предателя, который, отрекшись от Бога и Богом отверженный, «шед удавися». Отсюда понятно, что по нашим церковным и гражданским узаконениям сознательный и вольный самоубийца лишается церковного погребения и поминовения.[27]

на самоубийцах на том свете сам сатана разъезжает таким образом, что запрягает одних вместо лошадей, других сажает за кучера править, а сам садится на главном месте в развалку, понукает и подхлестывает. По временам заезжает он на них в кузницы [. . .] Когда же сатана сидит на своем троне в преисподней, то всегда держит на коленях Иуду, христопродавца и самоубийцу.[29]

Ежели кто сам себя убьет, то подлежит тело его палачу в бесчестное место отволочь и закопать, волоча прежде по улицам или обозу. [Воинский Устав 1716 года, статья 164.]

Ежели солдат пойман будет в самом деле, что хотел сам себя убить и в том ему помешали и того исполнить не мог, а учинит то от мучения, досады, чтобы долее не жить или в беспамятстве и за стыдом, оный, по мнению учителей прав, с бесчестьем от полку отогнан быть имеет: [. . .] а ежели ж кроме вышеупомянутых причин сие учинил, оного казнить смертью.[47] [Воинский Устав 1716 года, толкование к статье 164.]

Ежели сие убивство не намерено было или учинено от какого-либо мучения или несносной налоги или в беспамятстве, как то случится в огневых и меланхолических болезнях: то те, которые в той найдутся, вышеописанной казни не подлежат.[48] [Морской устав 1720 года, толкование к статье 117.]

392. кто, вознамерясь лишить себя жизни, недовершил сего предприятия или был в том воспрепятствован, таковаго, как помешавшагося в разуме, по излечении в больнице, предавать церковному покаянию.
395. в рассуждении тела самоубийцы надлежит поступать по церковным правилам и полицейским постановлениям.[51] [Проект уложения о наказаниях уголовных и исправительных 1813 года.]

347. Самоубийца лишается Христианского погребения, если доказано будет, что он лишил себя жизни не в безумии и не в беспамятстве.[52] [Свод законов Российской империи, 1835.]

348. Кто на самом деле изобличен в намерении лишить себя жизни, и в том воспрепятствован был токмо внешним обстоятельством: того наказывать, если сие намерение было предпринято не от мучения, несносной налоги, досады, стыда или в беспамятстве огневых и меланхолических болезней, как за покушение к смертоубийству. [Свод законов Российской империи, 1835.]

1943. Лишивший себя жизни с намерением и не в безумии, сумасшествии или временном от каких-либо болезненных припадков беспамятстве, признается неимевшим права делать предсмертные распоряжения, и потому как духовное завещание его, так и вообще всякая каким бы то ни было образом в отношении к детям, воспитанникам, служителям, имуществу, или к чему-либо иному изъявленная им воля не приводятся в исполнение и считаются ничтожными. Если самоубийца принадлежал к одному их Христианских вероисповеданий, то он лишается Христианского погребения. [Свод законов Российской империи; статья 1943 в издании 1845 года, статья 2021 в издании 1857 года, статья 1472 в последующих изданиях.]

1944. Изобличенный в покушении лишить себя жизни также не в безумии, сумасшествии или временном от какой-либо болезни припадке беспамятства, когда исполнение его намерения остановлено посторонними, независевшими от него обстоятельствами, предается, если он Христианин, церковному покаянию по распоряжению своего духовного начальства. [Статья 1944/2022/1473.]

С 1845 года наше право смотрит на него [самоубийство] преимущественно с религиозной точки зрения, хотя и проводит свой взгляд далеко не последовательно.[54]

когда кто-либо, по великодушному патриотизму, подвергнет себя очевидной опасности или и прямо верной смерти для сохранения государственной тайны и в других подобных случаях, а равно, если женщина лишит или покусится лишить себя жизни для спасения целомудрия и чести своей от грозившего ей и никакими другими средствами неотвратимого насилия.[56] [Статья 1945/2023/1474.]

Кажется удобнее и приличнее предоставить усмотрению духовного начальства разрешать в каждом особом случае, должен ли самоубийца быть лишен христианского погребения или нет?[58] [Проект уложения о наказаниях уголовных и исправительных 1844 года.]

Если самоубийца принадлежал к одному их Христианских вероисповеданий, то от усмотрения духовного начальства сего исповедания будет зависеть постановить: не должен ли он быть лишен христианского погребения.[58] [Проект.]

1016. Все духовные завещания должны быть составляемы в здравом уме и твердой памяти. Потому недействительны завещания 1) безумных сумасшедших и умалишенных, когда они составлены ими во время помешательства 2) самоубийц.[62] [Свод законов Российской империи, 1857, статья 1016.]

сие постановление равно несправедливо и неудобно в исполнении [. . .] сей закон, как с достоверностью известно, никогда не исполнялся.[63] [Проект.]

[область] правосудия божеского [. . .] совершенно независимую от права.[77]

Судебное преследование, в отношении к уголовной ответственности обвиняемого, не может быть возбуждено [. . .] за смертью обвиняемого. [Устав уголовного судопроизводства, 1864, статья 16.]

Покусившийся в здравом уме лишить себя жизни [. . .] предается, *если он христианин,* церковному покаянию по распоряжению своего духовного начальства.[79]

древними вселенскими постановлениями церкви, всегда долженствующими сохранить свою обязательную силу.[81]

Существует множество деяний, противных правилам нравственности и религии, не преследуемых однако ни в одном светском кодексе, для которого неуловим религиозный, внутренний мир человеческой души.[82]

врач, как лицо компетентное, может вскрыть труп и без следователя.[85]

от которого и будет уже зависеть признать самоубийцу или покусившегося на свою жизнь действовавшим в здравом рассудке или же под влиянием психической болезни.[86]

гражданский закон ставит решение вопроса, может или не может самоубийца быть похоронен по христианскому обряду, — в зависимость от отзыва врача и полиции.[88]

тело самоубийцы палач должен в бесчестное место отволочь и там закопать.[91]

медицинское — на основании вскрытия трупа данное свидетельство, что известное лицо лишило себя жизни по ненормальному состоянию душевных сил, делает для притча предание земле тела такого самоубийцы обязательным, как удостоверение того, что в данном случае смерть имела причиной не отчаянье или безверие.[93]

Ухо русского читателя давно уже прислушалось к толкам о важности статистических цифр во всех отраслях человеческой деятельности. Увлечение статистикой, какому предавалось наше общество лет пять назад, явилось одновременно с признанием важности реального принципа, который в настоящее время получил у нас полное право гражданства.[97]

в числе ее задач лежит один из важнейших основных вопросов для человека и человечества: отношение закона необходимости к тем действиям человека, которые люди привыкли рассматривать, как произвольные, самостоятельные и свободные.[99]

Человек во всех своих действиях, от самых важных до самых ничтожных, повинуется статистическим законам. [. . .] Роковые цифры [. . .] как древний рок управляют судьбами человека и не позволяют ему ни на шаг отступать от своих математических выводов.[101]

Если из 600 человек — *a*, *b*, *c*, *d* и т. д. — *один должен* совершить преступление, то можно ли считать, что он совершил его добровольно? Люди, говорящие о свободе воли и смотрящие на человека с драматической точки зрения, думают, что человек может противиться с успехом влечению своей плоти. Но положительный факт говорит нам, что из этих 600 человек один непременно *обязан* совершить преступление. Где же тут свобода воли? Кто может осудить эту безличную единицу, пока она остается безличной? А между тем, как скоро сделается известным, что преступление совершено *a*, то его судят и обвиняют, забывая, что если б *a* не совершил преступление, то его совершил бы *b* или *c*, что, следовательно, преступник должен непременно быть, что исключает совершенно возможность обвинения.[102]

наконец, скажем положительно, что всякое преступление, при каких бы обстоятельствах ни было совершенно, есть внешнее выражение физиологических или патологических явлений нашего организма и, следовательно, может так же мало влечь за собой ответственность, как какое-нибудь наружное уродство, например, горб или кривизна шеи. Нам уже доказали цифры, что преступления не зависят от человеческой воли, — следовательно, зависят от условий организма.[103]

В настоящей статье автор объясняет причины, порождающие самоубийства. Прежде всего он считает необходимым посмеяться над *древними мировоззрениями,* по которым человек есть существо привилегированное, управляемое особыми законами, независимыми от земных сил... Смотря на самоубийство с этой точки, он старается доказать, что оно, как и все другие явления человеческой жизни, есть действие непроизвольное, исключительно порождаемое гнетущими обстоятельствами и ненормальными условиями окружающей жизни... Затем следует ряд картин самоубийства из времен французского террора, с целью показать, что политические преследования в особенности умножают число самоубийств.[106]

Статью о исчислении смертоубийств и самоубийств, приключившихся в два минувшие года в России, почитаю не токмо ни к чему ненужною, но и вредною. Первое: какая надобность знать о числе сих преступлений? Второе: по каким доказательствам всякий читатель может удостоверен быть, что число сие отнюдь не увеличено? Третье: к чему извещение о сем может служить? Разве к тому только, что колеблющийся преступник, видя перед собою многих предшественников, мог почерпнуть из того одобрение, что он не первый к такому делу приступает? Мне кажется, подобные статьи, неприличные к обнародованию оных, надлежало бы к тому, кто прислал их для напечатания, отослать назад с замечанием, чтоб и впредь над такими пустыми вещами не трудился. Хорошо извещать о благих делах, а такие, как смертоубийство и самоубийство, должны погружаться в вечное забвение.[111]

разрабатывая статистику, общество как бы подвергает себя судебно-медицинскому вскрытию.[123]

Notes to Chapter 2

18. Аще человек небесен ся погубит, не пети над ним, но поверерничии (sic, читай: но повергнути и), а не погрести. [Устав Митрополита Георгия, XI век, правило 93.]

35. Народу присуще то воззрение, что человек не сам лишает себя жизни, а доводит его до самоубийства, иногда даже непосредственно убивает, топит, чорт, леший.

76. и коль скоро бывает доказано, что самоубийца лишил себя жизни в состоянии умственного расстройства — признает завещание самоубийцы действительным, в противном случае — недействительным.

94. Священник не может уклоняться от погребения умершего, если не имеет к сему особых законных причин.

Гражданского закона, который давал бы священнику право отказаться от христианского погребения самоубийцы и по получению от полиции удостоверения (после судебно-медицинского осмотра) о беспрепятственности его похорон, нет.

Chapter 3

31 июля в 10 часу утра, в Черной речке (Нарвск. Ч.4 кв.), всплыло мертвое тело неизвестного человека мужеского пола. По совершенной гнилости, тело предано земле [«Ведомости Санкт-Петербургской городской полиции», 9 августа, 1839].

В наше время, при развивающейся все более и более гласности, приходится беспрерывно слышать о новых случаях умопомешательства и самоубийства. Это, конечно, служит одним из несчастнейших признаков нездорового состояния общества.[8]

стоит только заняться чтением дневника происшествий и отчетов о заседаниях окружных судов — вас невольно охватывает какой-то ужас. [. . .] Если мы возьмем последний месяц старого и два месяца нового года, то увидим, что в одних только столицах застрелилось и зарезалось человек десять *благородных. Неблагородных* мы не берем уж в расчет, потому что их нужно считать дюжинами.[10]

Самоубийства у нас в последние годы — точно холера, забравшаяся в гнилое место, нарочно устроенное для ее постоянной поддержки. В городах открылись даже особенные постоянные еженедельные отчеты о самоубийствах.[11]

Мания самоубийства среди юношества, принимая с каждым днем все большие размеры, решительно становится общественным недугом; наши молодые люди исчезают один за другим; они, точно сговорившись по телеграфу, уходят из разных мест на тот свет одновременно, служа неиссякаемым материалом для хроники ежедневных происшествий.[13]

Самоубийства давно уже сделались обычным явлением нашей жизни. Никто теперь не удивляется встречая в каждом номере газеты несколько известий о том, что такой-то или такая-то пустили себя пулю в череп, приняли какого-нибудь яду, бросились под поезд железной дороги или иным путем покончили свои счеты с жизнью. Явились даже особые выражения, указывающие как на постоянство этого печального явления, так и на широкую степень его распространения: в редкой корреспонденции о самоубийстве мы не встретим выражения: «обычная весенняя или осенняя эпидемия самоубийств уже началась», или: «жертвами нынешнего сезона самоубийств являются» и т. д.[15]

В русской жизни самоубийства наблюдаются не сегодня и не вчера. Усиливается ли это явление и усилилось ли оно в 1888 году, достоверно неизвестно, потому что у нас нет точной статистики самоубийств. Но те, кому нужны самоубийства, как «материал», утверждают (тем более, что можно обойтись и без доказательств), что самоубийства увеличиваются.[16]

дело г-жи Сувориной, жены сотрудника «С-Петербургских Ведомостей», имя которой, как издательницы нескольких книг для детского чтения, небезызвестно и читающей публике.[18]

Рана довольно велика и с разорванными краями.[20]

Описывая во вчерашнем нумере кровавую драму в Бель-вью, мы признали необходимым, из совершенно понятного чувства деликатности и уважения к чести семейства г. Суворина, умолчать об одном важном факте [. . .] Факт этот заключается в том, что, как сказал нам владелец гостиницы Бель-вю, г. Ломач, в нумере, который был занят г. Комаровым, в момент убийства, все было в совершенном порядке и постели не тронуты.[24]

Одна газета дошла даже до того, что добровольно взяла на себя роль судебного следователя и с торжеством объявила публике, что, по наведенным ею справкам, в номере гостиницы, где случилось происшествие, вся оказалось в порядке и постель несмятою![25]

Частое повторение подобных фактов указывает отчасти на ненормальное состояние развитой части нашего общества, а причины такого состояния кроются, по нашему мнению, в тех переменах, которые испытало наше общество в течение последнего десятилетия.[26]

прозаической смерти одной бедной крестьянки, повесившейся на городском фонаре у Мытнинского двора.[28]

едва ли можно сомневаться, что они подчиняются известным законам, с такой же роковой, неуклонной правильностью, как и явления физического мира.[29]

Но разве эти убийцы из современной молодежи, распоряжающиеся чужой жизнью, как своею собственностью, лучше таких помещиков доброго старого времени, преданных вами проклятию?[30]

Тут уже статистика бросается в сторону и оседлывается другой модный конек — законы человеческого организма и психология. [. . .] с тех пор, как мы узнали, что существует наука статистика и еще несколько других наук, занимающихся исследованием законов органической и не органической природы [. . .] таких статей у нас расплодилось очень много.[34]

Настоящий строй общества — строй патологический.[35]

Напрасно стали бы мы искать той животворящей струи сильной, свежей и бодрой мысли, которая в иные эпохи подобно электрическому току, перебегая от индивида к индивиду, разветвляясь по различным слоям общественной формации, как бы образует коллективно мыслящее и чувствующее целое, в котором сливаются, возвышаясь и очищаясь, отдельные мирки индивидуальной мысли и чувства.[37]

человек чувствует под собою твердую почву, из которой он черпает свои жизненные соки, свою жизненную энергию.[40]

Не питаясь приливом жизненной силы из общества, их энергия слабеет и чахнет, и человек незаметно, день за днем, приходит к полной психической невозможности тянуть лямку дальше.[41]

все мы скорым или медленным процессом самообольщения и само-
разложения идем к самоубийству [. . .] нигилизм — это общая язва
нашего общества.[44]

взорам любопытных представилась какая-то окровавленная масса,
не похожая ни на какое живое существо. [. . .] верхняя часть тела
несчастного до пояса уже была измолота в сплошную окровавлен-
ную массу. О происшествии, конечно, составлен акт. Оказалось, что
самоубийца — мещанин города Самары. Причины, побудившие его
лишить себя жизни, неизвестны.[47]

в каюте 2 класса лежал труп пассажира-купца. Около трупа стоял
невысокого роста молодой человек, с русой бородкой, и испуганно
смотрел на обезображенное выстрелом лицо мертвеца. Это был при-
казчик покойного.[47]

Случайно только, через несколько месяцев или через год, при спаде
весенних вод, отыщут без вести пропавшего и напишут коротко: най-
дено совершенно сгнившее тело, по-видимому, мужчины или женщины [. . .] Иной раз просто поймают в воде, около пароходной конто-
ки, чью то отрубленную голову, а чья она? Какому бедняку принад-
лежала? Об этом и речи быть не может! Кто ж его знает, откуда он
и кто он такой, если так неосторожно потерял голову?[48]

2 августа, в 2 часа дня, на реке Волге, около мостков конторки паро-
ходнаго общества «Самолет» была *вынута из воды плывущая отруб-
ленная голова*, принадлежащая, по-видимому, мужчине. Волос на ней
нет. Наружные покровы на голове, лице и остатках шеи грязно-зеле-
ного цвета, ослизившиеся и разбухшие. Оболочки глаз сморщены.
Нос, губы и уши представляют признаки разложения. В верхней и
нижней челюсти недостает по четыре зуба; места, где помещались
зубы, не закрыты деснами. Черепные кости целы. При голове нахо-
дится только половина шеи, оканчивающаяся четвертым шейным позвонком. На нижней части этого позвонка отсечена часть кости в
горизонтальном направлении. Окружающие шейные позвонки мягкие
части оканчиваются параллельно с четвертым шейным позвонком.
Несмотря на разложение их, можно еще различить, что они рассече-
ны острым резущим орудием.[49]

смерть в виде раздробленного черепа, окровавленных покровов, при-
сохших к стене мозгов...[51]

одинокие могилы сравняются с матерью землею, а будущим летом
никто и не заметит, и не запомнит, что тут сгнили лучшие сердца и
лучшие мозги, которых только производила когда-нибудь Россия...[52]

вся почва Петербурга мало по малу обращается в общую помойную яму, испаряющую миазмы.[56]

великую ошибку сделал бы статистик, если бы, говоря, например, о самоубийствах в Петербурге, не обращал внимания на такие обстоятельства, о которых мы сейчас упомянули.[56]

и притом занятия в больнице с разложившимися трупами — и вы будете иметь прекрасно подготовленную почву для развития легочной чахотки.

Мудрено ли, что при подобной обстановке, число самоубийств в среде учащихся представляет собой значительную цифру?[57]

[пользуясь] только тем, что получили мы лично из хода жизни вообще и в особенности из данных судебно-медицинских вскрытий самоубийц.[62]

Хотя головной мозг, во всех психических расстройствах, и в том числе и при самоубийстве, и должен представлять соответствующие этим расстройствам материальные изменения, но эти изменения бывают иногда до того неуловимы или преходящи, что, даже при резких формах умопомешательства, не редко ускользают от надлежащего определения.

Проходимость, или неуловимость материальных изменений собственно головного мозга, при самоубийстве, есть явление почти постоянное, особенно при посягательстве на свою жизнь людей, по-видимому, психически здоровых.[65]

Но ничто нас так не поражало, как почти полное забвение у большинства студентов, оканчивающих медицинское образование, классических языков.[68]

Ведь это, по нашему мнению, есть ни что иное, как прямое издевательство над латинским языком и косвенное издевательство над временем, употребленным для изучения этого языка, — а ведь время-то — жизнь![69]

в Казани это уже не первый случай самоубийства из-за мертвых языков. [«Санкт-Петербургские Ведомости», no. 16, 1871.]

окружая самоубийц ореолом мученичества, сочиняя о них ряд статей, прославляя и оплакивая их [. . .] литература действует тлетворно и разрушительно, воспитывая в юношах идею о великости подвига лиц, лишающих себя жизни.[70]

Внутренний обозреватель Демерт — известен всем, кто интересуется явлениями внутренней, «черноземной» стороны русской жизни.[75]

а работа в качестве внутреннего обозревателя — дело трудное именно для впечатлительного человека.[79]

почти вся личная жизнь Демерта поглощена его делом, именно этим *внутренним обозрением.*[80]

А где его могила? И есть ли у него могила? Может быть, его, как безвестного арестанта, умершего в части, отправили в университетский анатомический кабинет и там распотрошили рядом с трупом одного из жуликов, с которыми он был захвачен.[83]

Увеличение за последнее время самоубийств привлекло к себе общее внимание. Настоящий год представляется в этом отношении исключительным. Мы встречаемся не только с значительным количеством самоубийств, но и с эпидемическим их характером.[85]

Можно сказать без преувеличения, что за последние три года в России свирепствует «эпидемия» самоубийств.[86]

Мы переживаем, можно сказать, эпоху самоубийств во всевозможных их видах.[87]

Наличность эпидемии самоубийств очевидна.[88]

1905-й год, — год подъема и надежд на близкое лучшее будущее, — не был благоприятным для самоуничтожения; люди дорожили жизнью, самоубийства везде или оставались на том же уровне, или даже падали, и мы видим, что печать откликнулась упоминанием лишь о 85 случаях за 7 последних месяцев этого года. С 1906 года начались разочарования, и самоубийства стали непрерывно возрастать, сделавши только временное исключение для мая и июня, месяцев первой Думы, когда кое-где опять вспыхнули надежды на возрождение и реформы. С июля рост уже не останавливается и особенно усиливается осенью этого года. В 1907 году все чаяния оказались окончательно рушившимися, и самоуничтожение неудержимо растет, сделавши сразу большой скачок в июне после роспуска второй Думы. Начавшись с 93 случаев в январе, этот год закончился 216 случаями в декабре, при чем созыв третьей Думы не оказал никакого влияния на подъем ценности жизни.[92]

самоубийство — болезнь заразительная, эпидемическая и наиболее послушная закону подражания.[93]

Ну, обычное «медицинское» объяснение... «Гоголь умер потому, что читал аскетические сочинения, а не Фейербаха и Молешотта» и проч. [. . .] Такая, подумаешь, премудрость в газетах и гражданской печати. Впрочем, что же: ведь «газеты» влияют даже на профессоров, наконец и на профессоров-психиатров, которые другой раз только «по газетам» и думают.[96]

Эта смерть, может быть, есть самое ужасное и самое значительное событие XIX в., куда важнее Наполеоновских войн! Как смерть Сократа была *потрясающее*, многозначительнее Полопенезской войны, *многоценнее и многопоследственнее* ее — так смерть этих терновских бедняков куда обильнее смыслом всей дипломатики XIX века, *воплощенной пошлости*. Такой народ, со способностью *такого восприятия, такого слышания*, — если этот *святой народ* услышит с Неба ли, от человека ли настоящее *живоносное* слово, он повернет около себя весь мир, всю мировую историю, как около оси вертится земля. Но *где* такое слово? увы, эта печальная смерть, непререкаемо убеждает, что «Слово», принесенное ему, которое он счел за «Слово Жизни» — на самом деле есть, было и будет «Словом Смерти»! Вот это-то доказательство, если б мы были к нему внимательны, и уравнивает смысл смерти тридцати терновских Сократов со смертью афинского мудреца.[97]

Самоубийство так же старо, как и само человечество. Изучением его занимаются врачи, статистики, философы, юристы и педагоги, но сих пор все еще не решен вопрос, что собственно представляет оно собой: проявление болезненного или здорового человеческого духа, преступление или естественное право человека, выражение свободной человеческой воли или же проявление общего мирового закона причинности и т. д. и т. д.[99]

мы не умеем еще расчленять душу на ее составные части подобно тому, как разлагаем сложные химические соединения на их простейшие элементы.[101]

[Durkheim] создает целую стройную теорию изучения самоубийства с точки зрения коллектива, который он рассматривает, как живое тело имеющее как бы свою душу, свои особенности и т. д.[102]

Все шли в разных отрядах великой армии, все жили коллективными чувствами. Слабые черпали силы из громадного резервуара общей воли, сомневающиеся заряжались электричеством общей веры. Смысл жизни был очевиден, почти осязаем. Великие цели, ясно видимые впереди на прямой, хотя и трудной дороге, звали к себе с покоряющей силой [. . .] В 1905 г. русское общество взошло на вершину исторической горы. [. . .] Начался спуск с перевала в долину политической и общественной реакции. Чем дальше под гору, тем быстрее. Ускорялся шаг, мешались ряды, а там густые тени долины окутали бегущих и скрыли их друг от друга, и закрыли от них горные вершины, к которым в одиночку, ощупью, в темноте все же инстинктивно продолжали и продолжают идти люди! Число самоубийств стало повышаться с чрезвычайной быстротой...[103]

Там — ушли жизненные силы, и естественно гибнет изжитой организм; здесь — утратился коллективный смысл жизни, и неистраченные силы, не находя исхода, не находя точки приложения, обращаются на носителя их и убивают его.[104]

распространение самоубийств, особенно среди молодежи, указывает на какую-то глубокую болезнь всего общественного организма, подтачивающую лучшие силы нации. Нельзя не задуматься над причинами и условиями развития этой непрерывно действующей эпидемии.[105]

Без этого всевозможные насилия, половая вакханалия и особенно опасный симптом обесценения жизни и внутреннего разложения — самоубийства не прекратятся.[107]

Революционный психоз сменился половым.[109]

вчерашний революционер облекается в одежды декадентства.[110]

Полубезумный художник весь в плену своей похоти... [. . .] Дальше... дальше... убийство... самоубийство... черная дыра.[111]

Эпидемия самоубийств среди молодежи — в тесной связи с теми настроениями, которые преобладают в литературе, и часть вины за истребление молодой жизни современная литература должна взять на себя. Несомненно, что некоторые явления в литературе должны были повысить число самоубийств.[114]

Кто знает? — не влияла ли инсценировка Карамазовых на рост самоубийств в Москве.[115]

в наших современных книгах свирепствует теперь, как и в жизни, эпидемия самоубийств. Удавленники и утопленники современнейшие нынче герои. И вот новая, небывалая черта: эти люди давятся и травятся, а почему — неизвестно. «Просто так». «Безо всякой причины». [. . .] Беспричинные самоубийства — таково новейшее открытие современной нашей словесности. Люди в наших книгах стали стреляться и вешаться не от горя или отчаянья, а и сами не знают отчего.[117]

Я отодвигаю эти книги, из которых все равно ничего не понять и беру ученую, тяжеловесную знаменитого социолога Дюркгейма.[117]

Оказывается, человек и вправду лишает себя жизни «просто так», почти без всякой причины, а все, что он почитает причиной, есть выдумка, иллюзия, фантом.[117]

«Мотивы,— пишет Дюркгейм, — приписываемые самоубийцей самому себе, не дают объяснений его поступку и в действительности являются в большинстве случаев лишь кажущимися причинами». [. . .] И мы думаем, что Дюркгейм прав.[118]

В этом-то и заключается то грозное и грандиозное, что в последние годы *незаметно* случилось со всеми нами: рвались, рвались какие-то ниточки, смыкавшие нас воедино, и нам это как будто даже нравилось.[118]

покуда твое сердце не только твое и руки — не только твои, покуда не я, но *мы* — твое обычное слово.[118]

с той самой минуты, когда он оторвался от вечного жизнедавца — общества.[118]

Да сбудется реченное Дюркгеймом: «Если распадаются узы, соединяющие человека с жизнью, то это происходит потому, что ослабела связь его с обществом». Дюркгейм, мы знаем, перебрал по порядку все — возможные и невозможные — причины добровольных смертей и, все их по порядку отвергнув, увидел эту одну, эту даже, в сущности, единственную у нас, когда тот цемент, который склеивал вас с каким-нибудь, безразлично с каким, коллективом, вдруг раскрошился, рассыпался, — и вы остались сами по себе.[118]

Notes to Chapter 3
89. Следовательно, по количеству ежегодных самоубийств мы, петербуржцы, занимаем первое место в мире.

Chapter 4

Да, если бы каждый самоубийца оставлял после себя описание того, как он учился и воспитывался; какой философии научила его школа и жизнь; в каких гигиенических условиях он жил и какое имел здоровье; наконец какие несчастные обстоятельства расстроили окончательно его нервную систему, навели его на мысль о самоубийстве; то многие почтенные немцы, разрабатывающие вопрос о самоубийстве, делали бы выводы более полезные и для общежития и для прогресса человеческой мысли, чем какие они делают до сих пор.[1]

написал два-три слова, приставил дуло пистолета ко лбу или к виску и... точно в другую комнату вышел! Нет сомнения, что этому последнему акту предшествовала долгая внутренняя борьба, но тайна ее обыкновенно уносится на тот свет, а на этом остается лишь мертвое тело...[2]

Чувство самосохранения и любовь к жизни так глубоко укоренены в человеке, а следовательно и в классах общества, что самоубийство всегда считается противоестественным поступком, патологическим явлением, — протестом против склада общественной жизни. Вследствии этого письма и записки самоубийц, с того момента, как самоубийцы приняли твердое намерение исключить себя навсегда из среды живых людей, перестают уже быть частными письмами.[6]

законодатель никогда не согласится отнять у семьи право сохранить тело ее члена, который лишил себя жизни.[8]

Нельзя не отметить этой особенности, что «множество народное», «толпа» в обезличеном ее значении, «чужие» чувствуют какое-то особенное право, и притом нравственное право, на «тело самоубийцы» и всегда горячо окружают его, со страшной силой вместе с тем приближая к себе и его душу или сближаясь сами с душою его... И как бы чувствуют вынутою, изъятою и эту душу, и это тело из рук близких, в особенности родных.[9]

далеко не все предсмертные записки самоубийц возбуждают чувство грустной боли, заставляют задумываться над несчастною судьбою этих жертв общественных условий. Иные записки самоубийц способны вызвать только неприятное, злобное чувство, иные — невольную улыбку, иные — чувство, граничащее с презрением.[11]

Я написал бы «в смерти моей никого не винить», — но чувствую, что эта стереотипная фраза мне не к лицу. И в самом деле, кому нужна моя смерть? Ни грабителям, ни наследникам. Кроме гадких лохмотьев, которые на улице становятся игрушкой ветра и невыразимого отчаянья, у меня нет ничего. Нет даже пера и чернил, чтобы в последний раз изложить свои мысли на бумаге немного связнее... Итак, биография моя в двух словах: хотел сделаться профессором, а сделался пугалом для ребят и самоубийцею. Некрасов говорит: «чтоб одного возвеличить, борьба тысячи слабых уносит, даром ничто не дается: судьба жертв искупительных просит». Это верно, но где же тут справедливость? Скажите, пожалуйста, чем же я хуже Ивана и Петра? Они кушают хлеб с маслом, а мне, вместо хлеба, судьба кидает камни!.. Нет, напрасно мы гибнем: общество обязано облегчить нам доступ к науке, оно мало нас поддерживает! Околеваю как собака, потому что на этом свете скверно и не любопытно теперь жить... Жаль матушки, невыразимо жаль!..[12]

записки неудачников, не смогших бороться с внешними, материальными условиями.[13]

М. г. В сегодняшнем нумере вашей газеты сообщено известие о моем отравлении, и сказано, что причиной, заставившей меня прибегнуть к самоубийству, были страшные внутренние страдания, причиненные болезнью. В действительности же это было делом ошибки. Я вовсе не рассчитывала лишить себя жизни, а только, страдая сильным расстройством желудка, приняла большой прием опия. [. . .] Благодаря усилиям докторов — Экка, Козырева, Веге и Дворянина, я в настоящее время почти совсем здорова.

Не откажитесь поместить мое заявление в следующем нумере вашей газеты.

Ольга Щавинская.[14]

Заявление мое, напечатанное в no. 287 «С-Петербургских Ведомостей» и перепечатанное в no. 205 «Петербургского листка», прошу считать недействительным.

Ольга Щавинская.[15]

Прощайте, дорогие родители! Причина смерти моей вам известна: я пережить не могу этого. Желаю вам всего хорошего, а главное — здоровья. Поклон всем родным и знакомым.[16]

Прощай, дорогой Ваня! Я застрелился после того, как провалился.[16]

Прощайте, дорогие читатели! Моя летопись коротка. Я гимназист, который наказан судьбою. Были гораздо хуже меня и пошли в гору! Ну, что же, не у всех одинаково счастье! Я перенесть не мог, потому что чувствовал, что буду напрасно страдать — лучше один раз, и конец. Хоть и тяжело расстаться с жизнью, но что же прикажете делать. Не я первый и не я последний. Еще раз прошу прощения.[16]

очень интересны[е] во многих отношениях.[16]

К вам мое слово: я одна из многих падаю жертвой для многих. Последнее мое слово — это проклятье богачам, бедности и безучастию.[17]

не материальные условия были причиной роковой развязки. Я всегда умел зарабатывать.[18]

Тяжко живется на Руси, когда все идейное, народное, культурное безжалостно уничтожается.[18]

Что пережил этот неизвестный Александр Крапухин раньше, чем формулировать весь опыт своей молодой жизни в словах: тяжко живется на Руси. Какой яд отравлял его душу? Кто изготовил этот яд? Что? Нет ответа.[18]

Иногда записки напоминают вариации одной и той же темы, разрабатываемые разными людьми, повторяются одни и те же словесные выражения, стиль и логические ходы рассуждения.[25]

Все мое имущество, платье, не исключая того, в котором я одет, белье, бумаги и револьвер, которым я имел счастие застрелиться, оставляю моим друзьям студентам N. и N.N. Причины моей смерти нет никакой: мне просто надоело жить. Тело мое, хотя и не очень вкусное, прошу бросить голодным собакам на съедение. Пусть будут сыты бедные скотины.[26]

Не забудьте велеть стащить с меня новую рубашку и чулки, у меня на столике есть старая рубашка и чулки. Эти пусть наденут на меня.

Мне было бы желательно, чтобы покупали эти мои вещи бабки, а если этого нельзя, то все равно — пусть, кто хочет, покупает.

Пожалуйста, Липарева, деньги 25 рублей и кофточку, что дали мне Чечоткины на дорогу, отвезите им, ведь я не еду же туда, куда они предполагают [. . .] Так как этих моих вещей быстро распродать нельзя, то можно оставить пока на хоронение деньги Чечоткиных, но, пожалуйста, как только продадите мой хлам, самое первое дело, это отдать двадцать пять рублей Чечоткиным. *Помните это*. Я вас еще раз прошу похоронить как можно дешевле. Лучше оставить живым, чем совать в землю на гниение.[27]

Кажется, я сказала все. Да вот еще: весь остальной хлам, не помеченный в списке, отдайте хоть Настасье Моисеевой, фельдшеровой матери или кому найдете нужным, так как она вероятно изъявит желание одевать покойную, отдайте капоты, солонку, ложку, кофейник маленький и образ (он у Лизанки остался), передайте сестре моей Марье, адрес ее знает Лизанька. Если придется вам тратить по моему делу на извозчиков, то это нужно высчитать из моих денег.

Теперь, Липарева, простите вы меня и пусть простит Петрова, в особенности Петрова. Я делаю свинство, пакость, — мало этого, делаю просто жестокость в отношении к ней, принимая во внимание ее нездоровье, но я не могу иначе: я устала, страшно устала, да и стрелянье в голове и ушах, которое по ночам иногда бывает очень сильно, мне надоело. Ах, как я устала! Где же лучше отдохнешь, как не в могиле.[27]

До странности занимают ее денежные распоряжения той крошечной суммой, которая после нее осталась.[28]

> Простите на вечно
> О счастье мечтанье
> Я гибну, как роза
> От бури дыханья.[29]

И вот, собравшись стреляться, он садится и долго потеет над длиннейшим и весьма нескладным стихотворением:

> Обманула ты, жизнь, обманула,
> Задавила меня и заснула,
> Дикой силы блудница — раба,
> И бессильна с тобою борьба.[30]

Я отставной подпоручик N.N., живу ... Избитая фраза: в смерти никого не винить, отправился на тот свет по собственному желанию.

Кто станет доискиваться причин или своим умом решит, что вследствие любви, разумея несчастную, будет дурак и да помянет его Бог в царствии своем.

Всем привет, кроме братьев.

Если наши ученые медики решат, что подох от пьянства или помешательства, то будет подлец и дурак, ибо подлипало он пред начальством.

Или Бог, или совесть да будет над вами, власть имеющими, Всего общества.

N.N.[31]

В первых числах августа в трактир селения Московская Ижора, Царскосельского уезда, вошел молодой человек, лет 26-ти или 27-ми, бедно одетый. Он потребовал чаю и ветчины, заперся в одной из комнат и зарезался в ней столовым ножом.[32]

Образ милой А. ни на минуту не покидает меня; прощай, моя радость![32]

Я предполагал, что в минуту перед самоубийством в голове у человека бывает множество дельных мыслей, но ошибся. Удивительно пусто в голове. Где мне судьба привела кончить жизнь?[32]

Я повесился. Не знаю от чего. Худого я ничего не сделал, но, кажется надо было повесится. Прощай моя дорогая мамочка, [уменьш. м. имя], Тетя [уменш. ж. имя], [уменш. м. имя]. Дайте знать купцу [адрес — улица, no. дома, фамилия], что я не буду ходить.

Прощайте дорогие

А все таки жить лучше чем умереть.[33]

Ты, N.N., как думаешь о телячьей голове, под острым соусом. Я был у тебя, а ты у меня. Ягор.

Завтра меня будут резать.[34]

Заявляю лицам, прибывшим для составления протокола и обязанным знать о всем случающемся в жизни, что я сегодня в пятницу 10 ноября сего 18** года, вечером в номере здешней гостиницы, вследствие собственного желания, но без всяких, положительно, особенных причин, а единственно только потому, что мне сильно надоела жизнь, в чем, однако, никто не виноват, и на что я уже давно решился, прекращаю свое существование посредством револьверного выстрела и одновременно с ним принятие дозы Cyanid'a de Potassium'a (орудия эти где достал, нахожу совершенно недолжным объявлять), обращаюсь к ним с всепокорнейшею просьбою приказать сделать возможное с их стороны распоряжение, или если не от них зависит, то оказать содействие к исполнению моего последнего желания, заключающегося в следующем: по составлении протокола и отправлении моего трупа, по принятому, вероятно, порядку, в ближайший приемный покой, не предавать его затем земле ни под каким видом и не смотря ни на какие, могущие возникнуть против этого, протесты моих родственников, а непременно отдать его, мой труп, хотя он, конечно, далеко не интересен, для научного анатомирования и вместе с тем в полное и неотъемлемое владение и распоряжение Медико-Хирургической Академии или так называемой Клинике. И это просьба моя, я льщу себя надеждою, по той причине, что последняя воля умирающего всегда исполняется, будет уважена и пунктуально выполнена. Затем, повторяя, что в смерти моей никто не виновен, прошу у лиц, коим я при жизни моей сделал зло–извинения. Для уплаты за номер со мною есть несколько денег, но в случае, если номерной найдет эту сумму недостаточною, то предлагаю ему обратиться за прибавкою в место моего жительства [адрес и подпись].[35]

* большинству писавших были неизвестны жестокие требования старого закона о недействительности посмертных распоряжений самоубийцы.

Очевидно он, как судебный следователь, усвоил себе идею, что душевные болезни находятся в тесной связи с органическими изменениями мозга, поэтому желание принести посмертную пользу науке и тем самым человечеству является весьма естественным.[36]

Я желаю, чтобы меня натомировали [sic] и посмотрели мою грудь.[37]

Покорнейшее прошу полицию не производить розысков или дозна-
ний о моей смерти, кроме разве анатомирования моего трупа. Я все
сказал откровенно.[38]

Наблюдение над действием морфия: 5 минут 1-го я начала прини-
мать морфий, который взяла в аптеке, в 15 минут уже было принято,
склянку бросила пустую в сортир, зашла в комнату Петровой, они
еще не спят. 20 минут 1-го немного тошно и в голове кружится...
половина 1-го вырвало... голова очень кружится... Не могу стоять на
ногах... часы трудно рассмотреть и писать трудно... все мелькает в
глазах... тошнота прошла... спать хочется... никак не могу разглядеть
— сколько теперь минут... не вижу, что пишу...[39]

может быть, действительно, бедная думала умереть «принеся науч-
ную пользу». Но какое бессмыслие! (23:231).

В половине 1-го принял яд. — 55 минут первого. Начинаю чувство-
вать шум в ушах и головокружение... — Я предпочел опиум револь-
веру, желая проследить, насколько возможно, ощущение при приближении смерти. — Час. В глазах темнеет; пишу с трудом; начинается
нервная дрожь; хладнокровие не покидает меня; желания жить нет.
— 10 минут 2-го часа. Глаза смыкаются; не много тошнит. — 1 час
20 минут. Странное явление: начинает сильно чесаться нос. — 1 час
30 минут. Теряю голос — вместо обыкновенных звуков с трудом
вырываются звуки глухие и хриплые. Мысли путаются; закрываются
глаза; начинаю бредить; в ушах звенит. — 1 час 35 минут. Закурил
папироску; тошнота увеличивается; не могу читать написанное,
потому что пишу буквы как бы в тумане. — 1 час 45 минут. Время
тянется, как кажется мне, идет чрезвычайно медленно. Пишу на
память, и чтоб не онеметь и не забыть потушить свечу и тем не
сделать пожара, тушу свечу. — Предметы двоятся; память, руки,
глаза отказываются служить. — 1 час 55 минут. ... (За тем следуют
еще две строки, которые совсем нельзя разобрать.)[40]

Для чего ему понадобилось это наблюдение? Зачем этот человек,
пожелавший умереть [. . .] пожелал вместе с тем «проследить ощу-
щения при приближении смерти»? Ближних, что ли, хотел он облаго-
детельствовать, оставив им в наследство свое исследование в качестве научного материала?[40]

просматривая длинный ряд всякого рода самоубийств нынешнего
лета, невольно наталкиваешься на эту молчаливость, как на наиболее
общую, наиболее типичную черту русских самоубийц. [. . .] Бывают,
конечно, и русские самоубийцы разговорчивые, даже болтливые. Но

в их предсмертных записках, часто очень искренних и трогательных, сплошь и рядом мотивы решения покончить с собой остаются в каком-то тумане, сквозь который посторонний человек ничего разглядеть не может.[43]

Эта вольная или невольная молчаливость наших самоубийц особенно бросается в глаза при сравнении с европейскими самоубийствами, по крайней мере, некоторыми.[43]

отравляюсь кислотой от невеселой своей жизни; на свете надоело жить. Максим.[44]

Молчаливый Максим оставил объяснительную записку и все-таки ничего не сказал.[44]

целую физиологию современного общества, целый трактат, сжатый, сильный, ясный. А у нас молчаливый Максим умирает просто от невеселой своей жизни, а то так и ровно ничего не оставляя в назидание современникам и потомству.[44]

всенародно обнажить свою душу.[44]

Сегодня я привожу в исполнение давно заветную мечту. Но прежде, чем отправиться в страну, где царствует Плутон, я изложу мотивы, побуждающие меня на самоубийство, ибо в современной журналистике часто слышатся сетования, что наши самоубийцы на святой Руси весьма отличаются от самоубийц западной Европы, где уж, если кто решился покончить с собою, то обыкновенно оставляет после себя ясно выставленные причины... Между тем, как наши самоубийцы гибнут бессловесно (конечно, здесь разумею не тех, кто замотал казенные деньги, но наших молодых самоубийц, лишающих себя жизни, по-видимому, без всяких причин). Вглядитесь поглубже в этих людей, якобы три греха совершивших, и вы найдете в них чистые и отзывчивые ко всему доброму души, которые более или менее ясно сознают, что надо вырваться из окружающей страшной тины, которые очень хорошо видят, что только пред другими, но не перед собственною совестью можно оправдаться пословицей: «с волками жить...»

И так, что прикажете делать такому человеку? Быть может вы скажите: заняться делом для пользы будущего развития человечества. Я с вами совершенно согласен, но при всем том не имею на столько силы воли, чтобы предаться этому и еще менее уверен в своих способностях к миссии, ибо сам нуждаюсь в миссионерах. Остаться жить на счет народа и в то же время сожалеть о его грубости, т.е. сделаться квасным либералом... А Боже избави, и без меня их теперь довольно. В то же время кругом не видишь никого, кто бы направил...[45]

даже самим себе не могли объяснить хотя бы только более пространно психический процесс, приведший их к мысли о [. . .] самоубийстве.[46]

сфера бессознательного вообще уже.[46]

и сам не знает [. . .] смутно, в глубине души, что-то копошится, но нет ни вполне сознательной мысли, ни, следовательно, слов...[46]

Где же искать этих умелых людей? Конечно, среди художников. Больше негде. Успехов научной психологии еще жди.[47]

В ней (книге) обобщены и научно освещены данные, почерпнутые не только из книг, письменных документов в виде писем, дневников и т. п., — всегда почти неискренних и не лишенных рисовки или, сознательно или бессознательно скрывающих истину, — а основанные на беспощадно-откровенной исповеди перед специалистами-врачами больных и людей, покушавшихся на самоубийство. Многое в ней продиктовано непосредственными переживаниями из глубины бессознательной душевной жизни самоубийц, — из той сокровенной глубины, где зарождаются и созревают главные импульсы жизни и смерти. В этой книге отразилась тайная, закулисная сторона душевной жизни, освещенная опытом, правда, еще молодой науки — психоанализа.[48]

Находясь в сферах, ближайших к земле, подобно привязанному шару, мы хотели бы ринуться вверх, в высшие сферы, но шар держится на крепком шнуре — это наша телесная связь, которая всегда нас соединяет с землею [. . .] Эти магические путы заставляют нас во что бы то ни стало возвращаться туда, где мы трусливо бросили свое земное тело, напоминают нам все ужасы самоубийства.
   — О, сколько муки, какое ужасное наказание!
   — Подожди, сказал он сдавленным голосом, это еще не все.[49]

Notes to Chapter 4

25. Совершенно оригинальные объяснения суицидального поступка встретились только у двух больных, лишивших себя жизни в состоянии психоза.

26. Записка интеллигентного молодого человека, бывшего переводчиком в редакции одной из газет.

34. Записка повесившегося кухонного мужика.

Chapter 5

— Бог необходим, а потому должен быть.

— Ну, и прекрасно.

— Но я знаю, что Его нет и не может быть.

— Это вернее.

— Неужели ты не понимаешь, что человеку с такими двумя мыслями нельзя оставаться в живых?

— Застрелиться, что ли?

— Неужели ты не понимаешь, что из-за этого только одного можно застрелить себя? (10:469)

Наши медики по вскрытии трупа совершенно и настойчиво отвергли помешательство (10:516).

я заметил, что развитие науки, что современное состояние ее *обязывает нас* к принятию кой-каких истин, независимо от того, хотим мы или нет; что, однажды узнанные, они перестают быть историческими загадками, а делаются просто неопровержимыми фактами сознания, как Эвклидовы теоремы, как Кеплеровы законы, как нераздельность причины и действия, духа и материи.

— Все это так мало обязательно, — возразил Грановский, слегка изменившись в лице,— что я никогда не приму вашей сухой, холодной мысли единства тела и духа, с ней исчезает бессмертие души. Может, вам его не надобно, но я слишком много схоронил, чтоб поступиться этой верой. Личное бессмертие мне необходимо.[5]

Маша лежит на столе. Увижусь ли с Машей? [. . .] Учение материалистов — всеобщая косность и механизм вещества, значит смерть (20:173, 175)

Это, говорят, так и следует. Такой процент, говорят, должен уходить каждый год... куда-то... к черту, должно быть, чтоб остальных освежать и им не мешать. Процент! Славные, право, у них эти словечки: они такие успокоительные, научные. Сказано: процент, стало быть и тревожиться нечего. Вот если бы другое слово, ну тогда... было бы, может быть, беспокойнее... А что, коль и Дунечка как-нибудь в процент попадет?.. Не в тот, так в другой?.. (6:43)

вопрошает труп [. . .] труп молчит или дает ответы, которые лишь приводят в сомнение о действиях жизни.[24]

Вспомни слова Биша — великого экспериментатора, опытного физика, убитого анатомическими опытами [. . .] Биша должен был сознаться, что «для тел органических надобно выдумать новый язык, ибо все слова, которые мы переносим из физических наук в животную или растительную экономию, напоминают нам такие понятия, которые вовсе не соответствуют физиологическим явлениям». Когда мы говорим, мы каждым словом вздымаем прах тысячи смыслов, присвоенных этому слову и веками, и различными странами, и даже отдельными людьми.[25]

Мое «Объяснение» достаточно объяснит все дело полиции. Охотники до психологии и те, кому надо, могут вывести из него все, что им будет угодно. Я б желал однако, чтоб эта рукопись предана была гласности. [. . .] Завещаю мой скелет в Медицинскую академию для научной пользы (8:342).

Наконец, и соблазн: природа до такой степени ограничила мою деятельность своими тремя неделями приговора, что, может быть, самоубийство есть единственное дело, которое я еще могу успеть начать и окончить по собственной воле моей. Что ж, может быть, я и хочу воспользоваться последнею возможностью *дела*? Протест иногда не малое дело... (8:344).

я старался вообразить себе психологическое состояние идущих на казнь (4:152).

А ведь главная, самая сильная боль, может не в ранах, а вот что вот знаешь наверно, что вот через час, потом через десять минут, потом через полминуты, потом теперь, вот сейчас — душа из тела вылетит, и что человеком уж больше не будешь, и что это уж наверно; главное то, что *наверно* (8:20).

Может быть, и есть такой человек, которому прочли приговор, дали помучиться, а потом сказали: «Ступай, тебя прощают». Вот этакой человек, может быть, мог бы рассказать (8:21).

всем нам прочли смертный приговор, дали приложиться к кресту, переломили над головою шпаги и устроили наш предсмертный туалет (белые рубахи). Затем троих поставили к столбу для исполнения казни. Я стоял шестым, вызывали по трое, следовательно, я был во второй очереди и жить мне оставалось не более минуты (28/I:161).

Ведь был же я сегодня у смерти, три четверти часа прожил с этой мыслию, был у последнего мгновения и теперь еще раз живу! (28/I:163–64).

* И помню я — Достоевский, сидя как умирающий Сократ пред друзьями, в ночной рубашке с незастегнутым воротом, напрягал все

свое красноречие о святости этого дела, о нашем долге спасти отечество, и пр. (18:191).

Об этой муке и об этом ужасе и Христос говорил (8:21).

На картине этой изображен Христос, только что снятый со креста. [. . .] это в полном виде труп человека, вынесшего бесконечные муки [. . .] лицо не пощажено нисколько; тут одна природа и воистину таков и должен быть труп человека, кто бы он ни был, после таких мук. Я знаю, что христианская церковь установила еще в первые века, что Христос страдал не образно, а действительно и что и тело его, стало быть, было подчинено на кресте закону природы вполне и совершенно. На картине это лицо страшно разбито ударами, вспухшее, со страшными, вспухшими и окровавленными синяками, глаза открыты, зрачки скосились; большие, открытые белки глаз блещут каким-то мертвенным, стеклянным отблеском. Но странно, когда смотришь на этот труп измученного человека, то рождается один особенный и любопытный вопрос: если такой точно труп (а он непременно должен был быть точно такой) видели все ученики его, его главные будущие апостолы, видели женщины, ходившие за ним и стоявшие у креста, все веровавшие в него и обожавшие его, то каким образом могли они поверить, смотря на такой труп, что этот мученик воскреснет? Тут невольно приходит понятие, что если так ужасна смерть и так сильны законы природы, то как же одолеть их? [. . .] Эти люди, окружавшие умершего, которых тут нет ни одного на картине, должны были ощутить страшную тоску и смятение в тот вечер, раздробивший разом все их надежды и почти что верования. [. . .] И если б этот самый учитель мог увидать свой образ накануне казни, то так ли бы сам он взошел на крест и так ли бы умер, как теперь? Этот вопрос тоже невольно мерещится, когда смотришь на картину (8:338–39).

о свободе и о свободном человеке (N.B. по апостолу Павлу) (9:120).

Поэт про обоготворение природы, язычник. [. . .] Бред, последние мгновения, «Götter Griechenlands». Смерть (9:120).

Он вывел, что русский народ есть народ второстепенный [. . .] которому предназначено послужить лишь материалом для более благородного племени, а не иметь своей самостоятельной роли в судьбах человечества. Ввиду этого, может быть и справедливого, своего вывода господин Крафт пришел к заключению, что всякая дальнейшая деятельность всякого русского человека должна быть этой идеей парализована, так сказать, у всех должны опуститься руки и... (13:44)

Сам Крафт изобразил смерть свою в виде логического вывода. [. . .] после него осталась вот эдакая тетрадь ученых выводов о том, что русские — порода людей второстепенная, на основании френологии, краниологии и даже математики, и что, стало быть, в качестве русского не стоит жить (13:134–35).

Я не атеист, но и не теист — для меня нет жизни будущей, а есть только жизнь атомов, выражающаяся в различных сочетаниях, производимых силою взаимного притяжения. Нынче известная масса составляет мою особу, а по смерти она уйдет на образование других организмов, но никогда не пропадет, а потому для меня все равно — жить ли под настоящим своим видом, или принять какую-либо иную форму. Вследствие вероятно особого склада мозга (я не признаю существования убеждений, и то, что другие называют убеждениями, считаю актом того или другого склада мозга) я пришел к заключению, что человеческая порода так же преходяща, как и все другие, и что даже самый земной шар не вечен, вечны только одни атомы с их взаимным притяжением. Но не это заставляет меня поднять на себя руку, эти мысли только дают мне силу расстаться с жизнью.[42]

я убедился, что [. . .] все его [русского народа] назначение в том только и состоит, чтобы сохранить и удобрить занимаемую им землю для другого народа.[43]

Последняя отметка сделана была в дневнике перед самым выстрелом, и он замечает в ней, что пишет почти в темноте, едва разбирая буквы; свечку же зажечь не хочет, боясь оставить после себя пожар. «А зажечь, чтоб пред выстрелом опять потушить, как и жизнь мою, не хочу», странно прибавил он чуть не в последней строчке (13:134).

Я громко удивился тому, что Васин, имея этот дневник столько времени перед глазами (ему дали прочитать его), не снял копии, тем более, что было не более листа кругом и заметки все короткие, — «хотя бы последнюю-то страничку!» Васин с улыбкой заметил мне, что он и так помнит, притом заметки без всякой системы, о всем, что на ум взбредет. Я стал было убеждать, что это-то в данном случае и драгоценно, но бросил и стал приставать, чтоб он что-нибудь припомнил, и он припомнил несколько строк, примерно за час до выстрела, о том, «что его знобит»; «что он, чтобы согреться, думал было выпить рюмку, но мысль, что от этого, пожалуй, сильнее кровоизлияние, остановила его». «Все почти в этом роде», — заключил Васин. [. . .]

— Но ведь последние мысли, последние мысли!

— Последние мысли иногда бывают чрезвычайно ничтожны. Один

такой же самоубийца именно жалуется в таком же своем дневнике, что в такой важный час хотя бы одна «высшая мысль» посетила его, а, напротив, все такие мелкие и пустые (13:134).

* жить мне оставалось не более минуты. Я вспомнил тебя, брат, всех твоих; в последнюю минуту ты, только один ты, был в уме моем. (28/I:161).

* Года полтора назад мне показывал один высокоталантливый и компетентный в нашем судебном ведомстве человек пачку собранных им писем и записок самоубийц, собственноручных, написанных ими перед самою смертию, то есть за пять минут до смерти (24:54).

Скоро 12 часов! Все готово. У меня легкий озноб, и я немного зеваю, но совершенно спокоен. Хотел выпить коньяку, но вино, говорят, усиливает кровотечение, а я и без того здесь напачкаю. Какая плохая книга «Анатомия Дондерса»! Два больших тома убористой печати, а нельзя найти, как с точностью определить место сердца.[46]

    Четверг 1 ч. 45 мин. ночи.
Я нисколько не чувствую ни волнения ни страха. Мне кажется, что я собираюсь лечь спать, меня даже очень клонит ко сну. Но меня почему-то сильно знобит, впрочем озноб я чувствую уже с месяц. Для того, чтобы согреться, я выпил несколько рюмок рому; но я знаю, что ром увеличит также кровотечение, как и все крепкие напитки, и потому я еще его пью, но вовсе не для того, чтобы в опьянении легче было застрелиться. Я чувствую в себе настолько твердости, что мог бы не закрывая глаз стать под дула направленных прямо в меня десятка ружей. Впрочем, для меня все равно, что бы обо мне ни думали.

    Чем тверже становится мой дух, тем более я начинаю себя уважать. Я понимаю теперь чувство Христа на кресте...
    2 ч. 45 мин. ночи.
Я удивляюсь физиологии Дрепера — она из 3 томов, а нет даже указания, как расположено сердце, а как на беду анатомия оставлена мною в Москве. Три часа приближается — я прошу прощения у владельца дома, что нарушаю покой в его доме.[47]

проследить, насколько возможно, ощущение при приближении смерти.[48]

Пишу на память и, чтоб не онеметь и не забыть потушить свечу и тем не сделать пожара, тушу свечу.[48]

Угнетенное состояние духа, вызванное самосознанием ничтожности своего общественного значения и нежелание расстаться с фиктивным величием, вызвали патологическое состояние мозговой деятельности. Ознобы, появлявшиеся уже в продолжении месяца, как указывает автор, и лечение ромом в день самоубийства дают право заключать, что психическое расстройство имело уже реальную органическую почву. . . .[50]

— Нынче безлесят Россию, истощают в ней почву [. . .] Все точно на постоялом дворе и завтра собираются вон из России. (13:54).

нет другой жизни, я на земле на одно мгновение, чего же церемониться.
[. . .] «Какое мне дело, хоть бы они провалились не только в будущем, но хоть и сию минуту и я с ними вместе, après moi le déluge». Параллель: как у нас истощение почвы и истребление лесов (16:8–9).

А зажечь, чтоб пред выстрелом опять потушить, как и жизнь мою, не хочу (13:134).

какие причины заставляют перед последними мгновениями чуть не всех (или очень многих) писать *исповеди* (N.B. так, что если бы у всех были средства, то все, может быть, писали бы исповеди) (16:68).

Истребляют себя от многочисленных причин, пишут исповеди тоже от сложных причин, а не одного тщеславия. Но можно отыскать и общие черты, напр[имер] то, что в такую минуту у всех потребность писать. «Голос»: зарезавшийся ножом в трактире: «Образ милой К. все предо мною». [. . .] Но вот что опять-таки общая черта: тут же, в этой же оставленной им записке (*несмотря на милую К.*, которой образ, *уж конечно*, не мог давать ему покоя, если из-за нее зарезался), — тут же у него и примеч[ание]: «Удивительно пусто в голове, думал, что в этакую минуту будут особые мысли». Умно или глупо подобное замечание — важно то, что все они чего-то ищут, о чем-то спрашивают, на что ответа не находят, о чем-то интересуются совершенно вне личных интересов. О каком-то общем (деле) и вековечном, несмотря даже на образ милой К., который, без сомнения, мог бы прогнать всякую общую идею и потребность самоуглубления и обратить действие *совершенно в личное* (16:68–69).

Во всем идея разложения, ибо все *врозь* и никаких не остается связей не только в русском семействе, но даже просто между людьми. [. . .] *Разложение* — главная видимая мысль романа (16:16–17).

Общество химически разлагается. [. . .] все эти семьи и вся эта народность разложится, даже образа от них не останется (16:16).

рубит образа [. . .] вынесть не может *образов* [. . .] застреливается (16:42, 43).

Планета с Богом соприкасаются целого и бессмертия (семейство уничтожается и предки, и личность (без Бога), остается род человеческий, ограничивается, стало быть, землею, а при воскресении свидание, познание) (16:170).

тип случайного семейства, в противуположность родового семейства (16:434).

* Я... я... я вас истреблю, вот что (он встал с места бледный). Belle vue (16:374). N.B. N.B. О том, что застрелить женщину, если она не соглашается, фельетон Суворина, ноября 3 no. 303 (16:195).

Все несчастье ЕГО, что ОН — атеист и не верует *воскресенью* (16:15).

Исчезла бы великая идея бессмертия и приходилось бы заменить ее; и весь избыток прежней любви к тому, который и был бессмертие, обратился бы у всех на природу, на мир, на людей, на всякую былинку. Они возлюбили бы землю и жизнь неудержимо и в той мере, в какой постепенно сознавали бы свою преходимость и конечность, и уже особенною, уже не прежнею любовью. Они стали бы замечать и открыли бы в природе такие явления и тайны, каких и не предполагали прежде, ибо смотрели бы на природу новыми глазами, взглядом любовника на возлюбленную (13:379).

Будет новый человек, счастливый и гордый, кому будет все равно, жить или не жить, тот будет новый человек. Кто победит боль и страх, тот сам бог будет. А тот Бог не будет (10:93–94).

— Старые философские места, одни и те же с начала веков, — с каким-то брезгливым сожалением пробормотал Ставрогин.
— Одни и те же! Одни и те же с начала веков, и никаких других никогда! — подхватил Кириллов с сверкающим взглядом, как будто в этой идее заключалась чуть не победа (10:188).

* Этот безумец словно воспроизводит на свой оригинальный лад знаменитое гегелевское положение: бытие или небытие — одно и то же (Sein und Nichtsein ist dasselbe).

был на земле один день, и в средине земли стояли три креста. Один на кресте до того веровал, что сказал другому: «Будешь сегодня со мною в раю». Кончился день, оба померли, пошли и не нашли ни рая, ни воскресения. [. . .] А если так, если законы природы не пожалели и *Этого* [. . .] для чего же жить (10:471).

Если нет Бога, то я бог (10:469–70).

— Если Бог есть, то вся воля его, и из воли его я не могу. Если нет, то вся воля моя, и я обязан заявить своеволие. [. . .] Я обязан себя застрелить, потому что самый полный пункт моего своеволия — это убить себя самому (10:470)

Я начну, и кончу, и дверь отворю. И спасу. Только это одно спасет всех людей и в следующем же поколении переродит физически. (10:472).

— Он придет, и имя ему человекобог.
— Богочеловек?
— Человекобог, в этом разница (10:189).

не в будущую вечную [жизнь], а в здешнюю вечную (10:188).

в теперешнем физическом виде, сколько я думал, нельзя быть человеку без прежнего Бога никак (10:472).

— Есть минуты, вы доходите до минут, и время вдруг останавливается и будет вечно.
— Вы надеетесь дойти до такой минуты?
— Да
— Это вряд ли в наше время возможно [. . .] В Апокалипсисе ангел клянется, что времени больше не будет.
— Знаю. Это очень там верно; отчетливо и точно. [. . .]
— Куда же его спрячут?
— Никуда не спрячут. Время не предмет, а идея. Погаснет в уме (10:188).

— Есть секунды, их всего зараз приходит пять или шесть, и вы вдруг чувствуете присутствие вечной гармонии, совершенно достигнутой. Это не земное; я не про то, что оно небесное, а про то, что человек в земном виде не может перенести. Надо перемениться физически или умереть (10:450).

К чему дети, к чему развитие, коли цель достигнута? (10:450–51).

* — Да разве нет способов умирать без боли?
— Представьте, — остановился он передо мною, — представьте камень такой величины, как с большой дом; он висит, а вы под ним; если он упадет на вас, на голову — будет вам больно?
— Камень с дом? Конечно, страшно.
— Я не про страх; будет больно?
— Камень с гору, миллион пудов? Разумеется, ничего не больно (10:93).

в углу, образованном стеною и шкафом, стоял Кириллов, и стоял ужасно странно, — неподвижно, вытянувшись, протянув руки по швам, приподняв голову и плотно прижавшись затылком к стене [. . .] Петр Степанович [. . .] мог наблюдать только выдающиеся части фигуры [. . .] Его, главное, поразило то, что фигура, несмотря на крик и на бешеный наскок его, даже не двинулась, не шевельнулась ни одним своим членом — точно окаменевшая или восковая. Бледность лица ее была неестественная, черные глаза совсем неподвижны и глядели в какую-то точку в пространстве. Петр Степанович провел свечой сверху вниз и опять вверх, освещая со всех точек и разглядывая это лицо. Он вдруг заметил, что Кириллов хоть и смотрит куда-то пред собой, но искоса его видит и даже, может быть, наблюдает. Тут пришла ему мысль поднести огонь прямо к лицу «этого мерзавца», поджечь и посмотреть, что тот сделает. [. . .] Едва он дотронулся до Кириллова, как тот быстро нагнул голову и головой же выбил из рук его свечку; подсвечник полетел со звоном на пол, и свеча потухла. В то же мгновение он почувствовал ужасную боль в мизинце своей левой руки [. . .] ударил револьвером по голове припавшего к нему и укусившего ему палец Кириллова. Наконец палец он вырвал и сломя голову бросился бежать из дому, отыскивая в темноте дорогу. Вслед ему и комнаты летели страшные крики:
— Сейчас, сейчас, сейчас, сейчас...
Раз десять. Но он все бежал и уже выбежал было в сени, как вдруг послышался громкий выстрел (10:475–76).

Описание самоубийства Кириллова — это одно из тех созданий Достоевского, где он переступает за пределы искусства; это то, о чем нельзя писать, почти говорить нельзя: это цинично, жестоко, может быть, преступно, не только художественно, но и нравственно преступно. Это своего рода вивисекция, анатомическое рассечение живой души: заглядывая в эту зияющую рану, окровавленные внутренности человеческой души, мы с отвращением и с любопытством ужаса следим за их последними содроганиями.[76]

Мне говорили, *что Кириллов* не ясен. Я бы вам рассказал про Малькова (24:163). Слышал о Малькове (22:162).

В ваше отсутствие я перестал быть «ветхим» человеком. Послушайте [. . .] вскройте и вы в себе «божественную душу». Сделайтесь христианином. Откажитесь от мысли — насилием уничтожить насилие.[80]

он вздохнул свою душу и сделал нас богочеловеками.[81]

Маленький сынишка Маликова, подпрыгивая на одной ножке, сообщил ему новость:
— А папка-м бог! А папка-м бог!..[82]

Христианин относится даже к дурному человеку как бы к недостаткам своего собственного тела, понимая, что они оба — части одного человечества, что все люди суть атомы социального организма, боготворимого ныне мною. Я убежден, что многие русские революционеры переродятся, если увидят и поговорят со мною![83]

Когда его ввели к нам, он заговорил о Боге, о социальном организме, которому и великие, и малые люди одинаково нужны, как каждому из нас нужен не только головной мозг, но и любой палец руки... Он тотчас же был освобожден.[84]

Да, тело сгорало... Но всегда ли?.. Можно себе представить еще шаг в этом направлении, еще большее напряжении веры, и огонь потеряет силу сжигать тело. [. . .] Неужели и вы допускаете, что под влиянием чисто нервных процессов тело человека может стать несгораемым?.. [. . .] Да, допускаю.[85]

* Я знаю, что мне надо бы убить себя, смести себя с земли как подлое насекомое; но я боюсь самоубийства, ибо боюсь показать великодушие. Я знаю, что это будет еще обман, — последний обман в бесконечном ряду обманов. Что же пользы себя обмануть, чтобы только сыграть в великодушие? Негодования и стыда во мне никогда быть не может; стало быть, и отчаяния (10:514).

от одной ошибки «на волосок» в критике познания — вся мудрость вдруг делается сумасшествием.[105]

Сверхчеловек, Человекобог превратился в человека-зверя. Страшный титан Заратустра-Антихрист — в жалкого калеку, бывшего немецкого доктора филологии, Фридриха Ницше, содержимого в лечебнице для душевно-больных.[106]

Сумасшествие Кириллова и Ницше — только первое слабое веяние этой неизбежной, всемирно-исторической заразы безумия.[107]

Notes to Chapter 5

43. Я думал было остаться еще на 5 или 6 лет для того, чтобы посвятить себя изысканию научных доказательств справедливости моих воззрений.

52. Один такой же самоубийца именно жалуется в таком же своем дневнике, что в такой важный час хоть бы одна «высшая мысль» посетила его, а, напротив, все такие мелкие и пустые (13:134).

Chapter 6

В 1876 году будет выходить в свет ежемесячно, отдельными выпусками издание Ф. М. Достоевского «Дневник писателя» [. . .] в формате еженедельных газет наших. Но это будет не газета; из всех двенадцати выпусков [. . .] составится целое, книга, написанная одним пером. Это будет дневник в буквальном смысле слова, отчет о действительно выжитых в каждый месяц впечатлениях, отчет о виденном, слышанном и прочитанном. Сюда, конечно, могут войти рассказы и повести, но преимущественно о событиях действительных (22:136).

Ей было двадцать пять лет. Фамилия — Писарева. Была она дочь достаточных когда-то родителей, но приехала в Петербург и отдала долг прогрессу, поступила в акушерки. Ей удалось, она выдержала экзамен и нашла место земской акушерки; сама свидетельствует, что не нуждалась вовсе и могла слишком довольно заработать, но она *устала*, она очень «устала», так устала, что ей захотелось отдохнуть. «Где же лучше отдохнешь, как не в могиле?» (23:24).

До странности занимают ее денежные распоряжения той крошечной суммой, которая после нее осталась: «те-то деньги чтоб не взяли родные, те-то Петровой, двадцать пять рублей, которые дали мне Чечоткины на дорогу, отвезите им» (23:25).

Эта важность, приданная деньгам, есть, может быть, последний отзыв главного предрассудка всей жизни «о камнях, обращенных в хлебы». Одним словом, руководящее убеждение всей жизни, то есть «были бы все обеспечены, были бы все и счастливы, не было бы бедных, не было бы преступлений. Преступлений нет совсем. Преступление есть болезненное состояние, происходящее от бедности и от несчастной среды» и т. д. и т. д. (23:25).

И почему это я раздумался о самоубийцах в этом здании, смотря [. . .] на этих младенцев? (23:24).

Позвольте Вас *спросить*, что Вы хотели сказать [. . .] упоминая часто в Вашем письме слова из Евангелия о камнях, обращенных в хлебы. Это было предложено дьяволом Христу, когда он его искушал, но камни не сделались хлебами и не обратились в пищу.[11]

Прошу извинения за то, что беспокою Вас подобным вопросом, но так как слово это вышло от Вас, то я лучше счел обратиться к Вам, я человек темный в этом, то и прошу Вас не вводить меня в искушение, Вам через науку господам открыто многое, от Вас разливается свет на людей темных.[12]

[они] извлекали бы из земли баснословные урожаи, может быть, создали бы химией организмы, и говядины хватило бы по три фунта на человека, как мечтают наши русские социалисты — словом, ешь, пей и наслаждайся (22:33).

Но вряд ли и на одно поколение людей хватило бы этих восторгов! Люди вдруг увидели бы, что жизни уже более нет у них, нет свободы духа, нет воли и личности, что кто-то у них все украл разом; что исчез человеческий лик. [. . .] И загнило бы человечество; люди покрылись бы язвами и стали кусать языки свои в муках, увидя, что жизнь у них взята за хлеб и за «камни, обращенные в хлебы» (22:34).

Настанет скука и тоска: все сделано и нечего более делать, все известно и нечего более узнавать. Самоубийцы явятся толпами, а не так, как теперь, по углам; люди будут сходиться массами, схватываясь за руки и истребляя себя все вдруг, тысячами, каким-нибудь новым способом, открытым им вместе со всеми открытиями (22:33–34).

В искушении диавола явились три колоссальные мировые идеи, и вот прошло 18 веков, а труднее, то есть мудренее, этих идей нет и их все еще не могут решить.

«Камни и хлебы» значит теперешний социальный вопрос, *среда*. Это не пророчество, это всегда было. «Чем идти-то к разоренным нищим, похожим от голодухи и притеснений скорее на зверей, чем на людей — идти и начать проповедовать голодным воздержание от грехов, смирение, целомудрие — не лучше ли *накормить* их сначала? [. . .]

Ты — Сын Божий, стало быть, Ты все можешь. Вот камни, видишь, как много. Тебе стоит только повелеть — и камни обратятся в хлеб.

Повели же и впредь, чтоб земля рождала без труда, научи людей такой науке или научи их такому порядку, чтоб жизнь их была впредь обеспечена. Неужто не веришь, что главнейшие пороки и беды человека произошли от голоду, холоду, нищеты и из всевозможной борьбы за существование [. . .]

На это Христос отвечал: «не одним хлебом бывает жив человек», — то есть сказал аксиому и о духовном происхождении человека (29/II:84–85).

Послушайте, отчего Вы так нападаете, отчего так сожалеете Писареву, сожалеете не просто, а кажется как-то особенно. Что же особенного? Это для Вас, может быть, Писарева аномалия? Таковое состояние некоторых из женщин в настоящее время удивительно?

Что находите Вы на этот раз большой кружок такого рода женщин?!

Отчего же Вы не направите Ваших стрел на причину, а не на следствие? А как скоро Вы причину найдете, Писарева Вас не удивит.

Я в сравнении с Вами — Ваш внук. Отнестись слишком свысока к моему письму с Вашей стороны будет не честно. Удовлетворите меня до некоторой степени и тем более, если Вы это можете, то сделайте немедленно. Прошу Вас очень.

Вам же должно быть понятно мое к Вам обращение.

П. Потоцкий.

Я убежден, что Вы мне ответите — это Вы должны (напишите, как я сказал, на равных) [. . .] Не смейтесь.[16]

[они] хотят жить *духовно*, хотят участвовать в деле человеческом, готовы на подвиги и на великодушие. Но, уходя из домов своих, попадаются в круги лиц, уверяющих их, что духовной жизни нет и что жизнь духовная — сказка, а не реализм. Что великодушия тоже нет, а есть только борьба за существование.

Писарева спрашивает тогда «что делать?» Ей отвечают: быть повивальной бабкой, по крайней мере будете полезны обществу. Уверовав, Писарева поступает в бабки: долгие годы учения, духовной пищи никакой. [. . .] Наконец, ее поражает мысль: «великодушия нет, а ступайте в повивальные бабки — будьте тем полезны». Но если нет великодушия, *не надо быть и полезным. Кому это?* Под конец полное разочарование (29/II:86–87).

то, что одни называют Богом, другие клеточкой, третьи неизвестным, недоступным духом — одним словом: *Великая Тайна*. Но тайна и остается тайной, и в этом-то именно и заключается весь смысл нашего существования, весь цикл условий, в котором стоит мир. Вы видите, это атеизм (по крайней мере, так понимают это), но я прошу Вас, не относитесь к этому слову с предвзятыми идеями и даже чувствами, так как в вас, как в христианине, и в глубоком христианине, чувство всегда идет вперед... Мне хочется лишь спросить Вас, прав я или нет, и для этого скажу предварительно два слова о себе.[19]

Ренан прельстил меня, *Милль* был глубоко симпатичен, *Бокль* открывал мне смысл истории, но *Дарвин*, вот кто все во мне перевернул, весь строй, все мысли. Я упивался этой новой, ясной и, главное, положительно-точной картиной мира! Я сделался другим человеком. *Фейербах* докончил в области духа то, что Дарвин начал в области фактов. Я потерял чувство (т. е. религию), но приобрел мысль и убеждения. Однако, случай меня в жизни не баловал. Целым рядом несчастно сцеплявшихся обстоятельств (уж, конечно, не без вин и ошибок с моей стороны) — я дошел до безвыходного положения. Я так ловко устроился, что пришлось убедиться, что я лишний человек, дурная, сорная трава, не опора, а бремя для семьи (а у меня 3-ое детей — вот кого жалко покинуть, а надо). Я здраво, математически верно определил безвыходность положения и весь вред моего существования — и решился умереть. (Семья, понятно, обеспечена более или менее — да и помощь ей нравственная и физическая тоже обеспечена).[19]

Поветрие самоубийства может быть лишь между гимназистами, жалкими, слабыми девушками, да еще между мучениками-пролетариями, — но самоубийство — результат всестороннего обсуждения всех шансов, самого смысла жизни и своего собственного *я* — это не преступление и даже не ошибка — это право.[19]

И жить-то на Русской Земле нельзя.[19]

Несколько дней осталось для деловых, необходимых распоряжений — и по тому, если хотите и найдете время, напишите словечко. Я вас очень полюбил и уважаю, даром что вы мистик, но — честная душа, а много ли таких? Делайте свое дело — человечество вас не забудет. Поверите ли, я в дверях могилы — а на сердце стало тихо, мирно и ясно! В мать-природу иду. Из нее и в нее. Вот и Тайна! не она ли?
     Уважающий Вас,
               N.N.[19]

Г-ну X.Y.Z, с девизом: «От веры к неверию» — или лучше: «*ответ на исповедь*».[19]

В самом деле: какое право имела эта природа производить меня на свет, вследствии каких-то там своих вечных законов? Я создан с сознанием и эту природу *сознал*: какое право она имела производить меня, без моей воли на то, сознающего? (23:146).

не буду и не могу быть счастлив под условием грозящего завтра нуля. Это — чувство, это непосредственное чувство, и я не могу побороть его (23:147).

Так как на вопросы мои о счастьи я через мое же сознание получаю от природы лишь ответ, что могу быть счастлив не иначе, как в гармонии целого, которой я не понимаю, и очевидно для меня, и понять никогда не в силах —

Так как природа не только не признает за мной права спрашивать у нее отчета, но даже не отвечает мне вовсе, и не потому, что не хочет, а потому, что и не может ответить —

Так как я убедился, что природа, чтоб отвечать мне на мои вопросы, предназначила мне (бессознательно) *меня же самого* и отвечает мне моим же сознанием (потому что я сам это все говорю себе) —

Так как, наконец, при таком порядке, я принимаю на себя в одно и то же время роль истца и ответчика, подсудимого и судьи [. . .]

То, в моем несомненном качестве истца и ответчика, судьи и подсудимого, я присуждаю эту природу, которая так бесцеремонно и нагло произвела меня на страдание, — вместе со мною к уничтожению... А так как природу я истребить не могу, то и истребляю себя одного, единственно от скуки сносить тиранию, в которой нет виноватого (23:147–48).

Только что появилась моя статья, и на письмах и лично посыпались мне запросы: что, дескать, значит ваш «Приговор»? Что вы хотите этим сказать и неужели вы самоубийство оправдываете? (24:45).

исповедь самоубийцы, последнее слово самоубийцы, записанное им самим [. . .] перед самым револьвером (24:44).

разъяснить ясными словами, от автора, цель с которою она написана, и даже прямо приписать нравоучение (24:44).

Статья моя «Приговор» касается основной и самой высшей идеи человеческого бытия — необходимости и неизбежности убеждения в бессмертии души человеческой. Подкладка этой исповеди погибающего «от логического самоубийства» человека — это необходимость тут же, сейчас же вывода: что без веры в свою душу и в ее бессмертие бытие человека неестественно, немыслимо и невыносимо (24:46).

отняв у человека веру в его бессмертие, хотят заменить эту веру, в смысле высшей цели жизни, «любовью к человечеству» (24:49).

совсем невозможна без совместной веры в бессмертие души человеческой [. . .]
любовь к человечеству *вообще* есть, как *идея*, одна из самых непостижимых идей для человеческого ума. Именно как идея. Ее может оправдать лишь одно чувство. Но чувство-то возможно именно лишь при совместном убеждении в бессмертии души человеческой. (И опять голословно.)

В результате ясно, что самоубийство, при потере идеи о бессмертии, становится совершенною и неизбежною даже необходимостью для всякого человека, чуть-чуть поднявшегося в своем развитии над скотами. Напротив, бессмертие, обещая вечную жизнь, тем крепче связывает человека с землей. [. . .] Без убеждения же в своем бессмертии связи человека с землей порываются, становятся тоньше, гнилее, а потеря высшего смысла жизни (ощущаемая хотя бы лишь в виде самой бессознательной тоски) несомненно ведет за собой самоубийство (24:49).

Я получаю очень много писем с изложением фактов самоубийств и с вопросами: как и что я об этих самоубийствах думаю и чем их объясняю? (24:50)

эти самоубийцы покончили с собой из-за одной и той же духовной болезни — от отсутствия высшей идеи существования в душе их (24:50).

Вопрос о самоубийцах и меня интересует уже давно. Он начал меня интересовать с тех пор, как я узнал о существовании теории, которая всех самоубийц признает психически больными. Мне это показалось очень странным. Неужели так-таки все самоубийцы психически больные люди? [. . .] Этот вопрос, говорю я, меня сильно интересовал и я стал искать другие причины, обусловливающие подобную аномалию в общественной жизни. Два года назад я случайно услышал рассказ о смерти одного киевского студента, который лишил себя жизни потому только, что не мог сделаться идеально честным. В таком смысле по крайней мере оставил записку. Находясь сам в настроении, близко подходящем к настроению этого несчастного студента, я решился логически последовательно разобрать подобное душевное состояние и таким [пропущено] добраться до какого-нибудь результата, вывести какое-нибудь заключение. Это мне было легко сделать, потому что, как я сказал, я был точно так же настроен, хотя в более общем смысле. Я что сделал; я выбрал форму рассказа, в котором мой герой, после сильных нравственных страданий, становится, наконец, на объективную почву и логически последовательно доказывает, что он должен покончить с собой: ни любовь, ни чувство долга, ни привязанность не в состоянии удержать его...[23]

Прочитав теперь Ваше рассуждение о самоубийцах и Ваш вывод, я, признаться, с одной стороны и обрадовался, что попался человек (и кто еще!), который тоже задается такими дикими вопросами; с другой стороны, я задумался и сильно задумался. Не там, значит, нужно было искать причины, где я искал, думалось мне: нужно было взять повыше... Ваш вывод о бессмертии души смутил меня окончательно.[23]

Вы говорите, человеколюбие есть чувство, а не идея. По-моему, это — громадная ошибка. Не будь человеколюбие идеею, до сих пор не было [бы] освобождения невольников, освобождения наших крестьян... Это самая реальная, самая положительная из всех идей и доступна всякому, кто сознательно относится к окружающей среде... [. . .] Вот от этой-то идеи и страдают наши интеллигентные самоубийцы, а не от недостатка веры в бессмертие души... Разве эта идея не выше идеи о бессмертии души, не реальнее, не доступнее для каждого смертного, разве она одна не достаточна для того, чтобы наполнить мир гармониею?..[23]

Правда, Вы бы с Вашим талантом в тысячу раз больше пользы принесли, если бы проповедовали идею человеколюбия в том смысле, на котором остановилось последнее слово науки, чем развивать идею о бессмертии души...[23]

Я хотел бы с Вами говорить насчет самоубийств. Я защищаю:
а) всякий человек имеет право самоубийства,
б) всякий человек в известных случаях должен,
в) с верою в будущую жизнь, в Бога, можно покончить с собою.

Почему у меня такие убеждения сложились — долго рассказывать; прилагаемая тетрадь, быть может, даст ответ.

Кроме вопроса о самоубийствах я хотел Вам еще рассказ представить (он в тетради) и спросить, стоит ли продолжать [. . .]

Если будете так добры — ответите, то в своем «Дневнике писателя» или — хоть это смело с моей стороны — по адресу [. . .] Отвечайте категорически «да» или «нет»: мне терять нечего.[24]

Четвертый год меня тянет с собой кончить и я дал слово некоторым знакомым — не кончать раньше 1880 г.; боюсь, что не сдержу этого.[27]

Но что я кончу самоубийством — несомненно. Мысль эта давно мелькает у меня, и я исполню ее. Не будь я — Воеводин!

Я в своем самоубийстве заинтересован со многих сторон. Я хочу этим самоубийством многое показать обществу, да при том и мне полезно будет это кровопускание. Но вот это-то, эту пользу для себя и для общества, я смутно понимаю, не могу вполне привести в ясность все это; меня вот это бесит, я хожу вокруг да около, не могу совершенно обхватить эти два мотива, решить эту задачу. Поймите, я в каком-то тумане, не могу схватить себя и уничтожить... Но будет, будет самоубийство...[28]

Конечно статистика эта не дает безусловно верных цифр и не объясняет причин самоубийств.[29]

Я не признаю жизни, как она есть, я не допускаю в ней многое, многое в ней меня тошнить, злоба, негодование, ненависть душать меня [. . .] Это *непризнание* жизни, основываемое мною на бесчисленных, окружающих меня, вас, примерах: на собственной моей жизни, жизни родных и близких моих, жизни, которую встречал [. . .] наконец на массе прочитанных мною книг, на социологических сочинениях.[32]

не слыхали ли вы про такие записочки:

«Милый папаша, мне двадцать три года, и я еще ничего не сделал; убежденный, что из меня ничего не выйдет, я решился покончить с жизнью...» (22:5).

Ночь была темная, не сверкали звезды [. . .] созвездие Большой Медведицы не сияло...[34]

подобные гимназисты вот и стреляются.[36]

в письме Вашем было для меня довольно много непонятного. Вы пишите: «отвечайте категорически: да или нет» и тут же прибавляете: «мне терять нечего». Но на что же отвечать? На Вашу тему о самоубийстве? Но не думаю, чтоб Вы предполагали получить от меня ответ в письме. Писать на эти темы письма совсем невозможно, тем более, что я не знаю Вас лично и не знаю Ваших мыслей. По тетради же Вашей очень трудно составить о Вас какое-нибудь понятие. [. . .] К тому же я хоть и прочел более половины Вашей тетради, но в ней такой беспорядок и так она интимно (то есть для Вас одного) написана, что, признаюсь, она задала мне много труда, а объяснений мало дала.

Относится ли наконец Ваш вопрос: «да или нет» до «Записок гимназиста»? (30/I:26).

* автобиография самого незначительного лица [. . .] может быть занимательной, да и как еще! [. . .] Пусть будет бессвязно, нескладно, нелепо [. . .] Кто угодно, говорю я, может быть писателем-автобиографом.

материальной, видимой, внешней причины (23:145).

потому что никак не могла приискать себе для пропитания работы (23:146).

и упала на землю, *держа в руках образ* [23:146].

Этот образ в руках — странная и неслыханная еще в самоубийстве черта! Это уж какое-то кроткое, смиренное самоубийство. Тут даже, видимо, не было никакого ропота или попрека: просто — стало нельзя жить, «Бог не захотел» — и умерла, помолившись. [. . .] Эта кроткая, истребившая себя душа невольно мучает мысль. Вот эта-то смерть и напомнила мне о сообщенном мне еще летом самоубийстве дочери эмигранта. Но какие же, однако же, два разные создания, точно обе с двух разных планет! И какие две разные смерти! (23:146).

То есть по-русски:

Предпринимаю длинное путешествие. Если самоубийство не удастся, то пусть соберутся все отпраздновать мое воскресение из мертвых с бокалами Клико. *А если удастся*, то я прошу только, чтоб схоронили меня, вполне убедясь, что я мертвая, потому что совсем неприятно проснуться в гробу под землею. *Очень даже не шикарно выйдет!* (23:145).

дочь и мать ненавидели друг друга и грызлись с утра до вечера. Конечно, дочь с детства воспитывалась в полном материализме и безверии.[41]

Убеждений своего покойного отца и его стремительной веры в них — у ней, конечно, не было и быть не могло, иначе она не истребила бы себя. [. . .] С другой стороны, сомнения нет, она возросла вне всякого вопроса о Боге в полном убеждении матерьялизма, даже, может быть, вопрос о духовном начале души, о бессмертии духа и не пошевелился в душе ее в уме ее во всю жизнь. [. . .] И вот что для отца было жизнью источником [жизни] мысли и сознания, для дочери обратилось в смерть (23:324–25).

В этот гадком, грубом шике, по-моему, слышится вызов, может быть, негодование, злоба, — но на что же? [. . .] На что же могло быть негодование?.. на простоту представляющегося, на бессодержательность жизни? Это те, слишком известные, судьи и отрицатели жизни, негодующие на «глупость» появления человека на земле, на бестолковую случайность этого появления, на тиранию косной причины, с которою нельзя помириться? Тут слышиться душа именно возмутившаяся против «прямолинейности» явлений, не вынесшая этой прямолинейности, сообщившейся ей в доме отца еще с детства (23:145).

с страданием, так сказать, животным и безотчетным (23:146).

Представьте себе мужа, у которого лежит на столе жена, самоубийца, несколько часов перед тем выбросившаяся из окошка. Он в смятении и еще не успел собрать своих мыслей. Он ходит по своим комнатам и старается осмыслить случившееся, «собрать свои мысли в точку» (24:5).

Все мгновение продолжалось, может быть, каких-нибудь только десять минут, все решение, именно когда у стены стояла, прислонившись головой к руке, и улыбалась. Влетела в голову мысль, закружилась и — и не могла устоять перед нею (24:34).

«что бы вы ни написали, чтобы ни вывели, чтобы ни отметили в художественном произведении, — никогда вы не сравняетесь с действительностью. Что бы вы ни изобразили — все выйдет слабее, чем в действительности» (23:144).

Это я знал еще с 46-го года, когда начал писать, а может быть и раньше, — и факт этот не раз поражал меня и ставил меня в недоумение о полезности искусства при таком видимом его бессилии. Действительно, проследите иной, даже вовсе и не такой яркий на первый взгляд факт действительной жизни, — и если вы только в силах и имеете глаз, то найдете в нем глубину, какой нет у Шекспира. Но ведь в том-то и весь вопрос: *на чей глаз и кто в силах?* (23:144).

Но и в действительность вглядывается поэт, а другой ничего не увидит (23:191).

Он забыл (Щедрин), что действительность определяют поэты (23:190).

Notes to Chapter 6

18. Милостивый Государь
          Федор Михайлович.
  Через час по столовой ложке
Но я скоро замолчу! Вы же долго еще будете жить. — Вы не удивляйтесь такой назойливости. — Ей Богу мне дорога жизнь, дорог каждый шаг, где видна жизнь. — А *нашу* жизнь никто лучше Вас не распознал. — У меня есть два брата: один европеец — человек практичный; другой Русский — человек теории, профессор [и] проч. И обоих этих братьев объяснили мне Вы. Поймите же, что я имею право Вас любить. —
          Опять таки
            Ваш Читатель
        Прощайте!

42. дочь Герцена все-таки должна была, кажется, быть почти непременно существом одухотворенным, имеющим хоть понятие о чем-нибудь высшем, чем бутылка Клико (23:325).

50. жизнь всей этой *семьи* была странная и не по силам этой молодой душе (23:324).

Пьет шампанское à la Herzen (16:50); герценская болтовня за шампанским (16:54); выпьем. Я как Герцен; да здравствует жизнь — шампанское! (16:418, 419).

Chapter 7

Вот хоть бы и в прошлую неделю: в знаменской гостинице повесилась немолодая уже женщина, госпожа Паж; в бане, что в доме Вяземского, в отдельном нумере, повесилась молодая женщина; чрез несколько дней зарезался отставной уездный врач Мейгров; в Царском Селе некий г. Р., принадлежащий, по словам газет, к высоко порядочному кругу, выстрелил из револьвера в свою жену — хотя рана была не смертельной, но у несчастной супруги, после выстрела, не досчитались нескольких зубов; отставной солдат, выбрав уединенное место, нанес себе две раны в горло... Это только в Петербурге; в провинции подобных случаев и не перечесть; да их никто и не считает.[2]

Из этого повального стремления самоубийствовать иной ученый выведет, пожалуй, заключение, что существует-де закон, перед которым все равны и которому все должны повиноваться, когда он приступает с своими требованиями! Ну, что тогда?..[3]

Просмотрите скорбный лист самоубийств и покушений на них за последние дни — ну, где тут и какая система? Тихон Герасимов, 24 лет — утопился; кухарка Фирсова — повесилась; акушерка бросилась с моста в воду, и, конечно, не ее вина, что ее спасли; Белов ранил себя в грудь; студент, на улице, среди белого дня, хотел застрелиться и, опять-таки, не по своей вине остался в живых; мещанин Ведерников застрелился в купальне в ту самую минуту, когда бывшая там с ним проститутка окунулась в воду; чиновник, лет 40, бросился в Неву с николаевского моста и, вопреки первоначальному своему намерению, был спасен. Где же в этом хаосе самоубийств найти систему?[3]

В этом году число утопившихся значительно превысило повесившихся, тогда как в предыдущие годы было наоборот. Почему способы самоубийства больше избираются простые — веревка и вода — будет более понятно, если скажем, что из числа самоубийств, около 70% приходится на долю простого класса жителей Петербурга и только 30% на долю привилегированных сословий.[4]

Кухарка потеряла 5 рублей заработной платы и решила, что ей жить больше незачем; акушерку же, вероятно, побудила к самоубийству не такая ничтожная причина; однако, кухарка повесилась, а акушерка бросилась в воду.[5]

Чего ему желать? Зачем ему жить? Кухарка 5 руб. потеряла. Какая пустая и глупая шутка.[6]

г. Достоевский берет готовых, живых людей, превращает их в идиотов и маньяков и заставляет их бредить на яву. Он не объясняет причины, двигающей их неопытными головами и толкающей их на безумие и погибель, а просто издевается над своими героями и заставляет их резать и вешать друг друга без всякого на то основания. Главный «курьез» романа состоит в том, что все почти герои его или с ума сходят или просто идиотствуют, или режут друг друга, или, наконец, сами стреляются и вешаются. [. . .] Нет, как хотите, а мне кажется, что г. Достоевский трудился исключительно для меня, чтобы я мог внести в свои «литературные курьезы» одним курьезом больше...[7]

прежде заботливая полиция скрывала эти «ужасы», а теперь печать ежедневно докладывает о них читателю. [. . .] Прежде, убился человек — кроме полиции никому до этого и дела не было, а теперь? Только развернешь газету — утопился, зарезался, повесился, даже в глазах зарябит! Прежде, пожалуй, самоубийствовали и больше, да говорили об этом меньше, потому что не знали, так что вопрос о самоубийствовании стал модным совершенно незаконно.[8]

этот человек поучал нас со столбцов газет и журналов требованиям общественной совести, которые он сам попрал таким преступным деянием. Бедное печатное слово, бедное![10]

Многоуважаемый Федор Михайлович!

Странная мысль пришла мне в голову — написать Вам настоящее письмо. Несмотря на то, что Вы получаете письма со всех концов России и между ними — без всякого сомнения — довольно глупые и странные, но от меня Вы никогда не могли ожидать писем.

Кто же, однако, этот «я»?

Я, во-первых, еврей,— а Вы очень недолюбливаете евреев (о чем, впрочем, будет у меня речь впереди); во-вторых, я был одним из тех публицистов, которых Вы презираете, который Вас (т.е. Ваши литературные труды) много, азартно и зло ругал. (Если я не ошибаюсь, то в одной статье во время редажирования Вами «Гражданина», Вы чрезвычайно метко отзывались обо мне — не упоминая впрочем моего литературного псевдонима — как о человеке, который всеми силами старался завести с Вами личную полемику, вызвать Вас на бой, но Вы проходили все мои выходки молчанием и не удовлетворили моего самолюбия); в третьих, наконец, я — преступник и пишу Вам эти строки из тюрьмы.

Вы, который так следит за всеми более или менее выдающимися явлениями общественной жизни вообще и процессами в особенности, давно, я думаю, догадались, что я — Ковнер, который писал в «Голосе» фельетоны под рубрикой: «Литературные и общественные курьезы», который затем служил в Петербургском Учетном и Ссудном банке и который 28 апреля 1875 г., посредством подлога, похитил из Московского Купеческого банка 168 000 рублей, скрылся, был задержан в Киеве со всеми деньгами, доставлен в Москву, судим и осужден к отдаче в арестантские роты на четыре года?[11]

* ответим только на несколько раз предлагавшийся нам со стороны вопрос: почему мы так мало или совсем даже не отвечаем на критики, нападения и ругательства, которые сыплются на нас беспрерывно [. . .]

Почему же не отвечаем? Во-первых и главное: не отвечать же всякому шуту?

О, без сомнения, есть и не шуты; есть люди умные, а иногда и остроумные, есть и литературно образованные, что так редко теперь и что ценишь. Но иным из них совершенно нельзя отвечать, хотя бы иногда и хотелось, — нельзя потому, что в конце концов не знаешь, чего сами они хотят. Не понимаешь, из-за чего они так кривят душой, так сами себе противуречат, какая их цель, что они преследуют, где их предания, в чем их будущее? [. . .]

Но зато есть такие, которым отвечать уже никак невозможно. [. . .] Это целая толпа пишущей братии, когда-то, от предков наследовавшая несколько либеральных мыслей, но в совершенной их наготе и наивности, без всякого их развития и толку [. . .] С фактами участившихся самоубийств или ужасного нынешнего пьянства они решительно не знают, что делать. Написать о них с отвращением и ужасом он не смеет рискнуть: а ну как выйдет нелиберально, и вот он передает на всякий случай зубоскаля. [. . .] Неужели же отвечать таким, пускаться с ними в полемику? Только развороти муравейник — беда! Впрочем, им, видимо, приятно бы было связаться, я замечал это по многим признакам. И уж как задирали! (21:156–57).

Но в чем собственно цель моего письма? Вы, как глубокий психолог, поверите мне, что я сам не могу себе выяснить этой цели и что очень может быть никакой цели у меня нет. Побудило же меня писать Вам Ваше издание «Дневника писателя», который читаю с величайшим вниманием и каждый выпуск которого так и толкает меня хвалить и порицать Вас в одно и то же время, опровергать кажущиеся мне парадоксы и удивляться гениального Вашему анализу.[12]

С прекращением издания «Дневника писателя» Вы перестали быть общественным достоянием, к которому каждый имел как бы право обратиться с своими письмами, сомнениями, печалями, даже личными интересами; теперь Вы частное лицо, недоступное всеобщему зондированию.[13]

Я должен Вам признаться, что, несмотря но то, что я Вас когда-то искренно ругал и издевался над Вами, читаю Ваши произведения с большим наслаждением, чем всех остальных русских писателей. [. . .] я считаю Вашим шедевром «Идиота»; «Бесов» я прочитывал много раз, а «Подросток» приводил меня в восторг. И люблю я в Ваших последних произведениях эти болезненные натуры, жизнь и действия которых нарисованы Вами с таким неподражаемым, можно сказать, гениальным мастерством. В то время, как другие находят последние Ваши романы скучными, я, напротив, буквально не могу оторваться от их страниц, каждый почти период я читаю по несколько раз и удивляюсь Вашему живому анализу всех поступков Ваших героев.[14]

Что касается моего *profession de foi*, то я *вполне* разделяю *все* мысли, высказанные (в вашем «Дневнике» за Октябрь) самоубийцей N., и *все* проистекающие от них выводы,— поэтому я не буду распространяться о них.[15]

Знаете, когда я недавно читал Ваш одиннадцатый выпуск «Дневника», т.е. «Кроткую», мне пришли в голову, думая о том, что хочу Вам писать, некоторые мысли, которые я внес в мой «дневник» и которые привожу здесь буквально. Судите сами, прав ли я или нет.

Вот что записано в моем «дневнике»:

«Я уверен, что величайшие психологи романисты, которые создают вернейшие типы порока и дурных инстинктов, анализируют все их поступки, все их душевные движения, находят в них искру Божию, сочувствуют им, верят и желают их возрождения, возвышают их до степени евангельского «блудного сына», — эти самые великие писатели, при встрече с настоящим преступником, живым, содержащимся под замком в тюрьме, отвернутся от него, если он станет обращаться к ним за помощью, советом, утешением, хотя бы он вовсе не был таким закоренелым преступником, какими они рисуют многих в своих художественных произведениях. Они посмотрят на него с удивлением, станут в тупик. «Что мол может быть общего между нашей нравственной чистотою и этой действительною грязью, опозоренной судом, тюрьмой, ссылкой, общественным мнением?» Это можно объяснить отчасти тем, что, создавая художественные отрицательные типы [. . .] наши писатели смотрят на них, как на собственное образцовое произведение, как на родное милое детище, и любуются ими, т.е. самим собою, своим умением верно схватить с жизни тип, художественно обработать его. [. . .] Но какое им дело до постороннего, живого существа, которое погряз в преступление, хотя бы оно и рвалось на свет божий, умолял о спасении, простирал к ним руки?..»[17]

Родился я в многочисленной нищей еврейской семье в Вильне, где, т.е. в семье, люди проклинали друг-друга за кусок хлеба; воспитание получил чисто талмудическое, до 17 лет скитался, по еврейскому обычаю, по маленьким еврейским городам, где существовал на чужих хлебах.[19]

проповедник обыкновенно начнет с какого-нибудь библейского текста и загромоздит его множеством вопросов, затем перейдет к другому тексту, который, казалось, никакого отношения к первому не имеет, и также облепит его разными вопросами, доказывая, что в нем нет ни логики, ни здравого смысла. После этого он останавливается на третьем тексте, в котором найдет массу противоречий и недоразумений, и т. д. Но вдруг, ссылаясь на какое-то изречение талмуда, он выскажет какой-то рогатый силлогизм, и смотришь после некоторого хитросплетения ума, все тексты оказываются согласными между собою, все противоречия исчезли, все вопросы разъяснены, и изречения библии и талмуда воссияли в объяснении проповедника ярче солнца.[20]

На 17 году меня женили на девушке гораздо старшей меня. На 18 году я бежал от жены в Киев, где начал изучать русскую грамоту, иностранные языки и элементарные предметы общего образования с азбуки. Я был твердо намерен поступить в университет. Это было в начале шестидесятых годов, когда русская литература и молодежь праздновали медовый месяц прогресса. Усвоив себе скоро, благодаря недурным способностям, русскую речь, я увлекся также, наравне с другими, Добролюбовым, Чернышевским, Современником, Боклем, Миллем, Молешоттом и прочими корифеями царствовавших тогда авторитетов. Классицизм я возненавидел и потому не поступил в университет. Зная основательно древне-еврейский язык и талмудическую литературу, я возымел мысль сделаться реформатором моего несчастного народа. Я написал несколько книг, в которых доказал нелепость еврейских предрассудков на основании европейской науки,— но евреи жгли мои книги, а меня проклинали. Затем я бросился в объятия русской литературы. [. . .] В 1871 год я приехал в Петербург. Тут я начал сотрудничать в «Деле», «Библиотеке», «Всемирном труде» Окрейца, «Петербургских ведомостях», а затем сделался постоянным сотрудником «Голоса». Разойдясь с Краевским [. . .] я поступил в Учетный банк.[21]

Неужели Вы не можете подняться до основного закона всякой социальной жизни, что *все* без исключения граждане одного государства, если только они несут на себе все повинности, необходимые для существования государства, должны пользоваться *всеми* правами и выгодами его существования?[22]

Ни над собою, ни вне себя, ни внутри себя он не признает никакого регулятора, никакого нравственного закона, никакого принципа. Впереди — никакой высокой цели, в уме — никакого высокого помысла, и при всем этом сила огромная.[24]

Я поступил в Учетный банк [. . .] Новая сфера, противная моему воспитанию, привычкам и убеждениям, заразила меня. Присматриваясь, впродолжении двух лет, к операциям банка, я убедился, что все банки основаны на обмане и мошенничестве. Видя, что люди наживают миллионы, я соблазнился и решился похитить такую сумму, которая составляет 3 процента *с чистой прибыли*, за один год, пайщиков богатейшего банка в России. Эти 3 процента составили 168 000 рублей.

Это было первое (и последнее) пятно, которое легло на мою совесть и которое погубило меня. В этом совершенном мною преступлении играла главнейшую роль любовь к одной честной девушке честной семьи. Будучи горяч от природы, пользуясь хорошим здоровьем и отличаясь очень некрасивой наружностью, я не знал что такое любовь хорошей женщины. Но в Петербурге меня полюбила чистая и славная девушка беззаветно, глубоко, пламенно (именно пламенно). Она меня полюбила конечно не за наружность, а за душевные качества, за некоторый умишко, за доброту сердечную, за готовность делать всякому добро и проч. Она была очень бедна, у нее была только мать (отец давно умер) и еще три сестры. Я хотел жениться на ней, но у меня не было никакого *верного* источника к существованию, так как в банке я служил без всякого письменного условия, и директор мог мне отказать каждую минуту. К тому [же] у меня были долги [. . .]

Не естественно ли после всего этого, что я посягал на вышеупомянутые 3 процента? Этими 3 процентами я обеспечил бы дряхлых моих родителей, многочисленную мою нищую семью, малолетних моих детей от первой жены, любимую и любящую девушку, ее семейство и еще множество «униженных и оскорбленных», не причиняя при этом никому *существенного вреда*. Вот настоящие мотивы моего преступления.

Я не оправдываюсь, но смело заявляю даже Вам, что у меня нет и не было никакого угрызения совести, совершив это преступление.[27]

С одной стороны, глупая, бессмысленная, ничтожная, злая больная старушонка [. . .] С другой стороны, молодые свежие силы, пропадающие даром без поддержки, и это тысячами, и это всюду! [. . .] Убей ее и возьми ее деньги, с тем, чтобы с их помощью посвятить себя потом на служение всему человечеству и общему делу [. . .] За одну жизнь — тысячи жизней, спасенных от гниения и разложения. Одна смерть и сто жизней взамен — да ведь тут арифметика (6:54).

так чисто и так тонко совершают операцию «выгрузки карманов» доверчивой публики, что ни к какому суду их не притянешь.[30]

В Петербурге, в первом месяце, я нанял себе комнату в одном семействе, в бедном семействе Кангиссер. [. . .] [семейство] состояло из матери, бедной вдовы, старшей дочери, вот ее (указывая на жену свою), еще двоих меньших детей и одного сына, который служил в мастерах по перчаточному ремеслу. Узнав, что они Евреи, я было хотел переехать, но увидев, что они очень бедные и честные, видя, что я составляю для них некоторый доход, я из сожаления остался. [. . .] Нищета была страшная, жили без всяких средств... (Подсудимая Кангиссер плачет.) Всеми силами я старался им помочь чем мог. София Кангиссер тоже не знала еще грамоты и просила чтоб я ее обучал. Она из благодарности привязалась ко мне, до этого она не имела никакого знакомства, одним словом, полюбила меня... Она была больна, постоянно страдала катарром легких и должна была пользоваться хорошим воздухом, но на квартире это было невозможно, и она не могла поправиться, хотя я и привозил ей различные лекарства... Одним словом, она жила моим трудом.[31]

Теперь я вам объясню мотив, который побудил меня совершить мой поступок. В нем виноваты исключительно вы, и никто другой! Я в душе честный человек, никогда я не совершил ничего похожего на преступление. Унизившись до того, чтобы просить у вас места, я думал, что вы будете знать различие между простым тружеником, который дальше своей конторки ничего не смыслит, и человеком, стоящим на высоте европейского образования, каков я. Но вы не обратили на это внимания, и я сделался личным злейшим вашим врагом. [. . .] И я решился отомстить вам, и я отомстил![32]

Вы теперь будете посмешищем, и я торжествую, потому что, когда вижу, что такой отвратительный эгоист, как вы, такой бездушный, тщеславный, безграмотный, оторванный от национальности и человечества, полусумасшедший жидок опозорен и сброшен с своей воображаемой высоты — это великое торжество для многих истинно мыслящих людей.[33]

Презирающий вас, А. Ковнер.[33]

Какая досада, три выстрела и ни одного удачного; я не буду жить, я не могу жить![35]

Ковнер жил у нас три с половиной года, он вел себя очень благородно. Моя дочь часто хворала, и он помогал ей. [. . .] Он нам помогал много, очень много помогал. Он меня жалел и жалел моих маленьких девушек. «Мамаша, говорила одна из них, это папаша наш встал из гроба». Я говорю: нет, это чужой, только очень добрый, он нас жалеет.[37]

Перед нами раскрывают картину корыстного преступления, нарушения чужой собственности, бесцеремонного ее похищения, а говорят, что все это совершенно ради высоких и честных нравственных целей.[40]

Рассуждение Ковнера в высокой степени оригинально и своеобразно. Московский Купеческий Банк, рассуждает он, получает на свой основной капитал огромные проценты. Сумма в 168.000 руб. для него ничего не значит. Употребление же из своих капиталов банк делает не особенно хорошее и полезное. Он, Ковнер, распорядился бы им гораздо лучше, и в его руках капитал в 168.000 руб. получил бы самое производительное употребление. Почему же бы ему — такова его логика — не изъять из Банка такой капитал и не распорядится им по своему? И он считает себя вправе сделать это, как вы видели, не стесняясь средствами. Да и зачем стесняться? Похищая 168.000 р. из банка, ведь он удовлетворит экономическим требованиям их наибольшей производительности и сделает из них лучшее употребление, словом, совершит дело общеполезное. [. . .] Страшно становится когда подумаешь к каким результатам и выводам они могли бы привести в своем развитии.[41]

Уж не считает ли он себя каким-то необыкновенным, непризнанным существом, у которого и самый подлог является геройством, в самом мошенничестве сквозят доблесть и честь? [. . .] Пусть же ваш строгий приговор покажет, что таких существ не бывает на свете или, лучше, что их отвергает общество и обвиняют присяжные.[42]

[ваши «Голословные утверждения»] никого из «тронутых» идеями N. убедить не могут. Конечно, предмет этот так глубок и так широк, что сотни томов недостаточно, чтобы разрешить эту мировую задачу, о которой пишут pro и contra столько умов и гениев в продолжении многих веков [. . .] Но все-таки не могу воздержаться от некоторых замечаний, которые, однако, надеюсь, дадут Вам понятие о почве противников Ваших «утверждений», и которые, хотелось бы, чтобы Вы их основательно опровергли.[45]

Я вполне сознаю, что существует какая-то «сила» (назовите ее Богом, если хотите), которая создала вселенное [sic], которая *вечно* творит и которая *никогда* не может быть постигнута человеческому уму. Но я не могу допустить мысль, чтобы это «сила» интересовалась жизнью и действиями своих творений и *сознательно* управляла ими, кем бы и чем бы эти творения ни были.

Не допускаю я этой мысли потому, что *знаю*, что весь мир, т.е. вся наша земля есть только один атом в солнечной системе, что солнце есть атом среди небесных светил, что млечный путь состоит из мириадов солнец [sic] (это все говорит наука, которой никто из мыслящих людей не может отрицать), что вселенная бесконечна, что наша земля живет, относительно, немногое число лет, что геология свидетельствует о бесконечных переворотах на ней, что гипотеза Дарвина о происхождении видов и человека весьма вероятна (во всяком случае разумнее объясняет начало жизни на нашей земле, чем все религиозные и философские трактаты, вместе взятые), что инфузории, которых мильоны [sic] в каждой капле воды, мушки, рыбы, животные птицы, словом, все живущее имеет такое же право на существование, как и человек; что до сих пор есть миллионы, сотни мильонов людей, которые почти ничем не отличаются от животных, что наша цивилизация продолжается всего каких-нибудь 4000 лет, что всевозможных религий бесконечное число (из которых одна противоречит другой), что идея о единобожия зародилась так недавно, и т. д., и т. д., и т. д.[46]

Вы скажите, что человек имеет искру Божию, поэтому он стоит выше всех. Но сколько этих людей? Буквально капля в море. Вы должны сознаться, что из 80 миллионов облюбованного Вами русского народа, в котором думаете находить лекарство [. . .], положительно 60 миллионов живут буквально животною жизнью, не имея никакого разумного понятия, ни о боге, ни о Христе, ни о душе, ни о бессмертии ее...[47]

Во всяком случае хотелось бы мне дожить до того времени, когда Ваши «утверждения» будут не «голословными». О, как бы я хотел убедиться в этих «утверждениях». Поверьте, что я первый буду преклоняться перед Вашими «истинами», когда будет доказано, что они «истины». Но боюсь, что никогда Вы этого не докажите.[49]

Я Вам долго не отвечал, потому что я человек больной и чрезвычайно туго пишу мое ежемесячное издание. К тому же каждый месяц должен отвечать на несколько десятков писем. Наконец, имею семью и другие дела и обязанности. Положительно жить некогда и вступать в длинную переписку невозможно. С Вами же особенно.[50]

Я редко читал что-нибудь умнее Вашего первого письма ко мне (2-ое письмо Ваше — специальность). Я совершенно верю Вам во всем там, где Вы говорите о себе. О преступлении, раз совершенном, Вы выразились так ясно и так (мне по крайней мере) понятно, что я, не знавший *подробно* Вашего дела, теперь, по крайней мере, смотрю на него так, как Вы сами о нем судите.[50]

N.B. Мне не совсем по сердцу те две строчки Вашего письма, где Вы говорите, что не чувствуете никакого раскаянья от сделанного Вами поступка в банке. Есть нечто высшее доводов рассудка и всевозможных подошедших обстоятельств, чему всякий обязан подчиниться.[50]

как же они могут не стать, хоть *отчасти*, в разлад с корнем нации, с племенем русским? [. . .] посмотрите, как Вы ненавидите русских, и именно *потому только, что Вы еврей*, хотя бы и интеллигентный. В Вашем 2-ом письме есть несколько строк о нравственном и религиозном сознании 60 миллионов русского народа. Это слова ужасной ненависти, именно ненависти, потому что Вы, как умный человек, должны сами понимать, что в этом смысле (то есть в вопросе, в какой доле и силе русский простолюдин есть христианин) — Вы в высшей степени некомпетентны судить.[50]

Об идеях Ваших о Боге и о бессмертии — и говорить не буду с Вами. Эти возражения (то есть все Ваши) я, клянусь Вам, знал уже 20 лет от роду![50]

* я в полном недоумении, с чего Вы взяли, что я «ненавижу» русских и еще «*именно потому что я еврей*»? Боже, как Вы ошибаетесь! Неужели Вы могли вынести такое убеждение из моего письма? почему Вы полагаете, что я, как еврей, «в высшей степени некомпетентен судить [. . .] насколько русский простолюдин христианин»? Я знаю очень хорошо историю христианства, смею думать, что знаю и дух его, знаю русскую историю, знаю, наконец, довольно близко жизнь русского народа. Почему же я не компетентен?

я хочу поговорить с вами, как я говорил уже однажды с Достоевским.[52]

Возможное продолжение бытия человека после смерти в какой-нибудь форме ни к чему его не обязывают.[55]

что касается положительного добра [. . .] то при устройстве общества на началах разума и справедливости, оно может осуществиться и без религиозных импульсов.[55]

Со всем этим я глубоко согласен. Это Достоевский наклеветал на человека, что «без Бога и веры в загробную жизнь люди начнут пожирать друг друга». Прежде всего, они при «вере» и «в Бога, и в загробную жизнь» жгли друг друга, — что едва-ли лучше пожирания; и жгли веками, не индивидуально, а церковно. Но оставим эти старые истории. Для меня совершенно очевидно и из непосредственных фактов мне известно, что люди совершенно неверившие в Бога и в загробную жизнь были людьми в то же время изумительной чистоты жизни, полные любви и ласки к людям, простые, не обидчивые, не завистливые. Мне ужасно грустно сказать, — ибо это есть страшное испытание для всякой веры, — что этих особенно чистых и особенно добрых, правдивых и ласковых людей, я встречал почти исключительно среди атеистов. Это до того страшно и непонятно, что я растериваюсь: но должен сказать, что видел. И у этих людей не никакой меланхолии, так что они «не от грусти добры», напротив — превеселые.[56]

Notes to Chapter 7

32. А главное — «Сонечка, вечная Сонечка»... мог бы буквально повторить этот отважный нарушитель уголовных запретов вслед за героем поразившего его романа: «Соня, Соня! Тихая Соня...»

Index

Index

Christ: death of, 7–9, 12, 14, 99,
131–32, 137, 144–46, 210n, 211n;
and Dostoevsky, 130–33;
Gethsemane prayer, 7–8, 12, 146;
mystical body of, 26–27; as paradigm
of death, 7–9, 132–33, 144, 161; and
Socrates, 7–8, 11, 16, 98–99,
144–45, 211n; as suicide, 7–8, 146,
156n, 210n
Chukovsky, Kornei, 102–3
Church: and suicide, 49–53, 55, 58–59,
63–66, 73; and law, 49, 55–60,
63–66, 73; and science 63, 73
Cicero, Marcus Tullius, 9
Cleombrotus, 7
Comte, Auguste, 31–32, 38
Condillac, Etienne Bonnot de, 34n
Corbin, Alain, 88

Darwin, Charles, 169, 231n
David, J.-L., *The Death of Socrates,* 11
Davydov, Iu., 247n
decomposition (*razlozhenie*), metaphor
of, 46, 82–88, 140–43, 157. *See also*
body social, disintegration of
Demert, N. A. (D.), 85, 92–94, 232n,
235n
Demert, Platon, suicide of, 91–92
De Quincey, Thomas, 210n
Diderot, Denis, 11
discursive strategies: in fiction, 143; in
press, 81–88, 94, 103–4
Dobroliubov, Nikolai, 192
Dobrovol'sky, V., 222n
Dolinin, A. S., on Dostoevsky, 142n,
245n, 252n
Donne, John, 7, 210n
Dostoevsky, Fyodor, 4, 97, 102,
123–84; *The Adolescent,* 133–43,
166, 182, 253n; *Brothers Karamazov,*
126, 160, 166, 176, 202–3, 242n,
250n, 251n; *Crime and Punishment,*
125–26, 195; *Diary of a Writer,* 4,
112, 117, 142, 162–84, 190; and
experimental method, 126–31; and
Grazhdanin, 75, 117, 118n; *The
Idiot,* 128–33, 171, 177; Ippolit,
128–33, 135, 171, 177; and Jews,
188, 201–2; and Kant, 124–25, 129,
148, 242n; Ivan Karamazov, 129,
166–67, 176, 202; Kirillov, 8–9, 123,
129, 143–51, 154–61; and Kornilova

case, 162–63, 171, 178, 199; and
Kovner, 185–205; Kraft, 133–39,
244n, 245n; *Krotkaia,* 182–83; letters
of suicides to, 168–70, 173–74,
175–78, 250n; Myshkin, 129–31; and
newspapers, 162, 187, 189, 249n;
and new paradigm of death, 8,
132–33, 149–50, 159–61; *Notes from
the Dead House,* 129; and personal
experience of death, 129–31, 136,
148, 150, 185, 204–205; *The
Possessed,* 8, 123, 143–51, 154–55,
250n; "Prigovor" (*Diary of a Writer*),
170–72, 180, 199, 250n;
Raskol'nikov, 125, 194–98, 201; and
his readers, 162–63, 165–78,
188–202, 249n, 251n; and "reality,"
151–53, 162–63, 182–84, 246n;
Stavrogin, 123, 144, 147–48, 154–55;
on suicide notes, 112, 135–40,
163–80, 187, 241n, 245n;
Svidrigailov, 226n; Verkhovensky,
123, 150; Versilov, 141–42, 166, 182
Douglas, Jack, 8, 40, 207n, 208n
Douglas, Mary, 234n
Drobisch, Moritz Wilhelm, 24, 216; in
Russia, 67
Dublin, L. I., 49n
Durkheim, Emile, 9, 17, 20, 25–26, 32,
36–43; in Russia, 99–100, 102–4,
237n

Elizabeth, Empress, and suicide
legislation, 56
Engelstein, Laura, 225n, 226n, 228n
Espinas, A., 31
Esquirol, Etienne, 20–21, 37, 213n; in
Russia, 72–73, 228n
experimental method, 22, 153; in
literature, 126–31, 243n, 246n; and
suicide notes, 117–18

Falret, J.-P., 20–21
Faresov, A. I., 151
Fedden, H. R., 61, 209n
Ferri, Enrico, 61
Feuerbach, Ludwig, 98, 130, 141,
146–48, 157, 169
Filaret, Metropolitan (Drozdov), 52
Foucault, Michel, 5, 16, 33, 61, 204
Fotii, Metropolitan, 51
Fraanje, Martin, 214n

Index

Frankenstein, 36
freedom of will, 2, 16–17, 19, 22–24, 67–68, 145–46, 216n
Freud, Sigmund, 2, 204n, 211n

Gadamer, Hans-Georg, 204, 211n
Gallagher, Catherine, 220n
Gates, Barbara, 208n
Geertz, Clifford, 5, 235n
Gernet, M. N., 229n, 230n
glasnost, 45; and suicide, 75, 78
"God is dead," 144–45, 154, 157
Goethe, J. W., 12, 29n, 212n; *Werther*, 12–13, 177; *Werther* and Christ, 12–13; *Werther* and suicide epidemic, 13, 212n, 213n; *Werther* in Russia, 13–14, 213n
Gogol, Nikolai, 98
Golosovker, Ia. E., on Dostoevsky, 242n
Golubinsky, E., 50, 52
Gordon, G. I., 99
Gorky, Maxim, 102
Granovsky, Timofei, 124
Great Reforms, 45–46; and suicide legislation, 61–64
Gregory Palamas, 140
Griesinger, Wilhelm, 235n
Grimm, Jacob, 10, 11
Gübner, Iu., 71, 229n
Guerry, A. M., 216n; in Russia, 67
Gvozdev, Ivan, 21, 88–90

Hacking, Ian, 21, 215n, 216n
Hamlet, 12, 177
Hegel, G. W. F., 8, 11, 144–46, 157, 161, 247n
Helvétius, Claude, 16
Herrmann, Ch.-Th., 70–71
Herzen, Alexander, 124; family of, 156n, 180–82, 252n, 253n
Herzen, Liza, suicide of, 179–82
Holbach, Paul Henri, 16, 226n
Holbein, Hans, *The Dead Christ*, 131–32
Hotel Belle Vue case, 77–82, 142n
Hugo, Vicor, 31; *Le Dernier jour d'un condamné*, 130, 151, 183, 243n
Hume, David, 226n

immortality: of the body/matter, 28, 134–35, 148–49, 152; of the soul, 2, 6, 8, 16, 19, 46–47, 124–25, 129, 142, 146, 149, 165, 172, 174, 180, 199–203
Iser, Wolfgang, 208n

Jacob, Ludwig Heirich von, 56–57
Jerome, 210n
Jordanova, Ludmilla, 34
Judas, 53–54

Kablitz, I., 152, 220n
Kanigisser, Sofia, 195–97, 199
Kant, Immanuel, 124–25, 129, 146, 148, 158, 242n
Kantorowicz, Ernst, 26–27
Karakozov, Dmitrii, 69
Katkov, M. N., 75
Kaufmann, Walter, 156n, 248n
Knapp, Liza, 242n-246n, 253n
Kojève, Alexandre, 161, 248n
Koni, A. F., 116n, 125, 134, 137–38, 239n
Konradi, Evgeniia (E. K.), 78–81
Kopei, A., 226n
Korolenko, Nikolai, 152
Kovner, A., 5, 185–205
Kramer, 134, 136–38, 244n
Krapukhin, A., suicide note of, 109–10

Lamennais, Félicité de, 31
Lange, Frederick, 22
Lapshin, I. I., 244n
Lavrov, Petr, 81
law, 8–9, 27n; on attempted suicide, 56–58, 60, 225n; canon law, 49–53, 64–66; and Church, 49, 55–60, 63–66, 73; on insane suicides, 56–62; and medicine, 64; secular law, 55–60, 61–64; and science, 61, 73; sources on Russian law, 223n; on suicide's burial, 55–56, 57, 59, 62, 227n, 228n; on suicide's will, 58–60; in the West, 49, 53, 60–62, 224n
Leenaars, Antoon, 2, 111, 239n
Lermontov, Mikhail, "I skuchno i grustno," 175, 181, 187
Letourneau, Charles, 181
Likhachev, A. V., 35–36, 72–73, 106, 134, 239n
Likhacheva, Elena, 78n, 229n
Lilienfeld, Paul von, 31, 38, 219n; as Russian author, 221n
Lilly, Ian, 241n

315

Index

Index